# Old Evidence
# and Core International Crimes

**Morten Bergsmo, Cheah Wui Ling
and Antonio Angotti (editors)**

**Second Edition**

**2024**
**Torkel Opsahl Academic EPublisher**
**Brussels**

**Editors of this volume:**

**Morten Bergsmo** is the Director of the Centre for International Law Research and Policy (CILRAP). **Cheah Wui Ling** is Associate Professor at the Faculty of Law of the National University of Singapore (NUS), where she is also a Research Fellow at the NUS Centre of International Law. **Antonio Angotti** is a CILRAP Fellow, the Secretary of the Coalition for International Criminal Justice (CICJ), and an attorney at the Bar Association of Florence.

*Front cover: Just as time has eroded the old wall by* Fontana del Mascherone *in Via Giulia, Rome – its materials reacting differently to the passage of time – so old evidence of core international crimes tends to disintegrate. War injustices linger on in the memory of nations for generations, but criminal justice requires living suspects and witnesses. Photograph: CILRAP.*

*Back cover: Modern criminal justice is polished, technology-prone and mass-produced. Perhaps it reminds us more of these concrete pavements on Manhattan (1st Avenue and East 49th Street) than the intricate, eroding wall in Via Giulia, Rome. Photograph: CILRAP.*

# PREFACE TO THE SECOND EDITION BY THE EDITORS

With the passage of time, sources that inform us about past incidents of wrongdoing age. This book is about such aged sources which we have given the generic label of 'old evidence', information relevant to old incidents. It refers to information which may or may not have been used in criminal proceedings, so the book uses the term in a wider sense than evidence proper that has been judicially admitted by a criminal jurisdiction.

Core international crimes going back several decades have been subjected to criminal justice processes relevant to a number of countries the past 30 years, including Argentina, Bangladesh, Bosnia and Herzegovina, Cambodia, East Timor, Kosovo and Indonesia. There are expectations of a criminal justice component in transitional justice mechanisms contemplated for several other countries where violations occurred in the 1980s–90s or early in the twenty-first century. Challenges linked to aging sources of information are relevant to decision-makers who determine whether an accountability mechanism should be set up, as well as to investigators, analysts, prosecutors and judges who must assess the relevancy, credibility and weight of sources of information. We would like the book to be useful to both constituencies.

Against this background, we have sought to include chapters from a variety of actors who have dealt with questions of old evidence in their work. Our objective was to interrogate the question of old evidence in a multi-perspective manner, by examining it through the lens of different actors with input into the prosecutorial and adjudicative processes. We have been fortunate to obtain contributions from national and international judges, prosecutors, counsel of victims, investigators, analysts and academics, with experience from widely different jurisdictions.

A common take-away from the contributions is that old evidence should not be automatically seen as an obstacle to delayed prosecutions – or an excuse not to pursue justice. A rigorous and critical approach in locating and analysing evidence is necessary. For example, the amount and quality of documentary evidence may actually increase over time, as mentioned by Siri S. Frigaard in her foreword. Each situation should be carefully analysed on its own merits, with a view to designing and implementing the best possible solution to the evidentiary challenges at hand. Fair criminal justice needs to be based on evidence that meets a standard of beyond reasonable doubt. This may be difficult, but such challenges may be overcome by tapping into the accumulated experience of national and international jurisdictions. As Ambassador Rapp notes in his foreword, "[a]ll can benefit from the experience of those who have participated in and studied these processes". It is our hope that this anthology will contribute to this common pool of shared knowledge.

When the book was first conceptualized, we realized that criminal justice processes in several Asian countries have encountered the problem of old evidence. The Centre for International Law Research and Policy (CILRAP) therefore decided to hold a seminar in 2010 on "Old Evidence and Core International Crimes" in Dhaka, Bangladesh, to directly engage colleagues who face the related challenges on a daily basis, so that the discussions were grounded in practice, by examining how issues of old evidence play out in real jurisdictions. Bangladesh was at that time starting to investigate atrocities perpetrated in the 1971 war. This explains the focus on Bangladesh in Chapters 12 and 13 and the last foreword.

The second edition is restructured into three parts, and an important new Chapter 7 ("The Time Variable in Relation to Insider Witnesses: Quantitative and Qualitative Analysis of International Criminal Court Cases") by Moa Lidén has been added. Chapter 14 by Otto Triffterer in the first edition has been taken out of the book, in consultation with the publisher, as it makes a better fit in the second, expanded edition of *Historical Origins of International Criminal Law*. Most chapters have been updated, and all have been copy-edited in accordance with the latest standards of the publisher. URLs are hyperlinked to legal sources in the open access ICC Legal Tools Database, thus widening the utility of the book as a knowledge-base.

Several people helped to bring this project to fruition. First and foremost, we would like to thank all the authors for their contributions. We would also like to thank Temme Lee Wei Wei, Abeer Yusuf and Cheah Wui Jia for having assisted with proof-reading. We are grateful to Khondoker Mehdi Maswood, Elisa Novic and Alf Butenschøn Skre who assisted in connection with the Dhaka seminar, and to Dr. Rosalynd C.E. Roberts who contributed to the editorial process. Finally, our thanks go to Rohit Gupta, Fan Yuwen and Kiki A. Japutra for their copy-editing support on behalf of the Torkel Opsahl Academic EPublisher.

Morten Bergsmo<br>
Cheah Wui Ling<br>
Antonio Angotti<br>
*Editors*

# FOREWORD TO THE FIRST EDITION
# BY STEPHEN J. RAPP

This anthology highlights and addresses challenges associated with old evidence when investigating, prosecuting and adjudicating core international crimes. Old evidence is of particular concern for the investigators and prosecutors of such crimes because these prosecutions often take place many years or decades after they were committed. Criminal justice actors find themselves having to deal with aging accused persons, witnesses with fading memories, disintegrating physical evidence, and documents reflecting decisions taken in a world different from that of today. To be able to deal effectively with such old evidence, those involved should have an awareness of potential problems, understand the issues involved and have requisite analytical skills. This anthology brings together a spectrum of experts – judges, policy-makers, prosecutors, lawyers, scientists, jurists – who discuss problems of old evidence and offer a variety of practical solutions for overcoming challenges inherent in dealing with old evidence in cases of core international crimes.

These crimes have been defined by custom and convention over the course of more than a century, but prosecutorial efforts remain relatively young. As many of the authors in this anthology point out, the start of modern-day prosecutorial efforts is often traced to the post-World War II period. Nevertheless, the idea and practice of ensuring individual accountability for these crimes has rapidly spread, with numerous and increasing efforts being undertaken at the national as well as the international levels. As we pursue our joint efforts to achieve accountability for atrocities, we can learn from each other and benefit from the expertise developed by those who have faced similar challenges. This is particularly important for judicial actors at the national level so that the societies most affected can be equipped and empowered to conduct trials on their own terms.

All of us, regardless of our nationality, and all States, whether presently Parties or non-Parties of the Rome Statute, should stand together behind the pursuit of individual accountability for atrocities by national and international authorities. Wherever possible, challenges should be met head on, and addressed through respectful international co-operation and assistance. National prosecutorial efforts should be supported and assisted in line with the needs and circumstances of the society concerned. As the burden and responsibility of prosecuting grave atrocities is increasingly taken up by national authorities, it is inevitable that these efforts will be shaped by each country's own national legal culture and circumstances. Such familiarity will make trial efforts more relevant to national populations. There may be types of challenges commonly encountered by practitioners across borders, such as that of old evidence, but the precise solution chosen by each national authority needs to be tailored to the country's culture and circumstances. This does not mean relativism or an abandonment of international standards. The basic rights guaranteed by treaties such as the International Covenant on Civil and Political Rights must be upheld in all proceedings.

In recognizing that the trials need to be relevant to a nation's population, it is also important to note that the process must be undertaken in a way that will be recognized as just and equitable by fair-minded persons from all parts of that population. These core international crimes have generally been committed against victims targeted on the basis of religion, ethnicity or political affiliation. Years after their commission, memories of specific events may have faded, but not the passions. Persons from a group whose members were victimized may be ready to believe the worst about members of a group associated with the perpetrators. Persons of the latter group may find it hard to believe that its members committed such crimes and view the process as one designed to marginalize the group politically.

This is why a clear prosecution strategy and strong public information and outreach programme can be at least as important in dealing with old crimes as they are with those committed more recently. The prosecution of crimes committed decades in the past will necessarily be limited to those who remain alive, competent and within the reach of the court. The criteria for deciding which of these living persons are to be investigated and prosecuted is a matter of vital public interest. It is important that a prosecution strategy be clearly announced that explains case selection in terms of level of responsibility of the alleged perpetrators or the representative nature of their alleged acts. Information about the trials should not just be available but widely disseminated through a programme of public outreach, so that all parts of the population can see and hear the evidence and understand the factual basis for the verdicts. Such efforts are critical to avoiding the perception that such trials are an exercise in political marginalization and will help ensure their acceptance in future years no matter what political transitions will follow.

For justice to be done, and seen to be done, after the commission of mass atrocities, judicial actors can benefit from the experience of those who have participated in and studied these processes. This anthology brings together resources and references that have proved effective. By providing a wide range of views and practical solutions on how to overcome the challenges of old evidence when investigating and prosecuting atrocities, it can be an invaluable tool for practitioners seeking to achieve justice for core international crimes.

Stephen J. Rapp

*Formerly Ambassador-at-Large*
Office of Global Criminal Justice,
United States Department of State

# FOREWORD TO THE FIRST EDITION
## BY SIRI S. FRIGAARD

This book deals with a *problématique* that I have encountered several times in my work as a prosecutor, also in core international crimes cases. Criminal justice can lead to deprivation of liberty as a punishment. Raising the shadow of incrimination and imposing punishment are serious acts of State. Indictments, prosecutorial pleadings and judgements must therefore be firmly based in the best available facts. Witnesses should be reliable, documents authentic, sites uncontaminated and experts credible. The passing of time affects each of these categories of evidence. Access to archives may actually improve over time, especially when peace replaces war. This may strengthen the knowledge and understanding of expert witnesses. But the same is not necessarily true for other types of witnesses, and normally not for the condition of crime scenes.

This volume contributes significantly to our understanding of these challenges in the context of the investigation, prosecution and adjudication of war crimes, crimes against humanity, genocide and aggression. It brings together experts and practitioners, with experience from a broad range of international and national war crimes prosecutions. It is particularly valuable that the book seeks to address the topic of old evidence with focus also on the situation in a jurisdiction such as that of Bangladesh. It gives the book a very real character.

I encourage national war crimes actors to not only use this book in their work, but to take forward the discourse which has now been started by the editors and the publisher, acknowledging their pioneering effort.

Siri S. Frigaard

*Former Chief Public Prosecutor and Director*,
Norwegian National Authority for Prosecution
of Organised and Other Serious Crime

*Former Deputy General Prosecutor for Serious Crimes*,
East Timor

# FOREWORD BY
# H.E. SHAFIQUE AHMED

The Centre for International Law Research and Policy ('CILRAP') – a neutral international non-profit organization – has made a laudable endeavour to focus on the use of old evidence in core international crimes cases by holding a seminar in Dhaka on 11 September 2011, which has resulted in this anthology.

A civilized society must recognize the worth and dignity of those victimized by abuses of the past. Co-existence between the *hostis humani generis* and victims of war crimes should end, and thus, from a restorative justice perspective, trials should be held, even after 40 years. As early as 1948, the Convention on the Prevention and Punishment of the Crime of Genocide defined this international crime and spelled out the obligations of States Parties to prosecute. Bangladesh considers that the perpetrators of crimes against humanity, crimes against peace, genocide and war crimes should be tried. The State has an obligation to remedy serious violations of human rights, as stated by Article 8 of the Universal Declaration of Human Rights and Article 2(3) of the International Covenant on Civil and Political Rights, which ensure the right to an effective remedy for violations of human rights, and to which Bangladesh has subscribed. Bangladesh acceded to the Rome Statute of the International Criminal Court in March 2010. We were the third Asian country, and the first in South Asia, to become a State Party. This amply demonstrates Bangladesh's commitment to the rule of law and international justice, and our efforts to end impunity for genocide, crimes against humanity and war crimes at all levels. This is a reflection of our State's values, seeking to uphold the progressive and humane values of democracy, justice and human rights everywhere in the world. This conviction stems from our national experience.

Bangladesh was born out of a sustained struggle for representative inclusion, democracy and rights, which shaped our collective aspiration for statehood and identity. Our experience during the 1971 War of Liberation brought us face to face with genocide inflicted by the occupying forces. Bangladesh, therefore, is naturally committed to promoting all efforts at all levels to prevent such crimes and bring an end to impunity for crimes of genocide, crimes against humanity and war crimes.

The government elected in 2008 has shown its commitment to bringing an end to the culture of impunity at the national and international level, and has initiated the trial of perpetrators who committed crimes against humanity, crimes against the peace, genocide, war crimes and other crimes under international law during the 1971 War of Liberation. The trials will undoubtedly bring justice to the victims, heal the wound that we have been carrying for the last decades, end the shameful legacy, and help Bangladesh to move forward with its agenda of development.

Bangladesh is proceeding with the trials of criminals alleged to have committed crimes during our liberation struggle, as per the provisions of the International Crimes (Tribunals) Act of 1973 ('1973 Act') and the rules framed on the basis of that Act. The government is determined to conduct these trials in accordance with international legal and human rights standards, and has already made some amendments to the 1973 Act in order to achieve the desired standards and transparency. A Tribunal has been set up to independently conduct the trials (the 'ICT-BD'). The government has also established an Investigation Agency and appointed a team of prosecutors in accordance with the provisions of the 1973 Act. The Tribunal consists of three judges, including learned Justices of the High Court Division of the Supreme Court. The Tribunal shall be independent in the exercise of its judicial functions and shall ensure fair trials according to the provisions of Section 6(2)(A) of the 1973 Act.

A number of international organizations and eminent experts have come forward to extend support and constructive suggestions to the ICT-BD. As an independent tribunal with a statutory obligation to ensure fair trials, it has welcomed the technical support provided by CILRAP through its department Case Matrix Network. Training sessions have also been held in Dhaka, organized by CILRAP and aimed at strengthening the capacity of ICT-BD investigators and prosecutors. All these activities clearly indicate that the perpetrators of war crimes must be brought to justice, in a manner, needless to say, that maintains fairness and due process of law. CILRAP's expert meeting on "Old Evidence and Core International Crimes", held in Dhaka on 11 September 2011, and this book provide important support to professionals working in national criminal justice, such as the ICT-BD. The seminar has benefited from its distinguished contributors. I was honoured to have been included in the programme, having been afforded the opportunity to share my views on the topic with distinguished international and national experts and participants. I extend heartfelt thanks and gratitude to Professor Morten Bergsmo, CILRAP, and to the Torkel Opsahl Academic EPublisher for organizing the seminar and publishing this book, both of high international quality.

H.E. Shafique Ahmed

*Former Minister of Law, Justice and Parliamentary Affairs of Bangladesh*

# TABLE OF CONTENTS

## Part II:
## Analysis and Forensic Perspectives on Old Evidence

# PART I:
## OLD EVIDENCE, DISCOURSE AND PRACTICE

# 1

## Old Evidence and Core International Crimes on the Agenda of Criminal Justice for Atrocities

**Morten Bergsmo, Cheah Wui Ling and Antonio Angotti**[*]

### 1.1. The Challenges of 'Old Evidence'

The investigation, prosecution and adjudication of core international crimes often take place years or decades after their actual commission. Such delay usually results as societies recovering from mass atrocity are faced with a variety of more pressing reconstructive needs, a fragile political environment, a lack of criminal justice capacity or a desire to move on without dwelling on the past: "Although there are open wounds that undermine deeper reconciliation in the societies affected by the crimes, the younger generations may have limited knowledge of the victimization caused by the crimes".[1] Much time may be required before post-atrocity societies are able and willing to implement fair and effective criminal trials.

Such delays can generate a variety of challenges:

> Witnesses in such cases are old. Their memory may be affected. They may have told their story many times, including in the form of interviews that have been made public. They may have spoken extensively with other victims or potential witnesses. Documents and other physical evidence have sometimes passed through many hands. The chain of custody can be unclear. Archives are occasionally broken up, destroyed or have become illegible. Mass-graves and crime scenes may have been interfered with. Experts and other persons with particular knowledge of the context in which the crimes were committed may have died. Potential witnesses will often have moved on to such an extent in their

---

[*] **Morten Bergsmo** is the Director of the Centre for International Law Research and Policy (CILRAP). **Cheah Wui Ling** is Associate Professor at the Faculty of Law of the National University of Singapore (NUS), where she is also a Research Fellow at the NUS Centre of International Law. **Antonio Angotti** is a CILRAP Fellow, the Secretary of the Coalition for International Criminal Justice (CICJ), and an attorney at the Bar Association of Florence.
[1] Morten Bergsmo, "Using Old Evidence in Core International Crimes Cases", FICHL Policy Brief Series No. 6 (2011), Torkel Opsahl Academic EPublisher, Brussels, 2011, p. 1 (https://www.toaep.org/pbs-pdf/6-bergsmo).

lives that they do not wish to reopen a traumatic past by co-operating with criminal justice.[2]

The undertaking of such delayed prosecutions is nevertheless supported by arguments made by various international legal actors that domestic statutes of limitations do not apply to such crimes. There may in fact be an increase in such prosecutions as the pursuit of individual accountability for such crimes becomes more common and less exceptional, with several societies around the world showing signs of being willing and able to investigate atrocities perpetrated in their past. Even when such prosecutions are undertaken by international criminal courts, such as the International Criminal Court ('ICC'), experience shows that it may take many years before investigations are effectively initiated or an accused person is actually brought to trial.

Investigators can, however, rely on an ever-evolving set of tools in their inevitable confrontation with the passage of time. This book addresses one of the challenges associated with delayed criminal justice for core international crimes, namely the location, treatment and assessment of evidence of conduct that occurred some time ago, referred to as 'old evidence' for the purposes of this anthology. Do such delays create insurmountable obstacles to criminal justice accountability? What are the main problems caused? When published in 2012, the book was the first to address the cluster of issues it groups under the topic of 'old evidence'; and it still is at the time of this second edition, even though a number of legal-academic works focusing on evidence have covered related matters, such as reliability, the passage of time *viz.* memory, witness inconsistencies and preservation of evidence.[3]

The anthology draws on contributions by some of the most experienced prosecutors and judges in international criminal justice, as well as leading international academic expertise on questions related to 'old evidence'. Several

---

2   *Ibid.* See also European Court of Human Rights, *Case of Varnava et al. v. Turkey*, Grand Chamber, Judgment, 18 September 2009, Applications nos. 16064/90 *et al.*, para. 161 (https://www.legal-tools.org/doc/1a9124/): "With the lapse of time, memories of witnesses fade, witnesses may die or become untraceable, evidence deteriorates or ceases to exist, and thus the prospects that any effective investigation can be undertaken will increasingly diminish". The quote is relayed in ICC, *Request Under Regulation 46(3) of the Regulations of the Court*, Pre-Trial Chamber I, Decision on the "Prosecution's Request for a Ruling on Jurisdiction Under Article 19(3) of the Statute", 6 September 2018, ICC-RoC46(3)-01/18-37, para. 86 ('ICC, 6 September 2018') (https://www.legal-tools.org/doc/73aeb4/).
3   Among them, Mark Klamberg, *Evidence in International Criminal Trials: Confronting Legal Gaps and the Reconstruction of Disputed Events*, Martinus Nijhoff, Leiden, 2013; Rodney Dixon and Karim A.A. Khan KC, *Archbold International Criminal Courts: Practice, Procedure and Evidence*, 4th ed., Sweet & Maxwell, London, 2014; Nancy A. Combs, *Fact-finding Without Facts: The Uncertain Evidentiary Foundations of International Criminal Convictions*, Cambridge University Press, 2010.

chapters were first presented at the international expert seminar on old evidence convened by the Centre for International Law Research and Policy ('CILRAP') on 11 September 2012,[4] in Dhaka, Bangladesh. The seminar aimed to base its discussions on the use of 'old evidence' in atrocity cases in a region that has seen several domestic accountability processes where 'old evidence' is a real challenge, notably in Bangladesh, Cambodia and East Timor. The seminar discussions considered and were, in this manner, informed by the range of real issues confronting war crimes justice actors. This lent additional credibility to the seminar exchanges and the presented papers. It also provided an opportunity to consider more closely national war crimes processes, to which Part 3 and the anthology is dedicated, and it gave a further dynamic potential to the book as it evolves through new editions.

## 1.2. Some Insights Gleaned From the Book

A number of insights are articulated in the book, making it a relevant publication on the topic for practitioners with a mandate to investigate, analyse, prosecute or adjudicate old core international crimes as well as for policy- and decision-makers who find themselves considering whether the prosecution of aged atrocities should be jurisdictionally enabled. Regrettably, several states saw the commission of core international crimes between 1980 and 2010, without having yet embraced criminal justice accountability for those concerned.

A number of themes are discussed by contributors to this anthology, as invited by the conceptualization of the CILRAP project. Some of the challenges when 'old evidence' is used are common to all crimes. Others are particularly pertinent to core international crimes due to their characteristics, such as their socio-political context, the disorder and stress accompanying such crimes, and an unstable post-atrocity environment. It is important that we improve our understanding of how such features impact assessments of the quality of evidence, *inter alia*, by benefitting from existing scientific research and avoiding succumbing to common general beliefs.

- *Simplistic 'truths' are often proven to be approximations by in-depth scientific research.* One such belief is that stress always compromises one's ability to serve as a credible witness.[5] Looking closer, this appears

---

4   See https://www.fichl.org/activities/old-evidence-and-core-international-crimes.

5   The book by Combs, 2010, see *supra* note 3, Section 1.B. of Chapter 1, provides an overview of the literature along with observations particularly tailored to the field of international criminal justice. The book takes into account jurisprudence suggesting that horrific events may be harder for witnesses to forget (pp. 15–16), although it underlines that stress negatively impacts perception and memory (see p. 15 along with the many social-science references in footnotes 44, 45 and 46). ICC case law notes the "profound impact and detrimental

to be an approximation. Research has focused on victims affected by post-traumatic stress disorder ('PTSD') – which presents memory-related issues by itself[6] or due to its "high co-morbidity with other psychiatric disorders associated to PTSD" – and reached differing results, explained in Chapter 6 by Anya Topiwala (Senior Clinical Lecturer, University of Oxford) and Seena Fazel (Professor, University of Oxford).[7] There is also apparent contradiction with an existing body of evidence "suggesting an enhancement of memory after trauma. Pre-clinical, animal and human studies demonstrate that arousal increases adrenaline levels that, in turn, enhance memory". It might not be obvious that "there is some evidence that memory is consolidated after one week", that is, *some* time can help memory recall.[8] Another example of the conclusions that can be reached when research looks into preconceptions is that, while old witnesses may be worse at identifying tasks such as line-ups, research has shown that they are "more likely to correctly identify an individual who is closer to their age (same age bias) as well as of the same race (same race bias) than are younger adults".[9] The relation between time, trauma and memory is more complex than what a commonly held simple 'truth' can convey.

---

effect that the length of time between the occurrence of the crimes and the moment in which evidence is presented at trial can have on the reliability of evidence" and that victims "who suffered trauma, may have had particular difficulty in providing a coherent, complete and logical account", see ICC, 6 September 2018, para. 86, see *supra* note 2, which references ICC, *Prosecutor v. Thomas Lubanga Dyilo*, Trial Chamber I, Judgment Pursuant to Article 74 of the Statute, 14 March 2012, ICC-01/04-01/06-2842, para. 103 (https://www.legal-tools.org/doc/677866/), and *Prosecutor v. Germain Katanga*, Trial Chamber II, Judgment Pursuant to Article 74 of the Statute, 7 March 2014, ICC-01/04-01/07-3436-tENG, para. 83 (https://www.legal-tools.org/doc/73aeb4/).

6. See Chapter 6, Section 6.3., which provides references to research that surveys sexual violence and abuse survivors and found that PTSD-affected victims "demonstrated increased false recognition of words" and "performed significantly worse than non-PTSD victims and controls on recall using a standardized test". Other research has found that war veterans are more impaired in verbal memory, compared to sexual or physical assault victims.

7. Chapter 6, Section 6.2., illustrates how, while inconsistencies are more prevalent in trauma narratives, memory impairments appear to be related to emotions, rather than directly to the traumatic events.

8. See Chapter 6, Section 6.4.

9. Helene Love, "Aging Witnesses: Exploring Difference, Inspiring Change", in *The International Journal of Evidence & Proof*, 2015, vol. 19, no. 4, p. 211 (the author refers to persons aged 60 or older). It is interesting to read (p. 221) that older witnesses perform better in line-up tasks when *interrogated in the morning*, and that the simple *reinstatement of the context* can mitigate how the elderly are "more likely to forget where a piece of information came from": both seem to be efficient efforts for investigators to make, before surrendering to the assumption that 'too much time has passed'.

Another common belief is that contradictions are always an indicator of unreliability: "legal actors tend to view inconsistent or contradictory witness evidence with much skepticism, often regardless of whether the inconsistencies were related to central or peripheral details and sometimes without sufficient consideration of the range of possible explanations of such inconsistencies and/or contradictions", writes Moa Lidén (Associate Professor, Uppsala University) in Chapter 7. However, "research into eyewitness testimony has firmly concluded that the relationship between accuracy and consistency is weak".[10]

- *Nuanced and non-superficial assessments of witness reliability are essential tools when working with 'old evidence'.* Criminal justice actors are mandated to make the necessary closer assessments of inconsistencies, probably more so when working with old evidence,[11] to study alternative explanations alongside the presupposed lack of reliability. In Chapter 9, Martin Witteveen (Appeals Prosecutor, the Netherlands) observes that, "[a]lthough a level of detail in a witness statement is necessary to assess the credibility of that information, the lack of details does not necessarily constitute an insurmountable hurdle in assessing the truth". Among other topics, David Cohen (Professor, Stanford University) in Chapter 2 analyses how international justice institutions have learned to distinguish between those discrepancies which are minor and do not impact credibility, and more significant discrepancies that impact "the essence of the incident changed in acceptable detail",[12] that is, the test of 'essence' or 'fundamental features' *versus* 'periphery' or 'minor details'. The case law of the *ad hoc* tribunals – extensively referred to in the subsequent chapters – reflects the need for nuanced evaluations of the reliability that can distinguish between central and less relevant details, such as in the 2010 *Nchamihigo* appeals judgment:

---

[10] See Chapter 7, Section 7.1. This resonates with the "'essence' versus 'periphery'" test for such inconsistencies explained by David Cohen in his Chapter 2 (see *infra* note 12) and with Chapter 9's argument that "[t]here is a need for judges to openly recognize and transparently discuss" the underlying reasons for cultural, linguistic and trauma-related factors.

[11] The *Orić* Trial Chamber Judgement noted that, when many years pass between facts and indictment (in that case 12 years), the reliability-assessment of evidence affected by time (in *Orić*, the identification of the accused) must be done with "particular caution". The passage of time is the first of four factors justifying said caution (see International Criminal Tribunal for the former Yugoslavia ('ICTY'), *Prosecutor v. Naser Orić*, Trial Chamber, Judgement, 30 June 2006, IT-03-68-T, para. 17 (https://www.legal-tools.org/doc/37564c/)).

[12] See Chapter 2, Section 2.3., quoting ICTY, *Prosecutor v. Kunarac et al.*, Trial Chamber, Judgement, IT-96-23-T and IT-96-23/1-T, 22 February 2001, para. 564 (https://www.legal-tools.org/doc/fd881d/).

it is not unreasonable for a Trial Chamber to accept the substance of a witness's evidence notwithstanding the witness's inability to recall certain details, especially when a significant amount of time has elapsed since the events to which the witness's evidence relates.[13]

And in the 2006 *Muvunyi* trial judgment:

When the effect of trauma is considered alongside the lapse of time from 1994 to the present the Chamber believes that the mere fact that inconsistencies exist in a witness's story does not mean that the witness is not credible. Such inconsistencies go to the weight of the evidence rather than the credibility of the witness.[14]

A more nuanced and structured evaluation of reliability is the approach that the *ad hoc* tribunals appear to have adopted with regards to the admission of statements of deceased witnesses. The requirement of 'indicia of reliability', necessary for such statements to be admitted, has been articulated by the ICTY in a way that allows for more complex assessments of reliability:

(a) the circumstances in which the statement was made and recorded, including (i) whether the statement was given under oath; (ii) whether the statement was signed by the witness with an accompanying acknowledgement that the statement is true to the best of his or her recollection; (iii) whether the statement was taken with the assistance of an interpreter duly qualified and approved by the Registry of the Tribunal; (b) whether the statement has been subject to cross-examination; (c) whether the statement, in particular an unsworn statement never subject to cross-

---

[13] International Criminal Tribunal for Rwanda ('ICTR'), *Prosecutor v. Siméon Nchamihigo*, Appeals Chamber, Judgement, 18 March 2010, ICTR-01-63-0345, para. 149 (https://www.legal-tools.org/doc/4b3598/), which in turn refers to ICTY, *Prosecutor v. Kvočka et al.*, Appeals Chamber, Judgement, 28 February 2005, IT-98-30/1, para. 591 (https://www.legal-tools.org/doc/006011/), where "substance" is expressly mentioned in a seemingly relevant context for the arguments in Chapter 2 of this book: "It was therefore not unreasonable for the Trial Chamber to accept the substance of the evidence notwithstanding the differences between the two accounts".

[14] ICTR, *Prosecutor v. Tharcisse Muvunyi*, Trial Chamber, Judgment and Sentence, 12 September 2006, ICTR-00-55A-T, para. 14 (https://www.legal-tools.org/doc/fa02aa/), where the court also states that the "mere fact that inconsistencies exist does not mean that the witness completely lacks credibility", further referring to ICTR, *Prosecutor v. Sylvestre Gacumbitsi*, Appeals Chamber, Judgement, 7 July 20006, ICTR-01-64-0246/1, paras. 74 and 93 (https://www.legal-tools.org/doc/aa51a3/), the latter of which reads: "it was reasonable for the Trial Chamber to accept Witness […]'s testimony despite some inconsistencies with his prior statement […] the Trial Chamber has wide discretion to determine whether discrepancies discredit a witness's testimony".

examination, relates to events about which there is other evidence; and (d) *other factors, such as the absence of manifest or obvious inconsistencies in the statements.*[15]

In this framework, inconsistencies are evaluated among "other factors" rather than as a sort of roadblock. The need for nuanced assessments of reliability – emphasized by Lidén in Chapter 7 and Cohen in Chapter 2 – is addressed by such a structured evaluation, as opposed to simplistic considerations on the presence or absence of inconsistencies.

- *The impact of community understandings on their members' memory must be assessed, and relevant cultural differences bridged, by justice actors.* Chapter 2 also examines the relationship between individual memory, collective memory and the passage of time, pointing to the case law of *ad hoc* and hybrid tribunals.[16] While "in many societies, the memory of events is shaped by community understandings of the past that influence the way in which individuals recount past events", and even if "it is far from clear how to disaggregate common knowledge from personal eyewitness experience",[17] it is still the courts' duty to do so, and they bear the responsibility "to bridge that cultural divide" if it negatively affects a case.[18] Sometimes, narrowing the bridge can be as straightforward as asking culturally-sensitive questions: "'What did you see?' and not 'What happened next?'", as Cohen recounts from personal experience.[19] Lidén also considers the substantial impact that community understandings have, over time, on Within Insider Reliability (that is, "the extent to which one and the same insider, over time, remembers and accounts for the same event in the same way, either between different

---

[15] ICTY, *Prosecutor v. Zdravko Tolimir*, Trial Chamber, Decision on Prosecution's Motion to Admit the Evidence of Witness No. 39 Pursuant to Rule 92 *quater*, 7 September 2011, IT-05-88/2-T, para. 18 (emphasis added), with references in footnote 28 (https://www.legal-tools.org/doc/98b425/). See also Dixon and Khan, 2014, pp. 787–788 with further references, see *supra* note 3, including relevant ICTR case law such as *Prosecutor v. Bagasora et al.*, Trial Chamber, Decision on Admission of Statements of Deceased Witnesses, 19 January 2005, ICTR-98-41, para. 15 (https://www.legal-tools.org/doc/26a957/).

[16] For example, see ICTR, *Prosecutor v. Jean Paul Akayesu*, Trial Chamber, Judgement, ICTR-96-4-T, 2 September 1998, para. 155 (https://www.legal-tools.org/doc/b8d7bd/) and Special Panel for Serious Crimes ('SPSC'), *Prosecutor v. Florenco Tacaqui*, District Court of Dili, Judgement, 20/2001, 9 December 2004, p. 42 ('*Tacaqui* judgment') (https://www.legal-tools.org/doc/864bbe/), both quoted in Chapter 2, Section 2.2.

[17] Chapter 2, Section 2.2.

[18] Cohen refers to the *Tacaqui* judgment, p. 5, see *supra* note 16, in which the SPSC seemingly attributes the responsibility for certain challenges in evidence-acquisition to the Timorese culture and public.

[19] Chapter 2, Section 2.2.

statements or within one and the same statement"),[20] particularly in the context of ICC cases: it is yet another possible explanation for inconsistencies, beyond the simple passage of time. Furthermore, just as trauma affects individual memory, "a traumatic series of events in a small-scale traditional community may become the subject of ongoing and intense discussion and interpretation".[21] The two factors behind forgetfulness described in Chapter 6, memory vividness and rehearsal, are inevitably impacted: "rehearsal makes memories more resistant to decay, but also offers the opportunity for distortion or errors to be assimilated into memory",[22] more so when community narratives are established and repeated over time.

- *Professionalism is essential to how evidence ages, especially when politically-charged contexts or actors are involved in evidence collection and analysis.* Several of the authors point out the need to be sensitive to the constructed nature of local knowledge and how this impacts the evidence put forward by witnesses, non-governmental organizations ('NGOs'), and other trial actors. "If old evidence should not be an excuse not to prosecute, it requires great caution. The fact that it relates to events carrying highly emotional burdens may render it more fragile."[23] Due to the politically and emotionally charged nature of these crimes, their narratives are usually subject to contestation or societal pressures to conform. Criminal justice actors should be aware of this political dimension, and the legal framework should have sufficient safeguards.

Practice has shown that investigators working on old crimes are sometimes left to work with what was recorded shortly after the incidents in question. Such statements are often recorded by non-judicial actors, and not originally intended for use in a criminal tribunal, as illustrated in Chapter 3 by Alphons M.M. Orie (formerly ICTY Judge).[24] Agnieszka Klonowiecka-Milart (Judge, United Nations ('UN') Dispute

---

[20] Chapter 7, Section 7.4.3. The referenced definition of Within Insider Reliability is offered in Section 7.1.

[21] Chapter 2, Section 2.2.

[22] Chapter 6, Section 6.2.

[23] Bergsmo, 2011, p. 4, see *supra* note 1.

[24] Such was the case in various instances at the ICTY, as Chapter 3 mentions in Section 3.3.3.: "Such evidence is at risk of being unreliable and therefore sometimes inadmissible. Major qualitative flaws were sometimes established" as the authors of non-investigative reports, such as civil society or international agencies, could be working without "any legal training, which means that they may pay far more attention to certain less important aspects of the events that occurred, while forgetting elements which are essential for the legal evaluation at a later stage".

Tribunal; formerly Supreme Court, ECCC) points out in Chapter 8 the important contributions of civil society actors (such as helping in the involvement of victims), but also that they risk playing a role in how collective memory is recorded "through the influencing of witness testimonies and the establishing of certain versions of events" or by exercising pressure on prosecuting authorities to go in a certain, perhaps unsubstantiated, direction.[25] The passage of time after atrocity crimes may signify State inaction or reluctance, but it should not lead civil society actors to "take over State functions, such as investigation and punishment". Regardless of whether investigative work is done by non-institutional actors or justice institutions, professionalism is an essential requirement for work with old evidence, as elaborated below.

- *Defining potential evidence as 'old' should not be a value judgment, but rather a helpful categorization in order to figure out how to best use it.* Klonowiecka-Milart notes that, along with the challenges of ageing evidence, "there are some benefits of approaching the crime from a long-ago perspective. The passage of time makes available the established historical record. Some elements are at least ascertained – maybe partially – in the public conscience [...]. Facts that make up contextual elements of international crimes have been argued upon by generations": "the quantum of knowledge, or opinion, is accumulated, layered and settled over a period of time".[26] If the past is like a foreign country, writes Patrick J. Treanor (formerly chief analyst at the ICTY Office of the Prosecutor) in his Chapter 5, we "therefore need to make an effort to learn about the past just as we do to learn about foreign countries": this effort consists in finding and adopting working methods that mitigate the impact of the passage of time. For example, when dealing with old crimes, the "search for documents begins with identifying the possibly relevant types of documents", maintaining the "original order of collected documents [...] whenever possible", and avoiding the "easy trap to fall into", namely "to look for evidence relating only to 'the period of the indictment'".[27]

---

[25] See Chapter 8, Sections 8.2.3. and 8.3.

[26] Chapter 8, Section 8.1.1.

[27] See Chapter 5, Section 5.2. The author describes how some forms of evidence, such as mass-graves or execution sites, are more at risk, as the case of the Sang Prison and Memorial: decades of lack of preservation (in that instance, ending with the demolition of the site) cannot be remedied. On the contrary, evidence that was preserved over the decades, such as execution records of the Tuol Sleng (or 'S-21') prison or photographs of its prisoners, were instrumental to the work of the ECCC.

- *Documentary analysis relies on the availability of archives, which – contrary to what happens to other sources of evidence – may actually improve with time.* Treanor recounts how, when the Unites States Office of Special Investigations ('OSI') began its investigations of Nazi crimes in 1979, it found that not only many old documents had been microfilmed, catalogued and organized by experts, but there was also a wealth of academic literature around them; even resources found on the Internet helped the OSI in the pursuit of justice.[28] In this context, it should be mentioned that the ICC Legal Tools Database first released online the archive of the United Nations War Crimes Commission. At the time of writing for the second edition, the Database held close to 300,000 documents. Investigators and analysts working today have in other words an advantage compared with those working in the field one or more decades ago.

- *Working with 'old evidence' is often a technical challenge and is thus aided by technology – particularly evidence preservation – and capacity-development.* 'Old evidence' may sometimes lose its probative value, because of decomposition or other factors. This may be a technical challenge: "well-preserved old evidence can benefit from new technological methods", such as the increased availability of DNA expertise with regards to, for example, bodies. But if many years pass between the taking of the statement and the exhumation of the body, then much evidence can be lost (for decay, or human intervention).[29] In fact, as Andrew T. Cayley KC (Principal Trial Attorney, ICC; formerly International Co-Prosecutor, Extraordinary Chambers in the Courts of Cambodia) writes, "merely documenting evidence is not enough; that documentation must be preserved in a form that will permit it to be understood and interpreted, and its original sources as well as its chain of custody proven, at a time long after the evidence has been collected".[30] As Chapter 5 illustrates, documentary evidence that is well-preserved does not change the story it tells, and "can be 're-interrogated' many times".[31] As mentioned above, it was instrumental in the work of the Unites States OSI on Nazi cases.[32]

---

[28]  Chapter 5, Section 5.2.

[29]  See Chapter 3, Section 3.4.

[30]  See Chapter 4, Section 4.6.

[31]  See Chapter 5, Section 5.1.

[32]  Conversely, for example, the International Military Tribunal for the Far East faced more substantial challenges with regards to the suppression of documents, which might be explained by the passage of time between the surrender and occupation of Japan, see Klamberg,

Technical and work-challenges can be addressed by building adequate capacity in skills, knowledge and professionalism. Ultimately, delivering justice (investigating, prosecuting, defending and adjudicating) by making use of old evidence

> is primarily a challenge of professionalism, which is shared by all criminal jurisdictions that deal with atrocities or core international crimes. As such, it is a common standard of achievement and responsibility. Investigators, prosecutors and judges should rise to this challenge whether they pursue war crimes justice for reasons of deterrence or reconciliation; whether the alleged crimes occurred a long time ago or more recently. In this light, working with old evidence is primarily a technical challenge to professionals involved in investigation, prosecution, defence and adjudication.[33]

The objective of administering justice presupposes impeccable professionalism on the institutional side, regardless of the age of evidence. As Witteveen remarks, "if evidence is unprofessionally collected, flawed, untested and then used for political purposes, turned into one-sided historical narratives, or used for personal agendas, truth is lost and justice not served".[34]

Self-awareness, capacity development and information-sharing among criminal justice actors are crucial in this regard. Apart from highlighting and explaining the challenges of using old evidence when prosecuting and adjudicating core international crimes, this anthology makes available a variety of knowledge and experience from different national and international contexts so that they may be applied, with proper contextual adjustment, by other criminal justice actors.

## 1.3. The Chapters of the Anthology

Part I of the anthology sets the framework for the discussion of 'old evidence', rooted in examples from past international practice. In the chapter that follows, Chapter 2, Cohen draws on a number of historical and contemporary cases to highlight some problems encountered in the use of old evidence when prosecuting and adjudicating atrocities. First, by using the *Demjanjuk* case that was repeatedly litigated over several decades in different countries and before a

---

2013, see *supra* note 3, p. 205, with references to research by May and Wierda, Piccigallo and Brackman.

[33] Bergsmo, 2011, p. 4, see *supra* note 1.

[34] See Chapter 9, Section 9.8. In Section 9.6.1., the author observes that a "witness who possesses crucial information for the case is not a guarantee of a successful prosecution if the information is not professionally taken by the investigators and recorded in a statement".

variety of courts, he describes how problems of obtaining a credible identification of the accused increasingly impeded prosecutions. Second, as mentioned above, he refers to a number of cases by the ICTR and the SPSC to demonstrate how courts have dealt with the effect of 'cultural factors' or collective memory on witness testimony. Third, he critically considers the judicial approach developed by the ICTY and ICTR towards the impact of trauma and memory on witness testimony.

In Chapter 3, Orie highlights problems commonly encountered when dealing with old evidence, and suggests how they may be overcome. The chapter explains that old evidence does not necessarily have to be 'bad' or inferior to new evidence, and that there is a need to subject all evidence to rigorous testing, such as by employing DNA tests. The chapter draws attention to issues that should be considered when dealing with witness evidence, such as the impact of stress on witness statements and the importance of establishing and following proper procedure from the very start when questioning witnesses or identifying suspects. Beyond the locating and testing of evidence, the chapter also emphasises the need to ensure that such evidence is presented, analysed and interpreted by defence counsel, prosecutors and judges in a fair and professional manner.

In Chapter 4, Cayley explains the real-life problems encountered when leading the prosecution of atrocity crimes before the ECCC, such as the destruction of crime scenes or physical evidence by forces of nature and the building of development projects. He emphasises the need to ensure that evidence is documented as soon as possible and as regularly as possible thereafter. He also notes the importance of retaining original documents and preserving the ability to prove the chain of custody.

Part II of the book is dedicated to analytical and forensic perspectives, highlighting the positive impact of research and analysis of working with 'old evidence'. Chapter 5 by Treanor discusses the challenges associated with using historical documentary evidence when investigating core international crimes. Documentary evidence is important as it becomes increasingly difficult to locate living witnesses in such cases. Such evidence is also particularly useful in establishing certain elements, such as organizational structure and locating leadership or individual responsibility. The location and analysis of such evidence, however, often requires historical training or the possession of requisite historical skills. This chapter is thus particularly useful in its exposition of approaches and practical tips that will facilitate the location and analysis of historical documentary evidence. For example, Treanor points out how while the relevant historical documentation is often found in public archives, much may also be found in the files of government agencies, in private hands, or with

NGOs. Some very valuable documentation was collected by the ICTY from private sources who had been contacted as witnesses. Also, he explains how expert reports may be used to facilitate the efficient and effective introduction of such large volumes of information into the trial. However, he cautions the need to give "clear and transparent instructions" to the expert, and highlights a number of these, which will ensure that such evidence will be accepted by the court.

Chapter 6, by Fazel and Topiwala, analyses scientific evidence on the effects of trauma on memory. It provides a preliminary survey of normal memory, and a summary of the effects of delay on autobiographical memory in normal persons. They highlight, among others, how traumatic memories are different from normal memories. Specifically, traumatic memories may be fragmented, with less recall of peripheral events, with occasionally vivid sensations and perceptions being remembered. However, they also note that there is no clear consensus on whether stress improves or worsens memory and that the relationship between memory and trauma is complex, dependant on an individual's psychosocial and biological characteristics.

Chapter 7, by Lidén, examines the general notion that 'time affects the reliability of testimonies', using ICC insider witness data to link empirical results to how and why the passage of time may, according to research, affect the consistency of testimonies in the first place. The chapter maps different types of inconsistencies along with their possible motivations and causes – including justice actors' acceptance and reactions to them, risk aversion or propension of the involved witnesses along with their security, their societal context and how these elements evolve with time. The chapter eruditely reminds readers that the passage of time changes many things, including memory, but also that 'memory fading' is but one of the many motivators and explanations for inconsistencies. Justice actors should not summarily accept that 'time made evidence unreliable' because, in doing so, they lose all opportunities to prevent and mitigate the many other possible motivators for inconsistencies.

Part III focuses on the investigation, prosecution and adjudication of atrocities from the perspectives of national jurisdictions. In Chapter 8, Klonowiecka-Milart draws on her judicial experience as a UN International Judge at the Supreme Court of Kosovo and explains how evidential assessments in atrocity cases are rendered particularly complex by the passage of time due to their politically contested nature and unstable post-atrocity environments. Due to the former, any use of collective knowledge or memory in the adjudication of atrocity cases should be undertaken with caution. Milart refers to certain legal frameworks that permit judicial notice to be taken of facts of 'common knowledge', 'objective truth' or 'public notoriety'. This allows the introduction of collective knowledge or memory. While these concepts facilitate trial expediency, they also *de facto* lower the standard of proof. It is therefore particularly important that the legal framework permits parties to contest them. Also, there is a need to ensure that judges do not rely exclusively on secondary evidence when dealing with the first case, which bears the burden of establishing the historical context for subsequent cases. Evidence collection and interpretation in atrocity cases is further complicated by the instability of post-atrocity environments which results in much evidence being lost or inadequately preserved. To facilitate evidence gathering, more inter-State co-operation is needed and evidence should be collected by those with proper training. There is also the need to be aware of how evidence collection and interpretation may also be influenced by politics, as demonstrated by the advocacy conducted by some political or civil society actors in Kosovo.

Witteveen, in Chapter 9, comprehensively traces and analyses the journey taken by old evidence from the field to the courtroom in atrocity cases. His chapter begins by providing an overview of the problems associated with old evidence. He focuses on issues of witness memory from a scientific perspective, elaborating on the problems associated with the 'encoding', 'retention', and 'retrieval' phases of memory. This part of Witteveen's chapter thus speaks to Fazel and Topiwala's chapter on memory, considered above. Witteveen then examines the unique challenges faced by investigators, prosecutors, and judges respectively. He emphasises the importance for criminal justice actors to be self-aware of these challenges, and for proper procedures to be put in place. He then describes the legal and institutional framework established by the Dutch authorities to deal with atrocity crimes. In doing so, he points out and evaluates a number of problematic issues, such as that related to the application of ordinary criminal procedure to atrocity crimes.

Sriyana (Head of Bureau of Law, Public Relations and Cooperation of the Indonesian Witness and Victims Agency), in Chapter 10, presents the institutional and operational set-up implemented in the inquiry undertaken by the Indonesian National Commission on Human Rights into a massacre that occurred in Indonesia in 1965–1966. By presenting the steps taken by the Commission in this case, Sriyana's chapter underscores the need for well-planned work processes, sufficient preparatory work prior to undertaking field investigations, and proper documentation of investigations.

The next chapter, by Mahdev Mohan (Global Policy and Standards team, Google; formerly Assistant Professor, Singapore Management University), deals with the challenges faced by civil party representatives in obtaining testimony from victims about historical crimes that took place in Cambodia and highlights lessons that may be applied to other national contexts, such as

Bangladesh, which hosted the 2012 seminar. Using an expressive justice framework, the author emphasises the need to manage the expectations of victims through the provision of adequate information, and ensure that their narratives are treated respectfully by the judicial process. Among others, his chapter puts forward a number of lessons drawn from Cambodia's experience, such as the need to work with local partners, identify focal sites as starting points, adopt a qualitative research approach, design clear interview questions, and provide independent legal representation to victims.

The two closing chapters focus on the national experience of Bangladesh, which at the time of the 2012 Dhaka seminar had begun prosecuting international crimes committed in 1971, thus necessarily relying on old evidence. In Chapter 12, M. Amir-Ul Islam (Senior Advocate, Bangladesh Supreme Court) offers a study of the International (Crimes) Tribunal of Bangladesh ('ICT-BD'), noting that the institution is in line with the spirit of the Rome Statute's declaration that perpetrators of atrocities not go unpunished and that "their effective prosecution be ensured by taking measures at the national level". The author sets out the historical context of Bangladesh's 1971 war, emphasises the need to ensure individual accountability for atrocities, and suggests how impunity had contributed to "the destabilisation of the constitution, democracy, and the rule of law". Chapter 13, by Md. Shahinur Islam (Chairman, ICT-BD), provides a comprehensive description and analysis of the substantive and procedural legal framework applicable to investigations and trials before the ICT-BD. This chapter provides valuable insight into the practice of the ICT-BD and highlights less-known aspects of the applicable legal framework beyond the 1973 Act, such as the domestic Jail Code. He argues for an understanding of the ICT-BD's legal framework in a 'holistic' manner. For example, though the right to interlocutory appeal is not expressly provided for, the ICT-BD nevertheless may intervene to correct any injustice upon assessing the process as a whole.

# 2

---

# The Passage of Time, the Vagaries of Memory, and Reaching Judgment in Mass Atrocity Cases

## David Cohen*

Other contributions to this volume analyse a wide variety of evidentiary issues that arise in prosecutions occurring decades after the commission of the crimes in question. This chapter takes up three interrelated problems as to the way the passage of time affects evidence and the ability to prove a case beyond a reasonable doubt. None of these problems is necessarily unique to long-delayed prosecutions. Indeed, they may all arise as normal evidentiary issues in all trials. This chapter, however, discusses to what extent these problems are affected or exacerbated by the passage of time and how this process impacts the need to establish guilt beyond a reasonable doubt. A 'devil's advocate' position might maintain that beyond a certain threshold, as the passage of time takes its toll, a reasonable doubt is almost necessarily present in the absence of other, less contestable, forensic evidence. This chapter examines the way in which judges have attempted to come to terms with such claims when advanced by defence counsel.

The three areas to be discussed are:

1. Establishing and documenting the identity of the accused. Here the *Demjanjuk* case will be the primary reference point.
2. What some courts have termed 'cultural factors', or problems of collective memory, as opposed to individuals' personal experience, that may taint the way witnesses describe what they saw and experienced. Here, the discussion will focus on the *Akayesu* case at the International Criminal Tribunal for Rwanda ('ICTR') and the *Tacaqui* case at the Special Panels for Serious Crimes in East Timor ('SPSC').

---

\* **David Cohen** is Professor at Stanford University's Doerr School of Sustainability. He previously taught at the University of California ('U.C.') Berkeley from 1979 to 2012. At U.C. Berkeley, he was the Ancker Distinguished Professor for the Humanities and the founding Director of the Berkeley War Crimes Studies Center, which later became the Stanford Center for Human Rights and International Justice. Since 2000, he has collaborated on human rights projects in Asia with the East-West Center in Honolulu, a federally-funded Asia-Pacific research centre.

3. The inter-relation of trauma and the passage of time on memory. Other contributions to this volume reflect cutting-edge scientific research on this issue. The analysis here will focus rather on how some cases at the ICTR and the International Criminal Tribunal for the former Yugoslavia ('ICTY') have attempted to conceptualize this problem and to assess its impact on the credibility of individual witnesses.

## 2.1. The *Demjanjuk* Case and the Legacy of World War II Prosecutions

World War II trials of alleged German war criminals have continued for many decades after Nuremberg. In Germany and Italy, for example, cases continued to be tried after 2010. Since the *Einsatzgruppen* trials in 1958 and the beginning of the *Auschwitzprozesse* in Frankfurt in the early 1960s, the German courts, in particular, have increasingly faced difficulties concerning both the credible identification of accused persons, especially because they were for the most part relatively low-level perpetrators rather than prominent public figures, and also the connection of individual accused to specific criminal acts. These became frequent grounds for acquittal or extreme mitigation of punishment.

Falsification or substitution of identity documents, together with the difficulty of witnesses in identifying a person 20 years or more after they saw them in a Wehrmacht or Schutzstaffel ('SS') uniform in a camp or killing site, proved to be stumbling blocks in a number of cases. The chaos following World War II contributed to the ability of some individuals to credibly establish false identities. In one of the most notorious cases, a famous German journalist in Hamburg simultaneously pursued his professional career in that city while under criminal investigation for war crimes in Frankfurt under a different name. It was only much later that his dual identity was revealed.

Such grounds also provided ample opportunity for some German judges who, in the Cold War atmosphere of the 1960s, were often not particularly interested in convicting Germans of war crimes.[1] In the *Auschwitz* and other mass-murder trials that began in the 1960s, dealing mostly with guards and security personnel in killing centres in Poland, judges often insisted upon an 'individuation' ('*Individualisierung*') of guilt to prove the crime of murder under German criminal law. In contrast to contemporary practice in crimes against humanity prosecutions at the ICTY or ICTR, the prosecution had to prove that the defendant had ordered, supervised or committed a particular murder, of particular persons, at a definite time and place. In one such case, for

---

[1]   As has been well documented in books such as Jörg Friedrich, *Die Kalte Amnestie* (Fischer Taschenbuch Verlag, 1984), a very significant percentage of judges sitting on the bench in the 1950s and 1960s had served as judges in the National Socialist period, producing a marked institutional 'reluctance' to convict or hand down harsh sentences.

example, the charges were dismissed against an SS officer in charge of a district in Poland where SS units under his authority murdered 15,000 Jews because it could not be shown at exactly which murders he was present. The court accepted his authority as the local SS commander responsible for seeing that the liquidation was carried out, and that he was at times present at the scene where the actual crimes were committed (it takes a long time to execute 15,000 persons at a mass grave site). The prosecution, however, could not satisfactorily establish exactly who had been killed when he was physically present and at which times and dates those specific killings took place. Hence, his guilt could not be 'individualized'.[2]

Needless to say, because of the very nature of systematic mass murder, such a standard made prosecution quite difficult, since those who would be prepared to provide such evidence were the objects of the executions and other SS officers present, if available as witnesses, were unlikely to incriminate their comrades or themselves.

The strange saga of one case in which issues of identity, documentation and the effects of the passage of time on witnesses' ability to recognize an accused person were litigated over many decades in three countries perhaps provides the most vivid and notorious example of these problems.

Ivan, or, as he later became known, John Demjanjuk, was born in the Ukraine in 1920. He was apparently taken as a prisoner of war ('POW') by German forces in the Ukraine in 1942. Recruited by the SS in the POW Camp in Chelm, Demjanjuk then served as a guard in various concentration camps. His 1942 SS-ID, or *Dienstausweiss*, provided important documentary evidence in his subsequent prosecutions, both for purposes of identification and for establishing where he served.

After training as an SS camp guard at Trawniki, his *Dienstausweiss* indicates that he was posted to the extermination centre at Sobibor in 1943. Exactly what he did at Sobibor proved to be a point of contention in subsequent litigation, but testimony from another SS guard, Ignat Danlichenko, alleged that he served in all parts of the camp, including where the unloading of the cattle cars, gassing and cremation took place. What is known with certainty is that Demjanjuk emigrated to the United States ('US') after World War II and was less than candid about his activities during the war.

Demjanjuk's legal difficulties in the US began in 1977, when he was accused of being a war criminal and citizenship revocation proceedings began against him. In 1981, he was stripped of his US citizenship and, in 1983, Israel

---

[2]     David Cohen, "Beyond Nuremberg", in Carla Hesse and Robert Post (eds.), *Human Rights in Political Transitions*, Zone, New York, 1999, p. 55.

requested extradition on the grounds that Ivan 'John' Demjanjuk was the notorious Sobibor camp guard known as 'Ivan the Terrible'. Demjanjuk fought the extradition request for several years, notably on the grounds that he was not in fact the man who had been known as 'Ivan the Terrible' and that the Israeli authorities had mistakenly identified him as such. Whether or not this identification was correct eventually turned out to be far from easy to establish beyond a reasonable doubt, but, in 1986, Demjanjuk was deported to stand trial in Israel.

Demjanjuk's defence that he had been inaccurately identified as 'Ivan the Terrible' proved to be in vain. Numerous Sobibor survivors identified him in the Israeli courtroom as such, and he was convicted on this basis in 1988. Demjanjuk appealed and new evidence indicated that 'Ivan the Terrible' was, in fact, a different person, Ivan Marchenko. Demjanjuk had been wrongly identified by numerous witnesses. The Israeli Supreme Court overturned his conviction, and, in 1993, he was returned to the US.

His legal troubles did not end here, however, as in 2001 he was again accused in the US of having served as a guard at the Sobibor and Flossenburg camps. He contested this accusation, but, in 2005, a deportation order was issued, against which he appealed.

Deported to Munich in 2009, Demjanjuk again stood trial, this time before a German court, where he was charged as an accessory to the murder of 29,000 persons at Sobibor. Unlike the trials of the 1960s, the prosecution did not connect him to specific crimes, but rather to his role at Sobibor. They alleged that by working as a guard at a death camp, he was a participant in the killings that took place there. When he was convicted in May 2011, the BBC commented that this was the first time that such an argument had been accepted by a German court.[3]

One of the striking things about the Munich trial was that there were no longer any living witnesses brought to court to identify Demjanjuk and testify against him. With the passage of so many decades, witnesses had died or were no longer in a position to testify. The prosecution, deprived of witness identification in court that in any event would have been highly contested, relied instead upon documentary evidence. They claimed that his *Dienstausweiss* showed both his training at Trawniki and his posting to Sobibor. The defence claimed that in the absence of corroborating witness identification, the documentary evidence was insufficient because his SS-ID was part of a forgery campaign by the KGB. They introduced a US Federal Bureau of Investigation report which they alleged supported their claim. The prosecution, on the other

---

[3]  "John Demjanjuk Guilty of Nazi Death Camp Horrors", *BBC*, 12 May 2011.

hand, produced evidence to show the genuineness of the SS *Dienstausweiss*. The court found that Demjanjuk was guilty as charged, sentenced him to five years of imprisonment, but released him pending an appeal on grounds of ill-health. He died on 17 March 2012, finally ending this long saga of contested identity.

If witnesses had been alive to testify against Demjanjuk, how reliable would have been their in-court identification, some 65-plus years later? In the end, Demjanjuk was convicted only on the basis of documentary evidence that showed that he was at the camp. No witnesses could either identify him or testify as to what he did there. Given that numerous witnesses had falsely identified him in Israel in 1988, how should a court have evaluated the credibility of witnesses whose memories were more than half a century old and who were seeing a man that bore scant resemblance to the young SS guard they had seen so long ago?

## 2.2. Collective Memory and 'Cultural Factors'

The problem of collective memory in the context of the effect of time on evidentiary testimony refers to how, in many societies, the memory of events is shaped by community understandings of the past that influence the way in which individuals recount past events. As has appeared in a number of cases in various tribunals, witnesses sometimes testify as if they had actually seen an event when, in fact, they have only heard about it. The interpretation that such a witness is lying may reflect a misunderstanding of the way in which knowledge and memory are shaped and expressed in some societies. Testimony of individuals about what they saw or experienced in such cases may merge with the collective understanding of their neighbours, kin or communities about what happened. This may be particularly the case for small, close-knit neighbourhood, district or village communities in traditional societies, such as in Rwanda, Sierra Leone or East Timor, with predominantly oral cultures. In such societies, the telling and retelling of the story of events is a way in which collective community memory and identity are shaped, transformed and transmitted over time. With the passage of time, a collective story that makes sense of the violence for the community that experienced it emerges. This can begin soon after the events as members of the community discuss what occurred and try to come to terms with it. Someone who was at the scene, but did not see X or Y, may testify that they saw it because that is what others have told them and the community (or part of it) has decided that it is what happened. Over time, they may come to believe it or may not appreciate the difference between having seen it themselves and having heard about it.

Such problems, as described above, sometimes become evident when, after direct examination about eye-witnessing, cross-examination reveals that the witness could not have seen the event in question. When monitoring the Special Court for Sierra Leone ('SCSL'), I experienced a striking example of this phenomenon when an insider witness was testifying about a campaign of violence in which he had participated. On direct examination, in response to the Prosecutor's repeated narrative of prompting questions of 'What happened next?', the witness would relate what he had seen and experienced. Or so it seemed, until the defence objected that no foundation had been laid for how the witness had come to know about what he was recounting. In response to a question as to how he knew that certain things had been done by the rebel forces, he revealed that he had not actually seen the event in question but had only heard about it. It took several reiterations of this pattern before the Prosecutor understood that she had to ask him 'What did you see?' and not 'What happened next?'. Similar issues arose routinely in trials at the ICTR and SPSC.

While it is clear that the passage of time plays an important role in the way in which collective memory develops in various societies, it is far from clear how to disaggregate common knowledge from personal eyewitness experience when witnesses may not be culturally equipped to appreciate fully the difference when they are testifying about events which they have both witnessed and intensively discussed with other witnesses and victims in their communities. A traumatic series of events in a small-scale traditional community may become the subject of ongoing and intense discussion and interpretation. The community discussion and interpretation in which individuals participate may in turn affect the way in which they remember what they experienced. This phenomenon has been noted in a number of cases, of which an example from the ICTR may prove illustrative.

In the very first trial at the ICTR, the *Akayesu* case, the Tribunal was confronted with the problem of whether witnesses were systematically lying and colluding to ensure convictions, as the defence claimed, or whether other factors were at work. This issue arose persistently at the ICTR in a number of cases.[4] While some observers believed that Rwandans participated in a culture

---

[4]    See, for example, ICTR, *Prosecutor v. Emmanuel Ndindabahizi*, Trial Chamber, Judgement, ICTR-2001-71-I, 15 July 2004, Chapter II, Section 3.5 entitled "Fabrication of Evidence and Collusion among Witnesses" (*'Ndindabahizi* case') (https://www.legal-tools.org/doc/d60956/). In paragraph 110, the Tribunal states: "Both the Prosecution and the Defense have alleged that witnesses appearing for the other side have conspired in the presentation of false testimony". Where such collusion in knowingly false testimony exists, this, of course, raises other issues than those under consideration here in regard to collective memory. For a discussion of the ways in which deliberate false testimony may operate in a social and culture context where it is condoned, regarded as natural or encouraged, see David Cohen, *Law, Violence, and Community in Classical Athens*, Cambridge University Press, 1995.

---

of falsehood, some trial chambers tried to come to grips with how 'cultural factors' exerted an impact on testimony over time.

The Tribunal in the *Akayesu* case considered these issues in a section of the judgment entitled *Cultural Factors Affecting the Evidence of Witnesses*. The Tribunal called expert witnesses to assist it in dealing with defence allegations of systematic lying. Dr. Mathias Ruzindana testified that:

> [...] most Rwandans live in an oral tradition in which facts are reported as they are perceived by the witness, often irrespective of whether the facts were personally witnessed or recounted by someone else. Since not many people are literate or own a radio, much of the information disseminated by the press in 1994 was transmitted to a larger number of secondary listeners by word of mouth, which inevitably carries the hazard of distortion of the information each time it is passed on to a new listener. Similarly, with regard to events in Taba, the Chamber noted that on examination it was at times clarified that evidence which had been reported as an eyewitness account was in fact a second-hand account of what was witnessed.[5]

At the ICTR, as at most tribunals, witnesses were typically testifying several years after the events they alleged to have witnessed. In recent cases, trials are taking place 15 years or more after the Rwandan genocide. Needless to say, with the passage of time, as more and more individuals participate in the shaping of the community memory of an event, the oral tradition of which this event becomes a part takes on a life of its own, as it is transmitted and re-transmitted again and again over time. Although Dr. Ruzindana opined that Rwandans, when asked, are able to distinguish between what they saw themselves and what they learned from others,[6] the way in which the passage of time affects this ability has been little studied. In post-conflict situations, this may be a particular problem because the narrative of events that develops in a community may also be shaped by post-conflict politics and provide additional incentives or motivations for individuals to come to believe that they have 'seen' something that they might not actually have witnessed, or, at the very least, to become increasingly reluctant to deviate from what has become the established 'history' of events in that community. This can impact every aspect of a case, including key identifications of the accused at crime scenes, as transpired, for example, in the *Ndindabahizi* case.[7]

---

5     ICTR, *Prosecutor v. Jean-Paul Akayesu*, Trial Chamber, Judgement, ICTR-96-4-T, 2 September 1998, para. 155 ('*Akayesu* case') (https://www.legal-tools.org/doc/b8d7bd/).

6     *Ibid.*

7     There are lengthy discussions of credibility where the judgment tries to sort out the various inconsistencies and contradictions in testimony and resolve to what extent they create rea-

This situation is similar to what occurred in a number of cases at the SPSC in East Timor. There were occasions where it appeared that witnesses who had testified to what they had seen were, in fact, testifying as to what they had heard from others in their communities. As noted above, this is a problem of traditional societies, especially in overwhelmingly oral cultures like that of East Timor, where literacy was low and Tetun, the most widely spoken indigenous language, was at the time, for the most part, not a written language. Many of the crimes prosecuted at the SPSC occurred in small or very small communities. Apart from the capital, Dili, there were no significant urban environments in East Timor in 1999, when the total population of the country was approximately one million.

The production of collective memory, of an accepted community version of events, can be particularly powerful in such small-scale traditional village societies, though it also operates in larger societal contexts. The situation in East Timor was compounded by the fact (also found in many other post-conflict societies) that the internal divisions within communities and families over allegiance to Indonesia produced competing narratives and operated to solidify those narratives within groups in ways that could directly impact testimony in the courtroom.

In a small community, an event like those that transpired in East Timor in 1999 (and 1974–1999) rends the fabric of social and familial relations. In the aftermath of such conflict, it is necessary for the community to come to terms with what has happened, for every family has been affected by such events and decisions will need to be made as to the accountability and reintegration of victims and perpetrators. In traditional Timorese communities where little was known of the outside world, or even of what was transpiring in the capital, events surrounding the conflict dominated the consciousness of the community and became a part of community identity. These events were intensely discussed, and inevitably the opinions of others, and particularly the collective interpretation that emerged, became what had happened. Many in the community will not readily distinguish between their personal experience and observations and the communal story that has emerged and been accepted. This may be less true for direct victims testifying as to the rape or torture that they themselves experienced, but it may be quite different for those asked to recount what they saw. As noted above, social pressure may operate to motivate individuals to conform their individual memory of events to the accepted community narrative. One of the judgments of the SPSC offers just such an

---

sonable doubt. See, for example, the *Ndindabahizi* case, *supra* note 4, paras. 128, 197 and 246, for a few examples of how such factors render identification of the accused or his presence at a crime scene unreliable.

---

explanation for the changes in the testimony of 14 witnesses to a massacre. In one example, such a change in testimony from before and after the witness' community learned of what he had said is instructive:

> Rather, the Court notices that the witness emphasized that in Dili and after years from the initial interview, he felt free to state the truth; the Court thinks that this new attitude of the witness, which can be put at the origin of the first change of version, may have dissolved when the witness was heard in Passabe, where the conditions of social pressure were clearly different: the witness didn't have the freedom to speak any more, surrounded, as he was, in the course of the testimony in the Police Station of Passabe, by villagers and eminent members of his community whose expectations he did not want to fail.[8]

The judgment quoted immediately above, from the *Florencio Tacaqui* case at the SPSC, repeatedly reflects the Court's frustration at trying to sort out what witnesses actually saw and what they later decided had occurred. This problem was not unusual in trials at the SPSC. What is unusual is the lengthy analysis that attempts, however clumsily, to deal with these issues, as opposed to most relatively abbreviated SPSC judgments that largely ignore or only deal cursorily with matters impacting credibility.[9]

Tacaqui was a local pro-Indonesian militia leader who was alleged to have been personally involved in a massacre of 47 persons. Almost none of the individuals who testified against him at trial even mentioned him in their initial interviews with investigators. They were not specifically asked about him at that point because he had not emerged as a suspect for investigators. Only after he had become the object of investigation did these individuals 'remember' that they saw him at the scene of the massacre. The Court attributed this shift to various cultural qualities of Timorese society such as a disposition to lie or a disposition to tell people what they think those persons want to hear.

What may have in fact transpired is that, with the passage of time, the community comes to attribute responsibility to certain persons and to adopt a particular interpretation of what happened. This is then what everyone believes occurred. For example, one witness changed his story when pressed by the presiding judge and retracted his earlier statement that he had seen Tacaqui.

---

[8] SPSC, *Prosecutor v. Florenco Tacaqui*, District Court of Dili, Judgement, 20/2001, 9 December 2004, p. 42 ('*Tacaqui* case') (https://www.legal-tools.org/doc/864bbe/). The judgment was written by a judge who was not a native English speaker, which accounts for the style.

[9] I have dealt with these issues extensively elsewhere. See David Cohen, *Indifference and Accountability: The United Nations and the Politics of International Justice in East Timor*, East-West Center, Honolulu, 2006.

---

When pressed to explain, he confirmed his earlier statement given in Court saying that "he did not know about the presence of the accused in Teolassi directly, but that my colleagues told me that he was there". The presiding judge then asked him, "when you were interviewed by the investigators you said that Florencio Tacaqui participated in the killing, now why this (double change of version) happen?". The witness replied significantly: "Because he was a commander of the militia […] he also killed people".[10]

It was striking that it was only many months into the investigation that the witnesses first named Tacaqui as the leader of the militia that perpetrated the massacre and attack. They did not mention him before, but soon all of them were able to recall his presence and his key role. What seems to have happened is that this understanding emerged in this community and soon all believed that they knew, or had seen, Tacaqui. The Court struggling to explain the contradictions in their various statements noted in regard to one such witness:

> Now, the Court notices (and will come on the issue again later) the unsolvable contradiction in which the witness fell and his changing attitude in referring the episode before and after the arrest of the accused: it is not necessary to spend words to underline the inconsistency of the two versions which can only find a solution in the radical negation of the trustworthiness of one of them […] Mateus Colo was unable to give any logical explanation.[11]

In analysing the testimony of some 14 witnesses who had placed the accused at the scene of the massacre, the Court reasoned:

> Hearing their testimonies as reading their deposition in Court leaves the listener astonished for the level of unreliability of such versions where the severity of the contradictions or incongruities is only balanced by the apparent naivety of all those who proffer them. All the witnesses but one in this batch were heard by investigators before the arrest of the accused but their declarations at the time, though detailed on the massacre in Teolassi, had not involved the accused whom they "discovered" only at the trial stage.[12]

The Court offers the following explanation for the evolution of the testimony on Tacaqui's presence at the scene of the massacre:

---

[10]  *Tacaqui* case, pp. 30–31, see *supra* note 8. The judgment italicizes quotations from the witnesses' testimony.
[11]  *Ibid.*, p. 35.
[12]  *Ibid.*, p. 44.

> The Court is not ready to state that someone specifically imposed
> or suggested the witnesses, after the arrest of Tacaqui, to go be-
> fore the investigators and tell them a specific version [...]. The
> members of the Panel have experienced, in several occasions in
> East Timor, how easy is for a witness, to be influenced and to fall
> victim of erroneous reconstructions of the facts, based on the
> need to satisfy the interlocutor. This is what the Panel believes
> has happened in the present case.[13]

The Court's ultimate explanation, then, is what it refers to as "collective suggestion". What this appears to involve, abstracting away from the particulars, is the impact of social context upon the recollection of witnesses as their testimony shifts over time to accommodate the expectations conveyed by the narratives dominant in the context in which they find themselves. As one of the examples above makes clear, the most powerful influence in those contexts is the small community in which they experienced the events and of which they continue to be a part. The normative expectations of that community and, in particular, as expressed through its leaders and what the Court calls its 'eminent persons', produce a coherent history of the past that individuals loathe to appear to contradict. More importantly, as the Court recognizes, they come to believe those narratives. Of course, as noted above, there may exist competing narratives that may be articulated by different parties in different circumstances. In other words, as time passes from the initial criminal event, a narrative history of the events evolves, and continues to evolve, reflecting the social and political dynamics of the community and the cultural practices of an oral culture in which history is not written, but is constantly recreated and re-instantiated through its role in the life of the community over time.

A war crimes tribunal enters this scene at a remove in time and in cultural space. In societies like that of East Timor, when asking witnesses, at the various stages of the judicial process, often many years after the event, to recount what they saw and experienced, judges unfamiliar with such traditional cultural practices may experience the confusion and frustration clearly, if inopportunely, expressed by the Italian judge who authored the *Tacaqui* judgment. One such section of the judgment bears quoting at length as it reveals the depth and impact of this cultural divide in mutual understanding and its effect upon the conduct of the trial and the apprehension of judicial proof by the judges:

> In general, on the collection of oral evidence, all the difficulties
> already met in previous trials before the Special Panels surfaced
> again in the present case: the interpretation of the words of the

---

[13]   *Ibid.*, p. 47.

witnesses, issues relating to their credibility and reliability, the capacity to understand the context in which their narrations are embedded are crucial and more troublesome in the Timorese cultural environment than in other jurisdictions. Most of the people who came before the judges to say what they saw of the facts and to give their contribution to the trial, were basically illiterate and scarcely able to narrate events in a congruent and exhaustive manner. Their ways to refer things appeared very often [...] obscure and numb, like a piece of wood or of stone in the process of being worked by the artisan to become an utensil or a decoration [...].

It has sometime happened that this exposure of some witnesses to the cross-examination and to the rules and customs of inquiry by the Parties [...] has brought confusion and contradiction, instead of clarity, with witnesses unable to come out from the bundle of contradictions created from their own words. In many cases the original version of a fact or of a detail regardless of relevance was modified during the course of testimony and the attempt to clarify the facts lead to renewed sources of confusion.

What's more, it should be noted that a pattern of behavior was noticed in many witnesses: the paucity of their culture was used by them as a defense. In other words, when a contradiction emerged, the excuse of the limited capacity to understand or remember was readily used by the same interviewed to justify even the most macroscopic of contradictions. Facing a request for clarification, or being asked which were the correct of two versions, the answer was often: "I don't know: we are simple people; we didn't go to school; we are illiterate; we are not like big people; we are son of God, what we know we say, what we don't know, we don't say".[14]

The *Tacaqui* Court tried to evaluate witness credibility while trying to understand how what the ICTR in the *Akayesu* case called 'cultural factors' had affected what the witnesses recounted in the courtroom. It is to the credit of this panel of judges that they did so, for most judgments at the SPSC paid scant attention to such issues and offered little analysis of credibility or justification of their factual findings. On the other hand, the failure to bridge that cultural divide made manifest by the *Tacaqui* judgment itself is apparent. The obvious sense of frustration of the Court, and the offensive parody of Timorese witnesses in the last paragraph of the quotation immediately above, are indicative of the depth of this failure.

---

[14] *Ibid.*, p. 5.

## 2.3. Assessing Credibility: Memory, Passage of Time and Trauma as Impacting Witness Testimony

As the contribution by Anya Topiwala and Seena Fazel to this volume deals in depth with the issue of trauma, memory and witness testimony from the standpoint of clinical psychology, the purpose of this concluding section is simply to review the way in which the ICTR and ICTY trial chambers have contributed to a judicial standard for dealing with such questions.

It is the nature of tribunals dealing with mass atrocity that many of the witnesses appearing before them have experienced horrific events that have left them deeply traumatized. Very often, they have also had no opportunity to receive treatment or support for the psychological effects of their experience. It is also the nature of contemporary tribunals that individuals are often interviewed by investigators years after they witnessed or suffered the criminal conduct that is the focus of the proceedings. Moreover, several more years typically pass before those individuals appear in a courtroom and testify as to what they saw and experienced. The section above has dealt with the way in which social and cultural factors and practices can, with the passage of time, have an impact upon the manner in which individuals remember or recount their experience. The present section deals with how judges have taken into account the effects of trauma and the passage of time on memory in assessing witness credibility and making factual findings based upon a standard of proof of beyond a reasonable doubt.

We can begin by returning to the *Akayesu* case. As noted above, the defence had argued that there had been systematic collusion among prosecution witnesses to provide false testimony. The Tribunal responded, however, by pointing out other factors that could produce the kinds of inconsistencies noted by the defence. The judgment notes that such discrepancies could be due to the fallibility of perception and memory, and the operation of the passage of time:

> The majority of the witnesses who appeared before the Chamber were eye-witnesses, whose testimonies were based on events they had seen or heard in relation to the acts alleged in the Indictment. The Chamber noted that during the trial, for a number of these witnesses, there appeared to be contradictions or inaccuracies between, on the one hand, the content of their testimonies under solemn declaration to the Chamber, and on the other, their earlier statements to the Prosecutor and the Defence. This alone is not a ground for believing that the witnesses gave false testimony [...]. Moreover, inaccuracies and contradictions between the said statements and the testimony given before the Court are also the result of the time lapse between the two. Memory over time naturally degenerates, hence it would be wrong and unjust for the

Chamber to treat forgetfulness as being synonymous with giving false testimony.[15]

*Akayesu* was the first trial completed at the ICTR. Some 10 years later, the issue becomes one which is seen to arise in every case as part of the more general issue of how to assess the credibility of witness testimony. By that time, however, the ICTY and ICTR have largely developed a standard approach for dealing with these questions. For example, the ICTR *Nchamihigo* case (trial in 2006–2007), was tried some 13 years after the genocide in Rwanda. How did the Trial Chamber deal with how this considerable lapse of time affected the ability of witnesses to recall facts with sufficient precision so as to meet the burden of proof? The Tribunal dealt with the passage of time and inconsistencies in testimony with what has become a routinized response:

> The jurisprudence on the recollection of details is also well formulated. The events about which the witnesses testified occurred more than a decade before the trial. Discrepancies attributable to the lapse of time or the absence of record keeping, or other satisfactory explanation, do not necessarily affect the credibility or reliability of the witnesses. The Chamber will evaluate the testimony of each witness in the context of the testimony as a whole and determine to what extent it can believe and rely on the testimony. In making this assessment, the Chamber will consider whether the testimony was inconsistent with prior statements made by the witness and, if so, the cause of the inconsistency. […] The Chamber will compare the testimony of each witness with the testimony of other witnesses and with the surrounding circumstances.[16]

This says little more than that such case will be handled in the same manner as judges handle any case in which there is a lapse of time: by assessing credibility according to the usual criteria. There is no special problem of memory and reliability acknowledged in such cases either because of the extreme lapse of time or because of the nature of the events. What happens, then, when the issue of trauma is sandwiched together with that of memory?

The ICTR *Nyiramasuhuko* case considers this issue:

> Many witnesses lived through particularly traumatic events and the Chamber recognises that the emotional and psychological reactions that may be provoked by reliving those events may have impaired the ability of some witnesses to clearly and coherently articulate their stories. Moreover, where a significant period of

---

[15] *Akayesu* case, para. 140, see *supra* note 5.

[16] ICTR, *Prosecutor v. Siméon Nchamihigo*, Trial Chamber, Judgement, ICTR-01-63-T, 12 November 2008, para. 15 ('*Nchamihigo* case') (https://www.legal-tools.org/doc/b3c6e0/).

> time has elapsed between the acts charged in the indictments and
> the trial, it is not always reasonable to expect the witness to recall
> every detail with precision.[17]

This paragraph acknowledges that there is a problem, but does little to resolve it, and in particular to resolve how that lack of precision and loss of ability to recount detail is to be dealt with in light of the presumption of innocence and the burden of proof beyond a reasonable doubt. How is reasonable doubt to be assessed, when it is acknowledged that the dual forces of time and trauma have eroded the ability to precisely recall the details of events?

It is the ICTY Trial and Appeals Chambers that have dealt with this issue in the greatest depth. The *Kunarac* case was a thematic sexual violence prosecution involving the sexual enslavement and repeated rapes and other severe mistreatment and torture of a large number of victims, typically over a period of many months. In addition to the problem of memory and trauma, the conditions under which the victims were held made it difficult or impossible for them to testify as to the details of the dates and times when specific events occurred. In some cases, because of the repetition by multiple perpetrators of the sexual violence to which they were subjected, it was also difficult for some witnesses to recall the chronology of events or to identify the accused with certainty. In deciding how to evaluate credibility in light of all of these issues, as well as the passage of some seven or eight years since the crimes occurred, the Trial Chamber acknowledged the same framework as articulated by the ICTR decisions noted above. But the *Kunarac* case went a step further in also setting out a test on which to base findings in particular cases where there were discrepancies between previous statements and in-court testimony.

The essence of the Tribunal's approach was to distinguish between details that were mere *minutiae* or peripheral, as opposed to the facts and details that made up the 'essence' of the event. They were prepared to disregard considerable inconsistencies as to details if the 'essence' was recounted with consistency and coherence. The Tribunal dealt, at some length, with its approach in general terms, and then applied it while examining the credibility of each witness in regard to each criminal act alleged in the indictment.

The Tribunal began by acknowledging the impact of trauma upon the victims and their ability to recount events with clarity and detail:

> By their very nature, the experiences which the witnesses underwent were traumatic for them at the time, and they cannot reasonably be expected to recall the minutiae of the particular inci-

---

[17] ICTR, *Prosecutor v. Pauline Nyiramasuhuko et al.*, Trial Chamber, Judgement, ICTR-98-42-T, 24 June 2011, para. 179 ('*Nyiramasuhuko* case') (https://www.legal-tools.org/doc/1d2476/).

dents charged, such as the precise sequence, or the exact dates and times, of the events they have described [...]. In general, the Trial Chamber has not treated minor discrepancies between the evidence of various witnesses, or between the evidence of a particular witness and a statement previously made by that witness, as discrediting their evidence where that witness has nevertheless recounted the essence of the incident charged in acceptable detail [...]. The Trial Chamber has also taken into account the fact that these events took place some eight years before the witnesses gave evidence in determining whether any minor discrepancies should be treated as discrediting their evidence as a whole.[18]

The Trial Chamber also explicitly acknowledged the burden placed upon the Prosecution by the particular circumstances of the victims. For example, in regard to the ability of women who were as young as 15 years at the time the crimes were committed, the Tribunal confirmed that they had scrupulously applied the test of proof beyond a reasonable doubt together with their standard of 'essence' *versus* 'periphery':

> [T]he absence of a detailed memory on the part of these witnesses did make the task of the Prosecution in providing proof to that degree of satisfaction more difficult, its absence in relation to peripheral details was in general not regarded as discrediting their evidence.[19]

Applying this standard to specific cases, the Trial Chamber in numerous instances attested that the inconsistencies or lapses in memory of the traumatized victims were serious enough that the Prosecution had not met its burden of proof in regard to those particular rapes or acts of sexual violence. In many other cases, however, the factual findings concluded that despite various inconsistencies the Prosecution's burden had been met. For example, in regard to the rape of witness FWS-95 by Kunarac, the judgment concludes that:

> The Trial Chamber regards this lapse of memory as being an insignificant inconsistency as far as the act of rape committed by the accused Kunarac is concerned. In particular, the Trial Chamber is satisfied of the truthfulness and completeness of the testimony of FWS-95 as to the rape by Kunarac because, apart from all noted minor inconsistencies, FWS-95 always testified clearly and without any hesitation that she had been raped by the accused Kunarac [...]. As already elaborated above, the Trial Chamber recognises the difficulties which survivors of such traumatic

---

[18] ICTY, *Prosecutor v. Kunarac et al.*, Trial Chamber, Judgement, IT-96-23-T and IT-96-23/1-T, 22 February 2001, para. 564 ('*Kunarac* case') (https://www.legal-tools.org/doc/fd881d/).
[19] *Ibid.*, para. 565.

events have in remembering every particular detail and precise minutiae of these events and does not regard their existence as necessarily destroying the credibility of other evidence as to the essence of the events themselves.[20]

If one systematically compares the way in which this standard was applied to different witnesses and events by the Trial Chamber in the *Kunarac* case, it is at times difficult to discern consistency in its application. One is left at times with the conclusion that the ultimate test is actually whether the judges, at some more instinctual level, were 'satisfied with the truthfulness and completeness of the testimony'. For in practice, it may indeed be difficult to distinguish between details that are so peripheral that they do not reflect upon the reliability of the memory of the accused and those which do. There is no need here to dwell upon this issue, however, for the main point is how the judges define their approach. It is interesting to see how their distinction between essential and peripheral events comports with the clinical findings reported elsewhere in this volume.

The approach followed in the context of sexual violence in the *Kunarac* case also reflects the general standard articulated by the ICTY Appeals Chamber in the *Delalić* case. There, the Appeals Chamber accepted the Trial Chamber's method of focusing on the "fundamental features" of the witness's testimony.[21] The Appeals Chamber concluded that the Trial Chamber was entitled to find that the fact that a witness might "forget or mix up small details is often as a result of trauma suffered and does not necessarily impugn his or her evidence given in relation to the central facts relating to the crime".[22] In the end, what the Appeals Chamber does is to follow the traditional approach of leaving fact-finding to the Trial Chamber in the exercise of its judgment and discretion to assess the credibility of witnesses. There appears to be a complete reluctance by the judges to relinquish any part of this exercise of judgment on particular accused and particular witnesses to medical experts on trauma and memory. Such experts may provide general testimony as to the nature and impact of trauma on memory, but not on how it has affected the particular memory of a specific witness. The test of 'fundamental features' or 'essence' as opposed to minor or peripheral details may seem unsatisfactorily vague and subjective to defence counsel, but it also operates to preserve the core function of the trial judge to assess credibility through the traditional experience of ob-

---

[20] *Ibid.*, para. 679.
[21] ICTY, *Prosecutor v. Zejnil Delalić et al.*, Appeals Chamber, Judgement, IT-96-21-A, 20 February 2001, para. 485 (https://www.legal-tools.org/doc/051554/).
[22] *Ibid.*, para. 497.

serving the witness and weighing his or her testimony according to a variety of factors and impressions that determine the ultimate finding.

# 3

---

# Adjudicating Core International Crimes Cases in Which Old Evidence Is Introduced

## Alphons M.M. Orie[*]

The purpose of this chapter is to participate in the discussion on the topic of old evidence. It will not be exclusively limited to the evidentiary problems encountered in the adjudication of *international* crimes, since evidence is evidence, whether it concerns the adjudication of international or domestic crimes. Therefore, international standards not only apply to international tribunals judging core international crimes, but also to national criminal courts.

To make the matters that will be discussed more understandable, the following hypothetical case will be used as a background illustration, which will be revisited in Section 3.6. at the end of the chapter.

In 1946, 'Mr. X' was convicted *in absentia* for collaborating with the German occupation as a *Quisling*, that is, not a war criminal but a *collaborator*. He first fled to South America where he lived a very decent life within a religion-based community before finally ending up in North America. In the early 1990s, approximately 50 years after the event, he was arrested and expelled to the Netherlands. He was described in the media as the "terror of his village". When examining his file, 50 years after the respective events, my attention was caught by some interesting evidentiary matters, in particular related to two incidents in which Mr. X had been involved. The first one related to a German soldier who had deserted his unit and was found shot. According to a witness statement in the file, Mr. X had ordered this person to stop as he ran away. The man had raised his hands but had nevertheless been shot in the head from a distance of 20–30 meters, as the witness told the investigator. The file also contained a medical report stating that this German victim died of a bullet

---

[*] Justice **Alphons M.M. Orie** (born in Groningen, the Netherlands) was previously a lawyer specializing in criminal law and was, at the time of publication of the first edition, one of the judges of the International Criminal Tribunal for the former Yugoslavia ('ICTY'). He spent seventeen years (until 1997) practicing at the bar, and then four years as a criminal chamber judge of the Supreme Court of the Netherlands. On 17 November 2001, he was elected to the ICTY. He was the presiding judge of the *Mladić* Trial Chamber which rendered its judgment on 22 November 2017. This chapter is based on Judge Orie's presentation at the conference in Dhaka on 11 September 2011 on which this anthology largely draws (the speech was informal and partially responded to what earlier speakers had said).

wound inflicted on the left of his head. The other incident involved the pursuit of someone who had tried to escape Mr. X's arrest. In the file there was a detailed sketch of the streets down which this person had been pursued and finally killed.

Before looking at these parts of the court file in more detail, the first question that needs to be answered when talking about old evidence is the following: what precisely is meant by the term 'old evidence'?

### 3.1. The Limits of the Legal Approach to 'Old Evidence'

The term 'old evidence' commonly refers to evidence concerning events that happened a long time ago. From a formal legal perspective – namely, that of the law of evidence – evidence is as fresh as it is presented. If someone gives testimony in court, it is quite hard to say whether it is 'old' or 'fresh' evidence. It is just 'evidence', presented at a certain point in time. It might therefore be that the legal approach does not bring us much when it comes to challenges encountered when dealing with 'old evidence', that is, evidence related to events that have long since passed.

Furthermore, the meaning of the word 'evidence' differs from one legal system to another, for instance whether one comes from the common law system or the civil law system. Within the former system, evidentiary material is formally admitted by virtue of a decision taken by the judge, or chamber, in court during trial. The material obtains the status of evidence in the proceedings and reaches the trier of fact, often a jury. Within the civil law system, the whole file, available to the judge who is most often the trier of facts, is accessible before the trial starts. It contains the results of the pre-trial investigations, often statements taken from witnesses, photographs, expert reports, reports by investigators and sometimes tangible objects seized. In short: the whole record of the history of the case and its investigation. Together with additional evidence presented at trial, this is the material from which the trier of fact can draw when deliberating on the facts to be established.

Within these two systems or traditions which I have briefly sketched there are a number of domestic versions which show a great variety of features.

### 3.2. Some Introductory Remarks on Evidence in Court

Evidence is the basis from which a trier of fact draws his conclusions, thereby truthfully establishing the factual elements of the offence with which the accused is charged. This raises a number of issues as illustrated by the following hypothetical example. A witness testifies that he has seen the accused at the scene of the crime stabbing another person. A dead body is found and the autopsy report determines that the cause of death were injuries resulting from stab wounds.

The inference seems to be very simple: the accused killed the victim by stabbing him. But before reaching such a conclusion one would have to critically analyse the evidence. Because it is the totality of the evidence that finally justifies drawing such an inference. None of the evidentiary elements could do without another.

Whatever a witness testifies, the question remains whether what he tells us is in accordance with the objective truth. He may have been mistaken. Or he may have lied on purpose. Could he identify the accused under the given circumstances (distance, light or darkness, vision of the witness)? Did he have any reason to not tell the truth, for example to cover up that a friend, or he himself, was the perpetrator? If the story is not truthful, the dead body and the autopsy report are still true and relevant but not conclusive as to whether this accused can be convicted.

A further search for evidence and thorough testing of the evidence already available may shed light on the probative value of the elements described above. If the DNA of the witness is detected on the handle of a knife found near the dead body, this may undermine his testimony – but not necessarily. The accused may have taken the knife from the witness' kitchen and he may have worn gloves. It is no surprise in such a situation that the handle of the knife bears the DNA of the innocent witness. While evidence that could be established objectively is often more reliable than witness evidence, the latter is often needed to put the objective elements in a logical context. A knife (even with the DNA of the accused), a dead body and an autopsy report could be insufficient to convict an accused even if he had been present at the crime scene. It is of great importance to also search for evidence which contradicts the hypothesis on which the charges are brought against the accused. This avoids a tunnel-view. Were the stab wounds indeed fatal, or was there a medical condition which was overlooked by the examiner of the body and may have caused the death?

That it is not necessarily what it looks like is demonstrated by a case that came before the ICTY.[1] The case involved the discovery, in a drainage canal, of several dozens of human corpses, with bullet wounds in them, near to each other and stretched over several hundred meters. It could be established for most of them that these people had been arrested by the enemy in the conflict, detained and questioned. The inference seemed to be relatively simple and logical: if someone is detained, his body found a couple of days later, and such an operation is repeated many times, always targeting the opponents of

---

[1]  ICTY, *Prosecutor v. Haradinaj et al.*, Trial Chamber, Judgement, 3 April 2008, IT-04-84-T, see, in particular, paras. 336–359 (https://www.legal-tools.org/doc/025913/).

one party to the conflict, it is likely that that members of the other party to the conflict were guilty of this crime. And that was what it turned out to be in these cases.

But if additional evidence was sufficient to confirm such a scenario in a large number of these cases, would that allow to draw the same inference for all these cases? Some evidence was brought to the attention of the Chamber in relation to one of the bodies found in the drainage canal. It was established through reliable witness evidence that this woman had indeed also been arrested and detained, but then, unlike the others, had been released. After her release, she went to a small town to buy a cell phone. She was then raped there and killed by persons who knew that many other bodies were deposited in the drainage canal. That is how this victim's body most likely ended up in that canal.

This example highlights the need to be very cautious when drawing inferences from a situation, even though such inferences may seem obvious at first sight. It also shows how witness evidence may change the impression given by the objective elements of being found in a hidden location, among other victims, with bullet wounds, and after arrest. For this particular victim, however, the story was a different one.

## 3.3. Witness Evidence

I have already observed that objective evidence is often more reliable than witness evidence, but I have also offered an example of how witness evidence can correct a first impression that objective facts created. If witnesses give evidence about events that happened a long time ago, that evidence is often even more vulnerable than witness evidence normally is. In order to rely on such evidence, the usual caution should apply: could the witness see what he says he saw (distance, light conditions)? Did he have any reason to tell lies? But the long time that has passed adds to the risk of flawed reliability. Has the witness been influenced by rumours spread in the long period after the events? I will further elaborate on some of such risks but want to already now point at the importance of recording witness statements in the early stages, close in time to the events. The fading memory of a witness or the influence of sources other than his own observations, as well as any other factor negatively impacting on the reliability of the evidence, may be more easily detected if statements are recorded in the early stages.

## 3.3.1. Issues of Intimidation and Reinforced Collective Recollection of Events

It is bad enough that witnesses are sometimes intimidated, but it happens. Especially in cases of violence between political parties or armed groups there is

a tendency to encourage witnesses with improper means to stick to what is favourable to the faction they belong to or that approached them. It does not
matter that much whether they were already inclined to give a false account of
the events or whether they were pushed or forced to do so. False testimonies
endanger the authority of the judgements delivered – irrespective of whether
the testimony favours the defence or the prosecution. The number of contempt
cases before the ICTY was relatively high. They involved attempts to train,
intimidate or bribe witnesses and in some of them even defence counsel or defence team members appeared.

It is important to establish whether a witness relies upon collective recollection rather than on what he observed himself. Often witnesses refer to
what they say was common knowledge in their village or region, but it is unclear what the source of such common knowledge is. Even worse, a witness
may reproduce what he has been told the truth should be as if it was based on
his own experience. It may be difficult for a witness to distance himself from
what is generally accepted in his social environment. Sometimes protective
measures are needed to make the witness feel comfortable to come forward
and testify in strict accordance with his own memory, rather than to reflect
what 'everyone knew' or what was suggested or dictated to them by others as
being the truth.

### 3.3.2. Probative Value of Witness Evidence

The use of witness testimony involves many assumptions regarding its probative value. Just because a witness says that something happened, that does not
necessarily mean that the said incident happened. This is true even if there is
every reason to believe that the witness thinks he is telling the truth. Was he
able to observe what he said he observed? It is not necessarily due to the bad
faith of the witness. It may be that the witness was really present and that he
saw the commission of the crime, but that he had not more than half a second
to see the perpetrator and the circumstances were not there for an accurate observation of the event. Comparing the testimony, given perhaps 50 years after
the event as may be the case, for example, in Bangladesh where crimes from
1971 are being tried, with any statement recorded immediately after the event
may assist in evaluating the probative value of the evidence. It may allow to
distinguish between what may have been lost over time but now comes back in
a refreshed memory, and what has never been there from the very beginning.
Such comparison may bring back details that the witness had forgotten about,
but it cannot fix circumstances that from the beginning were obstacles to an
accurate observation.

In this respect, it is interesting to note that Article 8(6) of the 1973 International Crimes (Tribunals) Act of Bangladesh ('ICT-BD Act') provides that

the "Investigation Officer may reduce into writing any statement made to him in the course of examination under this section".[2] It is of course a good thing that a written record remains for a longer period of time and can be used later. At the same time, the reduction into writing would easily cause considerable loss of details of the original statement. Audio- or video-recording is to be preferred and improves the potential of a comparative analysis of the original statement and the later testimony.

Even if an early statement is found to be unreliable, it does not mean that the witness lied. One should explore the reasons for its shortcomings. It can affect the totality of the statement, but sometimes only impacts on certain elements. It is a well-known fact that persons have sometimes difficulties in estimating distances. The accuracy of their estimates can often be verified later. But if the statement is in this respect unreliable that does not mean that in other respects (behaviour, colours, clothing, faces) the statement is also unreliable. The evidence of this witness (early statement or testimony in court) would be inaccurate anyhow, whether old or new. Discrepancies between early statements and later testimonies do not by themselves allow for a judgement on whether the old or the new evidence is better. It, first of all, requires a thorough analysis of its causes. Sometimes, however, it will be impossible to determine the relative quality of the old against the new evidence.

Old evidence is not necessarily bad; and new evidence is not necessarily good. For new evidence this is demonstrated by research in universities where lectures were suddenly disturbed by a violent event. Outsiders intruded the lecture room and attacked some of the students, who had no idea that it was all in fact staged. When the students were interviewed about what had happened no more than one hour after the event, they recalled the incident quite differently. Therefore, fresh recollection is not always better recollection. Rather, one should be very careful when dealing with the recollections of persons who have – and this is especially important for international crimes – made their observations under very stressful circumstances. Such circumstances may influence their ability to observe and to recall what really happened.

### 3.3.3. Impact of the Circumstances Around Evidence Collection

If a statement was taken at an early stage after the event occurred, apart from focusing on the content of the statement itself, it is important to learn more about the circumstances under which the statement was taken and recorded. What was the location? Was the statement taken by a professional investigator? Was sufficient time available for the interview? Was an opportunity given to

---

[2]    Bangladesh, The International Crimes (Tribunals) Act, 20 July 1973, Act No. XIX of 1973, Article 8(6) (https://www.legal-tools.org/doc/c09a98).

the witness to re-read the written version of his statement for review? Was a video or audio recording made or is the statement only put on paper? Is it or is it not a verbatim reflection of the words of the witness? At the ICTY, there have been various instances of witness statements being collected not specifically for use in court or by non-professionals, such as non-governmental organizations ('NGOs') . Such evidence is at risk of being unreliable and therefore sometimes inadmissible. Major qualitative flaws were sometimes established.

Article 19, Section 4 of the ICT-BD Act provides that:

> A Tribunal shall take judicial notice of official governmental documents and reports of the United Nations and its subsidiary agencies or other international bodies including non-governmental organisations.[3]

To take judicial notice of what exactly? Of the fact that the governmental document was created, that the United Nations ('UN') issued the said report? Or to take judicial notice of the facts described in the governmental document, the UN or the NGO report? When this provision is applied in relation to the accuracy of the content of such documents, one should not forget that these agencies may have overlooked certain important elements of the events described. The authors are often not professionals trained in the taking of statements, in collecting evidence which is admissible in court. Often, such persons have not had any legal training, which means that they may pay far more attention to certain less important aspects of the events that occurred, while forgetting elements which are essential for the legal evaluation at a later stage.

### 3.3.4. Technical Aspects of Witness Identification

One specific technical aspect to be considered relates to the identification of a person by a witness. Professor David Cohen's Chapter 2 above describes the *Ivan* cases. One of the results of the Israeli case against Mr. Demjanjuk was the publication of a book by Professor Willem A. Wagenaar in which he set out 50 essential rules for identification procedures.[4] For example, a photo spread or line-up identification of a perpetrator by a witness who already knew one of the persons presented to him from previous encounters, is useless. If a witness states to have seen his next-door neighbour committing a crime, what is the need of giving him a photo spread? If the witness has known the person he identifies as the perpetrator before, it is a rather useless exercise. This is because he has already established in his mind, when observing the event, who it

---

[3]  *Ibid.*, Article 19, Section 4.
[4]  Willem A. Wagenaar, *Identifying Ivan: A Case Study in Legal Psychology*, Harvard University Press, Cambridge, 1988, pp. xii and 187.

was that he saw perpetrating the crime, namely a person familiar to him as his neighbour. A photo-spread identification does not add anything of probative value. He would, of course, select from the line or from the photographs his next-door neighbour. Not on the basis of recognition of someone he saw at the crime scene, but because he would just repeat what he had observed already, that it was his neighbour, so well-known to him, whom he had seen at the crime scene as the perpetrator. Whether it indeed was his neighbour he had seen, or someone else, is not in any way strengthened by the photo-spread identification. If he made a mistake in his observation at the crime scene, that will not be corrected when later looking at the series of photographs.

There are, therefore, a number of rules that must be borne in mind so as to ensure the integrity of processes of identification. For instance, a session of photo-identification during which the witness is given only one picture will result in a totally unreliable identification. In the same way, if the witness is given a photo spread of six persons who all look very different – *exempli gratia*, one is an African and the others show clearly different racial characteristics – then, of course, even if he cannot recognize that person's facial features, he might recognize the skin tone of the person he saw, whereas the others logically are beyond consideration. The witness has no choice between persons of the same racial characteristics that he remembers the perpetrator owns. The result mainly would tell us that the witness recognized the perpetrator as a person of African origin, but not necessarily the African person in the photo spread. And once such defective identification has been made in the course of the investigations, repeating the exercise 'better' is also totally useless. Once the witness has identified one particular photo, he will not point to another one the next time, as he will remember which person he identified previously. So once the identification process has been wrongly conducted, the opportunity has been lost and it cannot be remedied.

Another set of questions to be raised in relation to witness evidence concerns the very specific elements that a witness can observe. For example, in the former Yugoslavia, women were often unable to identify which kind of uniform the perpetrators were wearing, let alone any insignia which might identify the individual as a member of unit A, B or C. In this regard, one should also be aware of potential bias, especially in the adjudication of international crimes. In the former Yugoslavia, the majority of the population is known as either a Serb, Muslim, Croat or Kosovar. Further, almost everyone is to some extent affiliated to a party to the conflicts, which may create a different kind of bias from what we often find in domestic adjudications. Therefore, witnesses who have no idea about uniforms may be biased in 'recognizing' specific features of the emblems they attribute to the enemy faction.

## 3.4. Preservation of Evidence and DNA Expertise

Sometimes old evidence loses its probative value. For instance, examining a corpse 15 years after it has been buried may result in an impossibility to draw any conclusions as to the cause of death. The weak parts of the body would have been subject to decay and putrefaction, preventing a clear view of what kind of injury the person might have endured. A bullet injury in a skull, however, would often allow for a conclusion, although we should keep in mind that bullets can also impact after the person has already died by other causes. Especially in mass graves, it may be hard to determine whether the bullet found next to the body was the bullet which killed person A to the left, or person B to the right.

Similarly, well-preserved old evidence can benefit from new technological methods. For example, a body or some tools used during the crime could have been found 25 years ago, when there was no DNA expertise available yet. However, such DNA expertise could now be applied to the body or the tools, and the relevant tests conducted. The availability of such technology will, however, be of no help if the evidence has not been properly preserved.

There were situations before the ICTY where the Prosecutor only managed to have bodies exhumed for DNA testing many years after a witness gave his statement regarding the location where that person was buried. It has also happened that instead of finding a male body where the witness said the body had been buried, only a female body was found. This could hint at a mistake made by the witness, but it is also possible that the male body was removed from the site where the witness had seen him being buried. This illustrates the importance of proper and timely preservation of evidence so that it is still available after a longer period of time for testing purposes. Well-preserved material evidence often provides a key to testing the reliability of witness evidence. Therefore, as far as old evidence is concerned, perhaps what matters most is not to miss any opportunity to preserve and test such evidence. Old evidence is not necessarily bad evidence. It can be tested against new evidence and the various evidentiary sources can be subjected to a comparative analysis. The probative value of separate evidentiary elements from different sources can thus sometimes be mutually reinforced, but the analysis may also undermine the probative value of one or more of these elements due to inexplicable discrepancies that were found.

## 3.5. Interpreting the Evidence and the Background of Judges

Apart from the technicalities described above, the human factor in the interpretation and evaluation of evidence cannot be ignored. The evidence is presented or commented upon by the parties. The better the analysis provided by the parties, the more the trier of fact is assisted in making his findings. Parties should, however, in their presentation and analysis of the evidence, not pretend more than they are actually able to achieve.

A particular feature of the adjudication of international cases is that counsel are sometimes unable to distance themselves from their own background. It is well known in my country, the Netherlands, that many counsel after World War II were reluctant to defend accused who had acted against the interests of the Netherlands. It was an unpopular job to undertake, and only courageous defence counsel were willing to serve justice by acting as defence counsel in cases of alleged war criminals or *Quislings*. This reluctance to assist and support the accused in his defence was also due to the risk of an appearance of siding with the accused. On the other hand, and generally speaking, counsel with a background similar to the background of the accused are at risk of losing the professional distance required to defend their client. It is tempting to manipulate the evidence and it requires professional self-discipline to resist an inclination or outside pressure to such improper practice.

Bearing this in mind, foreign counsel without any affiliation to the warring parties are not to be excluded from participating in the defence of the accused before national courts in cases dealing with a war situation. Allowing an international defence at trial avoids the impression that the war crimes trials are part of an internal revenge or retaliation exercise, flawed by not being transparent, open or not meeting international human rights standards of criminal procedure. Some foreign counsel have much experience in international criminal law trials which is not easily gained. To the extent foreign counsel would lack familiarity with the local circumstances and the history of the armed conflict that local counsel have at their disposal, mixed teams may be a perfect remedy.

The same issues also apply in some way to judges. They should ask themselves to what extent they are affiliated to any movement in the society which has undertaken to end impunity by prosecuting specifically its opponents. These are usually smaller or larger factions in society, which stand in opposition to the perpetrators' group. Even if this objective of ending impunity is to be praised, and even if judges are said to be – and are – independent and impartial, a door should be left open to allow the independence and impartiality of individual judges to be challenged.[5]

At the ICTY, for instance, there are judges from all over the world, so there is no *a priori* reason to think that they would be affiliated with one of the

---

[5]  At the time of writing, such a possibility is impossible under the ICT-BD Act, Article 6(8), see *supra* note 2.

parties that were involved in the conflicts in the former Yugoslavia. Nevertheless, the possibility has been left open to seek recusal of a judge – the disqualification of a judge can be sought by the parties. As a matter of fact, my disqualification was sought on a couple of occasions, once even successfully. This was not because I was found to be not independent or impartial, but because any *appearance* of partiality or a lack of independence should be avoided. A confident legal system, which believes in the quality of its judges, should be open to the possibility of seeking disqualification of the judges, not on political grounds, but on personal grounds. Once my disqualification was sought in a case in which the operations of DutchBatt played a role. DutchBatt was a contingent in the United Nations protection force (UNPROFOR) in Srebrenica in Bosnia and Herzegovina, where genocide was alleged to have taken place. Since I was Dutch, it was alleged that I could not be an impartial or an independent judge. I did not mind that my disqualification was sought because the best thing to do is to face the challenge and say: 'Well, if this is your argument, let us look at it: what does it mean that I am Dutch, what is my background, did I have any affiliation?'. It could be, for example, that a family member of mine was a member of DutchBatt and had been wounded. Such a circumstance would change the situation entirely. So I am only happy that these kinds of motions, seeking the disqualification of a judge, are openly discussed. Of course, the judge involved leaves the decision on such a motion to the judge or chamber assigned to dispose of the motion.

In Bosnia, for instance, if there is a panel of three judges – one Bosnian, one Croat and one Serb – it is understandable that people may think that if, for example, the accused is a Croat, the Serb and the Bosnian Muslim judges could join in making a majority finding and easily convict the accused. Therefore, to restore the balance – as was also the case with the Extraordinary Chambers in the Courts of Cambodia – international judicial involvement was considered to resolve this problem, intrinsic to the composition of benches in Bosnia and Herzegovina.

## 3.6. Concluding Remarks Based on the Example of the 1946 Case

Let me return to the case which I used as an illustration in the introduction to this chapter. In 1946 Mr. X was prosecuted for collaboration in a Dutch court; he was given a life sentence, which was reduced by partial pardon in the 1990s. The two instances of killing were only used as evidence of the collaboration he was charged with – he was not explicitly charged with those killings. In the late 1980s, the German authorities looked at the file again. They thought that his involvement in the killings was clear and that they could consider prosecuting him for having murdered the German deserter. They had the deserter's body exhumed and found that the impact wound was such that the weapon would have been discharged at a distance of no more than 20 centimetres from the head, so not 10 or 20 meters as stated by the witness. They also found the contemporaneous medical report, a *post mortem*, to be incorrect, because the bullet wound (the impact wound) was not on the left but rather on the right side of the head. These findings considerably affected the reliability of other evidence in this case. As a matter of fact, the doctor was not experienced enough to make the distinction between an entry and an exit wound. Similarly, the person who took the statement was not a trained police officer. Finally, the story of Mr. X – which he had upheld during all those years – that the victim was not surrendering but was using his pistol, raising his hand, to shoot himself, turned out to be the most likely course of events. It turned out that it was easier to establish what had happened 30 years after the event, when the body was exhumed, than to determine it at the time when the event took place.

As for the second incident in the case, the sketch happened to be – by pure coincidence – exactly the place where my primary school had been. My recollection could immediately establish that the sketch was utterly wrong. Every street on the sketch was wrongly situated and that could be easily proven, even after so many years had passed. Therefore, in the end, the old evidence, collected freshly after the events, was of very poor quality. Mr. X was not guilty of and could not reasonably be convicted of murder, if he had been charged with that crime. But he was still guilty of collaborating with the enemy.

This illustrates the evidentiary challenges when dealing with events that happened a long time ago, as considered throughout this chapter. In the case of Mr. X, the old evidence consisting of the fresh recollection of a witness and a contemporaneous medical report, upon being thoroughly tested decades after the events, turned out to be completely unreliable. The evidence that had been recently obtained – the obduction in the 1980s – had better probative value. One could say that the evidence presented in court in 1946 was 'new' in the sense of being freshly obtained. Then the findings in the 1980s and 1990s should be considered to be based on 'old evidence' in the sense that they revealed the truth only long after the tested materials (the obduction and the incorrect sketch) had been produced.

Freshly-produced evidence and evidence that is produced or reconsidered a long time after the events bring their own problems. Whether old or new, a thorough analysis of its content is essential. For such an analysis, the evidence – whether old or new – should be considered in its entirety. Old evidence can shed light over new evidence and the same is true in the opposite direction.

# 4

---

# Prosecuting and Defending in Core International Crimes Cases Using Old Evidence

### Andrew Cayley*

## 4.1. Introduction

With the prosecution of international crimes gathering pace across the globe, this anthology's topic is both timely and of increasing significance to the challenge of rendering justice for mass atrocity crimes. I have encountered the problem of old evidence at several points in my own career, and indeed, since my time as the International Co-Prosecutor at the Extraordinary Chambers in the Courts of Cambodia ('ECCC'), I dare say that I have, of necessity, developed a certain expertise in this area.

Physicists will tell you that the Second Law of Thermodynamics is one of the most fundamental laws of nature. This law states that the universe tends to move from order to disorder. In layman's terms, things fall apart. As a prosecutor who has extensively dealt with cases involving old evidence, I can tell you that the Second Law of Thermodynamics also applies to the problem of international crimes. Evidence of crimes is subject to entropy. It will eventually disintegrate and turn to dust.

This disorder can come about in many different ways. Individuals engaged in mass atrocity crimes often go to great lengths to destroy evidence of

---

* **Andrew Cayley** KC is Principal Trial Attorney, International Criminal Court; formerly Chief Inspector, United Kingdom Crown Prosecution Service and International Co-Prosecutor, Extraordinary Chambers in the Courts of Cambodia. At the time of publication of the first edition, he was the International Co-Prosecutor of the Khmer Rouge Tribunal in Cambodia having been nominated by the Secretary-General of the United Nations on 18 August 2009 and appointed by the King of Cambodia, His Majesty King Norodom Sihamoni, to that position on 27 November 2009. Prior to this, he was a Senior Prosecuting Counsel at the International Criminal Tribunal for the former Yugoslavia and the International Criminal Court in The Hague. He was admitted as a Solicitor of the Supreme Court of the Judicature of England and Wales in 1989, and in 2007, he was called by the Inner Temple to the Bar of England and Wales. He served with the British Army as an infantry platoon commander in Belize (on attachment to the Kings Own Royal Border Regiment) and as a military prosecutor and command legal adviser in Germany and the United Kingdom, having attended the Royal Military Academy Sandhurst.

their culpability. They can do this by operating in extreme secrecy, so that the existence of evidence is minimized from the start. They can burn or otherwise destroy documents and other traces of their acts. They can kill or intimidate witnesses. They can even make efforts to destroy entire crime scenes. But there are many other ways in which evidence ceases to exist over time, many of which do not involve the intentional destruction of evidence.

After mass atrocity crimes, society must rebuild, and the very act of re-building can destroy evidence at crime scenes. For example, believers will often be anxious to resurrect a desecrated religious structure, reconstructing it, re-consecrating and returning it to its original purpose. The imperative for people to live and to produce food can also result in the destruction of evidence, as when mass graves are ploughed over so that the land may be returned to agricultural productivity.

But even without the intervention of any human agency at all, evidence of mass crimes will still inexorably crumble over time. Animals, insects, mildew and rust all consume evidence unless it is carefully preserved – a luxury beyond the means of many developing countries. Tree roots and rain will destroy even solid structures, given passage of sufficient time. Rivers have the habit of not staying put, overflowing their banks in seasonal flooding, and even changing their course, damaging or destroying anything in their path. Thus, nature itself is one of the greatest threats to the longevity of evidence.

One of the greatest challenges of old evidence in mass atrocity cases is simply finding the evidence in the first place. It can become lost or be hidden. Evidence may be waiting for you in as yet unexplored places – in the basement at the Ministry of Home Affairs, in an old storehouse at the Ministry of Cultural Affairs, in a bunch of dusty boxes, long forgotten in a dark corner of the National Library. Beyond official sources, private individuals often hold on to useful evidence, waiting for the right moment, and the right person or institution to trust, before turning it over. Evidence might be hiding in a sealed metal box or buried under a tree just outside a small village, far from the capital. One simply has to find it.

Of course, when we are dealing with cases involving old evidence, a necessary corollary is that we will also be dealing with old defendants. At the ECCC, or the Khmer Rouge Tribunal, as it is commonly called, we faced precisely such a situation.

In 2009, the Khmer Rouge Tribunal completed its first trial. In 2011, the Trial Chamber convicted the defendant, Kaing Guek Eav, alias '*Duch*', for war crimes and crimes against humanity. The Trial Chamber sentenced Duch to 35 years of imprisonment for his role as chief of the Khmer Rouge regime's secret police. At the appeals stage, the Supreme Court Chamber decided to increase the sentence handed down by the Trial Chamber, sentencing Duch to life imprisonment.[1]

In June 2011, the Trial Chamber conducted initial hearings for the Court's second case, involving four defendants.[2] All of the accused in this case are elderly, in or on the verge of their 80s. Nuon Chea was the Deputy Secretary of the Communist Party and, the prosecution believes, was responsible for the regime's internal security apparatus.

Ieng Sary was the Deputy Prime Minister and Minister of Foreign Affairs, as well as a member of the Communist Party's Standing Committee, and the eldest of the accused persons before the Khmer Rouge Tribunal. Ieng Sary passed away on 14 March 2013, and the proceedings were terminated.

Khieu Samphan was the Head of State for Democratic Kampuchea and a member of the Communist Party's Central Committee. In many ways, he was the public face of the regime.

And finally, Ieng Thirith, who was the Minister of Social Affairs. The year prior to the commencement of trial in November 2011, the Trial Chamber found that Ieng Thirith was not mentally fit to stand trial and that she should be provisionally released. The Office of the Co-Prosecutors appealed that decision to the Supreme Court Chamber arguing that Ieng Thirith should continue with medical treatment and be re-evaluated in six months to determine whether or not she had improved sufficiently to stand trial. The Supreme Court Chamber decided that a new assessment of Ieng Thirith's fitness to stand trial should be made six months after medical treatment. That medical treatment did not improve Ieng Thirith's condition and later, on 13 September 2012, the Trial Chamber ordered a stay of proceedings and the release of Ieng Thirith on the basis of its finding that she remained unfit for trial. Ultimately, the proceedings were terminated as the accused passed away in August 2015.[3]

---

[1]  For more information about this case, see ECCC, *Prosecutor v. Kaing Guek Eav*, Trial Chamber, Judgement, 001/18-07-2007/ECCC/TC, 26 July 2010 (https://www.legal-tools.org/doc/dbdb62/); Supreme Court Chamber, Appeal Judgement, 001/18-07-2007-ECCC/SC, 3 February 2012 (https://www.legal-tools.org/doc/681bad/).

[2]  For more information about this case, see ECCC, *Prosecutor v. Nuon Chea and Khieu Samphan*, Case 002/01 Judgement, 002/19-09-2007/ECCC/TC, 7 August 2014 (https://www.legal-tools.org/doc/4888de/); Trial Chamber, Case 002/02 Judgement, 002/19-09-2007/ECCC/TC, 16 November 2018 (https://www.legal-tools.org/doc/8v76lk/); Supreme Court Chamber, Appeal Judgement, 002/19-09-2007-ECCC/SC, 23 November 2016 (https://www.legal-tools.org/doc/e66bb3/).

[3]  ECCC, *Prosecutor v. Ieng Thirith*, Trial Chamber, Termination of the Proceedings against the Accused Ieng Thirith, 002/19-09-2007/ECCC/TC, 27 August 2015 (https://www.legal-tools.org/doc/2332f2/).

The two, surviving accused in *Case 002*, Nuon Chea and Khieu Samphan, were found guilty of crimes against humanity, and sentenced to life imprisonment.

These four individuals in *Case 002* were charged with crimes allegedly committed during a regime which was established, and which ceased to exist, decades before the trials. Let me turn now to the matter of how the passage of time has created challenges for the assembling and evaluating of evidence pertaining to those alleged crimes. I will review four areas of evidence, including crime scenes, documents, witnesses and expert evidence, each of which has its own unique challenges and opportunities in respect of the passage of time.

## 4.2. Crime Scenes

Crime scenes include the places used to plan criminal acts or to conduct criminal activity, such as torture and execution sites. Of particular interest in this regard are locations where forensic evidence may still exist even long after the event, such as torture centres or mass grave sites.

In Cambodia, prior to the establishment of the Khmer Rouge Tribunal, researchers had identified the locations of more than 200 Khmer Rouge torture and execution facilities, and approximately 20,000 mass graves. However, with a few rare exceptions, after 30 years, these locations have been contaminated to such an extent that, from a forensic perspective, they no longer contain any useful evidence. Even so, the mere identification of the existence of these crime sites allows investigators to establish patterns of abuses so that the mass and systematic nature of these abuses becomes readily apparent.

Probably the most notorious of these types of locations in Cambodia is the infamous S-21 prison in Phnom Penh. Immediately after the regime was overthrown, this site was turned into a museum, and thus it has since been preserved. But it is the only one of more than 200 Khmer Rouge prisons which has been maintained in more or less its original condition.

Unfortunately, other locations, such as a Khmer Rouge prison in Phnom Srok District, Banteay Meanchey Province, were not maintained. After the regime fell, the building was rehabilitated, and used as the district administration office. No traces remained of its previous use as a prison.

In another instance, a cave, located in Dang Tong District of Kampot Province, was also used as a Khmer Rouge prison. A concrete factory was eventually built on this site. Since then, the entire cave has been ground up and crushed to manufacture concrete. The location no longer exists.

But it does not take only humans to destroy evidence of mass crimes. A site known as Ampe Phnom in Samrong Tong District of Kampong Speu Province contains numerous un-exhumed mass graves. This site sits on the banks of the Prek Thnoat River, and, as happened at Ampe Phnom, wandering rivers can and sometimes do consume mass graves. There are many rivers in Cambodia so this happens fairly often. It also happened on an island called Koh Phal in Kampong Cham Province, which sits in the Mekong River. Koh Phal was the location of a major massacre of Muslim Cambodians, and part of a series of acts which we allege constitutes genocide. But the evidence of a mass grave is long gone.

Many mass graves were exhumed in the immediate aftermath of the Khmer Rouge regime, often by families searching for lost loved ones, and also often by impoverished survivors looking for valuables, such as jewellery sewn into the clothing of victims. Those exhumations were haphazard, non-scientific and poorly documented or not documented at all, rendering the sites effectively useless from a forensic standpoint.

In preparation for the trials, a local non-governmental organization called the Documentation Centre of Cambodia carried out a nationwide survey of mass grave sites in 2002–2003. That project identified several undisturbed sites which were suitable for formal, multi-disciplinary forensic exhumation. The Khmer Rouge Tribunal's Office of Co-Investigating Judges studied this information and ultimately decided that the likely results of a forensic exhumation were not worth the time and expense which would have been required to carry it out.

A large execution site near the capital, Phnom Penh, which was used to dispose of prisoners from the infamous S-21 prison in Phnom Penh, was exhumed shortly after the fall of the Khmer Rouge. Many thousands of sets of human remains were recovered here. Those remains were arranged into a memorial. Unfortunately, however, since the remains were displayed in open air, and exposed to the elements for 10 years before they were moved to an enclosed structure, these bones deteriorated to the point where they are no longer useful as a source of forensic evidence. In the southwest region of Cambodia, the Khmer Rouge operated a torture and execution facility known as Sang Prison. We believe that at least 5,000 people were executed at this location, perhaps many more. A similar memorial to the one near Phnom Penh was created at this prison. There were an estimated 2,600 sets of remains in this memorial. By 1995, the Sang Memorial had fallen into disrepair, and the roof and doors of the structure had been stolen, so that the bones were exposed to rain, sun and animals. Cows, in particular, like to eat the bones, as they are rich in calcium. So the bones began to deteriorate and disappear rapidly. Within three years, by the end of 1998, the bones in the Sang Memorial had reached an advanced state of disintegration. Very few of the bones remained at this point, and those which did remain were literally falling apart.

By 2009, the entire area had been bulldozed and cleared to construct a motor pool for the provincial police department. The previous evidence of mass atrocity crimes at this site – the remnants of the prison, the mass graves and the exhumed human remains – are now nothing but a memory in the minds of surviving witnesses, except, of course, for photographs of the site that had been previously taken. This suggests the importance of documenting crime sites as soon as possible after the commission of the crimes, as well as at regular intervals thereafter.

In contrast to the previous examples, some crime scenes can survive for decades. For example, the Khmer Rouge used mass forced labour in 1977 at a dam construction site in Kampong Thom Province, Cambodia, which was called the First January Dam. Upwards of 40,000 persons, working almost entirely by hand, built a huge dam that was 52 kilometres long. Due to incompetent engineering, the dam collapsed almost immediately, but the project was so massive that much remains of that effort today.

The Khmer Rouge were proud of their forced labour projects, so those projects were a standard stop on tours for foreign dignitaries. One of the accused persons, Ieng Thirith, led a Laotian delegation on a visit to the First January Dam site on 22 April 1977. In recent years, a small portion of the First January Dam has been re-engineered and reconstructed, to serve as a functioning irrigation system.

Remote sensing utilizing space-based imaging satellites can be useful in dealing with old crimes sites as well. Remote imaging can, for example, be used to identify old mass-grave sites, or to observe the contours of a very large forced labour earthworks project like the First January Dam.

### 4.3. Witnesses

Let us turn now to witness evidence. Over time, the availability and quality of witness testimony naturally erodes, due to a variety of factors. Witnesses will die. Witnesses will forget, or their memories may become frail and unreliable with advancing age. Witnesses may also lose interest, and no longer be willing to recall traumatic events of long ago.

Over a long period, some witnesses may have told their story many times. Records of those recounted experiences may reveal shifts or contradictions over time in the story told by a particular witness, raising questions which can be exploited by the defence and which can create doubts in the minds of judges.

Another factor that can interfere with the memory of witnesses is their exposure to different versions of the story, told by other people. A variant of this effect can be observed in Cambodia, and arises from the fact that the political movement that replaced the Khmer Rouge has ruled Cambodia since 1979. This political movement, the Cambodian People's Party, has its own version of history, and that version of history has been constantly repeated in official propaganda for decades. The average Cambodian person has heard this official version of the Cambodian genocide story many times, perhaps hundreds of times.

Trauma itself, of course, is another issue altogether, one which may be exacerbated with the passage of time. This is particularly likely if traumatic experiences continue to accumulate in an individual's life, through ongoing violence, or through forms of structural violence such as poverty. Trauma can distort memory, and make a victim's recollection of events less reliable.

Despite these challenges, witnesses remain a key source of evidence. Witness evidence in old cases can be recorded, as oral histories or as testimonial evidence, and collected closer in time to the events in question. It is stating the obvious, of course. But witness accounts gathered closer in time to the actual event will generally be more reliable than those gathered at a later date. These witness accounts may be preserved in the form of writing, audio recordings, or video recordings. Even if a witness is unavailable at the time of trial to authenticate the statement, or to be cross-examined regarding their statement, the court may still consider such a testimony as probative and useful to ascertaining the truth.

In Cambodia, a great deal of witness testimony has been recorded over the decades, and the Khmer Rouge Tribunal relied extensively on this old evidence in building its case files. Similar examples might be testimony recorded in the book *Women's 1971*,[4] or in films such as Ananda's *The Village of Widows*, both concerning Bangladesh.[5] Another major source of previous witness testimony in Cambodia was the 1979 "People's Revolutionary Tribunal", a local trial which judged Khmer Rouge leaders Pol Pot and Ieng Sary *in absentia* in the immediate aftermath of the regime.[6] The records of that proceeding are available to the Khmer Rouge Tribunal, as the prosecution found some of them useful. This is akin to the trials conducted in Bangladesh during the mid-1970s; if the records are still available, such documents can be useful for the war crimes work being done in the past decade at the national level.

---

[4] Yasmin Saikia, *Women, War, and the Making of Bangladesh: Remembering 1971*, Duke University Press, 2011.

[5] For a brief account on recent documentaries addressing 1971, see "Bangladesh Through Audio-Visual Medium", *The Daily Star*, 11 February 2011.

[6] ECCC, "Have Any of the Khmer Rouge Senior Leaders Been Tried Before?" (available on its web site).

Long after a crime has taken place, witnesses can be hard to locate. Travel can be difficult – roads in rural Cambodia are often impassable except on foot or by using traditional means of transportation. Moreover, in Cambodia, people often change their names at significant passages during their life; this can make the tracking of witnesses more difficult. Khmer Rouge cadres changed their names frequently as a matter of policy, and they also used code-named aliases, such as 'Grandfather 15', 'Mr. Blue', or 'Uncle Fish Paste'. This makes the identification of witnesses that much more challenging, more so when working on old cases.

## 4.4. Documents

There are many kinds of potentially relevant documentary evidence in trials for mass atrocities, some of which fall into the category of old evidence. For example, there are original documents from organizations or individuals involved in carrying out atrocities, contemporaneous photographs and films, and contemporaneous domestic and international news accounts.

A challenge with contemporaneous but old documents is the chain of custody of the evidence. International courts have accepted the realities and had liberal rulings on admission and probity of these old documents, often relying on other evidence to corroborate the documents.

One example of this from Cambodia is the official journal of the Communist Party of Kampuchea, which was called 'Revolutionary Flag'. The Party leadership used this publication to convey the 'Party line' to rank and file members of the Party, that is, to indoctrinate their followers in the ideology and policy of the revolutionary organization. Many issues of this publication still exist, and they are invaluable in demonstrating the patterns of criminal activity ordered by the accused persons. While the prosecution has definitively been unable to prove the chain of custody for some documents, from their date of publication during the Khmer Rouge era up until today, it is still possible to support and corroborate those documents through other evidence. These publications may contain a great deal of material relevant to the charges; but again, if the parties attempting to introduce the document into evidence at the court cannot prove the chain of custody, it may be subject to challenge.

Another type of old evidence from Cambodia which can be useful is bureaucratic records of organizations engaged in violations of humanitarian law. One example is what the prosecution called an 'execution log' from the S-21 prison in Phnom Penh, written on 23 July 1977. It is a list that records the biographical details of 18 prisoners who were executed on that day, and it is signed by two senior officials of the prison. Handwritten at the bottom is a notation which states: "Also killed 160 children today, for a total of 178 enemies killed today". We are fortunate that a large number of documents from S-21 survive until today. At the same time, we are aware that a large number of documents from that institution also have been lost over the intervening years.

Indeed, one victim who filed a complaint at the Khmer Rouge Tribunal accidentally learned the fate of her disappeared father when, after the regime fell, she bought some food from a street vendor, only to discover that the food was wrapped in a page from her father's forced confession. This led to the discovery that he had been executed at S-21 as an 'enemy of the people'. This incident highlights the fact that for many societies in which the oral tradition is still strong, and appreciation for the written word is not widespread, documents may not be seen as significant in and of themselves, and instead may be much more valued as, for example, something in which to wrap fish, or to roll tobacco for a cigarette.

Photographs are also a highly probative form of documentary evidence. Bureaucratic records from the S-21 prison were photographs that include the name of the prisoner and the prisoner's date of arrest, which can then be corroborated with other records from the same institution. In fact, the prosecution assembled this kind of data for more than 12,000 prisoners at S-21, making it possible to understand a great deal about how S-21 functioned as an institution. Photographic evidence is also helpful for means other than identifying victims. One photograph in the prosecution's files shows several Khmer Rouge leaders in a railway carriage, with top Khmer Rouge leader Pol Pot in front. Seated directly behind him is one of the accused persons at the Khmer Rouge Tribunal, Nuon Chea. Pol Pot was known during the regime as 'Brother Number One', and Nuon Chea as 'Brother Number Two'. This type of photograph can help to establish hierarchical relationships and visually reinforce the rank of an accused.

Even when the provenance of particular images is unclear, under certain circumstances, they can still be useful as evidence. For example, the prosecution was not able to know who took one photograph, but, from the buildings in the background, it could identify the scene as the capital city of Kampot Province in south-western Cambodia. From the activity of the people pictured also, it was also possible to infer that the photograph was taken on 17 April 1975, as the Khmer Rouge were carrying out the forced evacuation of that city.

Another source for obtaining old evidence is in co-operation with third-party states. The Khmer Rouge Tribunal has obtained images of Phnom Penh's Central Market, as seen in United States Air Force surveillance photographs, five days before the evacuation of Phnom Penh and 10 days afterwards. In the before photograph, a viewer can see cars, trucks, buses, goods and even people bustling around the market. In the after photograph, the entire area is bereft of vehicles, and people are nowhere to be seen. These images provide strong visual reinforcement of the allegation that the Khmer Rouge entirely emptied the capital of its population.

## 4.5. Expert Evidence

Estimating death tolls in episodes of mass atrocity is a notoriously difficult issue, and inevitably there will be significant margins of uncertainty in even the most carefully constructed estimates. Furthering the parallel with Bangladesh, a quick look at the literature on the 1971 Liberation War, or Independence War, suggests that there is a very wide range of estimates on the number of people who were killed. The numbers routinely see ranges from a low of 200,000 to a high of 3,000,000.

Something had to be done to provide a clearer picture of the historical record and the scope of the alleged atrocities. The solution at the Khmer Rouge Tribunal was to bring in a team of independent expert demographers to carry out a focused study of the question. The demographers concluded that the death toll under the Khmer Rouge regime was between 1.7 million and 2.2 million, with between 800,000 and 1.3 million violent deaths. That is still a substantial range of uncertainty, but it is much better than the virtually open-ended estimates that had been previously circulating among the public. Thus, we can see the value of expert evidence in attempting to grapple with old and uncertain data.

Finally, another type of expert evidence is analytical evidence, which can be created either by the prosecution or defence, or by outside experts. Analytical evidence can be particularly valuable in old cases, when there are only fragmentary bits of information available regarding certain events, but when there are enough fragments with which skilled analysts can reconstruct aspects of the criminal events which may help judges understand the historical context. Organizational charts of the Khmer Rouge outlining hierarchical structures in a province, for instance, help us understand exactly who was in charge of particular areas at a particular time. The Khmer Rouge Tribunal assembled such charts for the entire country during the regime.

## 4.6. Conclusion

The following are a series of few lessons about old evidence, as taught by the experience of the Khmer Rouge Tribunal.

First, just because evidence has not been found yet, one should not conclude that the evidence does not exist. There is more evidence out there than investigators may realize at a certain time.

Second, it is crucial to begin documenting evidence of crimes as soon as possible after they occur, and then to regularly continue to document important sites over time.

Third, merely documenting evidence is not enough; that documentation must be preserved in a form that will permit it to be understood and interpreted, and its original sources as well as its chain of custody proven, at a time long after the evidence has been collected.

Fourth, with regards to old crimes, it is often the case that various types of interested persons and organizations, from civil society organizations to governments, may have been collecting evidence for a long time. This previously collected evidence should be sought – it can help reveal the truth in cases of mass atrocity crimes.

Fifth, the use of electronic data systems and other advanced systems to discover, preserve, organize, analyse and disseminate evidence of mass atrocity crimes provides invaluable tools to those who will either prosecute or defend accused persons in such cases.

And sixth, political, bureaucratic, social and other extra-legal considerations and pressures will often impact the survival of evidence in mass atrocity cases, as well as the ability of investigators to gather that evidence; the best responses to these pressures are diligence and persistence.

There are many similarities and parallels among various instances of mass atrocity crimes, and those similarities make it possible for us to learn across instances in order to do a better job of addressing accountability issues. By the same token, each situation is in many ways unique, and the mechanisms we devise to address them will always vary in some significant ways.

**PART II:**
**ANALYSIS AND FORENSIC PERSPECTIVES**
**ON OLD EVIDENCE**

# 5

---

# Old Documents and Archives in
# Core International Crimes Cases

## Patrick J. Treanor*

"The past is a foreign country: they do things differently there".[1] This well-known line reminds us of the truth that the past, even of our own countries, is often unfamiliar to us. We therefore need to make an effort to learn about the past just as we do to learn about foreign countries. Another truth, however, is not illuminated by our quote. Namely, with the past, as with foreign countries, most people think they already know something, or even a lot, about them. In fact, they very often simply share common misconceptions about both. Everyone in the world knows that in America the streets are paved with gold; and every American at least knows that the young George Washington chopped down a cherry tree. Unfortunately, neither piece of common knowledge is true.

So it is in international crimes cases. In the former Yugoslavia, everyone 'knew' that Slobodan Milošević was 'in charge' and therefore guilty. Unfortunately, what everyone knows is not evidence. As Louise Arbour, the then Prosecutor of the ICTY, lamented:

> This "general knowledge" is our worst enemy. I am told all the time, "why didn't you indict this man or that man? Everybody knows he is guilty". It is a long way from what everybody ostensibly knows to an indictment for crimes listed in the Statute of the Tribunal that will withstand the test before the court. When

---

* **Patrick Treanor** retired in 2009 as Senior Research Office and Team Leader, Office of the Prosecutor ('OTP') of the International Criminal Tribunal for the former Yugoslavia ('ICTY') (1994–2009). He led the leadership analysis team of that Office with more than 30 staff. Prior to that, he was, *inter alia*, Historian and (after January 1989) Senior Historian at the Office of Special Investigations, United States ('US') Department of Justice (1980–1994); and Intelligence Analyst, Federal Research Division, US Library of Congress (1977–1980). He holds an A.B. with Honours in Russian from the College of the Holy Cross, Worcester, US; an M.A. in Russian and East European Studies from Yale University Graduate School; and a Ph.D. in Bulgarian History from the School of Slavonic and East European Studies, University of London. He conducts research in over 10 languages. He has served as an expert witness in several cases before the ICTY, including in the *Karadžić* and *Mladić* cases. Treanor won the 2012 M.C. Bassiouni Justice Award. He is a Case Matrix Network (CMN) Senior Adviser.

[1] Leslie Poles Hartley, *The Go-Between*, New York Review of Books, New York, 2002, p. 17.

the accused are not famous personalities nobody asks us, "Why haven't you indicted them?" In those ostensibly notorious cases, there is always a suspicion that something is amiss if we don't act in accordance with the general perception.[2]

Trials of international crimes have a tendency to begin long after the alleged criminal conducts have taken place, rendering the past even more foreign – as evidence grows old. For example, the Bangladesh of 50 years ago was, if not a distant place for its own people, assuredly a far different one than today. The investigation and prosecution of international crimes will thus be confronted with the challenge of learning about important elements of the country's past. Failing to meet this challenge could prove costly in the courtroom. Fortunately, the experience of other jurisdictions shows that this challenge can be successfully met through the use of old documents.

The study of the past, or history, relies on the record of things said and done. This record, however, is imperfect. Not everything is recorded, some records are inaccurate, others have been destroyed, yet others are otherwise unavailable. Available records, or primary sources, typically include live witnesses, written documents, archaeological evidence, and audio and video recordings. I will here deal with old documents, or written records, and their use in international crimes cases. I will explore the purposes these documents can serve, how they may be obtained from archives or in the field, how their analysis should proceed in the office of a prosecutor, and how they may be presented in court.[3] I will conclude with some remarks that emphasize the importance of trained personnel, while recognizing that conditions and requirements vary between jurisdictions.

The exposition below draws on my own experience of over 29 years working on cases of international crimes in two specific contexts. In both instances, however, we faced problems of distance in space and time. At the Office of Special Investigations ('OSI') of the US Department of Justice, I worked as Historian and Senior Historian from 1980 to 1994. In this role, I investigated and litigated cases involving Nazi persecution of racial, religious and other minorities in Europe from 1933 to 1945. When the office was established in 1979, these crimes had occurred up to 46 years in the past; nevertheless, its efforts still continue to this day, 91 years after the establishment of the Nazi regime. The locus of these crimes, of course, lies an ocean away from America, with cases scattered all across Axis Europe. The OSI investigated

---

[2]  "Why Did Prosecution Fail to Prove What 'Everybody Knows'", *Sense Tribunal*, 7 April 2008 (available on the Sense Agency's web site).

[3]  What is said here about written documents naturally applies, *mutatis mutandis*, to the other types of records mentioned.

and litigated each of these cases individually pursuant to US immigration law. Although many of these cases were interrelated, they involved a myriad of different security, military and political organizations.

I also worked at the OTP of the ICTY as a Research Officer for over 15 years, dealing with cases beginning only three years after the Tribunal's creation in 1993, but which have now stretched to over 30 years. For us, the alleged crimes were, however, originally much more distant in place than time. Not only is the former Yugoslavia located in a part of Europe far removed from the seat of ICTY in The Hague, but its international judges, prosecutors and investigators are also almost totally unfamiliar with its political and economic systems, language, culture and history. Such *contextual unfamiliarity* adversely impacts the interpretation of old documents.

## 5.1. Purpose

The primary purpose of 'old documents' in international crimes cases is, of course, to serve as evidence to be used in criminal trials. More broadly, these documents can assist courts in the establishment of factual truth regarding complex and often obscure developments, and in understanding the background and context of cases.[4] An advantage of using documents as evidence over live witnesses is that the former do not change their stories, although they can be 're-interrogated' many times, in search of additional facts. Almost as importantly, these documents can be used during the investigation phase of a case for lead purposes, as well as for the preparation and conduct of witness interviews. At OSI, many leads on Nazi crimes and Nazi perpetrators came from old documents, such as guard rosters. The ICTY even has a special provision in Rule 70 of its Rules of Procedure and Evidence for the submission of documents to the OTP for lead purposes only.[5]

Documents played an important evidentiary role in both sets of cases referred to above. OSI's Nazi cases were almost entirely built around documents, rather than witnesses, as eyewitnesses to the actions of the alleged perpetrators were almost always unavailable. In the former Yugoslavia, cases targeting those allegedly most responsible for the crimes in the region were also largely document-based. This was due to the fact that these top political and military leaders were only rarely suspected of personal involvement in crimes.

---

[4] I will not here enter into issues related to the potential role of international crimes trials in contributing to peace and reconciliation or in the creation of a historical record. Suffice it to say that a courtroom, where it is necessary to avoid the type of interpretation and conjecture routinely practiced by professional historians, is a poor place to write history as such.

[5] ICTY, Rules of Procedure and Evidence, IT/32/Rev.50, as amended on 8 July 2015 (https://www.legal-tools.org/doc/30df50/).

In international crimes cases, documentary evidence may go to directly proving individual guilt, or proving contextual elements of the international crime concerned. As mentioned above, documentary evidence often plays an important role in the investigation of high-ranking leaders. However, documentary evidence can also serve as direct evidence regarding the guilt of low-level perpetrators. For example, local policemen in Nazi-occupied Poland produced reports accounting for their expenditures of ammunition, referred to as 'bullet reports'. Such reports, signed by the policeman involved, sometimes disclose the killing of Jews who were caught hiding during Nazi-ordered round-ups. Another example of documentary evidence often used is the service identification cards of guards at Nazi concentration camps or extermination centres. Such documents provide *prima facie* evidence of their owners' participation in the persecution occurring in these camps and centres.[6] In cases involving high-level officials, the signature of overtly persecutory Nazi laws or orders can constitute evidence of the individual's involvement.

Context, however, is also important. The term 'context' here refers to the events, organizational structures, legal frameworks and policies that surround the alleged crimes. In cases involving political leaders, context is particularly important as there is usually no direct evidence of these leaders' involvement in the crimes concerned. It therefore becomes necessary to reconstruct these leaders' scope of authority and responsibility, their goals and their activities to the extent possible on the basis of evidentiary materials. Such contextual evidence may include constitutional provisions, basic legislation, minutes or transcripts of meetings, orders, reports or correspondence. These documents may illuminate issues regarding the means and degree of control at the disposal of the individual concerned, as well as purposes motivating the said individual. At the ICTY, leadership cases are, in fact, largely based on such documentary contextual evidence, which provide links between leaders and direct perpetrators. During the trial of such cases, large volumes of documents are typically introduced into evidence by the parties concerned, which are often accompanied by extensive expert reports (on which, see further below). Court judgments therefore usually contain lengthy sections on context, which sometimes reach far back into pre-conflict history.[7]

---

[6] "[I]f petitioner had disclosed the fact that he had been an armed guard at Treblinka, he would have been found ineligible for a visa", United States Supreme Court, *Fedorenko v. United States*, Decision, 21 January 1981, 449 U.S. 490, para. 513 (https://www.legal-tools.org/doc/c7c51e/).

[7] On these points, see Richard Ashby Wilson, *Writing History in International Tribunals*, Cambridge University Press, 2011, especially pp. 73–77 and 128–39.

Even in OSI cases involving low-level perpetrators from the World War II era, it is still necessary to link the individuals concerned to Nazi policies of persecution by reconstructing the chains of command within which they operated, and proving the persecutory ends which their units served. This could only be done on the basis of the surviving records of German and German-sponsored security and military organizations.

## 5.2. Collection

In gathering any evidence, it is essential for investigators to have an idea of what they are looking for in at least general terms. Only by analysing all initially available evidence or information is it possible to formulate a preliminary hypothesis or set of questions. This is not necessarily the same as the theory of the case. These questions will then guide the hunt for new evidence. Investigations can then begin, and continue to proceed, on the basis of this substantive hypothesis. For example, the question may be which battalion was in a particular area at the relevant time or whether the party leader was really in overall control. The next step is to attempt to find out as much as possible about the actions, personnel, organizations and policies which figure in the hypothesis. It is here that documents can be helpful or even essential. It is necessary to emphasize that the process of collecting documents should not be just a search for 'smoking guns', and that possibly exculpatory evidence must not be neglected.

The search for documents begins with identifying the possibly relevant types of documents, some examples of which were mentioned above, and their locations. When common knowledge fails, the assistance of experts, informants and witnesses may be crucial in locating documents. Public archives located in various countries are the most common repositories for older documents generated by official bodies or donated by prominent, and sometimes not so prominent, individuals. Indeed, by far the single most valuable source of documentation for OSI was the National Archives in Washington, DC, literally a stone's throw from the Department of Justice, which housed well-known collections of captured German documents and Nuremberg trial materials. Many official records, especially but not always of recent date, are still held, however, by agencies, official bodies, or other organizations such as the United Nations. This is the type of documentation that proved so important for OTP investigations, with former Yugoslavia and United Nations agencies accounting for the bulk of the documents they collected. The advantage of these types of collections is that they tend to be well organized and catalogued. Private individuals, including former officials or political activists, may also have documents in their possession or know of those who do. They may also be able to alert investigators to the existence of particular documents, if not their location. Private diaries can likewise be an invaluable source of evidence and information. The OTP collected some very valuable documents on a voluntary basis from such private sources, usually retired international officials who were originally contacted as potential witnesses.

Nor should libraries be forgotten. National libraries and other large research libraries typically contain collections of official gazettes, other legal publications, newspapers and other contemporaneous periodicals, memoirs and secondary literature. Much material of this type may even be available *via* the Internet. All of these sources can provide valuable evidence or information. OSI was able to obtain many published documents and even Nazi era writings containing *prima facie* evidence of advocacy of persecution from the US Library of Congress, while libraries in the Netherlands and the Internet provided the OTP with much useful legal and political material from the former Yugoslavia.

In any case, it is always preferable to have direct access to documentary collections of any type so that investigators can do their own research and analysis. This may require travel to the site of documentary collections. The OSI sent many such research missions to archives in numerous countries, such as Germany, Poland, Israel and the former Soviet Union; and it almost goes without saying that OTP staff travelled to the former Yugoslavia on countless occasions to collect documents from agencies there. Such missions may involve one or more persons, but they must always be carefully planned to ensure adequate staffing as well as sufficient logistical and technical support. To limit expenses, costly missions should be organized to act on behalf of all investigations interested in the given collection. If requests are made to distant holders of possibly relevant documents for copies or originals of documents, they are best not framed as 'give us anything you have on so-and-so'. Instead, requests should ask for specified items whenever possible. If a collection is considered to be important, investigators should visit it personally for review.

When reviewing documents, it should be remembered that any document is better than no document. Even though relevant documents may seem scarce, one should still go through them meticulously as important information may be contained in one single page, for example, in the signature line or in a distribution list. Of course, the greater the number of documents that are available, the better the results of the investigation will be, although vast quantities may be a mixed blessing in view of the necessarily limited resources to handle them. Documents can be copied or, if conditions permit, seized. The use of portable copying machines, scanners or, these days, digital cameras, is much preferable to relying on even the most co-operative custodian to provide copies later. In order to avoid complicating authentication or the destroying of evidence, original documents should never be defaced. No useful material, including possibly exculpatory evidence or documents that may provide evidence in related cases or new leads, should be neglected. An easy trap to fall into is to look for evidence relating only to 'the period of the indictment'. Especially in leadership cases, such an approach can lead to the loss of material crucial to an understanding of facts regarding personnel, organizations and policies – the elements of which contribute to events that do figure in an indictment.

It must be said that the availability of old documents is heavily dependent on their timely seizure and subsequent careful preservation. These events may antedate an investigation by years, if not decades. The investigation of World War II era crimes in the US would have been virtually impossible were it not for the fact that American and other Allied Forces captured vast quantities of German documents at the conclusion of hostilities. Many of these documents were used in trials before the International Military Tribunal in Nuremberg and other courts immediately after the war. Later, experts in the US organized and prepared detailed catalogues of these documents, which were returned to Germany after being microfilmed. An extensive scholarly literature based on these documents was already in existence by the time the OSI began its investigations in 1979.[8] It therefore had the benefit of access to these important collections, as well as thorough archival guides, and much of the OSI's ground-breaking analytical work was based on both.

The case of the former Yugoslavia is different. Here, the conflict was still in progress when the ICTY was created, and all the most relevant documents were still held by various regional and international agencies and organizations. Ongoing hostilities and lack of co-operation by certain parties to the conflicts hampered efforts at collection in the region. Nevertheless, through persistent efforts over a period of years, the OTP managed to build up a huge collection of documents and other evidence. The establishment of co-operative relations with the parties, particularly after the Dayton Peace Accords, greatly facilitated collection efforts, but important material was also obtained through search warrants and court orders, sometimes even during trial.

The collection and analysis of documents and other evidence is assisted by building up a library of reference materials, such as geographical aids (maps and gazetteers), basic published documents (for example, laws and constitutions) and scholarly studies. Eventually, investigators will also build up their own archive of collected documents. These documents must be carefully

---

[8]    See, especially, Raul Hilberg, *The Destruction of the European Jews*, Harper and Row, New York, 1961.

indexed, organized and preserved in order to maximize their usefulness for investigatory and later trial purposes. The original order of collected documents should be maintained whenever possible.

## 5.3. Analysis

As indicated above, some analysis is necessary before proceeding to the collection of documents. This analysis must also continue during the document collection process. Conducting an ongoing analysis of the evidence that one accumulates, including old documents, is essential as this will help reveal the strengths and weaknesses in one's original hypothesis as well as the gaps in information and what further evidence is needed. The hypothesis which one starts with may, and indeed most likely will, change over time, but these changes should reflect and result from a deepening of knowledge based on constant analysis. This analysis should serve as a guide to the investigative process as a whole, as one proceeds with the gathering of fresh information and evidence, including additional documents. All relevant information and evidence must be continually integrated through analysis into the original or altered hypothesis. It is important to note that any inconsistent or irrelevant evidence should merely be put aside, but not forgotten, for later re-evaluation and possible use.

In this way, hard-won knowledge, obtained on the basis of steadily accumulating information and evidence, will not be ignored or forgotten. The ongoing analysis will constantly incorporate new knowledge into one's hypothesis while evaluating and re-evaluating this hypothesis and all available knowledge against each other. This reciprocal relationship between the hypothesis and knowledge gathered in the investigative process is extremely important, and the constant analysis that is required to establish and maintain this relationship is what should drive the investigation forward.

Ideally, of course, at the end of the investigative process, all information and evidence obtained will either be consistent with the final hypothesis or have been shown to be false or irrelevant. The initial hypothesis may not even have pointed to criminal liability. Indeed, the final hypothesis may not point to criminal liability, but it will at least be clear why this is so. The crucial thing is that, at any given point in time, the investigators should have a good command of what they know, and what they must still find out. This is especially important in order to avoid any duplication of evidence collection efforts. Investigators should, therefore, always have an overview of what documentary sources have been explored and what documents have been obtained. Having such a comprehensive overview will also help to prevent evidentiary gaps and to ensure the efficient use of resources by preventing the collection of duplicative evidence.[9]

The results of analysis can be set out in various formats, such as a Word document or by using inter-relational software such as Case Map or Case Matrix. Creating a narrative, such as might be found in a brief supporting an indictment or closing a case, will probably be necessary at some stage, in any event. Whatever format is adopted, the analytical product should always be made available to everyone involved in the specific investigation as well as other related investigations. Ideally, one person or a small group will be tasked with maintaining and updating this analysis. This will ensure its internal consistency. This shared analysis itself enables the creation of an institutional memory, which facilitates the addition of new staff and mitigates consequences resulting from the departure of experienced personnel.

## 5.4. Presentation

Old documents are used at trial in various ways. They may serve as trial exhibits, which are to be introduced as evidence along with the testimonies of appropriate fact witnesses whether on direct or cross-examination. If the court allows, they can also be introduced in dossiers. A very efficient way to exploit the evidentiary value of documents is by submitting substantive analytical expert reports based on these same documents, in conjunction with testimony by the author as an expert witness. This is especially useful when dealing with a large number of often lengthy documents.

For, as the analytical process will have shown, documents do not always speak for themselves, and the volume of collected documentation may be so high that it would be inadvisable to burden the court with all the documents concerned. A report, if accepted into evidence along with the testimony of the expert witness, can reduce the need to introduce the documents themselves. That is, the number of actual documents taken into evidence can be curtailed, sometimes dramatically, depending on the extent to which the report captures the relevant facts contained in them. The role of the expert is accordingly not to argue one side of a case but to explain the contents of the documents.

In commissioning such expert reports, clear and transparent instructions must be given to the expert concerned. Reports may be commissioned by either party or, in some jurisdictions, by the court itself. The instructions should specify the topics to be treated in the report (for instance, the chain of command and operations of a particular military unit over a particular time period, or the authority, structure and activities of the ministry of internal affairs). Ide-

---

[9] Sometimes multiple copies of the same document are useful to show, for example, its wide distribution.

ally, the instructions should be in writing in order to be available to a trial chamber or opposing party to help them appraise whether the report displays any bias toward the commissioning party. The methodology to be used in the report may best be left to the expert, and it has proven highly advisable for the expert to include a note on methodology and sources in a preface to his or her report in order to show how the instructions were carried out. The primary requirement is that the said expert should be given complete access to all relevant documents collected in the course of the investigation, including potentially adverse material. The expert must be given the full opportunity to analyse these documents as well as other sources that he or she considers suitable in light of the instructions. Reports must be carefully sourced through the use of footnotes or other citations to the sources used. This would be normal procedure for any academically trained expert, but ICTY trial chambers have actually received and rejected expert reports that failed to meet even this minimum professional standard. Trial chambers have also refused to accept reports based solely on open sources such as press stories or utilizing only one set of documents (such as minutes of meetings of a single body). They have been especially dismissive of reports that appeared to judge the ultimate issues of innocence and guilt in a case.

How can such experts be found? As indicated above, this depends on the overall availability of the documents concerned. Old documents that are preserved in public archives may have already been extensively exploited by reputable scholars. Published works that are based on and analyse these documents not only assist the investigation, but also establish the author's qualifications as an expert. In addition, these publications can sometimes be introduced as evidence along with a specifically commissioned report. It was the OSI's practice to utilize such outside experts in Nazi war crimes cases in the US. In instances where documents have not been publicly accessible, they may have been read and analysed only by investigation staff. Finding an outside expert with the time necessary to duplicate this effort may be next to impossible and probably prohibitively expensive. For these reasons and as further explained below, the ICTY eventually adopted a practice of using 'inside' experts at many trials.

## 5.5. Staffing

The foregoing considerations about the use of inside experts in court are related to the overall staffing requirements of the investigative offices concerned. Both the OSI and the OTP were combined investigative and prosecutorial offices that specialized in war crimes cases alone. That is, the prosecutors and investigators worked in the same office, were headed by a prosecutor and specialized in these types of cases. This model was pioneered by the OSI in the war crimes field and was later adopted in some, but not all, jurisdictions outside the US when pursuing international crimes cases from the World War II era.[10] Whether organizationally joined with the prosecution or not, virtually all the investigative organs concerned recognized, again following the lead of the OSI, the need to include and engage an additional area of substantive expertise possessed by a third professional group: analysts.

The successful collection, analysis and presentation of documentary evidence demand high levels of organizational, analytical and communications skills. Depending on the context of the given investigation, specific linguistic skills and background knowledge not possessed by prosecutors and criminal investigators may also be necessary. At the OSI, a group of historians provided this required skill set, while at the OTP, a corresponding group of Research Officers in the Leadership Research Team ('LRT') performed the same function. Both offices eventually created separate organizational units for these analysts.[11] At the OSI, in fact, the presence of the relatively large number of historians virtually supplanted the need for criminal investigators. This was certainly not true in the case of the OTP, as the contemporary nature of investigations facilitated the availability of many witnesses and other traditional forms of evidence that are best exploited by experienced criminal investigators.

In both the OSI and the OTP, however, the presence of academically trained researchers with the necessary skills and often extensive personal experience in the regions of their specialization proved to be invaluable assets to the organization. These researchers not only played major roles in the collection, analysis and presentation of documents but also assisted in many other aspects of investigation and litigation. At the OSI, each historian formed part of an effective, multi-disciplinary team that was created for each case or group of cases, working with others under a lead attorney. All members of these teams had clearly defined tasks in keeping with their professional backgrounds. The historians were responsible for the collection and analysis of all historical documents. They did not act as experts at trial, but consulted closely with the outside experts who did.[12] Within the OTP, individual members of the LRT and the Military Assessment Team similarly worked directly with the trial attorneys or investigators of one or more investigative or trial teams. As noted

---

[10] For example, Australia, the International Criminal Tribunal for Rwanda and the International Criminal Court, but not Canada and the United Kingdom.

[11] The OTP also had military intelligence analysts, organized in a separate Military Analysis Team and criminal analysts, working with the investigation teams proper.

[12] Including Raul Hilberg, whose monumental work was cited in Hilberg, 1961, see *supra* note 8.

above, many of these analysts also prepared expert reports and testified at numerous trials, in addition to the traditional outside experts.[13]

## 5.6. Conclusion

The use of old documents, as outlined above, must always be informed by a consciousness among all those concerned that it is frequently the accused who is, in fact, the leading expert on aspects of the distant events being considered by analysts, investigators, attorneys and judges. If these professionals neglect old documents, they run a serious risk of letting these accused provide their own self-serving and unchallenged versions of unfamiliar times and places.

---

[13] On the use of inside and outside experts at ICTY, see Wilson, 2011, pp. 121 ff., *supra* note 7.

# 6

---

# Memory and Trauma

## Anya Topiwala and Seena Fazel[*]

## 6.1. Introduction

Clinicians and researchers have investigated the reliability of witness accounts, particularly in individuals who have been subject to violence and aggression. In many legal settings, the reliability of witness memory is a key determinant in the outcome of cases. This chapter aims to provide a structured review of recent evidence on the effects of violence and trauma on memory, and outline some good practice guidelines.

Some studies have demonstrated memory impairments in individuals subjected to stress. Inconsistencies in trauma victims' narratives have also been reported. However, this work has methodological limitations, including a focus on victims with post-traumatic stress disorder ('PTSD'), with little information on other psychiatric diagnoses. Overall, a reasonable body of evidence exists in support of a specific type of memory deficit in victims of trauma. The loss of memory relates to the recall of verbal material, particularly autobiographical memory. This concerns recollections from an individual's life, a key element of witness memory. It is unclear to what extent this may undermine the credibility of the testimony of witnesses. There is a contradictory body of evidence suggesting some enhancement of memory under stress. Some studies report an increase in the retention of material with an emotional content, to the detriment of more peripheral details. This enhancement may be mediated by sleep and occur over a time period of a few days. In addition to summarizing the latest evidence, we propose clinical guidelines for professionals assessing victims prior to and in the courtroom.

---

[*] **Seena Fazel** is Professor in Forensic Psychiatry at the University of Oxford. He is an international authority on the mental health of prisoners, their suicide risk, and the relationship between severe mental illness and violence. He studied medicine at the University of Edinburgh before training in psychiatry at Oxford. **Anya Topiwala** is a Senior Clinical Lecturer in the Nuffield Department of Population Health at the University of Oxford. She graduated in physiological sciences and medicine from the University of Oxford before training in psychiatry and becoming a member of the Royal College of Psychiatrists. She has collaborated with the Forensic Psychiatry Group in Oxford, producing publications on topics such as the management of violence and the institutionalization of the mentally ill.

In a number of high-profile international criminal trials such as those of the former Yugoslavia, Rwanda and Cambodia, evidence has relied substantially on victims' memories. The cases of Rwanda and Cambodia are based on memories of events that occurred around eight and thirty years after the alleged criminal acts, respectively.[1] These cases raise two major issues in relation to the reliability of evidence. First, eyewitness memory in normal subjects is thought to be unreliable and, over time, it is known that memories decay. Second, PTSD, anxiety and depression are common in veterans,[2] remaining for some years after the traumatic events, and the contribution of these to memory decay is a contentious area. Therefore, the ability of some individuals to act as reliable witnesses in court needs clarification.

A 1992 review of the literature by Christianson[3] argued that the assumption that stress decreases brain processing capacity, and thus memory, was simplistic. This review suggested that emotional events are preferentially processed, and therefore memory was not necessarily adversely affected by trauma. Koss *et al.*, in a later review, concluded that memories for traumatic experiences typically contain more central than peripheral detail, are reasonably accurate, and are well-retained for very long periods, but are not completely indelible.[4]

A pertinent article reviewing the field centred around the trial of Anto Furundžija at the International Criminal Tribunal for the former Yugoslavia ('ICTY') in 1998.[5] Furundžija was a Bosnian-Croatian soldier accused of aiding and abetting the imprisonment and rape of a Muslim woman. The defence argued that the victim's memory was inaccurate because she had been diagnosed with PTSD. The article summarized the evidence of the defence and prosecution on this issue. It concluded that, as memories in all individuals are

---

[1]   Alexander Zahar, "Witness Memory and the Manufacture of Evidence at the International Criminal Tribunals", in Carsten Stahn and Larissa van den Herik (eds.), *Future Perspectives on International Criminal Justice*, T.M.C. Asser Press, The Hague, 2010, pp. 600–610.

[2]   Jillian Ikin *et al.*, "Anxiety, Post-Traumatic Stress Disorder and Depression in Korean War Veterans 50 Years After the War", in *The British Journal of Psychiatry*, 2007, vol. 190, no. 6, pp. 475–483.

[3]   Sven-Åke Christianson, "Emotional Stress and Eyewitness Memory: A Critical Review", in *Psychological Bulletin*, 1992, vol. 112, no. 2, p. 284.

[4]   Mary P. Koss, Shannon Tromp and Melinda Tharan, "Traumatic Memories: Empirical Foundations, Forensic and Clinical Implications", in *Clinical Psychology: Science and Practice*, 1995, vol. 2, no. 2, pp. 111–132.

[5]   Landy Sparr and Douglas Bremner, "Post-Traumatic Stress Disorder and Memory: Prescient Medicolegal Testimony at the International War Crimes Tribunal?", in *Journal of American Academy of Psychiatry and Law*, 2005, vol. 33, no. 1, pp. 71–78. See also International Criminal Tribunal for the former Yugoslavia, *Prosecutor v. Anto Furundžija*, Judgement, 10 December 1998, IT-95-17-T (https://www.legal-tools.org/doc/e6081b/).

subject to a range of inaccuracies, it was vital to obtain collateral information in cases involving both PTSD and non-PTSD victims.

Overall, these older reviews are somewhat contradictory in their conclusions, particularly regarding the accuracy of traumatic memories. They also have tended to focus on victims with PTSD. This review will attempt to update the literature, and propose evidence-based guidelines to assist professionals interviewing individuals in such cases.

## 6.2. Background

Memory has been categorized into implicit and explicit forms. Implicit memory comprises previous experiences that aid in the unconscious performance of a task, such as riding a bike. In contrast, explicit memory is the conscious, intentional recollection of previous experiences and information. Explicit memory includes autobiographical memory which includes memory for events ('episodic') and knowledge ('semantic'). Autobiographic memory for a normal event is verbal, sequenced (beginning, middle and end), recognized as being in the past, and may be recalled voluntarily. After 10 years, it is thought that memories can be highly accurate, highly inaccurate, or include both accurate and inaccurate reports relating to different aspects of the same episode.[6]

The main effect of a delay between an event occurring and it being recalled is forgetting. Two factors affect this: memory vividness and the amount of rehearsal. Vividness is determined by the comprehension and emotion at the time, its personal significance, and the extent to which it integrates with existing memories. Highly vivid memories may be retained for long periods and be more resistant to decay. Rehearsal makes memories more resistant to decay, but also offers the opportunity for distortion or errors to be assimilated into memory. The effects of delay are mediated by age, mental illness and trauma. This chapter will review the latter.

## 6.3. Methods

We searched the electronic bibliographic database 'MEDLINE' using search terms relating to memory and testimony. Publications were largely selected from the past 10 years (2013–June 2022), but commonly referenced and highly regarded older publications were not excluded. We also searched the reference lists of articles identified by this search strategy and selected those we judged relevant, focusing on key publications and review articles.

---

[6]    "Guidelines on Memory and the Law: Recommendations From the Scientific Study of Human Memory", British Psychological Society, Leicester, 2008.

## 6.4. Discussion

### 6.4.1. Normal Subjects Under Stress

There is evidence that subjecting normal humans to stress impairs memory. A meta-analysis of 113 studies found that stress prior to or during memory encoding was associated with memory impairments, except when the delay between the stressor and encoding was very short, when stress correlated with improved encoding.[7] A key study exposed 509 military survival school trainees to low- or high-stress interrogations.[8] A large number were unable to identify their interrogators despite being physically threatened by them for over 30 minutes. Those exposed to high-stress identified true positives only 30–49 per cent of the time and 51–68 per cent identified false positives. However, methodological criticisms have been levelled at these studies in that they do not entail the same degree of personal 'threat' as real-life trauma.[9] Hence, it is difficult to extrapolate these results to trauma victims, who may additionally be suffering from a consequential mental disorder.

### 6.4.2. Traumatic Experiences and Memory

Traumatic memories are often thought to be incomplete, unstable and triggered unexpectedly, providing fragments of details and emotions, or leading to freezing. Research has suggested that they are not complete in the sense of providing a temporal sequence of events. Trauma memory is characterized by vivid and distressing memories of the worst moments with jumbled and inconsistent recall of the remaining events.[10] In light of this, victims may be presented as unreliable in the courtroom.

A number of studies of victims have reported inconsistencies in their trauma narratives.[11] These have been found in those experiencing severe trauma, including Nazi concentration camp survivors, whose narratives were col-

---

[7] Grant S. Shields, Matthew A. Sazma, Andrew M. McCullough and Andrew P. Yonelinas, "The Effects of Acute Stress on Episodic Memory: A Meta-Analysis and Integrative Review", in *Psychological Bulletin*, 2017, vol. 143, no. 6, p. 636.

[8] Charles A. Morgan *et al.*, "Accuracy of Eyewitness Memory for Persons Encountered During Exposure to Highly Stressful Personally Relevant Events", in *International Journal of Law and Psychiatry*, 2004, vol. 27, no. 3, pp. 265–279.

[9] Steven Penrod and Brian Cutler, "Witness Confidence and Witness Accuracy: Assessing Their Forensic Relation", in *Psychology, Public Policy, and Law*, 1995, vol. 1, no. 4, p. 817.

[10] Amy Hardy, Kerry Young and Emily A. Holmes, "Does Trauma Memory Play a Role in the experience of Reporting Sexual Assault During Police Interviews? An Exploratory Study", in *Memory*, 2009, vol. 17 no. 8, pp. 783–788.

[11] Urs Hepp *et al.*, "Inconsistency in Reporting Potentially Traumatic Events", in *The British Journal of Psychiatry*, 2006, vol. 188, no. 3, pp. 278–283.

---

lected 40 years apart from the traumatic event.[12] Roemer and colleagues demonstrated "systematic inconsistencies" over time in the retrospective accounts of war zone events among Somalia veterans.[13] Such inconsistencies apparently caused problems in the Kupreškić case before the ICTY. The brothers, Zoran and Mirjan Kupreškić, were acquitted by the Trial Chamber of one count on the basis that the key witness to the incident had been embellishing his testimony over time. As the trial judges wrote:

> The difficulty concerning the credibility of this witness's evidence is that it was not until ten months after the incident that he firmly identified Zoran and Mirjan Kupreškić as the perpetrators of the massacre of his family.[14]

However, there may be other explanations for these discrepancies. For instance, more information can be recalled later (there is some evidence that memory is consolidated after one week), or information may have been given by others. It is also difficult to account for the severity and intensity of trauma.

Individuals exposed to trauma have been found to recall fewer specific memories on an autobiographical memory test in a meta-analysis, with a large effect size reported as a Cohen's d of 0.8 (95 per cent, confidence interval (CI) 0.4–1.1, $p<0.001$). However, substantial heterogeneity was observed.[15] Interestingly, memory impairments were greater in those exposed to trauma in adulthood rather than in childhood. Whilst many memories of traumatic events are rapidly forgotten, what is retained may be long-lasting. In a survey of survivors of the 9 September 2001 attacks, memories were not significantly changed after a 10-year delay.[16]

Cognitive impairments may relate to the emotional state of a subject. In a study of Colombian civilians exposed to urban violence or warfare more than a decade earlier, poorer short-term memory and cognitive control was only

---

[12] Willem A. Wagenaar and Jop Groeneweg, "The Memory of Concentration Camp Survivors", in *Applied Cognitive Psychology*, 1990, vol. 4, no. 2, pp. 77–87.
[13] Lizabeth Roemer *et al.*, "Increases in Retrospective Accounts of War-Zone Exposure Over Time: The Role of PTSD Symptom Severity", in *Journal of Trauma and Stress*, 1998, vol. 11, pp. 597–605.
[14] Stahn and van den Herik (eds.), 2010, see *supra* note 1.
[15] Tom J. Barry *et al.*, "Meta-Analysis of the Association Between Autobiographical Memory Specificity and Exposure to Trauma", in *Journal of Traumatic Stress*, 2018, vol. 31, no. 1, pp. 35–46.
[16] William Hirst *et al.*, "A Ten-Year Follow-Up of a Study of Memory for the Attack of September 11, 2001: Flashbulb Memories and Memories for Flashbulb Events", in *Journal of Experimental Psychology: General*, 2015, vol. 144, no. 3, p. 604.

observed in those recalling emotions of anxiety and fear connected to their experiences of violence.[17]

### 6.4.3. Post-Traumatic Stress Disorder and Memory

To date, much of the work examining the effects of trauma on memory has focused on PTSD victims.

Bremner and colleagues[18] reported that abused women with PTSD demonstrated increased false recognition of words (95 per cent) compared with abused women without PTSD (78 per cent) or the non-abused with PTSD (79 per cent). Jenkins *et al.* found that rape victims with a formal diagnosis of PTSD performed significantly worse than non-PTSD victims and controls on recall using a standardized test.[19] Vietnam veterans with PTSD were shown to have deficits on tasks of attention, working (short-term) memory and learning.[20] Impaired recall of words has also been found in a number of study populations with PTSD, including Holocaust survivors,[21] rape victims,[22] refugees from the former Yugoslavia,[23] earthquake survivors[24] and combat veterans.[25]

[17] Francesco Bogliacino, Gianluca Grimalda, Pietro Ortoleva and Patrick Ring, "Exposure To and Recall Of Violence Reduce Short-Term Memory and Cognitive Control", in *Proceedings of the National Academy of Sciences*, 2017, vol. 114, no. 32, pp. 8505–8510.

[18] J. Douglas Bremner, John F. Kihlstrom and Katharine Krause Shobe, "False Memories in Women With Self-Reported Childhood Sexual Abuse: An Empirical Study", in *Psychological Science*, 2000, vol. 11, no. 4, pp. 333–337.

[19] Melissa Jenkins *et al.*, "Learning and Memory in Rape Victims With Posttraumatic Stress Disorder", in *The American Journal of Psychiatry*, 1998, vol. 155, no. 2, pp. 278–279.

[20] Jennifer Vasterling *et al.*, "Attention, Learning, and Memory Performances and Intellectual Resources in Vietnam Veterans: PTSD and No Disorder Comparisons", in *Neuropsychology*, 2002, vol. 16, no. 1, p. 5.

[21] Julia Golier *et al.*, "Memory Performance in Holocaust Survivors With Posttraumatic Stress Disorder", in *The American Journal of Psychiatry*, 2002, vol. 159, no. 10, p. 1682–1688.

[22] Reginald Nixon *et al.*, "The Accumulative Effect of Trauma Exposure on Short-Term and Delayed Verbal Memory in a Treatment-Seeking Sample of Female Rape Victims", in *Journal of Traumatic Stress*, 2004, vol. 17, no. 1, pp. 31–35.

[23] Gunilla Kivling-Bodén and Elisabet Sundbom, "Cognitive Abilities Related to Post-Traumatic Symptoms Among Refugees From the Former Yugoslavia in Psychiatric Treatment", in *Nordic Journal of Psychiatry*, 2003, vol. 57, no. 3, pp. 191–198.

[24] E. Eren-Koçak *et al.*, "Memory and Prefrontal Functions in Earthquake Survivors: Differences Between Current and Past Post-Traumatic Stress Disorder Patients", in *Acta Psychiatrica Scandinavica*, 2009, vol. 119, no. 1, pp. 35–44.

[25] Rachel Yehunda *et al.*, "Learning and Memory in Combat Veterans With Posttraumatic Stress Disorder", in *The American Journal of Psychiatry*, 1995, vol. 152, no. 1.

Some studies suggest a correlation between symptom severity and the degree of impairment.[26]

A systematic review and meta-analysis of 28 such studies found a consistent impairment in verbal memory in victims compared to controls. The impairment was strongest in those with PTSD, but there was a modest effect in exposed non-PTSD controls. Perhaps surprisingly, stronger effects were found in war veterans than in sexual or physical assault victims.[27] In the longer term, there is an emerging evidence base for a link between PTSD and risk of dementia.[28]

Overgenerality in autobiographical memory, that is, a reduced ability to access specific memories of life events, has been demonstrated in individuals exposed to trauma.[29] Some have hypothesized that this is a protective mechanism that helps to attenuate painful emotions associated with trauma. Increased severity of post-traumatic stress has been associated with reduced autobiographical memory specificity in trauma-exposed samples.[30] Moradi *et al.* reported impaired retrieval of some aspects of autobiographical memory in trauma survivors with a past diagnosis of cancer.[31] The degree of impairment was associated with levels of both flashbacks and avoidance of the trauma. In refugees, a significant association was found between flashback frequency and reduced specificity for autobiographic memory. These studies, however, need to be interpreted cautiously. There is a high co-morbidity with other psychiatric disorders associated with PTSD, especially alcohol, substance misuse and

---

[26] Steven Southwick *et al.*, "Trauma-Related Symptoms in Veterans of Operation Desert Storm: A 2-Year Follow-Up", in *The American Journal of Psychiatry*, 1995, vol. 152.

[27] Grethe Johnsen and Arve Asbjørnsen, "Consistent Impaired Verbal Memory in PTSD: A Meta-Analysis", in *Journal of Affective Disorders*, 2008, vol. 111, no. 1, pp. 74–82.

[28] Sean A.P. Clouston *et al.*, "Incidence of Mild Cognitive Impairment in World Trade Center Responders: Long-Term Consequences of Re-Experiencing the Events on 9/11/2001", in *Alzheimer's & Dementia: Diagnosis, Assessment & Disease Monitoring*, 2019, vol. 11, no. 1, pp. 628–636; L.A. Rafferty, *et al.*, "Dementia, Post-Traumatic Stress Disorder and Major Depressive Disorder: A Review of the Mental Health Risk Factors for Dementia in the Military Veteran Population", in *Psychological Medicine*, 2018, vol. 48, no. 9, pp. 1400–1409.

[29] Sally Moore and Lori Zoellner, "Overgeneral Autobiographical Memory and Traumatic Events: An Evaluative Review", in *Psychological Bulletin*, 2007, vol. 133, no. 3, p. 419.

[30] Tim Dalgleish *et al.*, "Reduced Autobiographical Memory Specificity and Posttraumatic Stress: Exploring the Contributions of Impaired Executive Control and Affect Regulation", in *Journal of Abnormal Psychology*, 2008, vol. 117, no. 1, p. 236.

[31] Ali Moradi *et al.*, "Specificity of Episodic and Semantic Aspects of Autobiographical Memory in Relation to Symptoms of Posttraumatic Stress Disorder (PTSD)", in *Acta Psychologica*, 2008, vol. 127, no. 3, pp. 645–653.

depression, which may complicate the findings. Only a minority of studies have attempted to address this.[32]

Despite good evidence for specific impairments in victims with PTSD, such as in verbal memory, this is not thought to be necessarily indicative of a lack of credibility of testimony. One cannot extrapolate a compromised memory for past events from poor recall of words in an operationalized test. Nevertheless, PTSD may not account for all memory impairment after trauma. Memory can be decreased after trauma in the absence of PTSD symptoms.[33]

### 6.4.4. Enhanced Memory After Trauma

An apparently contradictory body of evidence exists suggesting an enhancement of memory after trauma. Pre-clinical, animal and human studies demonstrate that arousal increases adrenaline levels that, in turn, enhance memory.[34]

During autobiographical interviews with passengers who were aboard a flight which was nearly ditched at sea, memory was actually increased for episodic details.[35] Normal human subjects who have viewed slides and are then subjected to stress have increased cortisol levels (a stress hormone) and an increased memory for the emotionally arousing slides one week later.[36] Giving cortisol to subjects also results in an increased recall for emotionally arousing pictures.[37] Reist *et al.* found that recall after one week for an arousing narrated slide-story was enhanced.[38] This effect was blocked by propranolol, a drug that decreases cortisol levels. These studies suggest a possible biological ex-

[32] Jenkins *et al.*, 1998, p. 278, see *supra* note 19.

[33] Ariela Gigi, Merav Papirovitz and Masika Hagit, "Memory Functioning Following Terror Attack and the Suggested Immunization by Religious Faith", in *Stress and Health*, 2007, vol. 23, no. 3, pp. 199–204.

[34] John W. Haycock, Roderick van Buskirk, John R. Ryan and James L. McGaugh, "Enhancement of Retention With Centrally Administered Catecholamines", in *Experimental Neurology*, 1977, vol. 54, no. 2, pp. 199–208.

[35] Margaret C. McKinnon *et al.*, "Threat of Death and Autobiographical Memory: A Study of Passengers From Flight AT236", in *Clinical Psychological Science*, 2015, vol. 3, no. 4, pp. 487–502.

[36] Larry Cahill, Lukasz Gorski and Kathryn Le, "Enhanced Human Memory Consolidation With Post-Learning Stress: Interaction With the Degree of Arousal at Encoding", in *Learning and Memory*, 2003, vol. 10, no. 4, pp. 270–274.

[37] Tony Buchanan and William Lovallo, "Enhanced Memory for Emotional Material Following Stress-Level Cortisol Treatment in Humans", in *Psychoneuroendocrinology*, 2001, vol. 26, no. 3, pp. 307–317.

[38] Christopher Reist, John Gregory Duffy, Ken Fujimoto and Larry Cahill, "β-Adrenergic Blockade and Emotional Memory in PTSD", in *The International Journal of Neuropsychopharmacology*, 2001, vol. 4, no. 4, pp. 377–383.

planation for this effect, mediated by the corticosteroid hormone system and a part of the temporal cortex of the brain (the amygdala).[39]

How do we reconcile these apparently contradictory effects of stress on memory? One possible hypothesis is that trauma leads to an enhancement of central or emotional details of an event to the detriment of peripheral neutral aspects. In support, one study of psychology graduates who were shown a film of a simulated kidnapping demonstrated that the students remembered central actions, but were unable to recall descriptive details. In addition, and notably, they accepted false but plausible content with high levels of confidence – a finding that has implications for the suggestibility of witnesses in court.[40] In a similar experiment by Payne et al., students subjected to stress had significantly disrupted recall for the neutral but not the emotional content of a slideshow.[41] Herlithy et al. reported that the recall of details rated by the interviewee as peripheral to the account are more likely to be inconsistent than recall of details that are central to the account.[42] Therefore, such inconsistencies should not be relied on as indicating a lack of credibility.

In addition, the research evidence suggests that timing may be important. Consolidation of memory may occur after a number of days. Quevedo et al. found an enhanced memory for emotional slides after one week but not after one hour.[43] This process has been postulated to involve sleep.[44]

In summary, there is no clear consensus as to whether stress improves or worsens memory. Research findings imply the complexity of the relationship, which is moderated by many individual psychosocial and biological factors.

## 6.5. Summary

There is an apparently contradictory body of evidence supporting both an impairment and an enhancement of memory in normal humans subjected to ele-

---

[39] Benno Roozendaal, Bruce S. McEwen and Sumantra Chattarji, "Stress, Memory and the Amygdala", in *Nature Reviews Neuroscience*, 2009, vol. 10, no. 6, pp. 423–433.

[40] Malen Migueles and Elvira Garcia-Bajos, "Recall, Recognition, and Confidence Patterns in Eyewitness Testimony", in *Applied Cognitive Psychology*, 1999, vol. 13, no. 3, pp. 257–268.

[41] Jessica Payne et al., "The Impact of Stress on Neutral and Emotional Aspects of Episodic Memory", in *Memory*, 2006, vol. 14, no. 1, pp. 1–16.

[42] Jane Herlithy, Peter Scragg and Stuart Turner, "Discrepancies in Autobiographical Memories – Implications for the Assessment of Asylum Seekers: Repeated Interviews Study", in *The British Medical Journal*, 2002, vol. 324, no. 7333, pp. 324–327.

[43] João Quevedo et al., "Differential Effects of Emotional Arousal in Short- and Long-Term Memory in Healthy Adults", in *Neurobiology of Learning and Memory*, 2003, vol. 79, no. 2, pp. 132–135.

[44] Jessica Payne and Elizabeth Kensinger, "Sleep's Role in the Consolidation of Emotional Episodic Memories", in *Current Directions in Psychological Science*, 2010, vol. 19, no. 5, pp. 290–295.

---

vated levels of stress. One approach argument to reconcile this is that memory is enhanced for the central emotional aspects of an event but disrupted for peripheral non-emotional aspects of the same event. Therefore, the evidence suggests that inconsistencies in recall of peripheral details are not indicative of the unreliability of a particular witness. At the same time, there are a number of caveats to the research findings to date. First, many studies have been conducted involving normal persons and cannot be extrapolated to trauma victims. Second, when they focus on trauma, the research tends to focus on individuals with one particular diagnosis, that of PTSD. There is robust evidence for a deficit in verbal memory in this group. Finally, there are some notable gaps in the literature – whether or not verbal memory deficits in witnesses actually affect their testimony reliability and their autobiographical memory, a key requirement for witness recall, in an operationalized manner.

## 6.6. Practice Guidelines

Clinicians assessing and treating victims, as well as those working in the criminal justice system, may benefit from some clinical guidelines that have been suggested by professional bodies, such as the British Psychological Society.[45] Trauma victims have often undergone very distressing experiences and efforts should be made to reduce pressures on them during their journey through the judicial system. For example, it is recommended that one should be aware of cultural and language issues. Timing is of importance when scheduling interviews. Given the suggestion from the literature that memory may be enhanced after one week, compared to immediately post-trauma, a delayed assessment has been advised. Developing rapport with the victim is important, and may be encouraged by asking open-ended questions. It is recommended to reinstate the context of events by enquiring about the victims' thoughts, feelings and physical experiences at the time of the incident. Imagery techniques may aid in this endeavour, as they may recall the event in different temporal orders. Inconsistencies or omissions in testimony should be considered relatively common in the memory of traumatized victims, and should not necessarily undermine the entirety of their testimony. Criticism of any memory gaps should be avoided. Witnesses who have experienced trauma are potentially suggestible; hence, leading questions or proposing alternative hypotheses in court should be avoided. Inappropriate questioning styles, such as frequent interruption and over-talking, may decrease performance. Specific clinical presentations, such as the dominance of arousal and intrusive symptoms ('flashbacks'), may indi-

---

[45] "Guidelines on Memory and the Law: Recommendations From the Scientific Study of Human Memory", 2008, see *supra* note 6.

cate poorer intellectual performance, including of episodic memory.[46] Poor concentration is often a feature of PTSD; hence, simple questions, repetition and checking understanding are important. It has been recommended to allow sufficient time for responses and to avoid interrogative pressures such as challenges and negative feedback. Giving regular breaks in long interviews is also important. Such regular breaks should also be considered in any trial setting, as should submitting written questions in advance for particularly traumatized persons.

| Some Guidelines for Interviewing and Assessing Trauma Victims |
|---|
| Be aware of cultural and language issues. |
| Consider a delayed assessment. |
| Try to develop rapport. |
| Ask open-ended questions. |
| Attempt to reinstate the context of events. |
| Recall the event in different temporal orders. |
| Do not criticize memory weaknesses. |
| Abstain from using leading questions or proposing alternative hypotheses. |
| Avoid inappropriate questioning styles such as frequent interruption and over-talking. |
| Use simple questions, repeat them and check understanding. |
| Allow sufficient time for responses. |
| Give regular breaks. |

Table 1. Some Guidelines for Interviewing and Assessing Trauma Victims.

---

[46] Kivling-Bodén and Sundbom, 2003, p. 191, see *supra* note 23.

# 7

---

# The Time Variable in Relation to Insider Witnesses: Quantitative and Qualitative Analysis of International Criminal Court Cases

## Moa Lidén[*]

## 7.1. Introduction

> [...] the greater the passage of time [...] the greater the risk of deterioration of evidence and potential prejudice to victims, witnesses and the accused.[1]

While the time variable is a constant and unavoidable element in all jurisdictions and cases, it is, in national jurisdictions, most commonly discussed in relation to cold cases[2] and high-profile cases that become more time consuming than anticipated.[3] The time variable is also highly relevant to virtually all

---

[*] **Moa Lidén** is Associate Professor of Criminal Procedural Law, Uppsala University, and Honorary Researcher at the Department of Security and Crime Science, University College London. She is the Director and Principal Investigator of the International Centre for Evidence-Based Criminal Law (EB-CRIME), exploring multidisciplinary topics in both national and international jurisdictions. Her postdoctoral research was on the topic of "Reliability and Biasability of Criminal Evidence" and her Ph.D. thesis was titled "Confirmation Bias in Criminal Cases". The research conducted for this chapter was funded by the Swedish Research Council, the Bank of Sweden Tercentenary Foundation and the Knut and Alice Wallenberg Foundation.

[1] International Criminal Court, *Prosecutor v. Uhuru Muigai Kenyatta*, Trial Chamber V(B), Decision on Prosecution's Applications for a Finding on Non-Compliance Pursuant to Article 87(7) and for an Adjournment of the Provisional Trial Date, ICC-01/09-02/11-908, 31 March 2014, para. 96 ('*Prosecutor v. Kenyatta*, 31 March 2014') (https://www.legal-tools.org/doc/c2209e/). The full quote is:

> the greater the passage of time prior to the start of any trial, hypothetically including on any charges re-submitted to the Pre-Trial Chamber should the charges in this case be withdrawn, the greater the risk of deterioration of evidence and potential prejudice to victims, witnesses and the accused.

[2] See, for example, Jonathan Hughes and Monique Jonas, "Time and Crime: Which Cold-Case Investigations Should Be Reheated?", in *Criminal Justice Ethics*, 2015, vol. 34, no. 1, pp. 18–41, and Cheryl Allsop, *Cold Case Reviews: DNA, Detective Work, and Unsolved Major Crimes*, Clarendon Studies in Criminology, 2018.

[3] For example, the murder of Swedish Prime Minister Olof Palme in 1986 was investigated for 34 years, and the final conclusion at the closing of the investigation in 2020 was that the likely perpetrator was deceased, see the Swedish Prosecution Authority, "Decision in the In-

core international crimes cases as these investigations and proceedings last on average 4.9 years,[4] and with much longer time spans in individual cases.[5] As regards the context of core international crimes specifically, it has been pointed out that the passing of time is not uniquely associated with worse conditions for investigations and proceedings as, for example, in societies that are recovering from mass atrocities,[6] the availability to archives might, in fact, improve with time.[7] As such, the passing of time can enable the collection of essential documentary evidence,[8] which, for example, can form the basis of crucial interviews.

Another constant element in core international crimes cases is insider witnesses. Several researchers have emphasized the importance and reliance on insider witness testimonies in this context[9] as well as the often unpredicta-

---

vestigation into the Murder of Former Swedish Prime Minister Olof Palme", press release, 6 October 2020 (available on its web site).

[4]   Alette Smeulers, Barbora Hola and Tom van den Berg, "Sixty-Five Years of International Criminal Justice: The Facts and Figures", in *International Criminal Law Review*, 2013, vol. 13, no. 1, p. 18.

[5]   For examples, see Table 1 in Section 7.3.1.

[6]   While time delays are, thus, not uniquely associated with the international jurisdictions or core international crimes cases, the time variable is indeed relevant considering that the investigations concern societies that are faced with pressing reconstructive needs, a fragile political environment and a lack of criminal justice capacity, all potentially contributing to time delays, see Morten Bergsmo and Cheah Wui Ling, "Placing Old Evidence and Core International Crimes on the Agenda of the International Discourse on International Criminal Justice for Atrocities", in Morten Bergsmo and Cheah Wui Ling (eds.), *Old Evidence and Core International Crimes*, Publication Series No. 16, Torkel Opsahl Academic EPublisher, Beijing, 2012 (https://www.toaep.org/ps-pdf/16-bergsmo-cheah).

[7]   This was pointed out by, for example, Siri Frigaard in the first edition of this book, see Siri Frigaard, "Foreword", in Bergsmo and Cheah (eds.), 2012, see *supra* note 6. It has also been pointed out by Morten Bergsmo in a personal communication with the author.

[8]   Patrick J. Treanor, "Old Documents and Archives in Core International Crimes Cases", in Bergsmo and Cheah, 2012 (eds.), pp. 141–153, see *supra* note 6.

[9]   See, for example, Carla del Ponte, "Investigation and Prosecution of Large-Scale Crimes at the International Level: The Experience of the ICTY", in *Journal of International Criminal Justice*, 2006, vol. 4, no. 3, pp. 539–558; Xabier Agirre Aranburu, "The Contribution of Analysis to the Quality Control in Criminal Investigation", in Xabier Agirre Aranburu, Morten Bergsmo, Simon De Smet and Carsten Stahn (eds.), *Quality Control in Criminal Investigation*, Publication Series No. 38, Torkel Opsahl Academic EPublisher, Brussels, 2020 (https://www.toaep.org/ps-pdf/38-qcci); William Nardini, "The Prosecutor's Toolbox: Investigating and Prosecuting Organized Crime in the United States", in *Journal of International Criminal Justice*, 2006, vol. 4, no. 2, pp. 528–538; Gabriele Chlevickaité, Barbora Holá and Catrien Bijleveld, "Suspicious Minds? Empirical Analysis of Insider Witness Assessments at the ICTY, ICTR and ICC", in *European Journal of Criminology*, 2021, pp. 1–23.

ble and unreliable nature of this evidence.[10] This can not only cause major challenges to investigations that work on the basis of the information provided by insiders,[11] but can also, at a later stage, greatly impact on the International Criminal Court's ('ICC' or 'Court') outcome. In fact, research suggests that almost half of the insiders before the ICC were deemed seriously lacking in credibility and reliability, and thus were either dismissed, used in a limited manner or used only if corroborated.[12] These negative assessments have several possible explanations but two came out as particularly important, namely that the Court, in their official evaluations of the insiders, noted a number of inconsistences and contradictions[13] in how one and the same insider remembered and/or accounted for one and the same event across different interviews or within one and the same interview.[14] More specifically, among insiders who were negatively assessed before the ICC, inconsistencies with prior statements were mentioned in 62 percent of the cases[15] and contradictions were referred to in 56 percent of the cases.[16] These findings are in line with research pertaining to national jurisdictions, illustrating that legal actors tend to view inconsistent or contradictory witness evidence with much skepticism,[17] often regardless of

---

[10] Gabriel Chlevickaité and Barbora Holá, "Empirical Study of Insider Witnesses' Assessments at the International Criminal Court", in *International Criminal Law Review*, 2016, vol. 16, no. 4, pp. 676–677.

[11] See, for example, about the risk of, for example, sunk cost effect and confirmation bias, Moa Lidén, "Confirmation Bias in Investigations of Core International Crimes: Risk Factors and Quality Control Techniques", in Aranburu, Bergsmo, de Smet and Stahn (eds.), 2020, see *supra* note 9; Jessica Roth, "Informant Witnesses and the Risk of Wrongful Convictions", in *American Criminal Law Review*, 2016, vol. 53, p. 782.

[12] Chlevickaité, Holá and Bijleveld, 2009, pp. 1–23, see *supra* note 9.

[13] Note that it is uncertain exactly how the judges have used these two terms and how they relate to each other. When it is used in the following by the author, 'inconsistencies' refer to different accounts provided on the same exact topic between or within statements while not necessarily excluding each other, whereas 'contradictions' refer to the same situation, but the accounts do exclude each other in the sense that they cannot both be true at the same time. This coincides with how the terms were used by the Prosecution in the *Yekatom and Ngaïssona* case, see Section 7.3.2.

[14] Chlevickaité and Holá, 2016, pp. 676–677, see *supra* note 10.

[15] Chlevickaité, Holá and Bijleveld, 2009, p. 11, see *supra* note 9.

[16] *Ibid.*

[17] Garrett Berman and Brian L. Cutler, "Effects of Inconsistencies in Eyewitness Testimony on Mock-Juror Decision Making", in *Journal of Applied Psychology*, 1996, vol. 81, no. 2, pp. 170–177; Garrett Berman, Douglas Narby and Brian Cutler, "Effects of Inconsistent Eyewitness Statements on Mock-Jurors' Evaluations of the Eyewitness, Perceptions of Defendant Culpability, and Verdicts", in *Law and Human Behavior*, 1995, vol. 19, pp. 79–88; Neil Brewer *et al.*, "Beliefs and Data on the Relationship Between Consistency and Accuracy on Eyewitness Testimony", in *Applied Cognitive Psychology*, 1999, vol. 13, pp. 297–313; Alana C. Krix *et al.*, "Consistency Across Repeated Eyewitness Interviews; Contrasting Police

whether the inconsistencies were related to central or peripheral details[18] and sometimes without sufficient consideration of the range of possible explanations of such inconsistencies and/or contradictions. Arguably, individuals who report the same event in different ways must be wrong on at least one of the occasions[19] and thus we may presume that they are inaccurate or unreliable. However, research into eyewitness testimony has firmly concluded that the relationship between accuracy and consistency is weak.[20] This, of course, raises the question of how to interpret and properly evaluate what is here referred to as *Within Insider Reliability*, that is, the extent to which one and the same insider, over time, remembers and accounts for the same event in the same way, either between different statements or within one and the same statement.[21] The distinction between remembering and accounting for is essential as it highlights the many possible explanations for inconsistencies and contradictions, ranging from, for example, memory issues to threats or other security issues making the insider unwilling to stand by his or her previous statement.

---

Detectives' Beliefs with Actual Eyewitness Performance", in *PloS One*, 2015, vol. 10, no. 2; Aileen Oeberst, "If Anything Else Comes to Mind… Better Keep It To Yourself? Delayed Recall is Discrediting – Unjustifiably", in *Law and Human Behavior*, 2012, vol. 36, pp. 266–274; John Yuille and Judith Cutshall, "A Case Study of an Eyewitness Memory of a Crime", in *Journal of Applied Psychology*, 1986, vol. 71, pp. 291–301.

[18] Berman, Narby and Cutler, 1995, pp. 79–88, see *supra* note 17.

[19] Although this depends on how inconsistencies and contradictions are defined, as mutually exclusive accounts or just different versions, see *supra* note 13.

[20] Neil Brewer *et al.*, see *supra* note 17; Ronald Fisher and Brian Cutler, "The Relation Between Consistency and Accuracy of Eyewitness Testimony", in Graham Davies, Sally Lloyd-Bostock, Mary McMurran and Clare Wilson (eds.). *Psychology, Law and Criminal Justice: International Developments in Research and Practice*, De Gruyter, Berlin, 1995, pp. 121–136.

[21] This term has been inspired by the corresponding term 'within expert reliability' from Dror's "Hierarchy of Expert Performance" ('HEP') which is aimed at, for example, forensic expertise, and also distinguishes between their observations and conclusions, see Itiel Dror, "A Hierarchy of Expert Performance", in *Journal of Applied Research in Memory and Cognition*, 2016, vol. 5, no. 2, pp. 121–127. However the idea that different experts can be inconsistent with themselves, or with other experts assessing identical cases, has existed also before the HEP framework, not the least in the medical field, and in this framework the terms "Intra rater reliability" and "Inter rater reliability" are used, see, for example, in Inga Koerte *et al.*, "Inter- and Intra-Rater Reliability of Blood and Cerebrospinal Fluid Flow Quantification by Phase-Contrast MRI", in *Journal of Magnetic Resonance Imaging*, 2013, vol. 38, no. 3, pp. 655–662 and Charles McSherry *et al.*, "Second Surgical Opinion Program: Dead or Alive?", in *Journal of the American College of Surgeons*, 1997, vol. 185, no. 5, pp. 451–456. There is also some research into differences between different judges examining identical cases, for an overview, see Moa Lidén, "Inter-domar-reliabilitet – Är individuella skillnader i domares beslutsfattande ett löfte eller ett hot mot rättssäkerheten?", in *Ny Juridik*, 2021, vol. 2, no. 21, pp. 23–52.

---

Hence, while there may also be issues pertaining to *Between Insider Reliability*,[22] the focus of this chapter is Within Insider Reliability.

Lacking Within Insider Reliability is always, in one way or another, related to time. This correlation is fairly obvious when it comes to changes in memory over time,[23] but also because changes in insiders' testimonies often occur with repeated questioning, in interviews that are conducted at different points in time (maybe in different ways as well), or even within the same interview, using the time concept in a more minute to minute sort of fashion. But also other types of important changes can occur over time, including societal, political or other changes impacting on an individual's security and/or motivations. The passing of time is, in fact, a necessary requirement for inconsistencies and contradictions with prior statements to occur. It is therefore likely that inconsistencies and contradictions, and the many explanations for them, are best understood with close consideration of the time variable. Since the time variable has already been addressed in relation to insiders testifying before other international criminal courts and tribunals ('ICCTs'),[24] this chapter focuses on insiders testifying before the ICC, while occasional comparisons will be made.

Hence, the purpose of this research is twofold:

1. It empirically investigates Within Insider Reliability in cases before the ICC. This entails *quantitative analysis* pertaining to for example, the number of statements provided by insiders, time lapses between first and last statements, as well as total time lapses in the included cases and also the number of inconsistencies and/or contradictions noted in the in-

---

[22] That is, the extent to which different insiders remember and account for the same event in the same way, at the same or different points in time.

[23] See, for example, Nelson Cowan, *Attention and Memory: An Integrated Framework*, Oxford University Press, 1998; Aaron Benjamin, "Memory Is More Than Just Remembering: Strategic Control of Encoding, Accessing Memory, and Making Decisions", in Aaron S. Benjamin and Brian H. Ross (eds.), *The Psychology of Learning and Motivation: Skill and Strategy in Memory Use*, Academic Press, London, 2008.

[24] For examples pertaining to the International Criminal Tribunal for the Former Yugoslavia ('ICTY') such as ICTY, *Prosecutor v. Kunarac et al.*, Trial Chamber, Judgment, 22 February 2001, IT-96-23-T and IT-96-23/1-T (https://www.legal-tools.org/doc/fd881d/), from the International Criminal Tribunal for Rwanda ('ICTR') such as ICTR, *Prosecutor v. Jean-Paul Akayesu*, Appeals Chamber, 1 June 2001, ICTR-96-4-A (https://www.legal-tools.org/doc/c62d06/), and from the Special Panels for Serious Crimes ('SPSC') such as SPSC, *Prosecutor v. Florenco Tacaqui*, Judgment, 9 December 2004, No. 20/2001 (https://www.legal-tools.org/doc/864bbe/), see, for example, Andrew Cayley, "Prosecuting and Defending in Core International Crimes Using Old Evidence", in Bergsmo and Cheah (eds.), 2012, pp. 109–122, see *supra* note 6; David Cohen, "The Passage of Time, the Vagaries of Memory, and Reaching Judgment in Mass Atrocity Cases", in *ibid*, pp. 9–28.

sider statements by the Chambers and/or parties. The empirical investigation also entails *qualitative analysis* focusing on the nature of the inconsistencies and/or contradictions as well as what impacts they had on the investigations and proceedings.

2. It connects the empirical investigation to what is known from previous research about why, with time, testimonies may become inconsistent and/or contradictory. This includes memory deterioration and other cognitive factors (7.4.1.), interview-related factors (7.4.2.), societal and political factors (7.4.3.) and factors pertaining to the witness' motivation and security (7.4.4.). The implications of this research for ICC cases will be discussed as well.

## 7.2. Method

The two different purposes of this research required the use of essentially two different methods. Firstly, for the empirical investigation, a selection of ICC cases was made on the basis of previous research addressing insiders before this Court[25] as well as considerations regarding representation of different situations (Kenya, Democratic Republic of the Congo ('DRC'), Uganda, Ivory Coast, and so on) and of cases at different stages of the proceedings and/or with different outcomes (for example, charges withdrawn, acquitted, convicted, trial phase, and so on). However, the investigation is not, and should not be considered fully representative, neither of the range of cases before the Court, nor of the insiders who testify before the Court. When it comes to the closer selection of insiders subjected to quantitative and qualitative analysis, this was made largely on the basis of how much information about their testimonies that was publicly available, while, clearly, also confidential information or information that is unavailable for other reasons would have been relevant.[26]

Secondly, to connect the empirical investigation to previous related research, a database search was conducted focusing on studies addressing inconsistencies and contradictions in witness testimony and their relation to the time variable. While most of the available research concerns fact witnesses,[27] insid-

---

[25] Chlevickaité, Holá and Bijleveld, 2009, pp. 1–23, see *supra* note 9.

[26] For example, annexes to relevant documents have often been confidential, see, for example, ICC, *Prosecutor v. Muthaura, Kenyatta and Hussein Ali*, Office of The Prosecutor ('OTP'), Notification of the Removal of a Witness From the Prosecution's Witness List and Application for an Adjournment of the Provisional Trial Date, 19 December 2013, ICC-01/09-02/11-875, para. 5 ('*Prosecutor v. Muthaura, Kenyatta and Hussein Ali*, 19 December 2013') (https://www.legal-tools.org/doc/f017e7/).

[27] While the cited research concerns primarily witnesses in national jurisdictions, it coincides with what in the ICC practice is referred to as 'fact witnesses', that is, witnesses who have knowledge and testify about a course of event, some of them can be crimes-based witnesses

ers usually have more complex status as not only witnesses, but also some-times experts and/or potential suspects themselves. For example, the ICTY Appeals Chamber described insider witness testimony as accomplice evidence which should be viewed with caution.[28] There are also many descriptions of insiders as 'quasi-experts'[29] who are in a 'unique position' to provide evidence linking the organizers, order givers or planners of the atrocities.[30] To better account for insiders' multifaceted status, also other relevant research into in-consistencies and contradictions was reviewed, for example, that pertaining to suspect statements. This research was then connected and discussed in relation to the results of the empirical investigation of ICC cases.

## 7.3. Results

### 7.3.1. Quantitative Analysis: Number of Statements, Inconsistencies and Contradictions, Time Lapses

In Table 1 below, quantitative variables pertaining to the insiders' testimonies in the selected ICC cases are outlined. This includes the number of statements provided by each insider during the investigation ('I') and, where applicable, the number of (full or partial) days the insider was interviewed during trial ('T'). Also, the table outlines the time lapse between the first and the last statement ('S') as well as the total time lapse from the commencement of the alleged crimes, including the planning stages, to the concluded proceed-ings/last decision in the case ('T'). Furthermore, the number of inconsistencies and contradictions across or within the insiders' testimonies ('I-C') which were mentioned by the chamber or parties as significant are included. Note again that these numbers are based on public information, and that information per-taining to, for example, the number of interviews conducted during the inves-tigation, and when they were conducted, was often limited. As such, the real numbers are more or equal ('≥') to the stated numbers. For more comprehen-

---

when they have suffered harm and testify as witnesses about what happened to them and some of them can also hold the status of participating victims before the Court (dual-status witness), see the ICC, "Witnesses" (available on its web site).

28 See ICTY, *Prosecutor v. Kupreškić et al.*, Appeals Chamber, Judgment, 23 October 2001, IT-95-16-A (https://www.legal-tools.org/doc/c6a5d1/) and *Prosecutor v. Kordić and Čerkez*, Appeals Chamber, Judgment, 17 December 2004, IT-95-14/2-A (https://www.legal-tools.org/doc/738211/).

29 See Roth, 2016, p. 782, see *supra* note 11. More specifically, Roth describes how insiders occupy a particular position as quasi-experts, providing overview testimony and placing var-ious individuals and their actions into context, which increases the chances that an insider can influence the overall narrative of the case.

30 Nancy Amoury Combs, "Deconstructing the Epistemic Challenges to Mass Atrocity Prose-cutions", in *Washington and Lee Law Review*, 2018, vol. 75, p. 259.

sive details pertaining to, for example, how the time lapses were calculated, the reader is referred to Appendix 1 (7.6.).

| Case | Place | Insider | No. of Statements | Time Lapse | | No. of I-C | Custody Accused | Status |
|------|-------|---------|-------------------|------------|------|------------|-----------------|--------|
| | | | | S | T | | | |
| *Kenyatta* | Kenya | P-0004 | 7 (I) | 3yrs | 7yrs 4m | 4[31] | No | Charges confirmed but withdrawn |
| | | P-0012 | 5 (I) | 2yrs 6m[32] | | 2 | | |
| *Ruto and Sang* | Kenya | P-800 | 1(I) 7 days(T) | 2yrs 1m | 10yrs 3m | 1 | No | Charges confirmed, but case terminated |
| | | P-658 | 1 (I) 9 days (T) | NA | | 2 | | |
| | | P-356 | 1 (I) 7 days (T) | NA | | 3 | | |
| *Lubanga* | DRC | P-356 | NA (I) 3 days (T) | NA | 12yrs 3m | 1 | Yes | Convicted (AC) |
| *Mbarushimana* | DRC | P-542 | 2 (I) | NA | 2yrs 10m | 1 | NA[33] | Charges not con- |
| | | P-559 | 5 days (T) | NA | | 1[34] | | |

---

31  However, the defence alleged that the inconsistencies across Witness 4 were "wide-ranging" (para. 10) and "critical" (para. 14), without mentioning a specific number, see ICC, *Prosecutor v. Kenyatta and Hussein Ali*, Public Redacted Versions of the Defence 'Submissions Regarding the Prosecution's 11 April 2012 Disclosure of Material Relating to Its Initial Contact with OTP-4', 23 April 2013, ICC-01/09-02/11-719-Red ('*Prosecutor v. Kenyatta and Hussein Ali*, 23 April 2013') (https://www.legal-tools.org/doc/34737f/).

32  The first (screening) interview was held on 12 June 2011 and the fifth and last interview was held on 4 December 2013, see ICC, *Prosecutor v. Muthaura, Kenyatta and Hussein Ali*, 19 December 2013, paras. 6–10, see *supra* note 26.

33  Mr. Mbarushimana was transferred to the Hague on 25 January 2011 and released from ICC custody on 23 December 2011, but since the dates for the interviews with the insiders are not available, see Appendix 1. It is uncertain whether and to what extent this overlapped with the time period during which the insiders were providing their testimonies.

34  While the Chamber noted that Witness 559 "contradicts himself a few times" this seems to have been primarily in relation to whether the FDLR political leadership was aware of the crimes committed to the ground and/or what was reported to them, see ICC, Situation in the Democratic Republic of Congo, *Prosecutor v. Callixte Mbarushimana*, Pre-Trial Chamber I,

| | | | | | | | | firmed |
|---|---|---|---|---|---|---|---|---|
| *Ongwen* | Uganda | P-0205 | 2 (I) 5 days (T) | NA | 18yrs 7m | 1 | NA[35] | Convicted (AC) |
| *Gbagbo and Blé Goudé* | Ivory Coast | P-0009 | 11 (I) 9 days(T) | NA | 10yrs 3m | 3 | Yes | Acquitted all charges[36] |
| | | P-0435 | 4 (I) 10 days (T) | NA | | 8 | | |
| *Yekatom and Nga-ïssona* | CAR | P-0801 | 1 (I) 6 days (T) | 3yrs 3m | 9yrs 1m | 1 | Partly[37] | Trial phase (TC) |
| **Averages** | | | 3.78 (I) 6.78 days (T) | 2yrs 9m | 10yrs 1m | 2.33 | 28.57% resp. no, yes, NA, 14.29% partly | |

**Table 1: Quantitative Variables Pertaining to the Insiders'
Testimonies in Selected ICC Cases.**

*Note:* in the table, 'Custody Accused' refers to whether the accused was in ICC custody during the time period when the insider provided his or her testimony, and 'NA' means not available.

---

Decision on the Confirmation of Charges, 16 December 2011, ICC-01/04-01/10-465-Red, para. 313 (https://www.legal-tools.org/doc/63028f/).

[35] Mr. Lubanga was transferred to the ICC detention centre on 21 January 2015, but since the dates of P-0205's statements during the investigation are unavailable, it is not possible to say whether he was in custody at the time.

[36] ICC, *Prosecutor v. Laurent Gbagbo and Charles Blé Goudé*, Trial Chamber I, Dissenting Opinion Judge Herrera Carbuccia, 10 December 2018, ICC-02/11-01/15-1229-Anx, para. 47 ('*Prosecutor v. Gbagbo and Blé Goudé*, 10 December 2018') (https://www.legal-tools.org/doc/39a71d/).

[37] During the time period when P-0801 provided his first testimony (February 2018), neither Mr. Ngaïssona nor Mr. Yekatom were in ICC custody. However, as Mr. Ngaïssona was surrendered to the Court by French authorities on 23 January 2019 and Mr. Yekatom was surrendered to the Court by Central African Republic ('CAR') authorities on 17 November 2018, they were both in ICC custody when P-0801 provided his testimony before the Trial Chamber in May 2021, see ICC, Situation in the Central African Republic (CAR) II, *Prosecutor v. Alfred Yekatom and Patrice-Edouard Ngaïssona*, Pre-Trial Chamber II, Corrected Version of 'Decision on the Confirmation of Charges Against Alfred Yekatom and Patrice-Edouard Ngaïssona', 14 May 2020, ICC-01/14-01/18, para. 3 (https://www.legal-tools.org/doc/s5qfg5/).

As outlined in Table 1, the insiders provided on average 3.78 statements during the investigation and were interviewed for 6.78 days during trial. The average time lapse between their first and last statement was two years and nine months, while the average total time lapse in the cases was ten years and one month. The average number of inconsistencies and /or contradictions in their statements was 2.33 and it varied fairly equally whether the accused was in custody or not (or partly) during the time period when they provided their statements.

### 7.3.2. Qualitative Analysis: Nature of Inconsistencies and Contradictions, and Their Impact

The inconsistencies and contradictions outlined in Table 1 were of a range of natures and also had different impacts on the investigations and proceedings. As discussed at length in Section 7.4., the overall long time lapse between first and last statement as well as the total time lapse help understand these inconsistencies and contradictions, not only because of fairly straightforward reasons such as memory deterioration (7.4.1.), but also because interviews conducted at different points in time in different ways can generate different testimonies (7.4.2.) especially if also, with the passing of time, societal or political factors have changed in the community in which the insider resides (7.4.3.) as this is likely to impact on his or her motivations and/or security (7.4.4.). While some of these explanations are discussed at length and incorporated into the parties and/or Court's reasoning, as outlined below, the reasoning partially comes into different light in view of the research presented in Section 7.4.

In the *Kenyatta* case,[38] Mr. Kenyatta[39] and members of the *Mungiki* had, allegedly, created a common plan to commit widespread and systematic attacks against the non-Kikuyu population,[40] carried out from 24 until 28 January 2008 and resulting in around 1,300 people allegedly killed.[41] P-0004 had originally stated that he had attended a meeting at the Nairobi Members Club on 3 January 2008 and the Pre-Trial Chamber had relied upon P-0004 as key

---

[38]  ICC, *Prosecutor v. Kenyatta*, see *supra* note 1, formerly *Prosecutor v. Muthaura, Kenyatta and Hussein Ali*, ICC-01/09-02/11.

[39]  Mr. Kenyatta's contribution, allegedly essential to the implementation of the common plan, consisted of providing institutional support, on behalf of the PNU coalition, to secure: (i) the agreement with the Mungiki for the purpose of the commission of the crimes; and (ii) the execution on the ground of the common plan by the Mungiki in Nakuru and Naivasha, see ICC, *Prosecutor v. Kenyatta*, Case Information Sheet, see *supra* note 1.

[40]  Mostly belonging to the Lou, Luhya and Kalenjin ethnic groups, and perceived as supporting the Orange Democratic Movement ('ODM'), see ICC, *Prosecutor v. Kenyatta*, Case Information Sheet, see *supra* note 1.

[41]  ICC, *Prosecutor v. Kenyatta*, Case Information Sheet, see *supra* note 1.

evidence in the Pre-Trial Chamber's establishment of the charges.[42] Specifically, the Pre-Trial Chamber had used P-0004's testimony to establish Mr. Kenyatta's alleged attendance at this meeting which, in turn, was informative of Mr. Kenyatta's role in a common plan.[43] However, in an affidavit, sworn in May 2009 and signed for by a Prosecution member,[44] P-0004 admitted that he was, in fact, not present at the 3 January 2008 meeting,[45] but had instead heard of the meeting from someone else.[46] The defence, apart from raising the issue of non-disclosure by the Prosecution and challenging the confirmation decision,[47] also raised multiple other concerns pertaining to P-0004's statements.[48] Also, the Pre-Trial Chamber acknowledged such concerns in its Confirmation Decision, but still decided that "his evidence must be duly considered".[49] According to the Prosecution, two Prosecution staff members had reviewed the affidavit prior to the confirmation hearing but submitted that "one must be familiar with Witness 4's statements that he attended Nairobi Members Club meeting to spot the apparent inconsistency"[50] and that the significance of the sentence where Witness 4 stated that someone else told him about the meeting was not recognized "through an oversight".[51]

Furthermore, in a statement given to the Prosecution after the confirmation hearing, on 25 May 2012, P-0004 also recanted his evidence relating to a meeting at the Nairobi State House on 26 November 2007, a meeting allegedly

---

[42]  ICC, *Prosecutor v. Kenyatta*, Trial Chamber V, Public Decision on Defence Application Pursuant to Article 64(4) and Related Requests, 26 April 2013, ICC-01/09-02/11, para. 2 ('*Prosecutor v. Kenyatta*, 26 April 2013') (https://www.legal-tools.org/doc/da5089/).

[43]  *Ibid.*, para. 30.

[44]  The affidavit was, seemingly, received by the Prosecution on 27 September 2010 but not disclosed to the Defence until 19 October 2012, see *ibid.*, para. 27.

[45]  *Ibid.*

[46]  *Ibid*, para. 35.

[47]  ICC, *Prosecutor v. Kenyatta*, Defence Application to the Trial Chamber Pursuant to Article 64(4) of the Rome Statute to Refer the Preliminary Issue of the Confirmation Decision to the Pre-Trial Chamber for Reconsideration, 5 February 2013, ICC-01/09-02/11-622 (https://www.legal-tools.org/doc/560b4a/).

[48]  These are outlined in *Prosecutor v. Kenyatta and Hussein Ali*, 23 April 2013, see *supra* note 31.

[49]  For example, the Chamber noted that some other Mungiki members had testified that P-0004 was never a Mungiki member and they did not even know P-0004, see ICC, *Prosecutor v. Kenyatta*, Pre-Trial Chamber II, Public Redacted Version, Decision on the Confirmation of Charges Pursuant to Article 61(7)(a) and (b) of the Rome Statute, 23 January 2012, ICC-01/09-02/11-382-Red, para. 188 ('*Prosecutor v. Kenyatta*, 23 January 2012') (https://www.legal-tools.org/doc/4972c0/).

[50]  *Prosecutor v. Kenyatta*, 26 April 2013, para. 35, see *supra* note 42.

[51]  *Ibid.*

attended by Mr. Kenyatta and which was central to the Pre-Trial Chamber's findings on individual criminal responsibility.[52] In his May 2012 statement, Witness 4 had also admitted to lying about personally attending another meeting, on the 17 November 2007, at which Mr. Kenyatta also was present.[53] The Prosecution pointed out that Witness 4 had himself revealed that he had been offered and accepted money from individuals holding themselves out as representatives of the accused to withdraw his testimony, and that inconsistency therefore did not affect the Confirmation Decision or render the confirmation fundamentally unfair.[54] With reference to, for example, the Prosecution's duty to investigate incriminating and exonerating circumstances equally, following Article 54(1) of the Rome Statute of the ICC ('Rome Statute'), the Chamber reprimanded the Prosecution's failure to timely disclose P-0004's affidavit,[55] although P-0004 was later removed from the Prosecution witness list[56] and the Chamber was not persuaded that the non-disclosure had materially impacted on the confirmation process.[57]

Similarly, P-0012 had, seemingly, misled the Prosecution about his presence at a particular meeting, resulting in the Prosecution's decision to withdraw P-0012.[58] The witness admitted that he had provided false evidence regarding the event at the heart of the Prosecution's case against the accused.[59] In *Statements 1–3*, P-0012 described that he had attended a meeting at Nairobi State House on or about 30 December 2007 and that also Mr. Kenyatta had attended this meeting and participated in the organization and funding of violence that later unfolded against perceived ODM supporters.[60] In *Statement 4*, P-0012 stuck to his previous version of the course of events but stated another

---

[52]  *Ibid.*, para. 39.

[53]  *Ibid.*

[54]  *Ibid.*, paras. 57, 80. The Defence contended that the non-disclosure of Witness 4's Affidavit and post-confirmation withdrawal of his evidence, the confirmation decision was "based on an inherently flawed analysis of the evidence".

[55]  *Ibid.*, para. 128.

[56]  *Ibid.*, para. 35.

[57]  *Ibid.*, para. 101.

[58]  ICC, *Prosecutor v. Muthaura, Kenyatta and Hussein Ali*, 19 December 2013, see *supra* note 26.

[59]  *Ibid.*, para. 2.

[60]  KEN-OTP-0061-0187, at 196–197; KEN-OTP-0060-0112, at 115–117; KEN-OTP-0060-0299, at 313–314; KEN-OTP-0060-0426, at 428; KEN-OTP-0074-0590, at 597–598. See also ICC, *Prosecutor v. Muthaura, Kenyatta and Hussein Ali*, 19 December 2013, paras. 7, see *supra* note 26. The first interview was a screening interview on 12 June 2011, while the second and third interviews were full-length interviews conducted between 16–23 June 2011 and 2–4 May 2012.

time of the day for the meeting.[61] However, in *Statement 5*, P-0012 described that he had previously lied to the Prosecution since he had never personally attended the alleged 30 December 2007 meeting, but that he had learned about the meeting from someone else.[62] Hence, there were essentially two inconsistencies in P-0012's testimony, one seemingly non-essential, the change of time of the day, and one clearly essential; not having personally attended the meeting. Thus, overall, across time, P-0012's testimony, just like that of P-0004, went from incriminating to not providing any information about Mr. Kenyatta's responsibility. Furthermore, on the 1 November 2013, approximately one month before P-0012's *Statement 5*, another witness, P-0011 had informed the Prosecution that he was no longer willing to testify at trial.[63] It was also acknowledged by the Trial Chamber that yet other witnesses appeared to have withdrawn as a result of security concerns[64] and that the *Kenyatta* case presented particular evidential difficulties due to non-co-operation,[65] which, although not substantiated and formally acknowledged by the Chamber, was believed by the Prosecution to be because of that Mr. Kenyatta was himself, under the Kenyan constitution, as Head of State, responsible for compliance with international obligations.[66]

In fact, already at the confirmation of charges hearing, the defence or Mr. Kenyatta had challenged the credibility of witnesses P-0011 and P-0012 and described the two witnesses as "criminals" and "extortionists" who had given a "fully inculpatory account to the Prosecutor after having given a wholly exculpatory account to the Defence".[67] While the Pre-Trial Chamber was not persuaded by the defence argument,[68] the situation changed with *Statement 5* and

---

[61] KEN-OTP-0104-0383, at 395–400, KEN-OTP-0104-0383, at 399; KEN-OTP-0060-0426, at 429. During the fourth interview, undertaken on 16–17 May 2013, P-0012 stated that the meeting took place around 18:30–19:00 which was a departure from his earlier account that the meeting took place around 15:00–16:00.

[62] KEN-OTP-0123-0268, at 271 ff. The fifth and final interview was on 4 December 2013.

[63] ICC, *Prosecutor v. Muthaura, Kenyatta and Hussein Ali*, 19 December 2013, para. 2, see *supra* note 26.

[64] ICC, *Prosecutor v. Kenyatta*, Pre-Trial Chamber II, Decision on the Prosecution's Application for a Further Adjournment, 3 December 2014, ICC-01/09-01/11-981, para. 93 ('*Prosecutor v. Kenyatta*, 3 December 2014') (https://www.legal-tools.org/doc/731d89/).

[65] *Ibid.*

[66] *Ibid.*

[67] ICC, *Prosecutor v. Kenyatta*, 23 January 2012, para. 93, see *supra* note 49.

[68] According to the Pre-Trial Chamber, the Defence had alleged to be in possession of previous fully exculpatory statements which it attributed to P-0011 and P-0012 but did not present any such witness statement, instead they relied on what appeared to be notes taken during meetings with the individuals alleged to be P-0011 and P-0012. Also, the notes did not seem

the Prosecution 's withdrawal of P-0012.[69] The defence now argued that the Prosecution had created a narrative based on "false evidence",[70] that there were "fundamental inconsistencies"[71] in P-0012's evidence and that a continuation of the proceedings would lead to a miscarriage of justice. The Trial Chamber considered that the withdrawal of P-0012 was a "direct reason"[72] for the Prosecution's evidence falling below the standard required for trial.

Thus, while Pre-Trial Chamber II had already confirmed the charges against Mr. Kenyatta on the 23 January 2012,[73] the Trial Chamber rejected the Prosecution's request for further adjournment,[74] and following the Prosecutor's notice to withdraw the charges due to non-co-operation on behalf of the Kenyan government,[75] the Trial Chamber terminated the proceedings.[76]

---

to provide "fully exculpatory" information, see ICC, *Prosecutor v. Kenyatta*, 23 January 2012, para. 93–94, see *supra* note 49.

[69] ICC, *Prosecutor v. Muthaura, Kenyatta and Hussein Ali*, 19 December 2013, see *supra* note 26.

[70] ICC, *Prosecutor v. Kenyatta*, Public redacted version of the 13 January 2014 'Defence Response to the Prosecution's "Notification of the Removal of a Witness from the Prosecution's Witness List and Application for an Adjournment of the Provisional Trial Date"', 24 January 2014, ICC-01/09-02/11-878-Red, para. 21 (https://www.legal-tools.org/doc/9833f8/). See also ICC, *Prosecutor v. Kenyatta*, Trial Chamber V(b), Transcript of Hearing, 5 February 2014, ICC-01/09-02/11-T-27-ENG ET WT, p. 47, lines 12–21; p. 48, line 23; p. 49, line 6 (where it is submitted that that the Prosecution has created a narrative based on "false evidence" and that continuation of the proceedings would lead to a "miscarriage of justice") (https://www.legal-tools.org/doc/7e6374/).

[71] *Ibid.*

[72] ICC, *Prosecutor v. Kenyatta*, 31 March 2014, para. 90, see *supra* note 1.

[73] ICC, *Prosecutor v. Kenyatta*, 23 January 2012, see *supra* note 49. The judges declined to confirm the charges against Mr. Ali but did confirm the charges against Mr. Muthaura and Mr. Kenyatta and committed them to trial. Later, the charges against Mr. Muthaura were withdrawn, see ICC, *Prosecutor v. Kenyatta*, Case Information Sheet (available on its web site).

[74] In a previous decision from 31 March 2014, in relation to the Prosecution's first adjournment request, the Chamber found that strictly limited opportunity to pursue further investigations was justified at that stage. In the rejection of the request for further adjournment, the Chamber pointed out that the previous conclusion was premised on a finding that there had been unique circumstances beyond the Prosecution's control, which contributed to a loss of evidence in the case. However, such a finding did not provide a basis for open-ended investigations, see ICC, *Prosecutor v. Kenyatta*, 3 December 2014, para. 45, see *supra* note 64.

[75] See ICC, *Prosecutor v. Kenyatta*, OTP, Notice of Withdrawal of the Charges Against Uhuru Muigai Kenyatta, ICC-01/09-02/11-983, 5 December 2014 (https://www.legal-tools.org/doc/b57a97/). The Prosecution considered that the evidence was insufficient to prove Mr. Kenyatta's alleged criminal responsibility beyond reasonable doubt. The Prosecution submitted that the situation was unique in that the Kenyan Government had failed to comply with the Court's request for assistance and therefore potential lines of investigations had been thwarted. Furthermore, the Prosecution stated that only a fraction of the infor-

In the *Ruto and Sang* case,[77] the prosecution's case was built around a central allegation that a 'Network' had existed[78] with a common plan to punish perceived Party of National Unity ('PNU') supporters.[79] Allegedly, the plan was executed by expelling the civilian population, including Kikuyu, Kisii and Kamba communities, from the Rift Valley, by means of widespread and systematic attacks.[80] Mr. Ruto and Mr. Sang, allegedly, contributed to the implementation of the plan in different ways.[81] To support its allegations, the Prosecution aimed to prove, *inter alia*, that Mr. Ruto had arranged preparatory meetings aimed at mobilizing and co-ordinating Network members and the Kalenjin youth, obtaining weapons *etcetera*.[82] In this regard, the prosecution had relied on prior recorded testimonies from P-397, P-604 and P-495 which no longer formed part of the evidence in the case[83] and the Chamber therefore did not consider the preparatory meetings supported by the evidence.[84] After mul-

---

mation sought had been delivered by the Kenyan Government, see ICC, *Prosecutor v. Kenyatta*, OTP, Prosecution Notice Regarding the Provisional Trial Date, 5 September 2014, ICC-01/09-02/11-944, paras. 2–3 (https://www.legal-tools.org/doc/5d9c72/).

[76] ICC, *Prosecutor v. Kenyatta*, Trial Chamber V(B), Decision on the Withdrawal of Charges against Mr. Kenyatta, 13 March 2015, ICC-01/09-02/11-1005 (https://www.legal-tools.org/doc/2c921e/). However, this does not prejudice the right of the Prosecution to bring new charges against the accused at a later date, based on the same or similar factual circumstances, should it obtain sufficient evidence to support such a course of action.

[77] ICC, Situation in the Republic of Kenya, *Prosecutor v. Ruto and Sang*, ICC-01/09-01/11.

[78] ICC, *Prosecutor v. Ruto and Sang*, Trial Chamber V (A), Public Redacted Version of Decision on Defence Applications for Judgments of Acquittal, 5 April 2016, ICC-01/09-01/11-2027-Red-Corr, para. 25 ('*Prosecutor v. Ruto and Sang*, 5 April 2016') (https://www.legal-tools.org/doc/6baecd/).

[79] ICC, *Prosecutor v. Ruto and Sang*, Case Information Sheet (available on the ICC's web site).

[80] *Ibid.*

[81] *Ibid.* More specifically, Mr. Ruto was accused of Mr. Ruto was accused of being criminally responsible as in indirect perpetrator pursuant to Article 25(3)(a) of the Rome Statute for the crimes against humanity if murder, deportation of forcible transfer of population and persecution. He was believed to have provided essential contributions to the implementation of the common plan by way of organizing and co-ordinating the commission of crimes under the Statute. Mr. Sang was accused as an indirect co-perpetrator, of having otherwise contributed to the commission of the following crimes against humanity: murder, deportation, or forcible transfer of population and persecution. By virtue of his influence in his capacity as a key Kass FM radio broadcaster, Sang allegedly contributed tin the implementation of the common plan by placing his show Lee Nee Eme at the disposal of the organization, advertising the organization's meetings, fanning violence by spreading hate messages and explicitly revealing a desire to expel the Kikuyus and broadcasting false news regarding alleged murders of Kalenjin people in order to inflame the violent atmosphere.

[82] ICC, *Prosecutor v. Ruto and Sang*, 5 April 2016, para. 34, see *supra* note 78.

[83] *Ibid.*, para. 36.

[84] *Ibid.*

tiple witness statements (prior recorded testimonies) had been excluded from the proceedings, the remaining witness evidence that the Prosecution relied on to prove that training of youth had taken places was provided by P-800.[85] During examination in chief, P-800 stated that he had witnessed, first hand, youths leaving in lorries and that he saw them returning some time later.[86] However, in cross-examination P-800 confirmed that he had, in fact, received the information about the training from P-495, rather than making his own observations, and furthermore, that P-495, in turn, had received the information from another unnamed source.[87] Under oath, P-800 himself admitted involvement in witness interference and also testified that after he had provided his initial statement to the Prosecution in October 2012, he had a number of meetings with certain individuals, and in return for the payment of a bribe, he agreed to recant his statement.[88] The Trial Chamber pointed out that it had not been suggested that P-800 acted under duress or fear of retribution and that in circumstances like these where a witness has demonstrated "such a far-reaching willingness to manipulate the truth",[89] the Chamber could not rely upon the evidence as it was "incapable of belief".[90]

A similar course of event played out in relation to P-658 according to whom Mr. Ruto had provided funding for weapons used to commit crimes pursuant to the Network's alleged common plan to attack PNU supporters and the Kikuyu civilian population.[91] P-658, during the investigation stage, had told the Prosecution that he personally attended two crime-related events, but during his testimony before the Chamber, this witness also claimed to have obtained the relevant information from another source. The Trial Chamber noted in relation to P-658:

> The witness had initially offered a detailed, but apparently false, account of his personal involvement in both events and even

---

[85] *Ibid.*, para. 39.

[86] *Ibid.*

[87] More specifically, witness 800 confirmed that the information had been contained in a report that witness 495 had prepared for an organization that both these witnesses worked for at the time. Witness 800 stated: "I only even came to know about Boronjo and the people mentioned through that report". Witness 495 recanted his entire prior recorded statement at trial and expressly denied knowledge of any training of Kalenjin youths, see *ibid.*, para. 40.

[88] More specifically, he testified that he had signed a pre-written affidavit in which he recanted his earlier statement despite knowing most of its contents to be untrue. Moreover, he testified that he had agreed to approach other Prosecution witnesses, including Witness 495, in order to convince them to recant, see *ibid.*, para. 42.

[89] *Ibid.*, para. 43.

[90] *Ibid.*, para. 116.

[91] *Ibid.*, paras. 50–51.

went so far as to draw a layout of the relevant locations for the Prosecution's investigators, despite the fact that, according to his later in-court testimony, he had never set foot in at least one of those locations. This strongly suggests that Witness 658 deliberately tried to mislead the Prosecution, while knowing that the consequences of his false statements would be the incrimination of Mr. Ruto.[92]

Similarly, P-356, upon whom the Prosecution relied to prove that Mr. Ruto had acquired guns for the 'Network' with the purpose of using them in a criminal plan to attack Kikuyu and PNU supporters in the Rift Valley region, repeatedly changed his testimony about aspects, which in the view of the Chamber, were significant. This included aspects such as the number of weapons that were allegedly transacted,[93] the precise chronology of events on the day of the transaction, as well as the exact whereabouts and role of a number of individuals involved.[94] Judge Fremr noted that:

> [...] I accept that several years after the events, a witness may have trouble recalling details and that certain discrepancies inevitably arise when a story is reproduced on multiple occasions. Notwithstanding the foregoing, any difficulties in remembering the precise details cannot explain that the first time he made a declaration about the alleged gun transaction, when he was interviewed by an NGO, Witness 365 left out the most essential part of the information relevant to this case, by not mentioning that he allegedly had a phone conversation with Mr. Ruto shortly before the weapons were handed over. Instead, he talked about a rather similar conversation he had at that time, but with another interlocutor and after the alleged transaction had already taken place. During cross-examination, Witness 356 explained that he did not mention the accused to the interviewers of the NGO, because he did not trust them, but I find this explanation wholly unconvincing.[95]

---

[92] *Ibid.*, para. 53.

[93] ICC, *Prosecutor v. Ruto and Sang*, Trial Chamber V(a), Transcript of Hearing, 27 January 2014, ICC-01/09-01/11-T-81-Red-ENG, pp. 85–97 (*'Prosecutor v. Ruto and Sang*, 27 January 2014') (https://www.legal-tools.org/doc/355e79/).

[94] *Ibid.*, pp. 85–97; ICC, *Prosecutor v. Ruto and Sang*, Trial Chamber V(a), Transcript of Hearing, 28 January 2014, ICC-01/09-01/11-T-82-RED-ENG, pp. 11–21 (*'Prosecutor v. Ruto and Sang*, 28 January 2014') (https://www.legal-tools.org/doc/96641c/). Witness 356 also provided inaccurate information about his own background as well as his personal relationship and interactions with Mr. Ruto. See ICC, *Prosecutor v. Ruto and Sang*, Trial Chamber V(a), Transcript of Hearing, 24 January 2014, ICC-01/09-01/11-T-80-RED-ENG, pp. 5–77 (*'Prosecutor v. Ruto and Sang*, 24 January 2014') (https://www.legal-tools.org/doc/c93e4d/).

[95] ICC, *Prosecutor v. Ruto and Sang*, 5 April 2016, para. 58, see *supra* note 78.

Other than claiming to have been confused or to have made mistakes when giving different versions of events to Prosecution investigators and local non-governmental organizations ('NGOs'), Witness 356 was unable to provide a convincing explanation for the discrepancies, and the Chamber did not rely on his testimony.[96]

The inconsistencies and/or contradictions in these witness testimonies need to be considered in the context of the direct witness interference as well as indirect pressures on witnesses, acknowledged to have existed in this case and which are described in the Reasons of Judge-Eboe-Osuji as justification of why this case rightly should have been terminated on the basis of a mistrial.[97] These issues had been pointed out by the Prosecution even well before the commencement of the trial, and as described by Judge-Eboe-Osuji:

> [...] immediately upon the commencement of the trial, with the very first witness, it became clear that there had been a concerted campaign to troll witnesses on the Internet, by publishing their perceived identities. This was done by persons who had made clear their intention to frustrate the trial, by engaging in conduct aimed at intimidating witnesses.[98]

This, together with co-ordinated efforts to bribe witnesses[99] and possibly political meddling[100] (while not necessarily on the instruction or encourage-ment of Mr. Ruto or Mr. Sang)[101] constituted what Judge Eboe-Osuji referred to as direct witness interference. Also, there was a tangible indirect pressure on witnesses through the aggressive atmosphere created by influential voices within Kenya (including from within the Kenyan Parliament, expressing not only a Court hostile rhetoric, culminating in a vote in favour of withdrawing Kenya from adherence to the Rome Statute[102] and also the lobbying of other African States to withdraw *en masse* from the Statute).[103] While this was not explicitly intended to intimidate witnesses, it was reasonably likely to have

---

[96]   The Chamber noted that Witness 356 also appeared to have been deceitful in some of his dealings with the Prosecution, as well as the Victims and Witnesses Unit of the Registry, which, although not necessarily meaning that the witness lied about the gun purchase, showed that he was capable of acting in a mendacious manner, see ICC, *Prosecutor v. Ruto and Sang*, 5 April 2016, para. 60, see *supra* note 78.

[97]   ICC, *Prosecutor v. Ruto and Sang*, Reasons of Judge Eboe-Osuji, 5 April 2016, para. 2, see *supra* note 78.

[98]   *Ibid.*, para. 151.

[99]   *Ibid.*, para. 152.

[100]  *Ibid.*, para. 155.

[101]  *Ibid.*, para. 153.

[102]  *Ibid.*, para. 162.

[103]  *Ibid.*, para. 170.

that effect,[104] not the least considering the extensive media reports.[105] Noting that eight witnesses who potentially possessed evidence that the Prosecution considered relevant to the case never appeared before the Court, Judge Eboe-Osuji also emphasized the importance of witnesses' safety for the proper administration of criminal justice.[106]

Hence, overall, the time span between first and last statements for the witnesses who testified in the Kenya cases, have to be considered in view of the fairly dramatic societal and political developments in Kenya at the time, as this was an acknowledged reason for lacking Within Insider Reliability, probably not primarily because these witnesses remembered the events differently but because their motivations to account for the events differed (see 7.1., Introduction).

Compared to the Kenya cases, the *Lubanga* case[107] makes somewhat different references to lacking Within Insider Reliability. Even though it is clear that inconsistences and contradictions played an important role in other regards, for example, the Court's evaluation of age statements provided by alleged child soldiers,[108] the Defence in its appeal of Mr. Lubanga's conviction, in fact, submitted that the Trial Chamber had wrongly dismissed its submissions regarding conflicting witness evidence.[109] However, in the view of the Appeal's Chamber, the Trial Chamber had taken full account of such conflicting evidence, for example, in relation to P-0016,[110] a former Armée Populaire Congolaise soldier[111] who was appointed as a high-ranking official within the

---

[104] *Ibid.*, para. 164.

[105] Judge Eboe-Osuji referred to, for example, *The Nairobi Star*, "Hackers Steal ICC Witness Emails", 10 September 2011; *Daily Nation*, "Kenya AG Orders Probe on Ocampo Witnesses Claim", 15 March 2012; see ICC, *Prosecutor v. Ruto and Sang*, Reasons of Judge Eboe-Osuji, 5 April 2016, para. 173–175, see *supra* note 78.

[106] ICC, *Prosecutor v. Ruto and Sang*, Reasons of Judge Eboe-Osuji, 5 April 2016, para. 180, see *supra* note 78.

[107] ICC, Situation in the Democratic Republic of the Congo, *Prosecutor v. Thomas Lubanga Dyilo*, ICC-01/04-01/06.

[108] For more on this see Moa Lidén, "Child Soldier or Soldier: Estimating Age in Cases of Core International Crimes: Risk Factors and Quality Control Techniques", in Aranburu, Bergsmo, de Smet and Stahn (eds.), 2020, see *supra* note 9.

[109] ICC, *Prosecutor v. Thomas Lubanga Dyilo*, Appeals Chamber, Public Redacted Document, Judgment on the Appeal of Mr Thomas Lubanga Dyilo against his conviction, 1 December 2014, ICC-01/04-01/06-3121-Red, para. 481 (https://www.legal-tools.org/doc/585c75/).

[110] *Ibid.*

[111] ICC, *Prosecutor v. Thomas Lubanga Dyilo*, Trial Chamber I, Judgment Pursuant to Article 74 of the Statute, 14 March 2012, ICC-01/04-01/06-2842, para. 1082 ('*Prosecutor v. Lubanga*, 14 March 2012') (https://www.legal-tools.org/doc/677866/).

Forces Patriotiques pour la Libération du Congo ('FPLC') in 2002.[112] More specifically the Trial Chamber had concluded that there was "strong evidence that the accused provided support for the troops [...]" but that it did not accept the evidence of P-0016 as to the extent of Mr. Lubanga's control over operations as his account was "at least in part, inconsistent and it was difficult to follow [...]".[113] For example, P-0016 gave inconsistent evidence as to the number of guards he saw who were under the age of 15 years, but his evidence was that their youngest (of whom there were no more than four) were 13 to 14 years old.[114] There were also references made to inconsistencies in the testimony of P-0038[115] but this did not appear to be significant in the view of the Trial Chamber.[116] Possibly, this was because there was also other evidence which made the Chamber less reliant on the insider testimony. The Appeals Chamber pointed out that, in line with the practice of the *ad hoc* tribunals, "it is the Trial Chamber that has the main responsibility to resolve any inconsistencies that may arise within/and or amongst witnesses' testimonies".[117]

In the *Mbarushimana* case,[118] the Prosecution relied on statements by insiders, some of whom were former members of the Forces Démocratiques pour la Libération du Rwanda ('FDLR'), and had participated in the events charged.[119] The Chamber, in its decision to decline to confirm the charges by majority,[120] noted that the insiders involvement in the charged acts called it to

---

[112] *Ibid.*, para. 683.

[113] *Ibid.*, para. 1150.

[114] *Ibid.*, para. 1258.

[115] *Ibid.*, para. 1237.

[116] For example, in relation to Witness P-0011 who the Trial Chamber noted that "[e]ven though his accounts as a witness were inconsistent, and cannot be relied upon to convict the accused, I deem that he could have been recruited, albeit the contradictory evidence presented in this trial". See also the reasoning in relation to Witnesses P-0298 and P-0299, *ibid.*, paras. 28–29.

[117] ICC, *Prosecutor v. Lubanga*, Appeals Chamber, Judgment on the Appeal of Mr. Thomas Lubanga Dyilo against his conviction, ICC-01/04-01/06-3121-Red, 1 December 2014, para. 23 (https://www.legal-tools.org/doc/585c75/).

[118] ICC, Situation in the Democratic Republic of Congo, *Prosecutor v. Callixte Mbarushimana*, ICC-01/04-01/10.

[119] ICC, *Prosecutor v. Callixte Mbarushimana*, Decision on the Confirmation of Charges, 16 December 2011, ICC-01/04-01/10-465-Red, para. 51 ('*Prosecutor v. Mbarushimana*, 16 December 2011') (https://www.legal-tools.org/doc/63028f/).

[120] Although the Chamber found substantial grounds to believe that acts amounting to war crimes were perpetrated in five out of the 25 occasions identified by the Prosecutor, the majority found that the evidence submitted was insufficient to be convinced of the existence of substantial grounds to believe that such acts were part of a course of conduct amounting to "an attach directed against the civilian population" pursuant to or in furtherance of an organizational policy to commit such attack, within the meaning of Article 7 of the Rome Statute. Accordingly, the majority found that there not substantial grounds to believe that crimes

be "[…] mindful of the risks that attach to the statements of insider witnesses" and that it therefore should "exercise caution in using such evidence to support its findings".[121] The Chamber's evaluation of inconsistencies and/or contradictions in this case seem to have varied, depending on, for example, their nature. For example, in relation to P-542, the Chamber noted that he contradicted himself by first saying that the attack allegedly launched by the FDLR against Mianga took place in May and then instead saying the attack occurred in February.[122] Having noted this lacking Within Witness Reliability, the Chamber also noted a substantial lack of Between Witness Reliability regarding the date of the attack.[123] However, the Chamber assessed that the statements were "similar enough to conclude that they relate to the same event" and it therefore considered that there were substantial grounds to believe that the attack on Mianga occurred on or about 12 April 2009.[124] Similar assessments were made also in other situations when the Chamber had noted a lack of Between Witness Reliability, for example, regarding the name of the place where the soldiers were gathered before an alleged attack against Busuruni and surrounding villages.[125]

Furthermore, P-587, a former FDLR member, contradicted himself in that he first told the Chamber that he remembered that Mr. Mbarushimana talked on BBC Radio about the attack on Busurungi of 9–10 May 2009[126] but then continued by stating that he never heard the suspect speaking on the radio

---

against humanity were committed by the FDLR troops. The majority of the Chamber, with the Presiding Judge dissenting, further found that Callixte Mbarushimana did not provide any contribution to the commission of the alleged crimes, even less a "significant" one.

[121]  ICC, *Prosecutor v. Mbarushimana*, 16 December 2011, para. 51, see *supra* note 119.

[122]  *Ibid.*, para. 214, EVD-PT-OTP-00854, Summary Statement of Witness 542, at 1235.

[123]  More specifically, the Chamber noted that according to Witness 562 the attack took place after the attack on Busu rungi, Witness 632 said it happened "a little bit earlier" than Busu rungi, Witness 544 could not remember the month of the attack but said it happened during Umoja Wetu (which according to other information finished on 25 February 2009), and Witness 559 said the attack took place when the Umoja Wetu operation had already finished, see ICC, *Prosecutor v. Mbarushimana*, 16 December 2011, para. 214, see *supra* note 119.

[124]  *Ibid.*, paras. 214–215, see *supra* note 119.

[125]  In the *Mbarushimana* case, see *supra* note 118, the Chamber noted, in a footnote, that "there is some contradiction regarding the name of the place where the soldiers were gathered", Witness 561 refers to Gaseni, EVD-PT-OTP-00631, Transcript of Interview of Witness 561, at 1341, while other witnesses refer to Bucanga, EVD-PT-OTP-00762, Summary Statement of Witness 677, at 57; EVD-PT-OTP-00704, Transcript of Interview of Witness 562, at 1197; EVD-PT-OTP-00703, Transcript of Interview of Witness 562, at 1134; EVD-PT-D06-01332, Transcript of Interview of Witness 542, at 2153.

[126]  *Mbarushimana* case, see *supra* note 118, EVD-PT-OTP-00860, summary statement of Witness 587, at 1423, paras 68–70.

and the troops were not encouraged to listen to the radio.[127] The Chamber simply noted these contradictions and that they would be taken into account.[128] Similar contradictions were observed in relation to P-562[129] and P-559.[130] For example, the Chamber noted that P-559 "contradicts himself a few times" on the topic of whether Mr. Mbarushimana, or even the FDLR political leadership, was aware of the crimes committed on the ground.[131] More specifically, P-559 first reported that Mr. Mudacumura was informed of everything that happened on the ground, including crimes, and reported this to Mr. Murwanashyaka[132] and later said that not everything was reported by the commanders on the ground to the leadership.[133] The Chamber did not rely on this evidence as, in addition to the contradictions, it was unclear whether Mr. Murwanashyaka would have reported everything on to Mr. Mbarushimana.[134]

In this case, the Chamber seems to have been concerned also about Mr. Mbarushimana's right to be properly informed about the charges against him,[135] and interviewing techniques used by the OTP investigators. Since the

---

[127] *Mbarushimana* case, see *supra* note 118, EVD-PT-D06-01383, Transcript of Interview of Witness 587, at 1394.

[128] ICC, *Prosecutor v. Mbarushimana*, 16 December 2011, para. 326, see *supra* note 119.

[129] *Mbarushimana* case, see *supra* note 118, EVD-PT-OTP-00632, Transcript of Interview of Witness 561, at 1382; EVD-PT-D06-01314, Transcript of Interview of Witness 528, at 1178–80; EVD-PT-OTP-00854, summary Statement of Witness 542, at 1240. Witness 562 contradicts himself. He first states that the order to burn houses was not given prior to the attack but rather, during it and was directed only at the houses occupied by the Mai Mai, EVD-PT-OTP-00704, Transcript of Interview of Witness 562, at 1212–1214, but later he states that at the rally Kalume ordered them to set fire to the entire village, EVD-PT-OTP-00707, Transcript of Interview of Witness 562, at 1315.

[130] The Chamber noted that Witness 559 "contradicts himself a few times", see ICC, *Prosecutor v. Mbarushimana*, 16 December 2011, para. 313, see *supra* note 119.

[131] *Ibid.*

[132] *Mbarushimana* case, see *supra* note 118, EVD-PT-D06-01321, Transcript of Interview of Witness 559, at 1658; EVD-PT-D06-01323, Transcript of Interview of Witness 559, at 1723–1724; EVD-PT-OTP-00577, Statement of Witness 559, at 160.

[133] *Mbarushimana* case, see *supra* note 118. EVD-PT-D06-01318, Transcript of Interview of Witness 559, at 1533; EVD-PT-D06-01321, Transcript of Interview of Witness 559, at 1659; EVD-PT-D06-01322, Transcript of Interview of Witness 559, at 1708.

[134] ICC, *Prosecutor v. Mbarushimana*, 16 December 2011, para. 313, see *supra* note 119.

[135] For example, the Defence alleged that the charges against Mr. Mbarushimana were insufficiently specified and, following an assessment of the English proficiency of Mr. Mbarushimana, the Prosecution was ordered to disclose to the defence French translations of all witness statements which had not already been disclosed in Kinyarwanda, see ICC, *Prosecutor v. Mbarushimana*, OTP, Prosecution's Request for the Assessment of the English Proficiency of Callixte Mbarushimana, 28 April 2011, ICC-01/04-01/10-125 (https://www.legal-tools.org/doc/788870/) and *id.*, Pre-Trial Chamber I, Decision on the "Prosecution's request

---

Chamber's observations in relation to the interview techniques are indeed relevant for the risk of inconsistencies and contradictions, and thereby lacking
Within Insider Reliability, they are cited below:

> […] the Chamber wishes to highlight its concern at the technique
> followed in several instances by some Prosecution investigators,
> which seems utterly inappropriate when viewed in light of the
> objective, set out in article 54 (1)(a) of the Statute, to establish
> the truth by "investigating incriminating and exonerating circum-
> stances equally". The reader of the transcripts of the interviews is
> repeatedly left with the impression that the investigator is so at-
> tached to his or her theory or assumption that he or she does not
> refrain from putting questions in leading terms and from showing
> resentment, impatience or disappointment whenever the witness
> replies in terms which are not entirely in line with his or her ex-
> pectations. Suggesting that the witness may not be "really re-
> membering exactly what was said"[136] complaining about having
> "to milk out" from the witness details which are of relevance to
> the investigation,[137] lamenting that the witness does not "really
> understand what is important" to the investigators in the case,[138]
> or hinting at the fact that the witness may be "trying to cover" for
> the Suspect,[139] seem hardly reconcilable with a professional and
> impartial technique of witness questioning. Accordingly, the
> Chamber cannot refrain from deprecating such techniques and
> from highlighting that, as a consequence, the probative value of
> the evidence by these means may be significantly weakened.

Even with far less obvious pressure, and particularly with time and repeated questioning, it is likely that inconsistencies and contradictions will arise
(see Section 7.4.2. on interview related factors).

Similar to the *Lubanga* case, in the *Ongwen* case,[140] the Trial Chamber
rejected some of the defence's allegation that prosecution witnesses had pro-

---

for the assessment of the English proficiency of Callixte Mbarushimana", 12 May 2011,
ICC-01/04-01/10-145 (https://www.legal-tools.org/doc/2ea738/).

[136] *Mbarushimana* case, see *supra* note 118, EVD-PT-D06-01349, Transcript of Interview of
Witness 632, at 376, lines 492–493.

[137] *Mbarushimana* case, see *supra* note 118, EVD-PT-D06-01349, Transcript of Interview of
Witness 632, at 382, lines 717–718.

[138] *Mbarushimana* case, see *supra* note 118, EVD-PT-OTP-00668, Transcript of Interview of
Witness 564, at 1162, line 177.

[139] *Mbarushimana* case, see *supra* note 118, EVD-PT-D06-01322, Transcript of Interview of
Witness 559, at 1679, line 279.

[140] ICC, *Prosecutor v. Dominic Ongwen*, Trial Chamber IX, Decision on the Prosecution's Applications for Introduction of Prior Recorded Testimony under Rule 68(2)(b) of the Rules,
18 November 2016, ICC-02/04-01/15, para. 1 (https://www.legal-tools.org/doc/e9d9c4/).

vided inconsistent and/or contradictory statements. For example, P-0205 was a former Lord's Resistance Army ('LRA') fighter and commander, who testified about his knowledge of Mr. Ongwen, the attacks on Lukodi and Odek internally displaced persons camp relevant to the charges, as well as the treatment of women in the LRA.[141] The Defence suggested he had contradicted himself by recalling information in his testimony that were not discussed in his earlier interviews with the Prosecution[142] and more specifically whether Mr. Ongwen ordered an attack on civilians in Odek and Lukodi, and whether the witness reported seeing civilians deaths in Lukodi.[143] However, the Chamber's evaluation of this witness was overall positive, as it believed he was "a calm, restrained and forthcoming witness"[144] who "distinguished clearly between information he gained from personal experiences as opposed to events he was informed about".[145] Furthermore, the Trial Chamber added that his "testimony was as would be expected from a witness who testified to events he actually experienced".[146] This reasoning is related to research on reminiscent details, that is, the reporting of previously undisclosed details with repeated questioning over time,[147] and will be discussed in more detail in Section 7.4.1.

In the *Gbagbo and Blé Goudé* case, P-0009, 'General Mangou',[148] was considered a crucial insider witness,[149] for the claim made by the Prosecution that Mr. Gbagbo and his inner circle, of which Mr. Blé Goudé was a prominent member,[150] jointly conceived and implemented a common plan to keep Mr.

---

[141] ICC, *Prosecutor v. Dominic Ongwen*, Trial Chamber IX, Public Redacted Trial Judgment, 4 February 2021, ICC-02/04-01/15-1762-Red, para. 272 ('*Prosecutor v. Ongwen*, 4 February 2021') (https://www.legal-tools.org/doc/kv27ul/).

[142] *Ibid.*, para. 273 and ICC, *Prosecutor v. Ongwen*, Public Redacted Version of 'Corrected Version of "Defence Closing Brief", filed on 24 February 2020', 13 March 2020, ICC-02/04-01/15-1722-Corr-Red, paras. 366, 416 (https://www.legal-tools.org/doc/xibh9t/).

[143] ICC, *Prosecutor v. Ongwen*, 4 February 2021, paras. 272–273, including fn. 334.

[144] *Ibid.*, para. 272.

[145] *Ibid.*

[146] *Ibid.*

[147] See, for example, Krix *et al.*, 2015, see *supra* note 17.

[148] General Philippe Mangou was the Chief of Staff of Forces Armées Nationales de Côte d'Ivoire ('FANCI'), see ICC, *Prosecutor v. Gbagbo and Blé Goudé*, ICC-02/11-01/15 and *id.*, Pre-Trial Chamber I, Decision on the Confirmation of Charges Against Laurent Gbagbo, 12 June 2014, ICC-02/11-01/11-656-Red, para. 89 ('*Prosecutor v. Gbagbo and Blé Goudé*, 12 June 2014') (https://www.legal-tools.org/doc/5b41bc/).

[149] See, for example, ICC, *Prosecutor v. Gbagbo and Blé Goudé*, Pre-Trial Chamber I, Opinion of Judge Cuno Tarfusser, 16 July 2019, ICC-02/11-01/15-1263-AnxA, para. 85 ('*Prosecutor v. Gbagbo and Blé Goudé*, Judge Cuno Tarfusser Concurring Opinion, 16 July 2019') (https://www.legal-tools.org/doc/f6c6f3/).

[150] More specifically, according to the Prosecution, Mr. Blé Goudé was the "Général de la Rue" and he occupied an authoritative position in relation to pro-Gbagbo youth as he co-ordinated

Gbagbo in power,[151] including a widespread and systematic attack directed against civilians perceived as supporters of Alassane Ouattara.[152] However, P-0009's testimony was considered inconsistent and/or contradictory in multiple regards, for example, in relation to the information he told he had received from General Palasset about the shelling of Abobo in February[153] and also in that he mentioned different dates each time he was required to clarify the date on which General Palasset had informed him that mortars had been used by the Forces de défense et de sécurité ('FDS').[154] The majority, furthermore, noted that P-0009 General Mangou first said he knew the Garde Républicaine bunker very well but then stated he had never been there himself.[155] Also other types of inconsistencies were pointed out, for example, whether P-0009 had attended the meetings with Mr. Gbagbo and the generals[156] and whether Mr. Gbagbo had given any specific instruction regarding the RTI march,[157] by concurring Judge Tarfusser and dissenting Judge van den Wyngaert respectively. These

---

and directed their actions and served as a conduit between Mr. Gbagbo, the inner circle and the pro-Gbagbo youth. Allegedly, Mr. Blé Goudé used his oratorial skills and his charisma to mobilize the youth for violent acts, and also issues specific instructions and orders, see ICC, *Prosecutor v. Gbagbo and Blé Goudé*, Prosecution Pre-Trial Brief, 16 July 2015, ICC-02/11-01/15-148 para. 9 (https://www.legal-tools.org/doc/68aec0/).

[151] According to the Prosecution, Mr. Gbagbo, in his claimed capacity as both president and commander in chief, realized that freely contested presidential elections were inevitable in the following years and therefore the common plan to keep Mr. Gbagbo in power was necessary, *ibid.*, para. 9.

[152] *Ibid.*, paras. 9–16.

[153] P-009 had affirmed several times that that he learnt from General Palasset, commander of the Licorne forces, about the use of mortars in Abobo by the FDs in late February. However, he was considered inconsistent in his accounts of what information he received from General Palasset, see ICC, *Prosecutor v. Gbagbo and Blé Goudé*, Trial Chamber, Reasons of Judge Geoffrey Henderson, 16 July 2019, ICC-02/11-01/15-1263-AnxB-Red, para. 1352 ('*Prosecutor v. Gbagbo and Blé Goudé*, Reasons of Judge Geoffrey Henderson, 16 July 2019') (https://www.legal-tools.org/doc/j0v5qx/).

[154] *Ibid.*, fn. 2120.

[155] The majority, composed of Judge Tarfusser and Judge Henderson provided a detailed analysis of the evidence in ICC, *Prosecutor v. Gbagbo and Blé Goudé*, Reasons of Judge Geoffrey Henderson, 16 July 2019, para. 872, fn. 2120, see *supra* note 153.

[156] ICC, *Prosecutor v. Gbagbo and Blé Goudé*, Judge Cuno Tarfusser Concurring Opinion, 16 July 2019, para. 110, see *supra* note 149.

[157] ICC, *Prosecutor v. Gbagbo and Blé Goudé*, Trial Chamber, Dissenting Opinion of Christine van den Wyngaert, 12 June 2014, ICC-02/11-01/11-656-Anx, para. 6, fn. 7 (https://www.legal-tools.org/doc/f715a5/). More specifically, Judge van den Wyngaert stated that the Confirmation Decision had attached much importance to Mr. Gbagbo's alleged instruction during a meeting held on 14 December 2010 that the RTI march should not take place but yet this finding relied entirely on the testimony of P-0009 who also stated that Mr. Gbagbo did not give any specific instructions as to how this should be accomplished.

---

inconsistencies and/or contradictions seem to have occurred not only across different interviews but also within one and the same interview, as conducted before the Trial Chamber. For example, during the same day, General Mangou gave conflicting accounts as to when an operation in Abobo had ended,[158] by first stating that the FDS was forced to withdraw the same night (that is, 25 February 2011)[159] and then stating that the FDS operation and their control of the recaptured position lasted for more than one day.[160] The inconsistencies in P-0009's testimony was one of the reasons why the defence claimed that the Prosecution had:

> [...] built its narrative by assembling and selecting partial portions of individual testimonies, without taking into account the contradictions and the alternate narratives introduced by its own witnesses, some of them being insider witnesses.[161]

The Prosecution did acknowledge some challenges pertaining to P-0009's testimony,[162] and the majority which described them as one source of the "overall disconnect"[163] between the Prosecutor's narrative and the facts as progressively emerging from the evidence, unsurprisingly, acquitted both accused.

---

[158] For more on this operation, see ICC, *Prosecutor v. Gbagbo and Blé Goudé*, Reason of Judge Geoffrey Henderson, 16 July 2019, para. 1328, see *supra* note 153.

[159] ICC, *Prosecutor v. Gbagbo and Blé Goudé*, Trial Chamber, Transcript, 28 September 2017, ICC-02/11-01/15-T-196-Red-ENG, p. 40 (https://www.legal-tools.org/doc/7c30eb/).

[160] *Ibid.*, p. 43.

[161] ICC, *Prosecutor v. Gbagbo and Blé Goudé*, Public Redacted Version of "Corrected Version of 'Defence's Written Observations on the Continuation of the Trial Proceedings Pursuant to Chamber's Order on the Further Conduct of the Proceedings (ICC-02/11-01/15-1124)'", 25 April 2018, ICC-02/11-01/15-1158-Corr-Red, paras. 14 and 50 (https://www.legal-tools.org/doc/12d725/).The Defence argued, *inter alia*, that some of the insiders called by the Prosecution had already established that Mr. Blé Goudé had, in fact, not given inflammatory speeches calling for violence from the audience.

[162] For example, the Prosecution described how P-0009's testimony pertaining to his knowledge of any recruitment by the FDS of militia while he was in command, appeared to be "self-serving and must be treated with caution, given the indications of his own complicity with this recruitment and therefore his own responsibility, see ICC, *Prosecutor v. Gbagbo and Blé Goudé*, Public Redacted Version of "Annex 1 – Prosecution's Consolidated Response to the Defence No Case to Answer", 10 September 2018, ICC-02/11-01/15-1207-Anx1-Red, para. 159 (https://www.legal-tools.org/doc/187ba3/).

[163] The majority, composed of Judge Tarfusser and Judge Henderson provided a detailed analysis of the evidence in ICC, *Prosecutor v. Gbagbo and Blé Goudé*, Reason of Judge Geoffrey Henderson, 16 July 2019, para. 865, see *supra* note 153. Also, Judge Cuno Tarfusser used this expression in his concurring opinion, see ICC, *Prosecutor v. Gbagbo and Blé Goudé*, Judge Cuno Tarfusser Concurring Opinion, 16 July 2019, para. 5, see *supra* note 149.

Lacking Within Insider Reliability was observed or discussed also in relation to other insiders in this case, such as P-0483[164] and P-0435.[165] When it comes to P-0435, the defence argued that his testimony was the foundation of the Prosecution's case against Mr. Blé Goudé[166] and it listed no less than eight key facts regarding which P-0435 had provided inconsistent versions.[167] For example, P-0435 had not mentioned, in his previous statements to Prosecution investigators, that Mr. Ahoua Stallone had requested training of youth groups on the behest of Charles Blé Goudé.[168] Due to such inconsistences and contradictions, some of which were claimed to be because P-0435 was influenced by objections made by the parties during the proceedings[169] and that he had incentives to lie,[170] the Defence contended that P-0435's testimony was incapable of belief.[171] While the majority acquitted both of the accused,[172] dissenting Judge Herrera Carbuccia argued in relation to P-0435 that "there were no material or evident contradictions between his previous statement and his testimony in Court that rendered it incapable of belief"[173] and that his testimony was "inter-

---

[164] P-0483's testimony had been used by the prosecution to prove that a member of the Inner Circle had provided funds to Liberian mercenaries but this allegation was not reflected by P-0483's testimony before the Trial Chamber, ICC, *Prosecutor v. Gbagbo and Blé Goudé*, 12 June 2014, see *supra* note 148.

[165] ICC, *Prosecutor v. Gbagbo and Blé Goudé*, Public Redacted Version of "Corrigendum to the 'Blé Goudé Defence No Case to Answer Motion' (ICC-02/11-01/15-1198-Conf), 23 July 2018", 3 August 2018, ICC02/11-01/15-1198-Conf-Corr, 28 September 2018, ICC-02/11-01/15-1198-Corr-Red ('*Prosecutor v. Gbagbo and Blé Goudé*, 28 September 2018') (https://www.legal-tools.org/doc/4dc79e/).

[166] P-0435 was a former GPP member and the defence claimed that "the prosecution's theory is based almost exclusively on Witness P-0435's testimony, which proved to be uncorroborated, unreliable and patently incredible", see *ibid.*, para. 236.

[167] See version 1 and version 2 of key fact at issue no. 1 listed by the defence, *ibid.*, para. 239.

[168] *Ibid.*, para. 239.

[169] *Ibid.*, para. 247.

[170] *Ibid.*, para. 249.

[171] ICC, *Prosecutor v. Gbagbo and Blé Goudé*, 28 September 2018, para. 195, see *supra* note 165.

[172] ICC, *Prosecutor v. Gbagbo and Blé Goudé*, Trial Chamber I, Reasons for oral Decision of 15 January 2019 on the Requête de la Defense de Laurent Gbagbo afin q'un jugement d'acuittement portant sur toutes les charges soit prononcé en faveur de Laurent Gbagbo et que sa mise en liberté immediate soit ordonné, and on the Blé Goudé Defence No Case To Answer Motion, 16 July 2019, ICC-02/11-01/15-1263 (https://www.legal-tools.org/doc/440017/). The majority of the Trial Chamber decided to terminate the proceedings, while Judge Herrera Carbuccia believed that the proceedings should have continued, see ICC, *Prosecutor v. Gbagbo and Blé Goudé*, 10 December 2018, para. 47, see *supra* note 36.

[173] *Ibid.*, paras. 39–42.

nally consistent".[174] Also issues pertaining to lacking Between Witness Reliability were noted in this case.[175]

In the ongoing *Yekatom and Ngaïssona* case,[176] during the questioning of witness P-0801,[177] the Prosecution confronted the witness with what it perceived of as deviations between his testimony before the Court[178] and the testimony P-0801 had provided on the same matter in February 2018 to the OTP.[179] Presiding Judge Bertram Schmitt intervened and said:

> […] I don't see a contradiction to his interview here because I think if I – if I see the transcript correctly, he has said that there was a conversation between the prime minister and Mr. Yekatom and that he was present. So I think he has said that today.[180]

The Prosecution responded:

> I'm not pointing out a contradiction, Mr. President. I'm pointing out what's an inconsistency, which is a difference between what he's saying now and what he said then. But that doesn't mean that it's contradictory. It's just different. And what he's saying now is that he – he's saying now that he doesn't know why Yekatom was on that mission, although he said he was able to do that. He said (speaks French) and then he turned around and said he can't do that after he spoke to his lawyer.[181]

---

[174] *Ibid.*

[175] ICC, *Prosecutor v. Gbagbo and Blé Goudé*, Judge Cuno Tarfusser Concurring Opinion, 16 July 2019, para. 99, see *supra* note 149. This entailed more specifically the following observation:

> On document CIV-OTP-0043-0226, referring to the use of the camp in Akouedo as a shooting base, Witness P-0009 stated that the Akouedo camp had – and could - not have been used for these purposes since his appointment as Chief of staff, since houses had been built in the area. Witness P-0010, instead, confirmed it had been signed in his name and that these exercises were necessary for the purposes of testing the repairs carried out on some of the weapons which regularly fell out of order. Neither in the Trial Brief, nor in the Response did the Prosecutor raise the issue of the inconsistency between the two testimonies, or otherwise address Witness P-0009's specific challenges to the document.

[176] ICC, Situation in the Central African Republic (CAR) II, *Prosecutor v. Alfred Yekatom and Patrice-Edouard Ngaïssona*, ICC-01/14-01/18.

[177] P-0801 was member of the Government (special adviser) and member of the Anti-Balaka.

[178] More specifically, the Prosecution was asking about why Mr. Yekatom and the witness had gone on a mission together. In his previous statements witness P-0801 had stated that Mr. Yekatom was known to be the chief who controlled the south.

[179] ICC, *Prosecutor v. Alfred Yekatom and Patrice-Edouard Ngaïssona*, Transcript, 27 May 2021, ICC-01/14-01/18-T-036-ENG, p. 22, lines 4–7 ('*Prosecutor v. Yekatom and Ngaïssona*, 27 May 2021') (https://www.legal-tools.org/doc/vg6jky/).

[180] *Ibid.*, p. 22, lines 4–7.

[181] *Ibid.*, p. 20, lines 15–20.

Judge Schmitt, in turn, responded that the judges did not share this view and that there was "no need to get any tension into the questioning".[182]

Since this is an ongoing case, and the judges apparently did not share the Prosecution's view, it is uncertain (or even unlikely) that the deviations will be of any vital importance, but the example highlights one important point; namely that inconsistencies and/or contradictions are not a phenomenon that exists fully independently of its observer(s). Rather, the perception of when an insider is inconsistent and/or contradictory can vary between different observers, for example, depending on the overall impression of an insider or case.[183]

The questioning of P-0801 before the Trial Chamber also highlights the unique symbiosis of insider witness testimony as that of a witness, expert and potential suspect simultaneously. The shift in how the insider is questioned, moving continuously between these roles sometimes becomes clear. While the parties may be fully dependent on the insider as a witness, this witness is sometimes, indeed, questioned as a suspect. For example, when the Prosecution confronted P-0801 with a document[184] as well as an interview with Mr. Ngaïssona[185] indicating that P-0801 had been a military co-ordinator of the Anti-Balaka,[186] P-0801 indicated that this role had been offered to him but that he had rejected it[187] and he reminded that he had already said that he was not a member of the co-ordination of the Anti-Balaka.[188] Under circumstances such

---

[182] *Ibid.*, p. 21, line 10.

[183] The interdependence between the assessment of the quality of a statement and the impression of the insider has also been empirically studied and found, see, for example, Gabrielė Chlevickaitė, "What Matters for Assessing Insider Witnesses? Results of an Experimental Vignette Study", in *The Journal of Evidence and Proof*, 2023, vol. 27, no. 3, pp. 192–210; Gabrielė Chlevickaitė, "Towards a Model of (Insider) Witness Assessments in International Crime Cases: An Experimental Vignette Study", in *International Criminal Justice Review*, 2023.

[184] *Yekatom and Ngaïssona* case, see *supra* note 176; CAR-OTP-2001-3372; the document was signed by Mr. Ngaïssona, see ICC, *Prosecutor v. Yekatom and Ngaïssona*, 27 May 2021, see *supra* note 179.

[185] ICC, *Prosecutor v. Yekatom and Ngaïssona*, 27 May 2021, p. 7, lines 7–9, see *supra* note 179.

[186] *Ibid.*, p. 5, lines 9–17.

[187] P-0801 also added that some weeks later Mr. Maxime Mokom had been appointed the role, ICC, *Prosecutor v. Yekatom and Ngaïssona*, 27 May 2021, p. 5, lines 13–15, see *supra* note 179.

[188] According to P-0801, he was a member of the Anti-Balaka, but not a member of the co-ordination, ICC, *Prosecutor v. Yekatom and Ngaïssona*, 27 May 2021, p. 5, lines 5–14, see *supra* note 179. Prior to the hearing the Defence had submitted that the Prosecution had violated its obligation to disclose exculpatory evidence; more specifically the involvement of an insider (redacted) "in the fabrication of false evidence", see ICC, *Prosecutor v. Yekatom and Ngaïssona*, OTP, Public Redacted Version of Prosecution's Response to the Ngaïssona De-

---

as these, and regardless of whether the insider has committed any crime or not, it is unsurprising if he or she is unable to be fully consistent with previous statement, as he or she, just like other witnesses who are treated directly or indirectly as suspects, will do their best to distract from any suspicions, for example through adjustments and avoidance[189] (see more on interview related factors in Section 7.4.2.).

## 7.4. Discussion

In the following, the results from the empirical investigation of ICC cases will be discussed in relation to previous research about explanations of lacking Within Insider Reliability, that is, why the same insider may remember or account for the same event differently across time. Also, references will be made to observations made in this regard in relation to cases before other ICCTs. The previous research examined here has been divided into the four main categories outlined below: Memory Deterioration and Other Cognitive Factors (Section 7.4.1.), Interview-Related Factors (Section 7.4.2.), Societal and Political Factors (Section 7.4.3.), Factors Pertaining to the Witness' Security and Motivation (Section 7.4.4.). While understanding Within Insider Reliability would usually require considerations pertaining to all the categories simulta-

---

fence Motion to Strike REDACTED From the Final List of Witnesses and for the Exclusion of his Anticipated Evidence, 12 February 2021 ICC-01/14-01/18-840-Red (https://www.legal-tools.org/doc/3rczrz/). The motion was preceded by a letter from the Defence to the Prosecution, as of 23 August 2019, asking why it had not disclosed information in its possession that a Prosecution witness had engaged in the fabrication of evidence and requesting disclosure of all such information in the prosecution's possession. As a consequence, the Chamber, in its confirmation decisions, refrained from entering findings based entirely on that witness and has only referred to this witness for the purpose of corroborating findings otherwise established to the relevant standards, see ICC, *Prosecutor v. Yekatom and Ngaïssona*, Pre-Trial Chamber II, Corrected Version of 'Decision on the Confirmation of Charges Against Alfred Yekatom and Patrice-Edouard Ngaïssona, 28 June 2021, ICC-01/14-01/18-403-Corr-Red, para. 34 (https://www.legal-tools.org/doc/ruddqn/). It was noted that in "it is clear from the jurisprudence of this Court that a Trial Chamber may rely on witness's testimony or aspects thereof even when credibility issues arise", see ICC, *Prosecutor v. Yekatom and Ngaïssona*, OTP, Public Redacted Version of Prosecution's Response to the Ngaïssona Defence Motion to Strike REDACTED From the Final List of Witnesses and for the Exclusion of his Anticipated Evidence, 12 February 2021, ICC-01/14-01/18-840-Red, para. 168 (https://www.legal-tools.org/doc/3rczrz/).

[189] See, for example, Sandra Guerra Thompson, "Judicial Gatekeeping of Police-Generated Witness Testimony", in *Journal of Criminal Law and Criminology*, 2012, vol. 102, no. 2, pp. 329–396; Stella Bain and James Baxter, "Interrogative Suggestibility: The Role of Interviewer Behaviour", in *Legal and Criminological Psychology*, 2000, vol. 5, no. 1, pp. 123–133; Rachel Roper and David Shewan, "Compliance and Eyewitness Testimony: Do Eyewitnesses Comply with Misleading "Expert Pressure"", in *Legal and Criminological Psychology*, 2010, vol. 7, no. 2, pp. 155–163.

---

neously, and there are many logical connections between the categories, they are presented separately in the following for legibility purposes.

### 7.4.1. Memory Deterioration and Other Cognitive Factors

It is fairly intuitive and also fairly widely acknowledged in memory research that, as time passes, some level of inaccuracy or inconsistency is to be expected in autobiographical memory reports such as those provided by insiders relating to an event that they themselves have experienced.[190] Although, for natural reasons, a memory expert may be more forgiving in relation to such variations than critical evaluators determining whether someone has committed a crime.[191] Judges in many different jurisdictions, including the ICTY[192] and the ICC,[193] have acknowledged that minor discrepancies are to be accepted without diminishing the probative value of the account.[194] This however raises several follow-up questions; what are minor rather than major discrepancies? How many and how extensive discrepancies would occur naturally, that is, purely from memory deterioration or variation in how one and the same story is told over time? As pointed out in relation to the *Yekatom and Ngaïssona* case above, inconsistences and contradictions do not exist fully independently of their observers, and whether there is at all a relevant inconsistency or contradiction is sometimes far from self-evident.

For example, in the *Mbarushimana* case it seems the Chamber was willing to accept contradictions across P-542's statements regarding the date of the attack by the FDLR against Mianga (May or February).[195] However, the accumulation of multiple inconsistencies of which one concerns dates, but also regarding who attended meetings, whether the insider had visited certain places

---

[190] For now presuming that the insider is testifying truthfully and therefore has an autobiographical memory of a crime relevant event. For more on this research see, for example, Elizabet Olson and Gary Wells, "What Makes a Good Alibi? A Proposed Taxonomy", in *Law and Human Behavior*, 2004, vol. 28, pp. 157–176.

[191] Heather Price and Leora Dahl, "Investigator Sensitivity to Alibi Witness Inconsistency After a Long Delay", in *Behavioral Science and Law*, 2017, vol. 35, p. 72.

[192] See ICTY, *Prosecutor v. Prlić et al.*, Trial Chamber III, Judgment, 29 May 2013, IT-04-74-T, para. 285 (https://www.legal-tools.org/doc/2daa33/); *Prosecutor v. Mrkšić et al.*, Trial Chamber II, Judgment, 27 September 2007, IT-95-13/1-T ('*Prosecutor v. Mrkšić et al.*, 27 September 2007') (https://www.legal-tools.org/doc/32111c/).

[193] See, for example, the citation of Judge Fremr in relation to the *Ruto and Sang* case, in Section 7.3.2. above.

[194] ICC, *Prosecutor v. Prlić et al.*, 29 May 2013, para. 285, see *supra* note 192; *Prosecutor v. Mrkšić et al.*, 27 September 2007, see *supra* note 192.

[195] *Mbarushimana* case, see *supra* note 118, EVD-PT-OTP-00854, Summary Statement of Witness 542, at 1235 and *Prosecutor v. Mbarushimana*, 16 December 2011, para. 214, see *supra* note 119.

---

himself or only heard of them, *etcetera*, seemed to have tipped the balance to the negative side when it comes to P-0009's testimony in the *Gbagbo and Blé Goudé* case.[196] Similarly, without being able to provide, from the Chamber's viewpoint, an acceptable explanation for inconsistencies, P-356's testimony was not relied upon in the *Ruto and Sang* case since his testimony varied as regards the number of weapons that were allegedly transacted,[197] the precise chronology of events on the day of the transaction, as well as the exact whereabouts and role of a number of individuals involved.[198]

As outlined in Table 1, the average (minimum) number of statements provided by the insiders during the investigation phase was 3.78 and they testified on average for 6.78 days, with an average time lapse from first to last statement of two years and nine months, and an average total time lapse of ten years and one month from the commencement of the alleged crimes to the concluded proceedings. Also, the average number of inconsistencies and contradictions in their statements, as noted by the Chamber and/or parties (see the part on limitations in 7.1., Introduction), was 2.33. Overall, in research where memory has been tested on several occasions, the majority of interviewed individuals reported contradictory, inconsistent information across the repeated memory tests.[199] In research addressing repeated questioning of witnesses in low-stake settings, with two interviews, the first immediately after having witnessed a staged theft, and the second just ten minutes later, there was a total of 11.21 percent (233 out of 2079) of the responses that changed between the two interviews.[200] While this research highlights that also the type of feedback obtained from the interviewer was significant (see Section 7.4.2.), the following are the overall results, across all conditions/feedback types. Overall, among the

---

[196] P-009 had affirmed several times that that he learnt from General Palasset, commander of the Licorne forces, about the use of mortars in Abobo by the FDs in late February. However, he was considered inconsistent in his accounts of what information he received from General Palasset, see ICC, *Prosecutor v. Gbagbo and Blé Goudé*, Reason of Judge Geoffrey Henderson, 16 July 2019, para. 1352, see *supra* note 153.

[197] ICC, *Prosecutor v. Ruto and Sang*, 27 January 2014, pp. 85–97, see *supra* note 93.

[198] *Ibid.*, pp. 73–124; *Prosecutor v. Ruto and Sang*, 28 January 2014, pp. 11–21, see *supra* note 94. Witness 356 also provided inaccurate information about his own background as well as his personal relationship and interactions with Mr. Ruto. See ICC, *Prosecutor v. Ruto and Sang*, 24 January 2014, pp. 5–77, see *supra* note 94.

[199] Neil Brewer *et al.*, 1999, pp. 297–313, see *supra* note 17; Fisher and Cutler, 1995, pp. 21–28, see *supra* note 20; Tom Smeets, Ingrid Candel and Haralad Merkelbach, "Accuracy, Completeness, and Consistency of Emotional Memories", in *American Journal of Psychology*, 2004, vol. 117, pp. 595–609.

[200] Linda Henkel, "Inconsistencies Across Repeated Eyewitness Interviews: Supportive Negative Feedback Can Make Witnesses Change their Memory Reports", in *Psychology, Crime and Law*, 2017, vol. 23, pp. 97–117.

changed responses, 87 (37 percent) were changed towards accuracy, that is, from wrong answers to right answers, 102 (44 percent) were changed away from accuracy, that is, from right answers to wrong answers, and 44 (19 percent) were changed from one wrong answer to another wrong answer. Importantly, there was no significant difference between the proportion of times participants changed a wrong answer to a right answer than vice versa.[201] This is consistent with prior work showing that response changes do not necessarily systematically move towards or from accuracy.[202] Since the average time lapses in the selected ICC cases extend far beyond ten minutes, and even though forgetting is not necessarily linear,[203] it is likely that the risk of inconsistencies and contradictions, based on memory factors alone,[204] is fairly pronounced. Note, however, that this does not necessarily mean that a different response provided at a later point in time is always the inaccurate response.

Furthermore, also already between two interviews; the first immediately after a staged event (also theft) and the second one week later,[205] witnesses frequently reported reminiscent details, that is, details previously unrecalled, and contrary to experienced police officers' beliefs, a large proportion of the reported reminiscent details were in fact accurate.[206] Although reminiscence may seem at odds with the fact that memory declines over time, these findings are in line with previous research highlighting that reminiscence is a widespread phenomenon[207] that is not precluded by forgetting curves.[208] This highlights the

---

[201] t (167) = 0.46, p. =.64, see *ibid.*, p. 103.

[202] Allan McGroarty and James Baxter, "Interrogative Pressure in Simulated Forensic Interviews: The Effects of Negative Feedback", in *British Journal of Psychology*, 2007, vol. 98, pp. 455–465; Allan McGroarty and James Baxter, "Interviewer Behaviour, Interviewee Self-esteem and Response Change in Simulated Forensic Interviews", in *Personality and Individual Differences*, 2009, vol. 47, pp. 642–646.

[203] That is humans do not seem to forget at a constantly steady pace, but most of the forgetting occurs in the beginning, see for example, Jaap Murre and Joeri Dros, "Replication and Analysis of Ebbinghaus' Forgetting Curve", in *PLOS One*, 2015, vol. 10, no. 7, e0120644, although this research tests a different type of learning situation.

[204] See, for example, Søren Risløv Staugaard and Dorthe Berntsen, "Retrieval Intentionality and Forgetting: How Retention Time and Cue Distinctiveness Affect Involuntary and Voluntary Retrieval of Episodic Memories", in *Memory and Cognition*, 2019, vol. 47, pp. 893–905.

[205] Krix *et al.*, 2015, see *supra* note 17.

[206] *Ibid.*

[207] See, for example, Petra Brock, Ronald Fisher and Brian Cutler, "Examining the Cognitive Interview in a Double-Test Paradigm", in *Psychology, Crime and Law*, 1999, vol. 5, pp. 29–45; Julian Gilbert and Ronald Fisher, "The Effects of Varied Retrieval Cues on Reminiscence in Eyewitness Memory", in *Applied Cognitive Psychology*, 2006, vol. 20, pp. 723–739; Lorraine Hope *et al.*, "Protecting and Enhancing Eyewitness Memory: The Impact of an Initial Recall Attempt on Performance in an Investigative Interview", in *Applied Cognitive Psychology*, 2014, vol. 28, pp. 304–313.

importance of distinguishing between actual contradictions, which more often imply that at least one of the reported details are incorrect, and reminiscent details, where this is not necessarily the same.[209] Furthermore, a likely explanation of reminiscence is a change of retrieval cues,[210] which has an undeniable connection to how the insider is interviewed across different interviews or by different interviewers within one and the same interview (see Section 7.4.2.). This research is relevant in relation to, for example, P-0205's testimony in the *Ongwen* case and P-0435's testimony in the *Gbagbo and Blé Goudé* case, since both of them provided reminiscent details in subsequent interviews.

So far, the focus has been on autobiographical (episodic) memories presuming that insiders have, in fact, experienced the events they account for themselves. While this is a good starting point, there is also a clear risk, as illustrated by, for example, P-0012's testimony in the *Kenyatta* case, that insiders are in fact not accounting for self-experienced events but rather events told to them by others. Such a memory is not autobiographical but rather semantic, that is, knowledge of facts, vocabulary, and concepts acquired through everyday life but not drawn from personal experience as such.[211] To illustrate, semantic memory is the memory students use when they try to remember sections from a book to accurately account for the book's content in an exam. Is there any scientific basis for claiming that the prevalence or nature of inconsistencies and contradictions across time are somehow different between episodic self-experienced memories and semantic memories? If this was the case, research into lie detection would have identified systematic and significant differences between statements pertaining to self-experienced memories and semantic memories. However, this research has firmly concluded that the relationship between accuracy and consistency is weak[212] and that consistency,

---

[208] Matthew Hugh Erdelyi, "The Ups and Down of Memory", in *American Psychologist*, vol. 65, no. 7, pp. 623–633; David La Rooy *et al.*, "Do We Need to Rethink Guidance on Repeated Interviews?", in *Psychology, Public Policy, and Law*, vol. 16, no. 4, pp. 373–392, Ellen Scrivner and Martin Safer, "Eyewitnesses Show Hypermnesia for Details about a Violent Event", in *Journal of Applied Psychology*, 1988, vol. 73, pp. 371–377.

[209] Krix *et al.*, 2015, see *supra* note 17.

[210] This is based on the cognitive theory of memory, see Ronald Fisher and Gregory Mitchell, "The Relation Between Consistency and Accuracy of Eyewitness Testimony: Legal Versus Cognitive Explanations", in Ray Bull, Tim Valentine and Tom Williamson (eds.), *Handbook of Psychology of Investigative Interviewing: Current Developments and Future Directions*, John Wiley, Chichester, 2009, pp. 121–136.

[211] Endel Tulving, *Episodic and Semantic Memory – Organization of Memory*, Academic Press, New York/London, 1972, pp. 381–403; Larry Squire, *Memory and Brain*, Oxford University Press, New York, 1987.

[212] Neil Brewer *et al.*, 1999, pp. 297–313, see *supra* note 17; Fisher and Cutler, 1995, pp. 121–136, see *supra* note 20.

---

therefore, should not be used as a proxy for accuracy.[213] There are also individual differences in long-term memory ('LTM'), both episodic and semantic memory[214] as well as context related factors pertaining to encoding, storage and retrieval to take into account. Since such memory aspects are addressed in other chapters in this volume, for example, in Chapter 6 by Anya Topiwala and Seena Fazel, they will not be addressed further in this chapter.

However, as pointed out by Professor Shepherd, with the passing of time and repeated questioning, the human memory every time reconstructs the event, and it is always increasingly imperfect.[215] Also, due to a possible confirmation bias, stemming from, for example, societal narratives (see Section 7.4.3.), with time, some details may drop out while others acquire more salience.[216] As a result, if an insider is pressed for details in an interview (see Section 7.4.2.), he or she may confabulate or fill in details from other sources than the own memory, a process which can be more or less subconscious.[217] Therefore, when pressed for details, it is expected that an insider's account may not be accurate and consistent with previous versions.[218]

Hence, while evaluators may believe that witness testimony should be consistent over time[219] and that a changed testimony may be an indication of deception,[220] a fully consistent witness testimony is, in fact, fairly difficult or even impossible to provide.[221] However, it is also clear that evaluation of With-

---

[213] Deryn Strange, Jennifer Dysart and Elizabeth Loftus, "Why Errors in Alibis Are Not Necessarily Evidence of Guilt", in *Zeitschrift für Psychologie*, 2014, vol. 222, no. 2, pp. 82–89.

[214] Nash Unsworth, "Individual Differences in Long-Term Memory", in *Psychological Bulletin*, 2019, vol. 145, no. 1, pp. 79–139.

[215] Professor Eric Shepherd, "Interviewing Witnesses in International Criminal Investigations a Conversation with Professor Eric Shephard", Bedford Row's Webinar, 7 June 2021 (available on YouTube's web site).

[216] *Ibid.*

[217] *Ibid.*

[218] *Ibid.*

[219] Tara Burke, John Turtle and Elizabeth Olson, "Alibi Evidence in Criminal Investigations and Trials", in Michael Toglia, Don Read and Rod Lindsay (eds.), *Adult Eyewitness Testimony: A Handbook*, Erlbaum, Hillsdale, 2003, pp. 157–174; Scott E. Culhane and Harmon M. Hosch, "Changed Alibis: Current Law Enforcement, Future Law Enforcement, and Layperson Reactions", in *Criminal Justice and Behavior*, 2012, vol. 39, pp. 958–977; Jennifer Dysart and Deryn Strange, "Beliefs About Alibis and Alibi Investigations: A Survey of Law Enforcement", in *Psychology, Crime and Law*, 2012, vol. 18, pp. 11–25.

[220] Dysart and Strange, 2012, see *supra* note 219.

[221] Drew Leins and Steve D. Charman, "Schema Reliance and Innocent Alibi Generation", in *Legal and Criminological Psychology*, 2016, vol. 21, pp. 111–126; Elizabeth Olson and Steve D. Charman, ""But Can You Prove It?" Examining the Quality of Innocent Suspects' Alibis", in *Psychology, Crime and Law*, 2012, vol. 18, pp. 453–471; Strange, Dysart and Loftus, 2014, pp. 82–89, see *supra* note 213.

in Insider Reliability involves more than just an understanding of memory processes. For this reason, the following sections examine what is known about how statements may vary with time, even if there is no memory loss or other cognitive factors impacting on how a story is told.

## 7.4.2. Interview-Related Factors

As outlined above, there may, because of how human memory and cognitive processes function, at times, be benefits to repeated questioning such as adding correct information to one's report.[222] However, there may also be costs to overall accuracy, including forgetting originally reported details, changing details, adding incorrect information, and misattributing the source of the reported information.[223]

Further, research addressing the effect of the type of questions that are asked across repeated interviews has found that interviewees are more vulnerable to changing their responses when repeatedly questioned with linguistically complex or even deliberately confusing styles like 'lawyer-ese' and cross-examination type questions.[224] Also, when interviewees are given negative feedback or exposed to other types of interrogative pressures suggesting that the interviewee's answers are unsatisfactory,[225] they are more prone to change their responses.[226] This goes both for direct[227] and more subtle[228] negative feed-

---

[222] Geralda Odinot *et al.*, "Are Two Interviews Better than One? Memory Across Repeated Cognitive Interviews", in *PLoS One*, 2013, vol. 8, no. 10, e76305.

[223] Linda Henkel, "Memory Trust and Distrust in Elderly Eyewitnesses: To What Extent Do Older Adults Doubt Their Memories?", in Michael Toglia, David Ross, Joanna Pozzulu and Emily Pica (eds.), *The Elderly Eyewitness in Court*, Taylor and Francis, London, 2014, pp. 232–262.

[224] Though adults are better to resist the pressure to change their responses than are children, see Fiona Jack and Rachel Zajac, "The Effect of Age and Reminders on Witnesses' Responses to Cross-Examination-Style Questioning", in *Journal of Applied Research in Memory and Cognition*, 2014, vol. 3, pp. 1–6; Mark Kebbel and David Giles, "Some Experimental Influences on Lawyers' Complicated Questions on Eyewitness Confidence and Accuracy", in *Journal of Psychology: Interdisciplinary and Applied*, 2000, vol. 134, pp. 129–139; Tim Valentine and Katie Maras, "The Effect of Cross-Examination on the Accuracy of Adult Eyewitness Testimony", in *Applied Cognitive Psychology*, 2011, vol. 25, pp. 554–561; Jacqueline Wheatcroft and Louise Ellison, "Evidence in Court: Witness Preparation and Cross-Examination Style Effects on Adult Witness Accuracy", in *Behavioral Sciences and the Law*, 2012, vol. 30, pp. 821–840.

[225] Richard Ofshe and Richard Leo, "The Decision to Confess Falsely: Rational Choice and Irrational Action", in *Denver University Law Review*, 1997, vol. 74, pp. 979–1122.

[226] Jack and Zajac, 2014, pp. 1–6, Kebbel and Giles, 2000, Valentine and Maras, 2011 and Wheatcroft and Ellison, 2012, see *supra* note 224.

[227] Direct in the sense that interviewees are told they got a number of aspects wrong and to try again, which resulted in a greater number of responses being changed than neutral feedback did, see Gisli Gudjonsson, *The Gudjonsson Suggestibility Scales Manual*, Psychology Press,

---

back, even when the feedback is provided in a supportive manner.[229] Such communications can trigger anxiety and doubt in interviewees who then come to focus on managing the social pressures and are left vulnerable to interrogative suggestibility, sometimes resulting in memory distrust or even false accounts.[230] Although different individuals vary in compliance[231] and vulnerability to interrogative suggestibility, overall, significantly higher numbers of interviewees changed their responses as a result of negative feedback compared to neutral feedback.[232]

While the ICC staff conducting interviews receive continuous training in investigative interviewing, a framework designed to avoid, for example, interrogative suggestibility, it is unknown to what extent the staff abides by this training in practice. Research from national jurisdictions suggest that adherence rates vary and that personal or pseudoscientific beliefs among individual interviewers is one possible explanation for lacking adherence.[233] In this regard, the Pre-Trial Chamber's observation in relation to interview techniques used

---

Hove, 1997; Gisli Gudjonsson, *The Psychology of Interrogations and Confessions: A Handbook*, Wiley, West Sussex, 2003.

[228] For example, even in the absence of overtly leading or misleading questions, or not explicitly claiming that the interviewee's responses are incorrect but instead implying that this is the case and providing an excuse for such a memory failure, a tactic alleged to be used in actual interrogations; Henkel, 2017, see *supra* note 200, p. 106; Bain and Baxter, 2000, pp. 123–133, see *supra* note 189; Linda Henkel, "Do Older Adults Change Their Eyewitness Reports When Re-Questioned?", in *The Journals of Gerontology Series B: Psychological Sciences and Social Sciences*, 2014, vol. 69, pp. 356–365; McGroarty and Baxter, 2007, pp. 455–465, see *supra* note 202; McGroarty and Baxter, 2009, pp. 642–646, see *supra* note 202.

[229] More specifically, the supportive negative feedback was the interviewer sympathetically suggesting why many people's memory may be inaccurate, see Price and Dahl, 2017, p. 72, see *supra* note 191.

[230] Gisli Gudjonsson *et al.*, "The Role of Memory Distrust in Cases of Internalized False Confession", in *Applied Cognitive Psychology*, 2014, vol. 28, pp. 336–348.

[231] When interviewees are compliant, they are aware that they are making changes and, presumably, are doing so for some immediate instrumental gain like alleviating social pressure, which is different from when interviewees exhibit suggestibility, because they then may not realize that they have changed their responses, see Gudjonsson, 2003, see *supra* note 227.

[232] $t(61) = 2.19$, $p = .03$. Among those given supportive negative feedback (total 145), 51 moved towards accuracy, 68 away from accuracy and 26 neither to or from accuracy, while among those given neutral feedback (total 88), 36 moved towards accuracy, 34 away from accuracy and 44 neither to or from accuracy, see Henkel, 2017, p. 104, see *supra* note 200.

[233] See, for example, Scott Lilienfeld and Kristin Landfield, "Science and Pseudoscience in Law Enforcement: A User-Friendly Primer", in *Criminal Justice and Behavior*, 2008, vol. 35, no. 10, pp. 1215–1230; Nicole Adams-Quackenbush, Robert Horselenberg and Peter van Koppen, "Where Bias Begins: A Snapshot of Police Officers' Beliefs About Factors that Influence the Investigative Interview with Suspects", in *Journal of Police and Criminal Psychology*, 2019, vol. 34, pp. 1–8.

---

by OTP investigators in the *Mbarushimana* case, deserve to be briefly re-quoted, as the Chamber was under:

> the impression that the investigator is so attached to his or her theory or assumption that he or she does not refrain from putting questions in leading terms and from showing resentment, impatience or disappointment whenever the witness replies in terms which are not entirely in line with his or her expectations.[234]

The Chamber further described the technique as "utterly inappropriate when viewed in light of the objective, set out in Article 54(1)(a), to establish the truth by "investigating incriminating and exonerating circumstances equally"".[235] Although it deserves to be emphasized again that there is no systematic empirical and official investigation into adherence of ICC staff to the investigative interviewing framework, similar concerns in relation to interviews have been made also in other cases. For example, in her Dissenting Opinion in the *Bemba Gombo* case, Judge Ozaki noted that:

> Witness statements at the ICC are not taken in neutral, impartial circumstances. Rather they are taken by a party (often by an investigator) mainly in order to gather evidence to mount a case against an accused, and without the supervision of any impartial arbiter.[236]

Importantly, interrogative suggestibility is not always apparent to the interviewer, so that even those who perceive themselves as conducting impartial interviewing may more or less subconsciously push for a preferred hypothesis.

On a related note, and with reference to the *Kenyatta* case, Professor Shepherd describes how it is essential for prosecutors and judges to carefully consider "the journey of an account"[237] or, in other words, to analyse the reasons behind an interviewee's statement, including any inconsistencies and/or contradictions. On the basis of his analysis of interviewing techniques used in the *Kenyatta* case, Shepherd also identified multiple interview related factors which could help explain lacking Within Witness Reliability, namely:

1. the high number of interviewers conducting the interviews; for example, prosecutors, counsels, and investigators; and

---

[234] ICC, *Prosecutor v. Mbarushimana*, 16 December 2011, para. 51, see *supra* note 119.

[235] *Ibid.*

[236] ICC, *Prosecutor v. Jean-Pierre Bemba Gombo*, Trial Chamber III, Dissenting Opinion of Judge Kuniko Ozaki on the Decision of the Admission into Evidence of Materials Contained in the Prosecution's List of Evidence, 23 November 2011, ICC-01/05-01/08-1028, para. 11 (https://www.legal-tools.org/doc/9eca75/).

[237] Professor Eric Shepherd, 2021, see *supra* note 215.

2. the high number of topic changes, for example, 23 changes in one of the analysed interviews, which would be challenging for any interviewee to deal with.

While the more specific reasons are unknown, it can be noted that in the *Gbagbo and Blé Goudé* case, the Defence claimed that P-0435 was influenced by objections made by the parties during the proceedings and that this was one reason why he changed his testimony.[238] Also, in the *Kenyatta* case, the Defence claimed that P-0011 and P-0012 had given a "fully inculpatory account to the Prosecutor after having given a wholly exculpatory account to the Defence".[239]

Furthermore, Shepherd described how, even though it was clear that the interviewee in the *Kenyatta* case[240] was incapable of providing a sensible reply,[241] this seem to have been ignored and the interviewers (investigators in this instance) instead seemed to focus on the responses that confirmed their beliefs, that is, they displayed a confirmation bias.[242] The prevalence of such a bias also became apparent through the investigators use of leading, suggestive and false option questions,[243] while, when asked open ended questions, the interviewee again, failed to provide a narrative himself.

It is also unknown what importance the interpretation process has for Within Insider Reliability, but this is potentially of great practical relevance for multilingual trials such as those before the ICC. The potential for error was pointed out by Judge Herrera Carbuccia, who, following objections to the consistency of translations by the defence, in her dissenting opinion in the *Gbagbo and Blé Goudé* case stated that translations:

> [...] although helpful and often necessary for judges who do not
> understand one or more of the languages used in trial, may still

---

[238] ICC, *Prosecutor v. Gbagbo and Blé Goudé*, Trial Chamber I, Public Redacted Version of "Corrigendum to Blé Goudé Defence No Case to Answer Motions, 28 September 2018, ICC-02/11-01/15-1198-Corr-Red, para. 247 (https://www.legal-tools.org/doc/4dc79e/).

[239] ICC, *Prosecutor v. Kenyatta*, 23 January 2012, para. 93, see *supra* note 49.

[240] Shepherd did not specify who this interviewee was, but the analysis was conducted within the frame of the *Kenyatta* case, Professor Eric Shepherd, see *supra* note 215.

[241] For example, the interviewee kept repeating 'what?' in relation to the interview questions, and he provided no less than four different and fully incompatible versions about how he had killed his wife, see Professor Eric Shepherd, see *supra* note 215.

[242] For research on the importance of confirmation bias in criminal cases in general as well as in interviews specifically, see Moa Lidén, "Confirmation Bias in Criminal Cases", *Uppsala Universitetsförlag*, 2018 and Moa Lidén, 2020, see *supra* note 11.

[243] For more on different question types see, for example, Brent Snook *et al.*, "Let'em Talk!: A Field Study of Police Questioning Practices of Suspects and Accused Persons", in *Criminal Justice and Behavior*, 2012, vol. 39, no. 10, pp. 1328–1339.

distance judges from the original meaning of a word or message.[244]

Translation errors have been acknowledged as a potential source of
wrongful outcomes,[245] and if errors in the interpretation are made in one interview, then it should come as no surprise that in another interview conducted at
a later point in time, with another interpreter, the insider comes across as inconsistent or contradicting his or her previous statement. Shepherd explains
how interpreters may adopt direct or indirect approaches which to different
degrees account for the exact words said by an interviewee and whether trans-
lational issues are detected or not varies depending on, for example, cultural
factors pertaining to the witness compliance as well as whether the translation
is contested by others.[246] It can also be discussed whether the interpreter should
be familiar with or even part of the interviewee's social and cultural background,[247] a question which is all the more important if, with time, social narratives are formed which impact on the insiders testimony in many different
ways, as discussed in the next section.

### 7.4.3. Societal and Political Factors

> [...] the telling and retelling of the story of events is a way in
> which collective community memory and identity is shaped,
> transformed and transmitted over time.[248]
>
> *David Cohen, 2012*

> Naturally, credit must go to flashes of heroism whenever they oc-
> cur. But it will be too much to expect the average Kenyan witness
> to adopt a heroic stance in support of a criminal trial that may re-
> sult in the conviction of the accused; when community leaders,

---

[244] ICC, *Prosecutor v. Gbagbo and Blé Goudé*, 10 December 2018, para. 51, see *supra* note 36.

[245] For more on this in a national context see, for example, Ana Aliverti and Rachel Seoighe, "Lost in Translation? Examining the Role of Court Interpreters in Cases Involving Foreign National Defendants in England and Wales", in *New Criminal Law Review: An International and Interdisciplinary Journal*, 2017, vol. 20, no. 1, pp. 130–156, and for the context of in-ternational criminal justice, see, for example, Leigh Swigart, "Linguistic and Cultural Diver-sity in International Criminal Justice: Toward Bridging the Divide", in *Pacific Law Journal*, 2017, vol. 48, pp. 197–217.

[246] More specifically, with the direct approach, the translator says exactly what the interviewee said while, with an indirect approach, the translator edits the interviewee's statement in dif-ferent ways, see Eric Shepherd, 2021, see *supra* note 215.

[247] *Ibid.*

[248] Cohen, 2012, p. 14, see *supra* note 6.

religious leaders, the Kenyan Parliament, and the Government
have so vocally and aggressively stood against that inquiry.[249]

*Judge Eboe-Osuji, in the Ruto and Sang case, 2016*

With the passing of time, community understandings and cultural factors
may shape the memory of events, so-called 'collective memory' and this impacts the way in which individuals recount past events.[250] This is particularly
the case in small close-knit neighborhoods, districts, or village communities in
traditional societies, with predominantly oral cultures.[251] While it may vary
what the practical living arrangements for insider witnesses are during the time
they testify, many will, in one way or another, remain parts of their societies.
Furthermore, in these societies there may also be more or less explicit and official viewpoints which by themselves or in concert with collective memories,
shape and impact both on how insiders remember and account for certain
events over time, thus potentially relevant for both the memory and account
aspects of Within Insider Reliability.

There is much to suggest that lacking Within Insider Reliability in the
*Kenyatta* and *Ruto and Sang* cases was significantly stronger related to account than memory aspects, following, for example, "the aggressive atmosphere created by influential voices within Kenya, including the Kenyan Parliament".[252] However, the observation that insiders first tell a story as if they
have personally experienced it (for example, personally attending a meeting),
and then instead acknowledge that the information was obtained from someone else, has been made before at the ICCTs, and then emphasizing more the
memory aspects. For example, in cases before the Special Court of Sierra Leone ('SCSL'), it was noted that witnesses, sometimes, formed their statements
more on the basis of collective memory, that is, what they heard from others in
their home communities rather than what they personally experienced.[253] Furthermore, as pointed out by the expert witness Dr. Mathias Ruzidana in the
*Akayesu* case before the ICTR,[254] in societies with predominantly oral tradi-

---

[249] ICC, *Prosecutor v. Ruto and Sang*, Trial Chamber V(A), Public Redacted Version of Decision on Defence Applications for Judgments of Acquittal, Reasons of Judge Eboe-Osuji, 18
July 2013, ICC-01/09-01/11-817-Anx ('*Prosecutor v. Ruto and Sang*, 18 July 2013')
(https://www.legal-tools.org/doc/6c9a91/).

[250] Cohen, 2012, pp. 13–14, see *supra* note 6.

[251] *Ibid.* Cohen exemplifies these societies with, for example, Rwanda, Sierra Leone and East
Timor.

[252] ICC, *Prosecutor v. Ruto and Sang*, 18 July 2013, para. 162, see *supra* note 249.

[253] Cohen, 2012, p. 14, see *supra* note 6.

[254] ICTR, *Prosecutor v. Jean-Paul Akayesu*, Trial Chamber I, Judgment, 1 June 2001, ICTR-96-
4-T ('*Prosecutor v. Jean-Paul Akayesu*, 1 June 2001') (https://www.legal-
tools.org/doc/c62d06/), cited in Cohen, 2012, p. 15, see *supra* note 6.

---

tions and where many people are illiterate there is a "hazard of distortion of the information each time it is passed on to a new listener".[255] This expert was hired as a response to the Defence's allegations that witnesses were systematically lying.[256] The shaping and expression of memory in this way,[257] matches poorly the definition of lying as an "act that is intended to foster in another person a belief or understanding which the deceiver considers to be false".[258] Hence, if a witness is inconsistent with an original statement provided, one possible explanation is the development of such a collective memory over time. Hence, there are many examples of cases before the ICCTs which have resulted in difficulties with sorting out what witnesses actually saw themselves and what they later, based on what they had heard, decided had happened. This was evident also in the *Tacaqui* case[259] before the SPSC in which, interestingly enough, witness statements, unlike those outlined in Table 1, went from exonerating to incriminating over time.[260] More specifically, none of the individuals who testified against Mr. Tacaqui at trial had even mentioned him in their initial interviews during the investigation.[261] This was connected to the fact that

---

[255] Cited by Cohen, 2012, p. 15, see *supra* note 6. The original text comes from the ICTR Chamber I's Judgment in *Prosecutor v. Jean-Paul Akayesu*, where Dr. Ruzindana's testimony is recounted in the following way:

> [...] most Rwandan's live in an oral tradition in which facts are reported as they are perceived by the witness, often irrespective of whether the facts were personally witnessed or recounted by someone else. Since not many people are literate or own a radio, much of the information disseminated by the press in 1994 was transmitted to a larger number of secondary listeners by word of mouth, which inevitably carries the hazard of distortion of the information each time it is passed on to a new listener.

see *Prosecutor v. Jean-Paul Akayesu*, 1 June 2001, para. 155, see *supra* note 254.

[256] Cohen, 2012, pp. 14–15, see *supra* note 6.

[257] *Ibid.*, p. 14.

[258] Robert Krauss, "Impression Formation, Impression Management and Nonverbal Behaviors", in E.T. Higgins, Peter Herman and Mark Zanna (eds.), *Social Cognition: The Ontario Symposium*, Hillsdale, Erlbaum/Zuckerman, 1981, pp. 323–341; Bella DePaulo and Robert Rosenthal, "Verbal and Non-Verbal Communication of Deception", in Leonard Berkowitz (ed.), *Advances in Experimental Social Psychology*, Academic Press, New York, 1981, pp. 1–57.

[259] SPSC, District Court of Dili, *Prosecutor v. Florencio Tacaqui*, Judgment, 9 December 2004, 20/2001 (https://www.legal-tools.org/doc/864bbe/). Florencio Tacaqui was a local pro-Indonesian militia leader who was alleged to have been personally involved in a massacre of 47 individuals. For more on this case see, for example, Cohen, 2012, pp. 14–15, see *supra* note 6.

[260] The statements analysed here moved from incriminatory to exculpatory or, perhaps more accurately, to not providing any or barely any crime relevant information at all, while at other times the changes were just between different details, not necessarily in any specific direction, see Table 1 and Section 7.3.2.

[261] Cohen, 2012, pp. 17–18, see *supra* note 6.

---

investigators had not asked witnesses about Mr. Tacaqui specifically as he did not emerge as a suspect until later, and then, when asked about him, the witnesses "remembered" him as the leader of the militia that perpetrated the massacre.[262] The SPSC, noting an "unsolvable contradiction" attributed this shift to various cultural qualities of Timorese society such as a disposition to lie or a disposition to tell people what they think that person wants to hear.[263] As pointed out by Cohen in relation to the *Tacaqui* case:

> What may have in fact transpired is that with the passage of time the community comes to attribute responsibility to certain persons and to adopt a particular interpretation of what happened. This is then what everyone believes occurred.[264]

This highlights the impact of what the SPSC referred to as *collective suggestions*, that is, the social context impacts the recollection of witnesses as their testimony shifts over time to accommodate the expectations conveyed by the narratives dominant in the context in which they find themselves.[265] That means that insiders, on the basis of their original testimony, may very well be testifying against what is perceived to be the national interest of an ethnic group or similar, which seems to provide an understandable motivation to shift and provide inconsistent testimony. This highlights the possibility both of more subtle memory distortion and more conscious adjustments to be consistent with social narratives. The latter possibility also has ties to the witness security and motivation, discussed in more detail in the next section.

### 7.4.4. Factors Pertaining to the Witnesses' Motivation and Security

Psychological research suggests that humans have a few main motivations that drive their behaviours, including needs as fundamental as hunger, thirst and safety, that is, the security of body, of employment, of resources, of family, and of health,[266] but also of personal or social origins such as social approval, acceptance, the need to achieve and the motivation to take or avoid risks, to name a few.[267]

---

[262] *Ibid.*

[263] *Ibid.*, p. 18.

[264] *Ibid.*, p. 20.

[265] *Ibid.*

[266] This originates from Abraham Maslow's 'Hierarchy of Needs', which he first introduced in 1943, see for example, Abraham Maslow, "A Theory of Human Motivation", in *Psychological Review*, 1943, vol. 50, no. 4, pp. 370–396 and Abraham Maslow, *Motivation and Personality*, Harper and Row, New York, 1954. This hierarchy suggests that people are motivated to fulfill basic needs before moving on other more advanced needs.

[267] See, for example, Ezequiel Morsella *et al.*, *Oxford Handbook of Human Action, Social Cognition and Social Neuroscience*, Oxford University Press, 2009.

If there are direct or indirect threats against an insider, or even if the societal context more implicitly expects him or her to account for an event in a certain way (see Section 7.4.3.), then it seems fairly clear that motivators such as security and social approval will make the insider willing to consciously account for an event differently than what he or she has done before. It was acknowledged by the OTP that in the Kenya cases, there were "significant security concerns"[268] in relation to insiders following "difficulties with the witness protection program at that time".[269] Although the OTP in its own review, on the basis of an external expert review, claimed that "OTP thinking is now, in fact, far ahead of the recommendations, in relation to witness risk assessments, screening methods, and field craft regarding evidence collection",[270] the security of insiders, and particularly if the security situation changes over time, is an obvious and tangible source of lacking Within Insider Reliability. Reasonably, not only the actual but also the perceived availability and sufficiency of protective measures is important, primarily witness protection programs[271] during the investigation and closed session testimony, use of pseudonyms, facial and/or voice distortion.[272] There are also documented cases in international criminal law, for example, at the ICTY, of leaking of confidential information.[273]

There may also be somewhat more subtle motivators that prompt lacking Within Insider Reliability, and many of them can be explained with references to human general risk aversion,[274] that is, humans prefer outcomes with low uncertainty to those outcomes with high uncertainty, even if the average outcome in the latter case is better. As such, individuals are inclined to prefer situations that are more predictable, even if it results in a lower payoff, rather than another situation with a highly unpredictable but possibly higher payoff.

---

[268] "ICC OTP Kenya Cases: Review and Recommendations – Executive Summary of the Report of the External Independent Experts", p. 4, para. E20, Annex I to ICC OTP, "Full Statement of the Prosecutor, Fatou Bensouda, on External Expert Review and Lessons Drawn From the Kenya Situation", 26 November 2019 ('ICC OTP, 26 November 2019') (https://www.legal-tools.org/doc/32p2hy/).

[269] ICC OTP, 26 November 2019, p. 5, see *supra* note 268.

[270] *Ibid.*, p. 14.

[271] del Ponte, 2006, p. 546, see *supra* note 9.

[272] *Ibid.*

[273] *Ibid.*

[274] Daniel Kahneman and Amos Tversky, "Prospect Theory: An Analysis of Decision Under Risk", in *Econometrica*, 1979, vol. 47, no. 2, pp. 263–291; Jan Werner, "Risk Aversion", in Macmillan Publishers Ltd. (ed.), *The New Palgrave Dictionary of Economics*, Palgrave Macmillan, London, 2018, pp. 1–6; Levy Moshe, "An Evolutionary Explanation for Risk Aversion", in *Journal of Economic Psychology*, 2015, vol. 46, pp. 51–61.

In the context of criminal cases, risk aversion is an important motivator and explanation as to why defendants, also those who are innocent, so frequently accept plea bargains,[275] with plea rates well above 90 percent in some jurisdictions,[276] and counsel advice pertaining to the risk of accepting or rejecting a plea is an important factor in this regard.[277] Since plea bargains are also known to be important predictors for wrongful outcomes,[278] it seems reasonable to claim that risk aversion can be an important source of error in the context of criminal justice. This seems to apply also to risk aversion in insiders, although the risks they are averse to may be somewhat different. When it comes to informants, three main risks have been identified in this regard, including perhaps the most obvious reason: (i) to avoid punishment, (ii) allegiance to the suspect, and (iii) fear of retaliation.[279]

That insiders, just like other humans, generally and usually, wish to avoid punishment seems fairly straightforward. While insiders may originally think that providing an incriminatory statement is the best way to distract attention from themselves, insiders' perceptions of the potential benefits of doing so can change with time, for example, if they receive legal advice or gain other insights into the criminal proceedings which causes them to reconsider their positions. For example, for insiders who themselves have committed

---

[275] While plea bargains are a common element in some jurisdictions they are not in the ICC jurisdiction. Whether the ICC should use plea bargains has been discussed by a few scholars, see, for example, Gallia Daor, "When the Devil Won't Bargain – The Relevance and Potential Implications of Plea Bargaining in the International Criminal Court", in *Eyes on the ICC*, vol. 11, no. 1, pp. 29–54 and Regina Rauxloh, "Plea Bargaining in International Criminal Justice – Can the International Criminal Court Afford to Avoid Trials?", in *The Journal of Criminal Justice Research*, 2011, vol. 1, no. 2, pp. 1–25.

[276] United States Department of Justice, "Bureau of Justice Statistics", 2009.

[277] Vanessa Edkins, "Defense Attorney Plea Recommendations and Client Race: Does Zealous Represenation Apply Equally to All?", in *Law and Human Behavior*, 2011, vol. 35, no. 5, pp. 413–425; Erika Fountain and Jennifer Woolard, "How Defense Attorneys Consult with Juvenile Clients About Plea Bargains?", in *Psychology, Public Policy, and Law*, 2018, vol. 24, no. 2, pp. 192–203.

[278] See, for example, Ronald Huff and Martin Killias, *Wrongful Convictions and Miscarriages of Justice: Causes and Remedies in North American and European Criminal Justice Systems*, Routledge, 2013; Besiki Kutateladze and Victoria Lawson, "Is a Plea Really a Bargain? An Analysis of Plea and Trial Dispositions in New York City", in *Crime and Delinquency*, vol. 64, no. 7, pp. 856–887.

[279] Michael Cassidy, "Soft Words of Hope: Giglio, Accomplice Witnesses, and the Problem of Implied Inducements", in *Northwestern University Law Review*, 2004, vol. 98, pp. 1–43; United States Court of Appeals, *United States v. Cervantes-Pacheco*, Fifth Circuit, Judgment, 826 F.2d 310, p. 315 (https://www.legal-tools.org/doc/ky82rf/); United States Court of Appeals, *United States v. Singleton*, Tenth Circuit, Judgment, 8 January 1999, 144 F.3d 1343 ('*United States v. Singleton*, 8 January 1999') (https://www.legal-tools.org/doc/804uvk/).

crimes, the passing of time offers a chance to remove or neutralize relevant evidence that could have been used against them, and after which they are no longer motivated to provide incriminating testimony due to other risks (for example, retaliation). Furthermore, it may in other ways become clear to them that legal proceedings against them are very unlikely, for example due to the focus on the most responsible perpetrators. As such, the perception of whether there is a risk of incriminating oneself, as well as how tangible that risk is, may change with time.[280] As Carla del Ponte pointed out in relation to cases before the ICTY:

> An incentive among lower level accused to cooperate is the reduction of sentence for testifying and providing information about other in the criminal enterprise. Building a case against the most senior persons responsible may involve a series of cases which "work up the ladder", prosecuting lower-level perpetrators in collection of evidence against the higher-level perpetrator, or in obtaining the substantive cooperation of insiders. The use of such witnesses, both lower level and higher-level insiders is a valuable tool in international prosecutions. But as the remaining indictment only reflect the most responsible perpetrators at the highest level, it remains to be seen whether lower-level perpetrators will feel there is an incentive to cooperate when there are not further or pending investigations and indictments.[281]

Furthermore, allegiance to the suspect, can take a variety of forms such as interpersonal closeness,[282] loyalty to ingroup members, that is, group cohesiveness[283] and/or affiliation due to shared experiences.[284] Clearly, it cannot be

---

[280] Notably however, as pointed out by del Ponte, 2006, p. 544, see *supra* note 9, in the prosecution of Slobodan Milošević, Milan Babić was included in the indictment as a member of the joint criminal enterprise. Babić spontaneously came forward for interviews with the ICTY Office of the Prosecutor and subsequently testified voluntarily in the *Milošević* proceedings despite the fact that he was incriminating himself. He also provided documentation to assist in bringing himself and others to justice. Babić later was indicted, entered into a plea agreement and pleaded guilty to the crime of persecution, a crime against humanity.

[281] del Ponte, 2006, p. 543, see *supra* note 9.

[282] Arthur Aron, Elaine Aron, Michael Tudor and Greg Nelson., "Close Relationships as Including Other in the Self", in *Journal of Personality and Social Psychology*, 1991, vol. 6, pp. 243–257.

[283] Kenneth Dion, "Group Cohesion: From Fields of Forces to Multidimensional Construct", in *Group Dynamics*, 2000, vol. 4, pp. 7–26; Michael Hogg, "Group Cohesiveness: A Critical Review and Some New Directions", in Wolfgang Stroebe and Miles Hewstone (eds.), *European Review of Social Psychology*, 1993, vol. 4, pp. 85–111; Rolf Holtz, "Group Cohesion, Attitude Projection, and Opinion Certainty: Beyond Interaction", in *Group Dynamics: Theory, Research, and Practice*, 2004, vol. 8, pp. 112–125.

generally stated how allegiance to the suspect is impacted by the passing of time. Since many insiders' testimonies over time went in an exonerating rather than an incriminating direction, this could be an indication that the allegiance increases. One possible explanation of this, in turn, would be that of the social context (see Section 7.4.3.), which with time comes to form social narratives about what happened, who has guilt in that, and who does not, and such shared notions in societies can increase group cohesiveness and affiliation due to shared experiences.

At the same pace that allegiance to the suspect increases, due to, for example, the social context, fear of retaliation for providing an incriminating testimony may also increase. Usually, individuals engage in a cost-benefit analysis when deciding whether to engage in behaviour that may harm or anger another person.[285] Therefore, an insider may be reluctant to maintain an incriminating statement if the costs include possible retaliation, for example, threats to one's person, that outweigh the possible benefits of testifying. However, there is, of course, no general trend in this regard, and the passing of time can also mean that the insider is more out of harm's way, and therefore more likely to disclose accurate information, which was before associated with greater risk taking.

If individuals are generally risk averse, there are many potential risks developing in different directions as time passes, and they are then also offered an incentive to provide a certain testimony, lacking Within Insider Reliability should come as no surprise. In fact, research regarding incentivized testimony[286] highlights the role of incentives offered during informant interviews, for the reluctance or willingness of informants to implicate a close other through a secondary confession.[287] More specifically, the offer of an incentive[288] signifi-

284 Stanley Schacter, *The Psychology of Affiliation: Experimental Studies of the Sources of Gregariousness*, Stanford University Press, 1959.
285 Hans Crombag, Eric Rassin and Robert Horselenberg, "On Vengeance", in *Psychology, Crime and Law*, 2003, vol. 9, pp. 333–344; Robert Bies and Thomas Tripp, "Beyond Distrust: 'Getting Even' and the Need for Revenge", in Roderick Kramer and Tom Tyler (eds.), *Trust in Organizations: Frontiers of Theory and Research,* Sage, Thousand Oaks, 1996, pp. 246–260.
286 See, for example, Swanner and Beike, "Incentives Increase the Rate of False but Not True Secondary Confessions from Informants with an Allegiance to a Suspect", in *Law and Human Behavior*, 2010, vol. 34, pp. 418–428 and Jeffrey Neuschatz *et al.*, "The Effects of Accomplice Witnesses, Jailhouse Snitches, and Other Bartered Testimony on Judicial Decision Making", in *Law and Human Behavior*, 2008, vol. 32, pp. 137–149.
287 A secondary confession is confession evidence provided by someone other than the suspect and purported to be direct information from the suspect, see, for example, Neuschatz *et al.*, 2008, pp. 137–149, see *supra* note 286. Note however, that some of this research was con-

cantly increased the number of participants willing to sign a secondary confession, and while legal actors are generally aware that the informants or insiders who receive an incentive for their testimony may have a motivation to lie,[289] it is, of course, not always clear in an applied setting, whether and what incentives have been offered. It is unlikely that all insiders will be as open and forthcoming about incentives as P-800 in the *Ruto and Sang* case was, when he himself admitted under oath that he had agreed to recant his statement in return for the payment of a bribe.[290] This circumstance, together with the fact that neither laymen nor experts are good lie detectors (and individuals are usually better liars than they think),[291] constitute an undeniable risk of wrongful outcomes. While in national jurisdictions, the problem of demonstrably invalid or false secondary confessions is widespread, and were, in fact, present in 46 percent of the wrongful convictions in death row cases,[292] the consequences of incentivized testimony, as discussed in the context of insider witness testimony seems more uncertain, but since inconsistent and contradictory insider testimony is usually not relied upon, it potentially constitutes a larger risk of

---

ducted using a student sample, see Swanner and Beike, 2010, pp. 418–428, see *supra* note 286.

[288] More specifically, participants were offered extra credit and a small monetary prize, in exchange for secondary confessions, see Swanner and Beike, 2010, pp. 418–428, see *supra* note 286. Among undergraduate students, the incentive of getting out of a required second experimental session was sufficiently powerful to motivate secondary confessions, however, unfortunately, this motivated only false rather than true secondary confessions, see Jessica Swanner, Denise Beike and Alexander Cole, "Snitching, Lies, and Computer Crashes: An Experimental Investigation of Secondary Confessions", in *Law and Human Behavior*, 2009, vol. 34, no. 1, pp. 53–65.

[289] United States Supreme Court, *Giglio v. United States*, Judgment, 24 February 1972, 405 US 150 (https://www.legal-tools.org/doc/fa6555/) and *United States v. Singleton*, 8 January 1999, see *supra* note 279.

[290] More specifically, he testified that he had signed a pre-written affidavit in which he recanted his earlier statement despite knowing most of its contents to be untrue. Moreover, he testified that he had agreed to approach other Prosecution witnesses, including Witness 495, in order to convince them to recant, see ICC, *Prosecutor v. Ruto and Sang*, 5 April 2016, para. 42, see *supra* note 78.

[291] Without using specialized tools, people judge lies correctly about 47 percent of the time and truths correctly about 61 percent of the time, see Charles Bond and Bella DePaulo, "Individual Differences in Judging Deception: Accuracy and Bias", in *Psychological Bulletin*, 2008, vol. 134, pp. 477–492.

[292] Brandon Garrett, "Judging Innocence", in *Columbia Law Review*, 2008, vol. 8, pp. 55–142; Warden, "The Snitch System: How Incentivized Witnesses put 38 Innocent Americans on Death Row", in *Northwestern University of School of Law*, Center on Wrongful Conviction, 2004, pp. 1–16.

---

wrongful acquittals than convictions.[293] While not directly comparable, it can be noted that incentives only seem to increase false secondary confessions while it had no impact on true ones.[294]

## 7.5. Implications and Conclusion

On the basis of the empirical investigation conducted within the frames of this research, it has been possible to obtain an overall quantification of the 'time variable' relevant here. On average, the examined ICC cases entailed a time lapse of ten years and one month from the commencement of the alleged crimes, including the planning stages that insiders often testify about, to the concluded proceedings or last decision. Although limited in terms of the number of examined ICC cases as well as insiders testifying in those cases, this research also provided some more specific numbers pertaining to the time variable. To begin with, the average time lapse between the first and last statement provided by insiders was two years and nine months, during which the insiders were, on average, interviewed 3.78 times (at the very least) during the investigation and for an average of 6.78 days in or before the Court.

Since research indicates that considerable variations in witness testimony can occur already between two interviews that are conducted ten minutes apart, significant variations in insider testimonies can be expected on the basis of memory factors alone. Hence, for prosecutors and judges, it appears relevant to actively evaluate whether and to what inconsistencies and contradictions can be expected already on the basis of the time lapse and the number of interviews. Furthermore, it seems relevant to determine whether information provided by the insider is different, incompatible or new, in relation to the previously disclosed information. For example, the available research suggests that the reporting of reminiscent details, that is, details not previously disclosed, is fairly common and not necessarily a sign that an insider should not be trusted. However, it is clear, not the least from the examined cases, that understanding and properly evaluating Within Insider Reliability involves far more than just an understanding of memory processes. How the insider has been interviewed across different interviews at different points in time is one example. This includes considerations relating to, for example, interrogative

---

[293] However, as pointed out by Professor Eric Shepherd, even inconsistent and contradictory insider testimony may be considered reliable, if investigators, prosecutors and judges, hold a confirmation bias whereby they focus only on the instances of the testimony which supports their prior beliefs and also makes them less skeptical of the testimony, see Eric Shepherd, 2021, see *supra* note 215. For more on confirmation bias in evaluations of witness testimony see Lidén, 2020, see *supra* note 11.

[294] Swanner, Beike and Cole, 2009, see *supra* note 288. This is unsurprising considering that incentives are selfish motivations, see Swanner and Beike, 2010, p. 427, see *supra* note 286.

suggestibility, number of interviewers, and number of topics covered. It also seems relevant for an interviewer as well as evaluator to know what social context as well as social narratives the insider has been subjected to. If the social context and narratives have changed with time, and the insider's testimony is consistent with such developments, this is a relevant explanation, especially combined with changed motivational factors, including not only security but also changes occurring over time that impact on the insiders' risk-taking behaviour.

Understanding why inconsistencies and contradictions occur is one important aspect but does not necessarily answer the question of what the legal significance is or should be. However, preferably, the likely explanations for lacking Within Insider Reliability should be integrated into decision making as to whether, for example, under Rule 68 of the Rules of Procedure and Evidence, submissions to include prior recorded testimony should be allowed. Indeed, such submissions have been made, for example, in the *Gbagbo and Blé Goudé* case,[295] the *Ongwen* case[296] as well as the *Yekatom and Ngaïssona* case.[297] While documents and recordings, unlike testimonies, do not normally change (in terms of content) with time, it has been questioned whether an increased volume and use of prior recorded testimony would interfere with the rights of the accused,[298] for example, when it comes to cross examination of

---

[295] In this case, the Prosecution attempted to use Rule 68(2)(b) to admit the written statements of three witnesses and multiple associated documents informing the Chamber that the examination of the three proposed witnesses was "unnecessary", see ICC, *Prosecutor v. Gbagbo and Blé Goudé*, Trial Chamber I, Public Redacted Version of "Prosecution Application to Conditionally Admit the Prior Recorded Statements and Related Documents of REDACTED, under Rule 68(2) and the Prior Recorded Statements and Related Documents under Rule 68(3), 26 April 2016, ICC-02/11-01/15-487-Red (https://www.legal-tools.org/doc/1f8e40/). The Trial Chamber observed that one of the proposed statements appeared to contain a distinct, first-hand perspective while another included decidedly unique information from the only eyewitness to a contested matter, see, ICC, *Prosecutor v. Gbagbo and Blé Goudé*, Trial Chamber I, Decision on the Prosecutor's Application to Introduce Prior Recorded Testimony Under Rules 68(2)(b) and 68(3), 9 June 2016, ICC-02/11-01/15-573-Red, para. 17 (https://www.legal-tools.org/doc/712c8d/).

[296] ICC, *Prosecutor v. Ongwen*, Trial Chamber IX, Decision on the Prosecution's Applications for Introduction of Prior Recorded Testimony Under Rule 68(2)(b) of the Rules, 18 November 2016, ICC-02/04-01/15-596-Red, para. 1 (https://www.legal-tools.org/doc/e9d9c4/). The application asked the Chamber to admit 38 such statements.

[297] There were multiple such submissions, but see, for example, ICC, *Prosecutor v. Yekatom and Ngaïssona*, Trial Chamber V, Public Redacted Version of "Prosecution's Request for the Formal Submission of the Prior Recorded Testimony of P-1074 pursuant to Rule 68(3), 22 April 2021, ICC-01/14-01/18-963-Red (https://www.legal-tools.org/doc/dbbzuf/).

[298] See, for example, ICC, *Prosecutor v. Ruto and Sang*, Trial Chamber V(a), Public Redacted Version of Corrigendum: Decision on Prosecution Request for Admission of Prior Recorded

---

the insider, following Rule 92 of the Rules of Procedure and Evidence.[299] Furthermore, the consequences for the principle of orality have been discussed in this regard.[300] In addition, it has been alleged that allowing large volumes of such submissions could "render the trials sterile, reduce the impact of prosecution evidence and may make the criminal process very difficult for the public to follow".[301] On top of that, some argue that it would be to recreate past mistakes by historical ICCTs,[302] before which large volumes of affidavit evidence made the post-World War II proceedings more efficient,[303] but also contributed to the perception of lacking legality or unfairness of the Nuremberg, as well as Tokyo, proceedings.[304] As such, it has been alleged that replacing oral evidence with written statements is a "risky maneuver at best".[305]

In this regard, it can be noted that numerous common law jurisdictions permit the admission of prior inconsistent statements under certain circumstances, including Canada,[306] Ireland[307] and Australia.[308] Among adversarial

---

Testimony, 19 August 2015, ICC-01/09-01/11-1938-Corr-Red2, para. 60 (https://www.legal-tools.org/doc/d18042/).

[299] Under Rule 92, the written statements of available witnesses are admissible only after meeting a host of technical requirements, including that the statement bet witnessed, sworn and provided under penalty of perjury. See ICC, Rules of Procedure and Evidence, 9 September 2002, Rule 92 (http://www.legaltools.org/doc/8bcf6f/).

[300] ICC, *Prosecutor v. Gbagbo and Blé Goudé*, Appeals Chamber, Judgment on the Appeals of Mr. Laurent Gbagbo and Mr. Charles Blé Goudé Against the Decision of Trial Chamber I of 9 June 2016 Entitled Decision on the Prosecutor's Application to Introduce Prior Recorded Testimony Under Rules 68(2)(b) and 68(3), 1 November 2016, ICC-02/11-01/15-744 (https://www.legal-tools.org/doc/34d0b3/). The ICC Appeals Chamber stated that "respect for the principle of orality" cannot be reduced to a purely mathematical calculation of the percentage of witnesses providing their entire evidence orally". In other words, even when the majority of witness testimony is in the form of out-of-court statements, an ICC trial may nevertheless comply with a statutory provision that "makes in-court personal testimony the rule".

[301] United Nations Secretary-General, "Comments on the Report of the Expert Group to Conduct a Review of the Effective Operation and Functioning of the International Tribunal for the Former Yugoslavia and the International Criminal Tribunal for Rwanda", UN Doc. A/54/850, 27 April 2000, para. 54 (https://www.legal-tools.org/doc/pfz5l8/).

[302] Megan Fairlie, "The Abiding Problem of Witness Statements in International Criminal Trials", in *International Law and Politics*, 2017, vol. 50, no. 75, pp. 75–158.

[303] For similar arguments in relation to the ICC, *Prosecutor v. Gbagbo and Blé Goudé*, Decision Adopting Amended and Supplemented Direction on the Conduct of the Proceedings, Annex A, 4 May 2016, ICC-02/11-01/15-498, para. 48 (https://www.legal-tools.org/doc/d25a23/).

[304] Fairlie, 2017, pp. 75–158, see *supra* note 302.

[305] *Ibid.*

[306] See, for example, Supreme Court of Canada, *R. v. B.* (K.G.), Judgment, 25 February 1993, 1 S.C.R. 740 (https://www.legal-tools.org/doc/8f54f5/), addressing prior inconsistent statements of recanting witnesses available for cross-examination.

systems, the United Kingdom ('UK') has adopted legislation that, like Rule 68(2)(d), admits prior statements of fearful witnesses even when the witness is completely unavailable for cross-examination and the accused played no role in the witness' unavailability to testify.[309] When the Grand Chamber of the European Court of Human Rights recently considered this UK approach, its analysis included comparative assessments of six other common law jurisdictions, none of which employed similar legislation.[310]

Other, partially overlapping suggestions included the videotaping of interviews as this would document early disclosures and help ensure that retractions and inconsistencies are evaluated in the context of the interview itself as well as the overall investigation.[311] Furthermore, pretrial hearing to expose witness contamination is a possibility, at least in theory, which would allow experts to testify, and the recording of all interviews to be viewed and evaluat-

---

[307] Ireland, Criminal Justice Act 2006, 16 July 2006, no. 26 of 2006 (https://www.legal-tools.org/doc/qti6ta/); United States of America, Federal Rules of Evidence, 1 December 2020, Rule 801(d)(1)(A) (https://www.legal-tools.org/doc/9anw7i/), addressing prior sworn statements of declarants who testify and are subject to cross-examination.

[308] See High Court of Australia, *Adam v. The Queen*, Judgment, 11 October 2001, 207 C.L.R. 96 (https://www.legal-tools.org/doc/8n123a/), addressing prior inconsistent statements of recanting witnesses available for cross-examination.

[309] Scotland, Criminal Justice (Scotland) Act, 2003, 26 March 2003, Clause 44, Section 116 (https://www.legal-tools.org/doc/m0qsuf/), permitting the admission of written statements of fearful witnesses "if the Court considers that the statement ought to be admitted in the interests of justice" and providing four factors the Court should take into account in making such a ruling including "any risk that its admission or exclusion will result in unfairness to any party to the proceedings, and in particular to how difficult it will be to challenge the statement if the relevant person does not give oral evidence. Scottish Law has a similarly broad approach to hearsay and would likewise permit the admission of prior statements, although it makes no reference to fear or recantation, see the Scotland, Criminal Procedure (Scotland) Act, 1995, 8 November 1995, Section 259(2)(e) (https://www.legal-tools.org/doc/r6bmk3/).

[310] See European Court of Human Rights, *Al-Khawaja v. United Kingdom*, Grand Chamber, Judgment, 15 December 2011, Application Nos. 26766/05 and 22228/06, paras. 69–87 (https://www.legal-tools.org/doc/45f9d8/), comparing the UK approach to that of Ireland, Australia, Canada, Hong Kong, New Zealand and the United States. The UK law, as well as laws applied in other domestic jurisdictions, have been criticized and described by Marny Requa as: "a practical approach to the admission of unavailable witness evidence, one that complements the statutory regime but, it has been contended here, risks fair trial rights", Marny Requa, "Absent Witnesses and the UK Supreme Court: Judicial Deference as Judicial Dialogue", in *International Journal of Evidence and Proof*, 2010, vol. 14, no. 3, p. 226. See also Fairlie, 2017, p. 149, see *supra* note 302, who stated that: "In other words, the closest domestic parallel to 68 (2) (d) is not only exceptional but controversial", as well as Mark Brodin, "The British Experience with Hearsay Reform: A Cautionary Tale", in *Fordham Law Review*, 2016, vol. 84, no. 4, pp. 1422–1423.

[311] Lindsay Malloy and Michael Lamb, "Biases in Judging Victims and Suspects Whose Statements are Inconsistent", in *Law and Human Behavior*, 2010, vol. 34, pp. 46–48.

ed carefully. Clearly, to the extent that deliberate interference is alleged, the onus is on the prosecution to substantiate this allegation and, as appropriate, to bring proceedings pursuant to Article 70 of the Rome Statute. In the *Kenyatta* case, while this possibility was pointed out by the Prosecution, with reference to Mr. Kenyatta's influential position in Kenya during the relevant time, no evidence was provided in support and the Chamber was not called upon to decide the issue of any such alleged interference.[312]

In conclusion, it is clear that the time variable is essential to understanding Within Insider Reliability. This does not preclude the fact that other factors are also relevant, for example, how legal actors form their perceptions of what constitutes a relevant inconsistency or contradiction.

For example, legal actors may be more or less sceptical or optimistic depending on whether the statement is aligned with their previous beliefs,[313] which has been studied for example in relation to alibi witnesses and witnesses providing incriminating information.[314] While it is unknown what more specifically goes on behind the scenes, during confidential analysis or deliberations pertaining to the insider testimonies, on the basis of the publicly available information, it appears that a more nuanced approach, more actively integrating the possible explanations of lacking Within Insider Reliability is needed. However, this would benefit greatly from more comprehensive and continuous empirical research on the topic, preferably with better access to information about interviews with insiders.

## 7.6. Appendix 1: Details Pertaining to Insider Witness Testimony as Outlined in Table 1

Below, the bases for the approximate time lapses and the number of statements provided by insiders and outlined in Table 1 are explained.

---

[312] ICC, *Prosecutor v. Kenyatta*, 3 December 2014, see *supra* note 64.

[313] Karl Ask and Pär Anders Granhag, "Motivational Bias in Criminal Investigators' Judgments of Witness Reliability", in *Journal of Applied Social Psychology*, 2007, vol. 37, no. 3, pp. 561–591.

[314] See, for example, Tara Burke and John Turtle, "Alibi Evidence in Criminal Investigations and Trials: Psychological and Legal Factors", in *Canadian Journal of Police and Security Services*, 2003, vol. 1, pp. 193–201; Price and Dahl, 2017, p. 16, see *supra* note 191; Culhane and Hosch, 2012, see *supra* note 219; Dysart and Strange, 2012, see *supra* note 219. This research suggests, for example, that police investigators may approach alibi evidence with more scepticism than they would other evidence and may be prone to look for inconsistencies and signs of deception in those providing such evidence. Thus, inconsistencies in alibi witness statements may be weighed even more heavily at least by investigators, than inconsistencies in eyewitness evidence.

The approximate total time lapses were calculated on the basis of the information provided in the documents containing the charges and the case information sheets for the respective cases and the approximate time lapse between first and last interview was calculated on the basis of the information provided about the interviews in judgments and other officially available documents.

### 7.6.1. *Kenyatta*

**Total Time Lapse**

*Commencement of alleged crime(s):* According to the Prosecutor, between at least November 2007 and January 2008, Mr. Kenyatta and members of the Mungiki allegedly created a common plan to commit widespread and systematic attacks against the non-Kikuyu population.

*Concluded proceedings:* Decision on withdrawal of charges against Mr. Kenyatta: 13 March 2015.

*Approximate total time lapse:* November 2007–March 2015 = 7 years, 4 months.

**Approximate Number of Statements and Time Lapse From First to Last Statement**

**P-0004**

- Statement 1: Screening, KEN-OTP-0096-0378;
- Statement 2: Statement to CIPEV, KEN-OTP-0005-0484;[315]
- Statement 3: Affidavit, May 2009;
- Statement 4: Telephone interview with Prosecution investigators, in 2010, KEN-OTP-0097-0003;[316]
- Statement 5: KEN-OTP-0043-0002;
- Statement 6: KEN-OTP-0051-1045;
- Statement 7: 25 May 2012.

*Approximate total time lapse*: May 2009–May 2012 = 3 years.

**P-0012**

- Statement 1: Screening interview on 12 June 2011;

---

[315] ICC, *Prosecutor v. Kenyatta and Hussein Ali*, Trial Chamber V, Public Redacted Version of the Defence 'Submissions Regarding the Prosecution's 11 April 2013 Disclosure of Material Relating to Its Initial Contact with OTP-4' (ICC-01/09-02-ll-719-Conf, 18-04-2013), 23 April 2013, ICC-01/09-02/11-719-Red, para. 25 (https://www.legal-tools.org/doc/34737f/).

[316] *Ibid.*, para. 12.

- Statement 2 -3: Full-length interviews conducted between 16–23 June and 2–4 May 2012;
- Statement 4: 16–17 May 2013;
- Statement 5: 4 December 2013.[317]

*Approximate time lapse from first to last statement*: June 2011–December 2013 = 2 years, 6 months.

### 7.6.2. *Ruto and Sang*

**Total Time Lapse**

*Commencement of alleged crime(s):* The Prosecution alleged that from at least 2006 until January 2008, Ruto and other including Sang planned to expel individuals, namely members of the Kikuyu, Kamba, and Kisii ethnic groups who were perceived to support other political forces, should these political forces win or rig the 2007 elections.

*Concluded proceedings:* The case was terminated on the 5 April 2016.

*Approximate total time lapse:* January 2006–April 2016 = 10 years, 3 months.

**Approximate Number of Statements and Time Lapse From First to Last Statement**

**Witness 800**

*Interview during the investigation:*

- Statement 1: The witness provided his initial statement to the Prosecution in October 2012;[318]

*Interviews during seven trial days:*

- Day 1: Transcript of hearing on 18 November 2014 (Examination in chief)
- Day 2: Transcript of hearing on 19 November 2014;
- Day 3: Transcript of hearing on 20 November 2014;
- Day 4: Transcript of hearing on 21 November 2014;
- Day 5: Transcript of hearing on 24 November 2014;
- Day 6: Transcript of hearing on 25 November 2014 (Cross examination);
- Day 7: Transcript of hearing on 27 November 2014.

*Approximate time lapse from first to last statement:* October 2012–November 2014 = 2 years, 1 month.

---

[317] See ICC, *Prosecutor v. Muthaura, Kenyatta and Hussein Ali*, 19 December 2013, paras. 6–10, see *supra* note 26.

[318] ICC, *Prosecutor v. Ruto and Sang*, 5 April 2016, para. 42, see *supra* note 78.

**Witness 658**

*Interview during the investigation:*

- Statement 1: During the investigation stage, the witness had told the prosecution that he personally attended two crime related events.[319]

*Interviews during nine trial days:*

- Day 1: Transcript of hearing on 28 November 2014, ICC-01/09-01/11-T-163-CONF-ENG;
- Day 2: Transcript of hearing: 1 December 2014;
- Day 3: Transcript of hearing 3 December 2014;
- Day 4: Transcript of hearing 4 December 2014;
- Day 5: Transcript of hearing 5 December 2014;
- Day 6: Transcript of hearing on 8 December 2014;
- Day 7: Transcript of hearing on 9 December 2014;
- Day 7: Transcript of hearing on 10 December 2014;
- Day 9: Transcript of hearing on 11 December 2014, ICC-01/09-01/11-T-173-CONG-ENG.

**Witness 356**

*Interviews during the investigation:*

- Statement 1: The Trial Chamber described that Witness 365 was interviewed by an NGO and left out that he had had a phone conversation with Mr. Ruto,[320] ICC-01/09-01/11-T-82-CONF-ENG, pp. 21–35 and EVD-T-D09-00111.

*Interviews during seven trial days:*

- Day 1: Transcript of hearing on 20 January 2014;
- Day 2: Transcript of hearing on 21 January 2014;
- Day 3: Transcript of hearing on 22 January 2014;
- Day 4: Transcript of hearing on 23 January, ICC-01/09-01/11-T-79-CONF-ENG;
- Day 5: Transcript of hearing on 24 January 2014, ICC-01/09-01/11-T-80-CONF-ENG;
- Day 6: Transcript of hearing on 27 January 2014, ICC-01/09-01/11-T-81-CONF-ENG;

---

[319] *Ibid.*, para. 53.
[320] *Ibid.*, para. 58.

- Day 7: Transcript of hearing on 28 January 2014, ICC-01/09-01/11-T-82-CONF-ENG.

### 7.6.3. *Lubanga*

*Commencement of alleged crime(s):* The Trial Chamber concluded that the armed wing of the UPC-FPLC, between 1 September 2002 and 13 August 2004, was responsible for the widespread recruitment of young people, including children under the age of 15 years, on an enforced as well as voluntary basis.

*Concluded proceedings:* On 1 December 2014, the Appeals Chamber confirmed the verdict and sentence.

*Approximate total time lapse:* September 2002–December 2014 = 12 years, 3 months.

**Approximate Number of Statements and Time Lapse From First to Last Statement**

**P-0016**

*Interviews during the investigation*:

- Information not available from the official case files.

*Interviews during three trial days:*

- Day 1: T-189-Red2-ENG;
- Day 2: T-190-Red2-ENG;
- Day 3: T-191-Red2-ENG.

*Approximate time lapse from first to last statement*: Not possible to calculate.

### 7.6.4. *Mbarushimana*

**Total Time Lapse**

*Commencement of alleged crime(s):* The Prosecution alleged that, in January 2009, the FDLR hierarchy launched a campaign aimed at attacking the civilian population and creating a 'humanitarian catastrophe' in the Kivu provinces of DRC, in order to draw the world's attention to the FDLR's political demands. According to the Document Containing the Charges, in his capacity as Execute Secretary of the FDLR, Mr. Mbarushimana was the individual responsible for part of the FDLR strategy.

*Concluded proceedings:* On 16 December 2011, Pre-Trial Chamber I declined to confirm the charges of crimes against humanity and war crimes.

*Approximate total time lapse:* January 2009–December 2011 = 2 years, 11 months.

**Approximate Number of Statements and Time Lapse From First to Last Statement**

**P- 559**

- Statement 1: EVD-PT-D06-01321;
- Statement 2: EVD-PT-D06-01322;
- Statement 3: EVD-PT-D06-01323;
- Statement 4: EVD-PT-OTP-00577;
- Statement 5: EVD-PT-D06-01318.

*Approximate time lapse from first to last statement:* Transcripts confidential or unavailable, dates not accessible.

**P-542**

- Statement 1: EVD-PT-OTP-00854;
- Statement 2: ICC-01/04-01/10-135-Conf-Exp-Anx6.

*Approximate time lapse from first to last statement:* Transcripts confidential or unavailable, dates not accessible.

### 7.6.5. *Ongwen*

**Total Time Lapse**

*Commencement of alleged crime(s):* The war crimes and crimes against humanity that Mr. Ongwen was convicted for by Trial Chamber IX were, according to the verdict, committed in Uganda between 1 July 2002 and 31 December 2005.

*Concluded proceedings-Last decision:* On 4 February 2021, Trial Chamber IX declared Mr. Ongwen guilty of 61 crimes characterized as war crimes and crimes against humanity.

*Approximate total time lapse:* July 2002-February 2021 = 18 years, 7 months.

**Approximate Number of Statements and Time Lapse From First to Last Statement**

**P-0205**

*Interviews during the investigation:*

- Statement 1 and 2: The Trial Chamber judgment mentions "his earlier interviews with the Prosecution".[321] While there is no specification of the number of interviews this must reasonably mean that at least two interviews were conducted with P-0205 during the investigation.

---

[321] ICC, *Prosecutor v. Ongwen*, 4 February 2021, para. 273, see *supra* note 141.

*Interviews during five trial days:*

- Day 1: T-47;
- Day 2: T-48;
- Day 3: T-49;
- Day 4: T-50;
- Day 5: T-51.

*Approximate total time lapse from first to last statement*: Not possible to calculate.

### 7.6.6. *Gbagbo and Blé Goudé*

**Total Time Lapse**

*Commencement of alleged crime(s):* The Prosecutor claimed that Mr. Gbagbo and Mr. Blé Goudé had committed crimes against humanity between 16 and 19 December 2010 during and after a pro-Ouattara march on the RTI headquarters, on 3 March 2011 at a women's demonstration in Abobo, on 17 March 2011 by shelling a densely populated area in Abobo, and on or around 12 April 2011 in Yopougon.

*Concluded proceedings:* On 31 March 2021, the Appeals Chamber confirmed, by majority, the acquittal decision of 15 January 2019.

*Approximate total time lapse:* December 2010-March 2021: 10 years, 3 months.

**Approximate Number of Statements and Time Lapse From First to Last Statement**

**P-0435**

*Interviews during the investigation:*

- Statement 1: CIV-OTP-0063-1801;
- Statement 2: CIV-OTP-0063-1765;
- Statement 3: CIV-OTP-0093-0060;
- Statement 4: CIV-OTP-0043-0175-R02.

*Interviews during ten trial days:*

- Day1: P-0435, T-87 dated 18 October 2016;
- Day 2: P-0435, T-88 dated 19 October 2016;
- Day 3: P-0435, T-89 dated 20 October 2016;
- Day 4: P-0435, T-90 dated 21 October 2016;
- Day 5: P-0435, T-91, dated 22 October 2016;
- Day 6: P-0435, T-92 dated 25 October 2016;

- Day 7: P-0435, T-93 dated 27 October 2016;
- Day 8: P-0435, T-94 dated 31 October 2016;
- Day 9: P-0435, T-96 dated 2 November 2016;
- Day 10: P-0435, T-97 dated 3 November 2016.

**P-009**

*Interviews during the investigation:*

- Statement 1: CIV-OTP-0051-1086;
- Statement 2: CIV-OTP-0051-0907;
- Statement 3: CIV-OTP-0051-0871;
- Statement 4: CIV-OTP-0011-0324;
- Statement 5: CIV-OTP-0051-0712-R01;
- Statement 6: CIV-OTP-0051-0556-R01;
- Statement 7: CIV-OTP-0051-0770-R01;
- Statement 8: CIV-OTP-0051-0830-R01;
- Statement 9: CIV-OTP-0051-0935;
- Statement 10: CIV-OTP-0006-0161;
- Statement 11: CIV-OTP-0011-0324.

*Interviews during nine trial days:*

- Day 1: P-0009, T-195 dated 17 September 2017;
- Day 2: P-0009, T-193 dated 25 September 2017;
- Day 3: P-0009, T-194 dated 26 September 2017;
- Day 4: P-0009, T-195 dated 27 September 2017;
- Day 5 P-0009, T-196 dated 28 September 2017;
- Day 6: P-0009, T-197 dated 2 October 2017;
- Day 7: P-0009, T-198 dated 3 October 2017;
- Day 8: P-0009, T-199 dated 4 October 2017;
- Day 9: P-009, T-200 dated 5 October 2017.

### 7.6.7. *Yekatom and Ngaïssona*

*Commencement of alleged crime(s):* The crime suspicions regard crimes against humanity and war crimes allegedly committed in CAR between December 2013 and December 2014.

*Concluded proceedings:* Since the trial is still ongoing, this cannot be stated but from the date this chapter was last reviewed, 3 January 2023.

*Approximate total time lapse (so far):* December 2013–January 2023 = 9 years 1 month.

**P-0801**

*Interviews during the investigation:*

- Statement 1: February 2018.[322]

*Interviews during six trial days:*

- Day 1: Transcript 24 May 2021;
- Day 2: Transcript 25 May 2021;
- Day 3: Transcript 26 May 2021;
- Day 4: Transcript 27 May 2021;
- Day 5: Transcript 28 May 2021;
- Day 6: Transcript 1 June 2021.

---

[322] ICC, *Prosecutor v. Yekatom and Ngaïssona*, 27 May 2021, p. 22, lines 4–7, see *supra* note 179.

# PART III:
## NATIONAL PERSPECTIVES

# 8

---

# Old Evidence in Core International Crimes Cases in Kosovo

**Agnieszka Klonowiecka-Milart***

As a preliminary statement, one should always keep in mind that the standard of proof in attributing individual criminal liability is 'beyond a reasonable doubt'. This concerns all the material elements of a crime. It is the onus of the prosecution to prove beyond a reasonable doubt both the broad contextual elements, high-level politician and commander liability for policies or silent approvals, and the identity and actions of the low-level soldiers who kill, rape or torture.

Yet, different evidence is being used in proving contextual elements of international crimes and the actual acts of the perpetrator – what constitute the *actus reus* and *mens rea* in the individual charges. Moreover, different means of evidence are employed to prove crimes based on command responsibility and those entailing direct execution. Each of these areas might give rise to specific problems, especially when they are encountered by a young court. And especially when it is old evidence.

## 8.1. Old Evidence of the Criminal Context

### 8.1.1. A Balanced Approach to Old Evidence

Is it possible, as a premise, to start with the praise of old evidence? As already discussed, witness evidence can be compromised by memory loss, a re-characterization of what happened helped along by express or implicit pressure from peers and interested groups, or not available at all. Physical evidence, if any, is very likely to have encountered degradation, loss due to its inherent temporary nature, or be omitted from the chain of custody. Archives might have been broken or evacuated, as it happened in Bosnia, or evidence 'booked'

---

* Judge **Agnieszka Klonowiecka-Milart** currently serves on the United Nations ('UN') Dispute Tribunal and was previously an international judge at the Supreme Court Chamber of the Extraordinary Chambers of the Courts of Cambodia ('ECCC'), a hybrid tribunal for international crimes committed during the period of the Khmer Rouge, 1975–1979. Prior to her appointment to the ECCC, she was a UN international judge on the Supreme Court of Kosovo, adjudicating, *inter alia*, charges of genocide and war crimes arising from the conflict 1998–1999 in the former Yugoslavia. Judge Klonowiecka-Milart started her legal career as an Assistant Professor at the Law Faculty of the University in Lublin, Poland.

in file drawers and boxes that are taken with the international forces who are repatriated, as in Kosovo.

At the same time, however, there are some benefits of approaching the crime from a long-ago perspective. The passage of time makes available the established historical record. Some elements are at least ascertained – maybe partially – in the public conscience: the parties who stood on each of the good and bad sides, who started or encouraged the armed violence, when did the armed violence start, and when did it end. There is a plethora of reports, analyses and commentaries, approaching the problems from all angles and proving, sometimes, opposing theses. Facts that make up contextual elements of international crimes have been argued upon by generations. Even if conflicting versions of the past continue to exist, their differences are more substantively articulated and are, as such, easier to verify and, where it is necessary, the courts may find it easier to choose among the alternatives.

Should old evidence therefore be considered as an advantage or a danger? The notion of 'collective memory' is an important element in this present discussion.

The body of evidence for core international crimes derives primarily from victimized societies and groups. In mostly illiterate societies, witness 'stories' and recounting repeated through oral tradition will in fact be the main source of collective knowledge; whereas in highly literate societies – and Bangladeshi and Cambodian urban societies fall in this category – the passage of time brings about a proliferation of secondary sources such as books, media articles and government documents. There may be television documentaries and even movies. One can, for instance, think of "The Killing Fields", an epic picture by Roland Joffe on the 1975–1979 events in Cambodia, which, when released in the mid-1980s, sparked a great interest in the Khmer Rouge tragedy in Europe. In the last decades, images and information – old evidence of the future – instantly reaches smartphone holders all around the globe. These various materials contribute to, and form, people's perceptions. They also constitute general knowledge about the context of international crimes in the minds of those who deliver evidence and those who hear it.

This process, therefore, happens through the media and through word of mouth. In these modalities, the *quantum* of knowledge, or opinion, is accumulated, layered and settled over a period of time. Against this background of facts accepted as true, there is a question of individual criminal responsibility that needs to be demonstrated and ascribed into that context in the criminal process.

Interestingly, the statements of the mechanisms of collective knowledge formation hold true also for statements about the legal framework. In particular, where the plane of reference is customary international law, the subjective element, *opinio juris*, that is, the perception and knowledge of what is law, is shaped and becomes fact with time, as scholars and activists over the time develop legal theories. Areas of disagreement are identified and narrowed down and ultimately the practice confirms the emergence of the norm. The context in which transitional justice is discussed and dispensed is usually characterized by political struggle and accompanying dynamic changes affecting the legal framework, the legal cadre, academia, rights activists and other stakeholders in justice systems. In this climate, legal notions may be hijacked to serve different interests. Similar to the transmittal of international norms into domestic governance that often occurs through the work of 'norm entrepreneurs', who "attempt to convince a critical mass [...] to embrace new norms",[1] activism plays a role in the subsuming of the facts under the notions of international criminal law, entering the sphere of legal discourse, legislation and jurisprudence, especially where incentives are created by the jurisdictional relationship between domestic and international institutions.

It is noteworthy that, as victimized societies express a particular need for their suffering to be acknowledged, this is sometimes put forth through the demand that the oppressive and traumatizing events concerned be qualified as an international crime. In particular, there is often a popular demand for the qualification of genocide to be attributed to the historical record of the victimized society. Contrary to what lawyers say,[2] genocide is commonly perceived as the most egregious of international crimes; there is a particularly emotional

---

[1]   William W. Burke-White, "The Domestic Influence of International Criminal Tribunals: The International Criminal Tribunal for the Former Yugoslavia and the Creation of the State Court of Bosnia & Herzegovina", in *Columbia Journal of Transnational Law*, 2008, vol. 46, p. 306.

[2]   M. Cherif Bassiouni, *Introduction to International Criminal Law*, Transnational Publishers, 2003, p. 119. Bassiouni notes:

> Neither conventions nor the writings of scholars establish a hierarchy among international crimes, except with respect to *jus cogens* [...]. Presumably, one can assume that all other international crimes are of equal standing and dignity, irrespective of the international interest they seek to protect and the international harm they seek to avert.

International Criminal Tribunal for the former Yugoslavia ('ICTY'), *Prosecutor v. Duško Tadić*, Appeals Chamber, Judgement in Sentencing Appeals, Separate Opinion of Judge Cassese, IT-94-1-A, 26 January 2000, para. 7 (https://www.legal-tools.org/doc/df7618/). Judge Cassese notes:

> In short, one cannot say that a certain class of international crimes encompasses facts that are more serious than those prohibited under a different criminal provision. *In abstracto*, all international crimes are serious offences and no hierarchy of gravity may *a priori* be established between them.

charge that it carries. Such a demand was, for instance, formulated and addressed to internationalized courts in Kosovo[3] and Cambodia.[4]

In legislation that seeks to respond to past atrocities, the targeted inclusion of the categories of international crimes poses a challenge to the principle of legality. In accordance with this principle, no one can be held guilty of any criminal offence on account of any act or omission which did not constitute a criminal offence, under national or international law, at the time when it was committed.[5] Accordingly, the enumeration of international crimes in statutes of the courts established to adjudicate past crimes is not itself a source of criminalization of conduct and, as such, does not constitute an autonomous basis for entering convictions.[6] For that matter, I note that the law establishing the International Crimes Tribunal for Bangladesh ('ICT-BD') contains the description

---

[3] See the comments about the judgment in the case of *Miroslav Vučković* of September 2001 in "Kosovo Assault 'Was Not Genocide'", *BBC News*, 7 September 2001. The report notes that:

> A United Nations court has ruled that Serbian troops did not carry out genocide against ethnic Albanians during Slobodan Milosevic's campaign of aggression in Kosovo from 1998 to 1999. The controversial ruling by the UN-supervised Supreme Court in the Kosovan capital, Pristina, has angered Albanians, and some UN officials are reported to be preparing to challenge it.

[4] See the exchange between Gregory Stanton, William A. Schabas and Suzannah Linton about whether what happened in Cambodia is to be qualified as genocide. William A. Schabas, "Should Khmer Rouge Leaders Be Prosecuted for Genocide or Crimes Against Humanity?", in *Searching for the Truth*, Documentation Center of Cambodia, 2001, no. 22, pp. 37–43; Gregory H. Stanton, "The Khmer Rouge Did Commit Genocide", in *Searching for the Truth*, Documentation Center of Cambodia, 2001, no. 23, pp. 32–33; Suzannah Linton, "An Internationalized Domestic Tribunal?", in *Searching for the Truth*, Documentation Center of Cambodia, 2002, no. 25, pp. 37–38. See also Julia Wallace, "Justice in the Dock at Khmer Rouge Trials", *Al Jazeera*, 30 September 2012: "Equally devastating for many Cambodians is the decision of the judges to hear just a few charges at a time against the three defendants [...]". She also reports on the concerns of victims: "I am so concerned about this, because the court is prosecuting only one issue, not all the issues", says Soum Rithy, 59, a survivor of torture in a Khmer Rouge prison and a plaintiff in the case, "[a]nd the issue they are prosecuting isn't even the most serious compared to other crimes like genocide and torture. They need to take those first".

[5] International Covenant on Civil and Political Rights, 16 December 1966, Article 15 (https://www.legal-tools.org/doc/2838f3/).

[6] See, for example, Report of the Group of Experts for Cambodia established pursuant to General Assembly resolution 52/135, 18 February 1999, para. 60 ('Commission Report') (https://www.legal-tools.org/doc/3da509/). The relevant portion of the report states:

> [...] any review of the law in a report such as this is oriented only towards determining whether the evidence justifies, as a legal matter, the inclusion of certain crimes within the jurisdiction of a court [...]. [T]his section does not make recommendations regarding which crimes should be included in the jurisdiction of a tribunal, but only as to which crimes appear to us legally justifiable for inclusion.

of acts underlying crimes against humanity that are broader than what would result from applying the Nuremberg Principles, judgments of the National Military Tribunals or other documents defining international crimes. While the ICT-BD law establishes *a priori* jurisdiction over the acts so listed, the actual exercise of its jurisdiction is subject to determining the definition of crimes against humanity as it stood under international law at the time of the alleged criminal conduct. Yet, one should bear in mind that the jurisdictional provision alone has the potential of forming perceptions and expectations, especially when fostered by politics or activist movement.

For example, the long-time taboo of acknowledging that rape was being systematically used as a tool in attacks against civilians has been lifted after the problem received due attention in the mid-1990s and led to the articulation of rape as a form of crime against humanity in the jurisprudence of the *ad hoc* Tribunals and then in the International Criminal Court's ('ICC') Statute. This relatively recent focus of the activist movement may, at times, manifest itself as a pressure to have rape emphasized not only in the factual panoply of charges but also in legal descriptions that, if accepted, would pre-date the emergence of rape as crime against humanity.[7]

Certain decisions of the internationalized panels in Kosovo exemplify the incursion of categories of international criminal law into the jurisprudence.[8] These examples concern the application of international customary law concepts directly in the sphere of domestic proceedings, contrary to the imperative provisions of the applicable legal framework which allowed the attribution of criminal responsibility solely pursuant to the statutes.[9] Such decisions cannot be readily explained by unfamiliarity with the applicable law. Rather, what could have occurred seems more likely connected to the congruence of

---

[7] This was an outright demand for attributing responsibility for sexual crimes in a pending case in Panel Recommendations to the ECCC following a truth-telling forum. See Alison Barclay and Beini Ye (eds.), *Women's Hearing: True Voices of Women Under the Khmer Rouge Regime on Sexual Violence*, Cambodian Defenders Project, Phnom Penh, June 2012. The publication recommends: "After having severed case 002, include sexual crimes in the first trial and hold the accused liable under the enemy policy for sexual crimes [...]" (p. 16).

[8] District Court of Gijlan, *Prosecutor v. Momčilo Trajković*, Judgment, P. Nr. 68/2000, 6 March 2001 ('*Momčilo Trajković*') (https://www.legal-tools.org/doc/7836ef/). In this case, a conviction was entered for crimes against humanity, which was not foreseen under the applicable criminal law. District Court of Priština, *Prosecutor v. Latif Gashi et al.*, Judgment, P. Nr. 425/2001, 16 July 2003 ('*Latif Gashi et al.*') (https://www.legal-tools.org/doc/lqf8vq/). In this case, a finding on command responsibility was made pursuant to a mode not foreseen by the applicable law, that is, applying a sentence not foreseen by the statute in invoking 'international standards'. Each of these cases was quashed on appeal.

[9] See Michael Bohlander, "The Direct Application of International Criminal Law in Kosovo", in *Kosovo Legal Studies*, 2001, vol. 7.

---

self-interest in enhanced visibility and popular demand attaching to the finding of an international crime. While the instances were corrected upon appeal, they illustrate the tendency that favours international crime qualification over the more 'mundane' options of domestic law.[10]

Another example emerged when an appeal against *Case 001* was brought before the ECCC. During the appellate hearings, the Court encouraged the parties to make submissions regarding the legal framework to be applied in assessing the acts attributed to the accused, in particular with respect to the definition of crimes against humanity. A defence counsel when referring to the nexus element at the time of the commission of the crime, stated that "everyone knows that nexus was dropped by then". This was actually not so universally accepted, as shown by the concurrent decision of the Pre-Trial Chamber, in which it expressed an opposite opinion[11] but indeed reflected views circulated fifteen years earlier, during the period of discussion over the Court's creation.[12]

This example illustrates well how discussions and statements about the law can over time settle and form the reality of the trial, reinforced by the passage of time and the repeating of information. There is, therefore, a strong potential for people's perceptions, especially when used by politics, to exert pressure on judicial decision-making where international crimes are concerned. This phenomenon needs to be addressed with a measure of caution, with compassion for the emotions involved but with respect for the letter of the law, in order to ensure the legitimacy of the decisions.

---

[10] Compare with the practice and legal framework in the Solomon Islands, where after the 'Times of Tension' internal armed conflict of 1998–2003 ended and the Regional Assistance Mission to the Solomon Islands ('RAMSI') arrived with advice and assistance for prosecution and defence, the Penal Code's murder, abduction and accomplice liability provisions were used. The Penal Code does not contain any provision prohibiting war crimes, crimes against humanity, including genocide. The Solomon Islands has bound itself to the Geneva Convention, but has not ratified or acceded to the ICC's Rome Statute.

[11] ECCC, *Prosecutor v. Ieng Thirith and Nuon Chea*, Pre-Trial Chamber, Decision on Ieng Thirith's and Nuon Chea's Appeals Against the Closing Order, Case File No. 002/19-09-2007-ECCC/OCIJ (PTC145 and PTC146), D427/2/l2, 13 January 2011, para. 11(1) (https://www.legal-tools.org/doc/d2b9ee/); *Prosecutor v. Ieng Sary*, Pre-Trial Chamber, Decision on Ieng Sary's Appeal Against the Closing Order, Case File No. 002/19-09-2007-ECCC/OCIJ (PTC75), D427/1/26, 13 January 2011, para. 7(1) (https://www.legal-tools.org/doc/d264ce/); *Prosecutor v. Khieu Samphan*, Pre-Trial Chamber, Decision on Khieu Samphan's Appeal Against the Closing Order, Case File No. 002/19-09-2007-ECCC/OCIJ (PTC104), D427/4/14, 13 January 2011, para. 2(1) (https://www.legal-tools.org/doc/226624/).

[12] Commission Report, 1999, para. 71, see *supra* note 6.

---

## 8.1.2. The Effects of Collective Conceptions on the Criminal Procedure

### 8.1.2.1. The Subject of Proof

If indeed largely accepted as true, some common conceptions may develop to the level of public notoriety, which may give rise to procedural consequences. First, national laws may exempt these facts from proof requirements. Let us recall the relevant provision of International Crimes (Tribunals) Act of 1973 ('ICT-BD Act'): "A Tribunal shall not require proof of facts of common knowledge but shall take judicial notice thereof". [13] The term 'common knowledge' denotes facts that are commonly accepted or universally known, such as general facts of history or geography, or the laws of nature. In the application to municipal crimes, the question of notoriety may not be universally approached, but does not carry a potential for major problems and is a useful tool for expediting the proceedings.

For that matter, to use a provision of which I am quite familiar on a professional level, the Polish Code of Criminal Procedure contains a provision that has similar effect to the one in the ICT-BD Act, although it also discloses differences typical of systems based on the doctrine of 'objective truth'. Thus, the Polish law permits a judge to accept facts commonly held as true without proof.[14] Nonetheless, certain conditions must be met. The court must give notice to the parties and allow them to contest its decision to admit said facts on the basis of public notoriety. In other words, the parties may challenge the court's proposition that the said facts are commonly accepted as true. In this case, the opposing party is allowed to offer a proof to the contrary. The Polish Supreme Court held that, considering consequences of the far-reaching finding of public notoriety, the interpretation of what constitutes public notoriety must be strict. In particular, the court must not accept as notorious facts that are known only to a limited circle, such as to specialists in a given subject area. The notorious facts must be reasonably beyond dispute. The source of common knowledge of the fact is immaterial; rather, common knowledge means that a reasonable and experienced person under the jurisdiction of the court should ordinarily arrive at this knowledge from a variety of sources.

The existence of such a 'public notoriety' test therefore helps preserve the expediency and the economy of trial proceedings, but is accompanied by

---

[13] Bangladesh, The International Crimes (Tribunals) Act, 20 July 1973, Article 19(3) (https://www.legal-tools.org/doc/c09a98/).

[14] Article 168 of the Polish Code of Criminal Procedure, 6 June 1997 (https://www.legal-tools.org/doc/43b23e/): "Facts commonly known shall not require proof; nor shall facts known ex officio, although the attention of the parties should be directed to these facts. It shall not exclude evidence to the contrary".

conditions which prevent the privileging of convenience over the interests of the party.

More problematic is the application of the public notoriety construct in the adjudication of international crimes, in particular where relevant historical facts, such as the existence of armed conflict or attack against civilians, are in themselves the elements of crime and as such are contested. The ICT-BD Act provision resembles the language of ICTY and the International Criminal Tribunal for Rwanda's ('ICTR') Rules of Procedure and Evidence[15] on the basis of which a considerable body of jurisprudence has been developed. This jurisprudence may be of relevance for the work of the ICT-BD.

The *ad hoc* Tribunals held that taking judicial notice of the facts of common knowledge is a matter of an obligation and not discretionary,[16] and that whether a fact qualifies as common knowledge is a legal question and so the deferential standard of appellate review to the trial court's assessment of evidence has no application.[17] In determining what constitutes common knowledge, the ICTR held that these are facts that are "so notorious, or clearly established, or susceptible to determination by reference to readily obtainable and authoritative sources that evidence of their existence is unnecessary".[18] It further elaborated that common knowledge concerns facts that are "generally known in the tribunal's jurisdiction"[19] and are "reasonably indisputable".[20] The requirement of reasonable indisputableness excludes the application of judicial notice to facts that, albeit widely accepted as true, could be challenged on the basis that they have support in sources whose accuracy and objectiveness could be called into question. This interpretation prevents the use of judicial

---

[15] Rule 94 of the Rules of Procedure and Evidence for the ICTR ('ICTR Rules') (https://www.legal-tools.org/doc/c6a7c6/), and its equivalent in the Rules of Procedure and Evidence for the ICTY ('ICTY Rules') (https://www.legal-tools.org/doc/30df50/), provide as follows: (A) A Trial Chamber shall not require proof of facts of common knowledge but shall take judicial notice thereof; (B) At the request of a party or *proprio motu*, a Trial Chamber, after hearing the parties, may decide to take judicial notice of adjudicated facts or documentary evidence from other proceedings of the Tribunal relating to matters at issue in the current proceedings.

[16] See, for example, ICTR, *Prosecutor v. Laurent Semanza*, Appeal Chamber, Judgement, ICTR-97-20-A, 20 May 2005, para. 194 (https://www.legal-tools.org/doc/a686fd/).

[17] ICTR, *Prosecutor v. Karemera et al.*, Trial Chamber, Decision on Prosecutor's Interlocutory Appeal of Decision on Judicial Notice, ICTR-98-44-AR733I, 16 June 2006, para. 23 ('*Karemera* decision') (https://www.legal-tools.org/doc/c7bd16/).

[18] ICTR, *Prosecutor v. Laurent Semanza*, Trial Chamber III, Decision on the Prosecutor's Motion for Judicial Notice and Presumption of Facts Pursuant to Rules 94 and 54, ICTR-97-20-I, 3 November 2000, para. 25 (https://www.legal-tools.org/doc/147ec1/).

[19] *Ibid.*, para. 23.

[20] *Ibid.*, para. 24, cited with approval in *Karemera* decision, para. 22, see *supra* note 17.

---

notice for the exercise of 'victor's justice' through accepting one-sided versions of historical events, no matter how popular.

Notwithstanding the agreement as to these elements of the doctrine, the practical application of judicial notice at the ICTR has resulted in diverse decisions regarding the same or similar factual propositions,[21] demonstrating in this way that the facts in question had not been 'reasonably indisputable'. The general trend that emerged, however, seemed to be that the Chambers were more inclined to find beyond reasonable dispute such facts when they: (i) constituted a more remote premise for the charge than those that in themselves were the elements of crime; (ii) were clearly identifiable events rather than clusters of facts and value judgements; and (iii) were plain facts rather than their legal assessment, such as the occurrence of genocide.

The criminal procedure in Kosovo, heavily marked by the tradition of the active role of the court in establishing the 'objective truth', initially did not explicitly provide for the judicial notice of commonly known facts.[22] The internationalized panels nonetheless applied it to a limited extent in relation to facts, such as to the North Atlantic Treaty Organization's ('NATO') strikes against the former Yugoslavia in March 1999,[23] UN Security Council resolutions, the time of the sunset in January,[24] and the existence of agreements between the United Nations Interim Administration Mission in Kosovo ('UNMIK'), the Council of Europe and Interpol published on the official web site.[25] Accepting without proof of broad statements concerning the origin, the nature and the course of the armed conflict in Kosovo, or facts alleged only locally and directly relevant for the specific accusations, was not adopted as of mid-2000s. At the end of 2003, the Supreme Court of Kosovo cautioned specifically:

---

[21] James G. Stewart, "Judicial Notice in International Criminal Law: A Reconciliation of Potential, Peril and Precedent", in *International Criminal Law Review*, 2003, vol. 3, no. 3, p. 251.

[22] Law on Criminal Procedure, Official Gazette of the Socialist Federal Republic of Yugoslavia No. 4/77, in 2004 replaced by UNMIK Regulation on the Provisional Criminal Procedure Code of Kosovo, UNMIK/REG/2003/26, 6 July 2003 ('PCPCK') (https://www.legal-tools.org/doc/8c2a74/). On this occasion, a proposal from international judges and prosecutors to introduce judicial notice concept in Kosovo was adopted, see Article 152, para. 3.

[23] *Momčilo Trajković*, p. 4, see *supra* note 8: "(3) the state of war was declared by the Yugoslavian government on 24 March 1999".

[24] District Court of Priština, *Prosecutor v. Zoran Stanojević*, Judgement, P. Nr. 43/2000, 18 June 2001, para. 196 ('*Račak* case').

[25] Supreme Court of Kosovo, *Prosecutor v. Bashkim Berisha*, Decision on Petition for Transfer of Luan Goci and Bashkim Berisha, PN-KR 335/2005, 30 January 2006.

> [T]here is a possibility for the court to accept certain circum-
> stances as generally notorious ["judicial notice"] thus not requir-
> ing formal proof. The Supreme Court realizes that until an objec-
> tive research on the facts of the armed conflict in Kosovo is doc-
> umented and confirmed, notoriety can apply only within a narrow
> range. Circumstances such as, *e.g.*, that there were NATO strikes
> against former Yugoslavia in March 1999, and was a mass out-
> flow of Kosovo Albanian population during the armed conflict,
> are popularly acknowledged as historical facts. In evoking gen-
> eral notoriety, however, especially in cases involving conflicted
> ethnic groups – like the case subject to this proceedings – courts
> need to ascertain that a claimed notoriety is genuine, *i.e.*, com-
> mon to both groups concerned. The Supreme Court also appreci-
> ates the role of judicial proceedings in the process of a creation of
> such notoriety and therefore stresses the importance of thorough-
> ness in establishing historical facts in landmark war crimes pro-
> ceedings.[26]

Still, such a resignation from the production of evidence in favour of judicial notice offers the opportunity to expedite trial proceedings in the interest
of all parties involved. Since the main risk involved in judicial notice lies in
lifting the burden of proof contrary to the presumption of innocence, the
agreement of the accused as to the facts encompassed by common knowledge
is of practical significance. Even though not legally required, such an agreement confirms that accepted facts are common knowledge and are indeed beyond a reasonable dispute. As such, it appeases concerns about the fairness of
proceedings.

This consideration brings us to a related but separate area of admitted or
agreed facts. The question is whether, other than judicial notice of commonly
known facts, the law may relieve from the requirement of proof based on admission of facts by the parties. Such a construct is typical of proceedings in the
civil procedure, but less usual in the criminal procedure, in particular of the
continental type. The issue was also disputed in the jurisprudence of the *ad hoc*
Tribunals.[27] Eventually, it seems that the pragmatism of accepting agreed facts
as proven prevails and provisions that allow resigning from the production of

---

[26] Supreme Court of Kosovo, *Prosecutor v. Anjelko Kolasinać*, AP-KZ 230/2003, 5 August
2004 (https://www.legal-tools.org/doc/3da647/).

[27] ICTY Rule 65*ter*(H) does not explicitly authorize the acceptance of agreed facts as proven;
it states: "The pre-trial Judge shall record the points of agreement and disagreement on matters of law and fact. In this connection, he or she may order the parties to file written submissions with either the pre-trial Judge or the Trial Chamber". Similar language is found in
ICTR Rule 108(C) concerning the pre-appeal judge. On contradictions in the application,
see Stewart, 2003, pp. 267–268, see *supra* note 21.

evidence have been adopted in the legal frameworks of the courts that adjudicate core international crimes.[28] Regarding the contextual elements of crime, the accused may give such admissions willingly, as he will rather focus on negating his own role in the events charged than question the context of the events. This actually often happened in Kosovo as part of defence tactics; unless the defence adopted a stance based on negating everything, the accused invoked the conditions of an armed conflict or a widespread attack against civilians to argue exigent circumstances or as demonstration of general openness and co-operation.[29] Again, just like many of the continental criminal procedures, the procedure applicable in Kosovo traditionally did not foresee dispensing with the production of evidence based on agreed facts, although it allowed explanations of the accused as source of evidence. Changes exempting agreed facts from proof have been introduced later, as part of guilty plea arrangements. Still, any plea or fact agreement is not binding on the court.[30] In any event, where the accused is silent about the elements of the context, it would be up to the court to solicit a clear representation as to whether the facts concerned are admitted or not. Ultimately, the court decides what needs to be proven through formal evidence.

Judicial notice and admission of facts may greatly assist in establishing the factual context of international crimes. Yet, the politicization accompanying the adjudication of international crimes may lead to the *de facto* lowering of the standard of substantiation of these elements. Even if material facts are dubious or contested, they may be accepted as proven without sufficient evi-

---

28    ICC, Rules of Procedure and Evidence, 9 September 2002, Rule 69 (https://www.legal-tools.org/doc/l3a64k/). This Rule states:

   The Prosecutor and the defence may agree that an alleged fact, which is contained in the charges, the contents of a document, the expected testimony of a witness or other evidence is not contested and, accordingly, a Chamber may consider such alleged fact as being proven, unless the Chamber is of the opinion that a more complete presentation of the alleged facts is required in the interests of justice, in particular the interests of the victims.

   In Kosovo, the possibility of accepting a guilty plea as basis for conviction has been introduced in PCPCK as part of the criminal law reform in 2004; see PCPCK, 2003, Articles 315 and 359, *supra* note 22. Similarly, the Cambodian Law on Criminal Procedure applicable to proceedings before the ECCC, which largely follows the French law, does not foresee basing a judgment on a guilty plea or agreed facts alone. The ECCC Internal Rules, however, allowed accepting the agreed facts as proven. See ECCC, Internal Rules (Rev. 8), 3 August 2011, Rule 87(6) (https://www.legal-tools.org/doc/f356ac/).

29    In the case of *Latif Gashi et al.*, factual circumstances of an internal armed conflict in Kosovo in the period preceding the NATO strikes against Yugoslavia were largely adduced through the explanations of the accused.

30    PCPCK, 2003, Articles 315 and 359, see *supra* note 22.

dence, while insufficient weight is given to evidence to the contrary. Experience in Kosovo shows that it may happen that the court accepts secondary sources, such as reports, journal articles or books, without attempting to collect and consider primary sources of the evidence. Here again, the lapse of time impacts on the quality of evidence in two ways: historical research and secondary sources pile up whereas the availability of direct evidence, especially witness testimony, diminishes with time.

### 8.1.2.2. The Importance of the First Case

The first case heard by the court necessarily carries the greatest burden of establishing the historical context of the crimes concerned. Subsequent cases, to a lesser or greater extent, may rely on the evidence adduced through primary sources in the first case.

The furthest going reliance is enabled when the law allows taking judicial notice of adjudicated facts. Such authorization is included in the Rules of Procedure and Evidence of the ICTY and ICTR.[31] The scope of this provision turned out to be highly controversial, especially regarding the taking of judicial notice of facts which constituted elements of crime. Certain chambers, for example, accepted adjudicated facts only in so far as to confirm the existence of authentic documents, the contents of which was subject to evaluation. Eventually, the Appeals Chamber of the ICTY affirmed that, in consideration of the right of the accused to hear and confront the witnesses against him, it is appropriate to exclude from the judicial notice of adjudicated facts those relating to the acts, conduct and mental state of the accused.[32] Pursuant to this approach, it results, *a contrario*, that deriving from prior cases' findings regarding the contextual elements of international crimes would be allowed. In any event, the existence of adjudicated facts provides, at minimum, the record of available human and documentary evidence to be sought for the direct production in a trial.

The burden on the first case or the initial wave of cases should be taken into consideration in any timeline or in any prosecutors' preparation strategy, namely, it may be reasonable to expect that, in the first case, the contextual element will need to be proven through primary sources.

---

[31] Rule 94 of the ITCR Rules (see *supra* note 15) and its equivalent in the ICTY Rules (see *supra* note 15): "(B) At the request of a party or *proprio motu*, a Trial Chamber, after hearing the parties, may decide to take judicial notice of adjudicated facts or of the authenticity of documentary evidence from other proceedings of the Tribunal relating to matters at issue in the current proceedings".

[32] *Karemera* decision, para. 50, see *supra* note 17.

In Kosovo, the internationalized panels had to struggle with this issue. In one of the early cases, *Prosecutor v. Mladenović*, the prosecution put forth several suppositions pertaining to the presence of an armed conflict, without, however, any supporting evidence.[33] In the case *Prosecutor v. Bešović*,[34] where the Court needed to examine and prove the circumstances of an armed conflict, with not much evidence being presented by the prosecution, the Court eventually decided to cut and paste into its opinion substantial fragments of reports by Human Rights Watch and the Organization for Co-operation and Security in Europe ('OSCE'), the latter entitled "As seen, as told", readily signalling the reliance on hearsay. The case was reversed by the Supreme Court of Kosovo,[35] on the basis of contradiction in evidence indicative of the actual participation of the accused in the events. Therefore, the question of whether it is enough to have only the mentions of reports, which are secondary sources, remains unresolved. This question was even more pregnant in this case as there was no other case law yet produced in Kosovo nor was there ICTY jurisprudence on Kosovo.

In 2005, however, the District Court, hearing the case of *Prosecutor v. Runjeva et al.*, was capable of finding the internal armed conflict proven using not only the same reports, but also well-documented ICTY material, direct witness evidence and the record of stipulated facts, that is, facts agreed as undisputed between the parties.[36]

A decade after the establishment of the international judiciary in Kosovo, there have been several proceedings instituted at the ICTY for acts which arose, at least partially, from the events in Kosovo.[37] The material gathered in these cases, even absent legal authorization to accept adjudicated facts or institutional co-operation between the ICTY and Kosovo judiciary, is an extremely valuable record of evidence. The use of this potential, however, depends on the

---

[33] District Court of Priština, *Prosecutor v. Aleksandar Mladenović*, Verdict, P. Nr. 26/2001, 23 November 2001, paras. 15–21 ('*Mladenović* case') (https://www.legal-tools.org/doc/8ofvol/).

[34] District Court of Peja/Peć, *Prosecutor v. Veselin Bešović*, Verdict, C/P 136/2001, 26 June 2003 ('*Bešović* case') (https://www.legal-tools.org/doc/e05c92/).

[35] Supreme Court of Kosovo, *Prosecutor v. Veselin Bešović*, Verdict, AP-KZ No. 80/2004, 7 September 2004 ('*Bešović* appeal') (https://www.legal-tools.org/doc/107371/).

[36] District Court of Priština, *Prosecutor v. Ejup Runjeva et al.*, Verdict, P. Nr. 215/04, 12 May 2005 (https://www.legal-tools.org/doc/8dtxsv/).

[37] ICTY, *Prosecutor v. Milošević*, Trial Chamber, Judgement, IT-02-54-T, 12 December 2007 (https://www.legal-tools.org/doc/e706e2/); *Prosecutor v. Milutinović et al.*, Trial Chamber, Judgement, IT-05-87-T, 26 February 2009 (https://www.legal-tools.org/doc/9eb7c3/); *Prosecutor v. Haradinaj, Balaj and Brahimaj*, Trial Chamber, Judgement, IT-04-84-T, 3 April 2008 (https://www.legal-tools.org/doc/025913/); *Prosecutor v. Đorđević*, Trial Chamber, Judgement, IT-05-87/1-T, 23 February 2011 (https://www.legal-tools.org/doc/653651/).

availability of primary evidence and access to ICTY case files, and there is a need for a balance between evidential rigour of the ICTY and evidential availability of the Kosovo courts to be struck adequately.

It would have been optimal if the Kosovo court could establish the historical truth on the basis of direct or primary evidence, rather than relying upon reports of others that are not tested by cross-examination in which the authors are required to explain their methodology and analysis in an adversarial oral process. By doing so, the Court would have been shaping history instead of allowing history to shape the Court's truth.

### 8.1.3. The Need for Co-operation Across Public Authorities of the State and Beyond

My experience in Kosovo shows that it may be difficult for a national court to gain access to primary sources of evidence. Such access requires governmental support and the existence of various related mechanisms, such as explicit and effective subpoena powers. This is necessary in order to facilitate the production of the high-profile witnesses to testify on organizational structures, hierarchies, strategies and policies. Even so, this assumes that the witnesses concerned are all willing to testify and participate in this specific process.

There is also a need for access to archives and databases, which are not always available. These might have been broken, misplaced or evacuated abroad. Primary sources may have sometimes been destroyed, though copies may be available elsewhere. Government support may be required for the court to access these archives and databases and to obtain resources to effectuate a meaningful search. The availability of old files – administrative decisions, written policies and guidelines, complaints, investigative files or any records and official documents – drawn up pursuant to old established procedures may be invaluable.

Finally, the court might also need to gain access to documents, including archival materials, through international co-operation. A broad range of documents are needed, even those of seemingly neutral character, such as law texts, administrative acts and organizational graphs. Particularly important are those documents that enable the assessment and establishment of lines of responsibility for commanders that would facilitate the determination of command responsibility or civilian responsibility. Another area is journalist material, which, even if already put in the public domain, is often unavailable to be reproduced in trial under the caveat of compromising journalist access to the conflict zone in the future.

There is, therefore, a need to put in place inter-State co-operation mechanisms to enable access to evidence located in other States. In this regard, the

Kosovo court encountered many difficulties. Insufficient regional co-operation persisted throughout the decade of the presence of UNMIK, hampering access to the accused who had fled and who were wanted for trial.[38] Moreover, the UNMIK internationalized judiciary could not count on co-operation even within the international 'family'.

In the *Simić* case,[39] for instance, the Red Cross was reluctant to render its documents to the Court, even when the documents required were of a neutral nature and not related to access to the zone of war and conflict. The Court had to resort to obtaining political support to subpoena the person concerned and obtain the disclosure of evidence that was entirely exculpatory, providing documentary evidence that impeached critical prosecution eyewitnesses by showing they were hundreds of kilometres away from the crime scene.

Even the ICTY was very reluctant to share information with the Kosovo internationalized court, as its teams were investigating cases in the area at the same time, and the records needed were not in the public domain. In one case, when the Kosovo court eventually obtained access to the relevant material, it had been so substantially redacted that it retained little probative value.[40]

Similarly, the international military presence in Kosovo, the Kosovo Force ('KFOR'), despite a decade of efforts aimed at streamlining the co-operation with UNMIK in the area of evidence gathering, did not manage to develop a modality for providing information to the UNMIK internationalized judiciary. The crucial missing element was an inability to convert intelligence into evidence that could be admitted in court. The international community remained divided on this issue for several years, engaged in designing bureaucratic structures aimed to serve as filter and relay institutions. Meanwhile, however, KFOR refused to disclose information even on issues as harmless as the Kosovo Liberation Army's command structures. Here again, this had to be adduced through back channels and information sought in official sources after publication. Frequent changes of command and great turnover among the military legal advisers effectively precluded institutionalizing direct co-operation

---

[38] As noted by the OSCE in "Kosovo War Crimes Trials: An Assessment Ten Years On", May 2010, p. 22:

> Insufficient regional co-operation has also hampered the process of trying war crimes cases. It is possible that some persons accused of war crimes have fled Kosovo and can be tried in another jurisdiction. However, in order to broaden this process and try the suspects who have fled Kosovo, prosecutors and investigators outside of Kosovo would need access to witnesses and evidence in Kosovo. That would require official co-operation between officials inside and outside Kosovo, which does not currently exist.

[39] District Court of Mitrovica, *Prosecutor v. Igor Simić*, Judgement, P. Nr. 44/2000, 1 April 2001 ('*Simić* case').

[40] *Račak* case, 18 June 2001, see *supra* note 24.

within the time needed for the production of evidence. This is a particular instance of accelerated 'aging' of the evidence.

## 8.2. Contemporaneously Adduced Evidence

The typical feature in proving core international crimes is that their evidence originates from the time of conflict and armed violence. And this bears two different sets of problems.

### 8.2.1. Physical Availability

The first problem concerns the physical availability of old evidence. The best opportunity to record and preserve this evidence arises during or in the immediate aftermath of the conflict concerned. However, such situations are characterized by an inevitable crisis of institutions, regress of legal procedures, and unavailability of expertise, in particular of forensic expertise.

Subsequently, there may be an opportunity to secure evidence when transitional justice mechanisms are established. However, such mechanisms again operate in circumstances of institutional deficiency, in which those responsible for collecting evidence and statements – military police, national guards, summary courts, *ad hoc* commissions – do not necessarily have the required qualifications, the necessary impartiality, or the adequate training or equipment to do so. Moreover, an inadequate legal framework may complicate the determination of what is to be considered necessary evidence and what is not; what needs to be preserved and kept may not be clear. All this requires a certain degree of institutional organization, technical knowledge and prospective vision. Even if evidence is available, it can be overlooked or lost due to the lack of infrastructure, for instance, as well as the lack of realization of its significance in the context.

To illustrate the problem: in Kosovo, where the possession of weapons, especially during the early years, was commonplace, in over 30 initiated war crime cases that resulted in suspect arrest, there was not one where the suspect weapon would have been seized and secured.

The already mentioned *Simić* case[41] well illustrates the type of issues that can arise from the paucity of physical evidence. A Kosovo Serb, Igor Simić, was accused of having killed 26 Kosovo Albanian civilians in an execution-style paramilitary slaughter of civilians. Years later, when the UNMIK and Kosovo police regained primacy for criminal investigations, the NATO military presence in Kosovo, KFOR, acted then as an *ad interim* law enforcement agency. On the crime scene, in 1999, a 'ski-mask', containing within it some hair, had been found, secured and booked into the KFOR Gendarmerie

---

[41] *Simić* case, 1 April 2001, see *supra* note 39.

premises on the KFOR military base in Mitrovica. The accused had allegedly abandoned it at the occasion of the commission of the act. Unfortunately, when the case came to trial a year later, that Gendarmerie unit had been rotated back to France, and with it, the mask disappeared, along with other physical evidence. The *ad hoc* evidence room had been lost. Many of the relevant files were either lost or were considered military intelligence, thus classified and not made available to the prosecution or courts.

## 8.2.2. Credibility of the Evidence

The credibility of the evidence also depends on the context of the crime, which may not yet be revealed or disputed as groups are struggling for power to claim the inception of history. These groups gradually begin to frame the context, the mindset of the witnesses, and finally that of the general public.

An interesting example of this phenomenon can be found in the case connected to the 'Račak massacre' of 43 Kosovo Albanian civilians,[42] which was allegedly committed by the Serb armed forces. This case, and the related judgement of the Priština District Court of Kosovo, shows very well how the early days following the perpetration of potentially international crimes can shape a crime's context and public perceptions.

Each body was quickly examined and photographed by a team composed of a doctor and a nurse.[43] In their written report, they concluded that half of the victims had been killed execution-style and thrown into the ditch. The report further identified that death resulted from shooting and mutilation: eyes had been gauged out and wounds caused by bayonets or other blunt force on the heads of the victims, evidencing bestiality. Later, three other autopsies were conducted on the bodies. These findings were inconclusive. Some of the mutilations or wounds found by that doctor were, however, qualified as caused by animals which had access to the corpses. The Court noted:

> Dr. Bajrami, admitted in the trial that team had had neither the necessary time, nor the necessary forensic expertise and equipment, which would make the findings accurate and reliable. Regardless of this, the report was later presented in a scientific symposium in Pristina. The photographs taken on the spot of the event were subsequently used in publications circulated in Kosovo and displayed in a public exhibition in Pristina.[44]

---

[42] *Račak* case, 18 June 2001, see *supra* note 24.
[43] *Ibid.*
[44] *Ibid.*, para. 101.

Moreover, the Court found "discrepancies and contradictions in witness evidence"[45] and "doubts as to the reliability of the witness testimony",[46] who had undergone great stress during the events. There was also evidence of ethnic hostility from the witnesses towards the accused.[47] All the witnesses had seen the exhibition and the report of the doctor. To this regard, the Court found that:

> […] findings of the report by Dr. Vezir Bajrami and photographs taken by his staff achieved local notoriety. It seems some of the witnesses might have accepted as true such rumors and widespread information, and consciously or not, let such distort their recounting of the critical events.[48]

There are also numerous instances of eyewitness testimony in trials that were proven to be significantly inconsistent with prior statements, demonstrating the role of societal pressure on the witnesses. For example, in *Bešović*, the Court has recognized that:

> having accepted that with the passage of time people naturally forget facts, the trial court should apply particular scrutiny where a pattern of increasing inculpation is detected in the witness testimony, particularly where the recognition of the accused is built into the testimony only in subsequent hearings.[49]

Many of these cases due to repeated remanding for re-trial could never reach finality.

---

[45]  *Ibid.*, para. 153.

[46]  *Ibid.*, para. 149.

[47]  *Ibid.*, paras. 150–151.

[48]  *Ibid.*, para. 152.

[49]  *Bešović* case and *Bešović* appeal, see *supra* notes 34 and 35. The Supreme Court of Kosovo went on to instruct the District Court:

> [T]he District Court should in its evaluation of the incriminating testimony relate in a more detailed way to the defence's claims about the fabrication of the charges, bearing in mind such factors as: that it was undisputedly established that there had been repeated attacks on the house of the accused; that there was evidence of a theft from the forest belonging to the accused; that war crime complaints against the accused were brought following his acquittal from a robbery charge; that the accused alleged specific motives on the part of some of the witnesses, in particular Haxhi Kastrati, which does not appear to have been disproved; that the record of the investigative hearing reflects that Haki Gashi threatened to kill the accused and finally that some of the witnesses who inculpated the accused in the events pertinent to the instant proceedings had not reported his involvement in their earlier statements.

### 8.2.3. The Actual Production of Evidence

Evidence is also vulnerable to politics in the aftermath of conflict. A number of cases in Kosovo demonstrate how political actors, including non-governmental organizations ('NGOs'), sought to impact collective consciousness and memory through the influencing of witness testimonies and the establishing of certain versions of events. These actors sought to advocate prosecution by submitting requests to the investigating judges. There were instances of such collective action aimed at building cases against particular ethnic groups in Kosovo.

The UNMIK international judiciary recorded and evaluated such instances of evidence submission by civil society actors or NGOs. In the case of *Kelanović*, the International Prosecutor was confronted with a the report submitted by the Council of Human Rights and Freedoms, a local NGO comprised of an ethnic Albanian unanimity, that specifically identified an ethnic Serb as the specific individual responsible for killings.[50] However, the International Prosecutor investigating Kelanović found, during that investigation, that his own witnesses in that case contradicted their earlier statements to the police, and, in the end, declined to file an indictment.

The Council for the Human Rights and Freedoms had more persuasion in the case of *Radivojević et al.*,[51] where five Serbs were charged with a war crime by the District Prosecutor who sought to initiate investigation and arrest based entirely on evidence gathered by the Council. This material consisted entirely in rumours. The panel of international judges passed a decision refusing to initiate an investigation.

Even a more advanced case of evidence production concerned the case of *Mladenović*. The District Court found that:

---

[50] Office of the Public Prosecutor of Mitrovica, *Case of Kelanović*, Decision on Rejection of Charges, 13 July 2002, p. 2. The decision notes:

That Albanian journalist Murat Muslim is the Coordinator for the Council of Human Rights, and he wrote with others the Report of the Council, which cites Mr. Arugi and others blaming Dejan Kelanovic with killings in Skenderaj/Srbica on that date. In that earlier journalist's story, obtained by the international prosecutor from the journalist who took it directly from his computer drive from his office, the original version of the murder Mr. Aruqi [did not implicate Dejan Kelanović as he said he had not seen the perpetrators who wore masks and the murder happened out of his sight anyways]. This journalist interview which does not identify the shooters pre-dated the police interviews and pre-dated the media reports of Dejan Kelanovic's arrest for unrelated charges.

[51] District Court of Priština, *Prosecutor v. Radivojević et al.*, Decision of the Investigating Judge on Refusal of Investigation and Referral to the Panel of Judges, Hep 386/2001, 14 December 2001.

> The coincidence of Mladenovic's arrest and the phenomenon of all injured parties filing their claims against him raises suspicion that it was an action resulting from a collective decision, or even a conspiracy. These fears are fortified by the fact that virtually none of the injured parties, including those who claimed to remember events from two years before in utmost detail [such as exact time in hours and minutes], could state from whom had they learnt about Mladenovic's arrest. [...] On the other hand, there is evidence that an agitation against Mladenovic was carried out by Hasim Salihu and his party among the witnesses. Ibrahim Haziri was told that there were already 15 witnesses ready to testify against the accused and therefore he decided to join them; the same concerned Besim Isuf Jashari.[52]

## 8.3. Concluding Remarks

There are a number of important conclusions that can be drawn from the developments outlined above with respect to the use of old evidence in core international crimes cases. First, my tentative conclusion is that the evidence used for low-level criminal actions and to prove those perpetrators' identities tends to be eyewitness testimony, while the evidence used for contextual elements and for high-level command and political liability tends to be documentary, or closer to a historical consensus or the focus of reports and studies that are sometimes accepted by the courts. Thus, in general, old documentary evidence holds up with age more reliably than eyewitness evidence.

Second, the previous developments lead us to considering the role of civil society. There are powerful arguments for the involvement of civil society and victims. It benefits victims to the degree that they actually want to be involved. NGOs may be helpful in identifying victims and disseminating information about the proceedings and the law. But this carries a degree of danger when the engagement of the victims and civil society actors purport to take over State functions, such as investigation and punishment. So, the decision about victim and civil-society involvement calls for careful development, regarding its role and competences, so that it does not impede the process, both logistically and in the terms of perceptions and the presumption of innocence. Old evidence is as it is: it is difficult, but it is important that it be tested in accordance with the principles of fair trial. This implies adversarial procedures and neutrality. Hence, means of enhancing adversarial and neutral procedures should not be dismissed lightly.

Finally, as this chapter was originally written for a conference in Dhaka, Bangladesh has made the choice to establish the ICT-BD as a national court

---

[52] *Mladenović* case, 23 November 2001, para. 94, see *supra* note 33.

without the use of international judges – and there is no good reason why it should not do so. But taking into account the historically charged circumstances in which justice is to be done, and is to be seen to be done, perhaps making room for some foreign input in the functioning of the defence should be given some thought.

# 9

---

# Dealing With Old Evidence in International Crimes Cases: The Dutch Experience as a Case Study

## Martin Witteveen[*]

### 9.1. Introduction: Our Increased Appreciation of Evidential Difficulties in the Investigation and Prosecution of International Crimes

The criminal investigation of international crimes[1] is no longer an exception today. It has in fact become accepted, and is increasingly carried out at the national and international levels. The international community has established internationalized courts, such as the International Criminal Tribunal for the former Yugoslavia ('ICTY'), the International Criminal Tribunal for Rwanda ('ICTR'), the International Criminal Court ('ICC') and a handful of other tribunals and special chambers. Apart from these more recent endeavours, one

---

[*] **Martin Witteveen** is an Appeals Prosecutor in the Prosecution Service in the Netherlands, specialized in international crimes cases and human trafficking and smuggling. He also served as an Investigation Judge for international crimes in the District Court in The Hague, the Netherlands. As such, he conducted pre-trial investigations for international crimes, which are adjudicated by the District Court. He heard witnesses in the presence of the prosecution and the defence attorneys mostly in the countries where the crimes have taken place. He has experience with witnesses from various countries and backgrounds. Between 2004 and 2008, he served as investigation team leader for the investigation into Northern Uganda and police analyst in the Office of the Prosecutor ('OTP') of the ICC. In 2021, he advised the Human Rights Commission of Ethiopia in its joint investigation on the war in Tigray. At the time of the publication of the second edition, he works with the Minister of Justice in the National Unity Government (NUG), Myanmar, on the collection of evidence and how to prepare for accountability for the crimes committed in Myanmar. He served as a public prosecutor in the Netherlands for almost 20 years, mainly in the field of organized crime and led a number of high-profile prosecutions against criminal organizations. He graduated from the Faculty of Law of Utrecht University (LL.M.). This chapter was written with the wonderful assistance of my intern Floris Gerritsen, Master's graduate of the University of Amsterdam, who researched the issue of reliability of witnesses in cases of international crimes from January until July 2009. Part of this chapter develops ideas first presented by Witteveen in "Closing the Gap in Truth Finding: From the Facts in the Field to the Judge's Chamber", in Alette Smeulers (ed.), *Collective Violence and International Criminal Justice*, Intersentia, 2010.

[1] I will refer to these crimes by using the generic term of 'international crimes'. For the purposes of this chapter, they include genocide, war crimes, crimes against humanity and torture.

---

should recall the number of international treaties since World War II which have served as a basis for states to apply forms of universal jurisdiction within their national jurisdiction before the Rome Statute.[2] Many countries have initiated investigations of international crimes that took place on their territory.[3] Others have adopted laws that permit them to exercise extra-territorial or even universal jurisdiction over these international crimes. Considering the headwind international criminal justice is facing, such developments are spectacular.

It is noteworthy that there have been a number of acquittals before national and international courts.[4] The prosecution has at times failed to prove, based on evidence presented in court, that the accused person was guilty beyond a reasonable doubt. This chapter examines reasons associated with the 'age' of evidence presented to and considered by courts, particularly witness testimony. The next two sections (9.2. and 9.3.) highlight a number of features commonly associated with international crimes that greatly increase the need for, but also the instability of, using old evidence in prosecutions. The fourth and fifth sections (9.4. and 9.5.) respectively deal with how trauma, commonly associated with international crimes, impacts the different stages of memory and witness testimony itself. The sixth section (9.6.) examines the roles played by different professionals in general. The last section (9.7.) evaluates the Dutch authorities' experience specifically, and makes the point that working with reliable witness evidence, even when old, implies more than applying the right technique. The chapter concludes by offering some reflections in Section 9.8.

---

[2]   The most important ones being the Geneva Conventions (the four treaties agreed in 1949: Convention for the Amelioration of the Condition of the Wounded and Sick in Armed Forces in the Field (https://www.legal-tools.org/doc/baf8e7/), Convention for the Amelioration of the Condition of Wounded, Sick and Shipwrecked Members of Armed Forces at Sea (https://www.legal-tools.org/doc/0d0216/), Convention Relative to the Treatment of Prisoners of War (https://www.legal-tools.org/doc/365095/), Convention Relative to the Protection of Civilian Persons in Time of War (https://www.legal-tools.org/doc/d5e260/); and the two additional protocols: Protocol (I) (https://www.legal-tools.org/doc/d9328a/), Protocol (II) (https://www.legal-tools.org/doc/fd14c4/)); the Convention on the Prevention and Punishment of the Crime of Genocide, 9 December 1948 (https://www.legal-tools.org/doc/498c38/); and the Convention Against Torture and Other Cruel, Inhuman or Degrading Treatment or Punishment, 10 December 1984 (https://www.legal-tools.org/doc/326294/).

[3]   Countries like Guatemala, Argentina, Chile, East Timor and states formerly being part of ex-Yugoslavia such as Bosnia and Herzegovina and Serbia.

[4]   A good overview of the results of the criminal trials around the world is available on the web site of TRIAL International. There seems to be a low number of acquittals in national jurisdictions.

---

## 9.2. Reality and Facts of International Crimes

International crimes cannot easily be compared with ordinary crimes. They are of an incomparable scale and seriousness. The word 'unimaginable' often used in the context of these crimes should be taken literally. In my own experience, I recall reading accounts of witness testimony of crimes committed or events having taken place where my immediate reflex was thinking: this cannot have happened. I had the feeling that my brain could simply not absorb the reality immediately.

One characteristic of these crimes is that they are very complex and involve multiple acts. Often, we are dealing with a series of events that took place in one single day, or even only part of a day, during which hundreds of people are attacked and killed or mutilated. Moreover, these killings and attacks normally involve a multitude of perpetrators. The attacks are often carried out by groups of people, consisting of tens of people or more. The attacks are rarely well-organized or -structured as in a regular army. Chaos is the proper way of describing these attacks and crimes committed within their context. Consequently, the victims of such attacks and crimes are in total disarray while the crimes are committed and the attacks carried out. The initial reaction of a victim or target of an attack is to flee and escape. The victims run around seeking shelter wherever they can find a place to hide and often go from one place to another. They usually have no idea of what exactly is going on, or who is doing what. Their focus is survival.

These crimes also impact their victims in the most horrible of ways. People are shot by guns, while others are hacked to death with machetes or knives. During some attacks, spears and clubs are used to kill people. Saddam Hussein used mustard or nerve gas in Iraq against the Kurdish population. Victims went through a gruesome death process, watched by loved ones and neighbours in the village where the attacks took place. Rape is rampant in crime scenes, and women more often fall victim to this crime than others. In any event, victims and witnesses of these events always experience an unprecedented agony in their lifetime. Trauma is most likely the lasting effect impacting victims and witnesses.

Special attention needs to be paid to the perpetrators usually involved in international crimes. The crimes are perpetrated by persons acting in groups, rather than as individuals. Sometimes the structures of the groups are quite loose and badly documented. Sometimes the perpetrators are senior figures in an army or a paramilitary group with a well-defined structure and meticulous documentation. International tribunals, as a policy, aim their efforts at prosecuting the most responsible for the crimes under investigation, most likely the leaders of these military or paramilitary groups. National systems, although

they base their jurisdiction on the nationality of the defendant or on their physical presence in the territory of that state, are also faced with leadership cases.
More often the most responsible persons or leaders were not involved in the
crimes directly in the sense that they personally killed or mutilated victims.
They may have ordered or otherwise instigated the killers and attackers. Often,
they are military commanders or political leaders, who may have a more indirect criminal responsibility for the crimes. This is a relevant factor for the collection of evidence and thus determines the prospect of a conviction or an acquittal. The countries and areas where these crimes take place and where the
organizations operate are not known for their meticulous record-keeping. And,
even if records were kept, they are often destroyed, not available, or kept away
from the investigators for reasons of state security. Consequently, in cases
where the facts of the field are extended to (para-)military organizations or
other (political) organizations, the investigation may be impeded from the
start.[5]

These features of international crimes make their evidential proof particularly difficult, and this is further compounded by circumstances emerging
in the aftermath of international crimes, as explained in the following section.

## 9.3. The Aftermath of International Crimes: Delayed Investigations and Consequent Problems

What happens next, in the aftermath of international crimes? Usually, societies
focus on more immediate reconstructive demands. Political dialogue and
peace-building trump the call for accountability. The crimes that took place are
incredibly complex, and victimized witnesses have undergone intense trauma.
Yet, the crimes have not been sufficiently recorded at the time of events. There
is a lack of sufficiently trained personnel to undertake investigation-related
activities, such as interviewing witnesses or performing forensic examinations.
Due to a variety of such factors, investigative and prosecutorial efforts are delayed.

### 9.3.1. The Consequences of Delayed Investigations and Prosecutions

Much time often passes before investigations and prosecutions are initiated.
Indeed, it often takes a few years before a criminal investigation begins. At the
ICTR and the ICTY, it took at least two to three years before the first investi-
gators got back to the field to unearth the facts and investigate the crimes. Still,

---

[5] The great exception is that of the Nuremberg trials, where the Prosecutor almost completely
relied on documentary evidence as the Nazis had meticulously documented the genocide on
the Jews and those documents were readily available. See Robert H. Jackson, *The Nürnberg
Case*, Alfred A. Knopf Inc., New York, 1947; Ann Tusa and John Tusa, *The Nuremberg Trial*,
Atheneum, New York, 1984.

---

the first trials before these tribunals did not take place before the latter part of the 1990s.[6] Yet, these first investigations and trials took place under relatively favourable circumstances. Later, investigations and trials at these tribunals did not get off the ground until some 10 years had passed.[7] The circumstances at the ICC are similar. By law, the ICC has jurisdiction over international crimes only from 1 July 2002 onwards. In Uganda and in the Ituri province of the Democratic Republic of the Congo ('DRC'), the investigations were announced by the Prosecutor in the summer of 2004. The crimes under investigation had occurred from 2002 until 2004. The investigations into the crimes in Darfur started in 2005 and focused on events in Darfur in 2003 and 2004. The investigations into the crimes in the Central African Republic ('CAR') started in 2006 and concentrated on the events in the CAR in 2002 and 2003. Subsequent investigations, such as into alleged crimes committed in Côte d'Ivoire in 2010 and 2011, in Libya in 2011, and in Kenya in 2007 and 2008, started relatively soon after the facts. Despite these relatively favourable circumstances, trials did not commence as regards to Darfur until 2022,[8] and, in the case of the DRC and the CAR, they have not started until 2009.[9] The trial against Dominic Ongwen in the Uganda situation was completed only in 2020. The Côte d'Ivoire and Kenya situation-trials were held in 2015 and 2016. In the Libya situation, no trials have been held so far.[10]

One can wonder what the effect on the witnesses' memory is when witnesses from such situations are called to testify in full court in The Hague many years down the line, while their first statements to the investigators, in some cases, have been taken between 2004 and 2006.

In national jurisdictions the situation is even worse, although the reason for the time lapse is different. In the Netherlands,[11] justice has been adminis-

---

[6] The first trial at the ICTR was the case against Jean Paul Akayesu. He was arrested 10 October 1995, but his trial did not commence until 1997. The verdict was given on 2 September 1998. The first case at the ICTY (although not the first verdict) was the case against Duško Tadić, arrested in 1994, but his trial commenced only in May 1996 and the verdict was given in May 1997.

[7] See, for example, the so-called *Government II* case against Bizimungu *et al.*, where the defendants' trials commenced in 2002 and the verdict was rendered on 30 September 2011.

[8] The trial against Ali Muhammad Ali Abd-Al-Rahman commenced on 5 April 2022 and is ongoing.

[9] The first trial at the ICC was against Thomas Lubanga Dyilo in the DRC situation and commenced with considerable delay in January 2009. Other trials in the DRC situation as well as the trial against Jean-Pierre Bemba Gombo in the CAR situation have commenced mostly after 2010.

[10] A complete overview of the cases is available on the web site of the ICC.

[11] In this chapter, only the cases in the Netherlands are mentioned. There have been investigations into international crimes in other countries as well. Belgium, for instance, has tried

---

tered in cases of international crimes by the District Court in The Hague, which is the only competent court in the Netherlands to try domestic cases of international crimes, 10 to 20 years after the facts occurred or even longer than that. In a case that was tried in 2008 and 2009, the defendant was charged with participation in the genocide that took place in Rwanda in 1994. The verdict was given almost exactly 15 years after the genocide, while the witness hearings took place between 12 and 14 years after the facts.[12] Another Rwandan national residing in the Netherlands was tried in the District Court in the Hague in 2012 and 2013 for her role in the genocide.[13] In other cases, the defendants were charged with their alleged involvement in torture committed by the Afghan Military Intelligence Service under communist rule in the 1980s, 20 years after the facts occurred.[14] One other case dealt with the alleged involvement of a defendant in the war in Liberia and Sierra Leone in 1991–1996. He was tried some 15 years after the facts[15] and, in one case, a Dutch busi-

---

several cases against defendants charged with involvement in the Rwandan genocide for years. In Canada, a verdict was given in a case against a Rwandan national convicted for his role in the genocide in Rwanda in 1994. Switzerland tried one defendant for involvement in the genocide, with a verdict in 2001. Several other countries such as Sweden and Finland have started investigations and trials against Rwandans as well. Germany tried persons from the former Yugoslavia, and more recently a number of high-profile cases related to crimes committed in Iraq, Syria (notably the trial against two alleged members of the Syrian government security apparatus accused of torture in one of Syria's notorious prisons) and against alleged ISIS members.

[12] District Court in The Hague, *Case against Joseph Mpambara*, Judgement, 23 March 2009, Case Nos. 09/750009-06 and 09/750007-07 ('*Mpambara* case') (https://www.legal-tools.org/doc/08057f/). In appeal, the Court of Appeal in The Hague, on 7 July 2011, sentenced Mpambara to life imprisonment.

[13] The defendant, Yvonne Ntacyobatabara, was convicted for incitement to genocide on 1 March 2013 to six years and eight months imprisonment with acquittals on other charges. See District Court in The Hague, *Case against Yvonne Ntacyobatabara*, Judgement, 1 March 2013, Case No. 09/748004-09 (https://www.legal-tools.org/doc/3f41c2/). Initial appeals were withdrawn.

[14] District Court in The Hague, *Case against Hesam and Jelalzoy*, Judgement, 14 October 2005, Case No. 09/751005-04 ('*Hesam and Jelalzoy* case') (https://www.legal-tools.org/doc/58bf72/); Court of Appeal in The Hague, *Cases against Hesam and Jelalzoy*, Appeal Judgement, 29 January 2007, Case No. 09-751005-04 ('*Hesam and Jelalzoy* appeal') (https://www.legal-tools.org/doc/31e38b/); District Court in The Hague, *Case against Faqirzada*, Judgement, 25 June 2007, Case No. 09/750001-06 ('*Faqirzada* case') (https://www.legal-tools.org/doc/65daa2/); Court of Appeal in The Hague, *Case against Faqirzada*, Appeal Judgement, 16 July 2009, Case No. 09/750001-06 ('*Faqirzada* appeal') (https://www.legal-tools.org/doc/g8eiij/).

[15] District Court in The Hague, *Case against Guus Kouwenhoven*, Judgment, 7 June 2006, Case No. 09/750001-05 ('*Kouwenhoven* case') (https://www.legal-tools.org/doc/61daa1/); Court of Appeal in The Hague, *Case against Guus Kouwenhoven*, Appeal Judgement, 10 March 2008, Case No. 09/750001-05 ('*Kouwenhoven* appeal') (https://www.legal-

nessman was charged with supplying Saddam Hussein with precursor chemicals to fabricate the chemical weapons he subsequently used against the Kurds in 1986.[16] The case was concluded in 2005, 20 years after the crimes were committed. In 2022, the Court of Appeals in The Hague convicted a former member of the Ethiopian communist military junta, the Dergue, to life imprisonment for crimes committed in the 1970s.[17] Lastly, the trial against an alleged former member of the Afghan military intelligence under communist rule, the Khad, has started before the Court of Appeal in The Hague in 2024 for allegedly being a prison commander of the infamous Pul-e-Charkhi prison in Afghanistan in the 1980s. The District Court sentenced him to 12 years imprisonment.[18] The time that has passed between the facts and the trial is mindboggling. However, in recent years a number of defendants have been convicted for international crimes committed within the last ten years.[19]

The lapse of time between the occurrence of the facts and crimes and the actual investigations and trials has consequences. First of all, evidence will have gone lost. In particular, the possibilities to execute forensic investigations are significantly reduced. Crime scene locations will have been rebuilt or completely demolished. Weapons used in the crimes are no longer there, or are hard to trace back. Burial sites are harder to find and, if they are found, exhumations and autopsies have limited use. The use of forensic evidence in the genocide cases before the ICTR has been very limited. The Tribunal has accepted some to prove that genocide did take place.[20] But forensic evidence has

---

tools.org/doc/49c55b/). After the Supreme Court quashed the acquittal, Kouwenhoven was retried by the Court of Appeal in Hertogenbosch, who sentenced him to 17 years imprisonment on 21 April 2017 (https://www.legal-tools.org/doc/8e3386/). Kouwenhoven's extradition from South Africa is still pending.

[16] District Court in The Hague, *Case against Frans van Anraat*, Judgement, 23 December 2005, Case No. 09/751003-04 ('*van Anraat* case') (https://www.legal-tools.org/doc/4966cf/); Court of Appeal in The Hague, *Case against Frans van Anraat*, Appeal Judgement, 9 May 2007, Case No. 09/751003-04 ('*van Anraat* appeal') (https://www.legal-tools.org/doc/d138be/).

[17] Court of Appeal in The Hague, *Case against Eshetu*, Appeal Judgement, 8 June 2022, Case No. 22-005503-17 ('*Eshetu* case') (https://www.legal-tools.org/doc/zgyxn8/).

[18] District Court in The Hague, *Case against Abdulrazaq*, Judgement, 14 April 2022, Case No. 09/748011-12 (https://www.legal-tools.org/doc/mohy55/).

[19] For example, a Syrian national was convicted for arbitrary detention and torture as crimes against humanity committed from 2011 to 2013 in Syria, District Court in The Hague, *Case against Mustafa*, Judgement 22 January 2024, Case No. 71/122211-22 (https://www.legal-tools.org/doc/uda3a7/).

[20] See, for example, ICTR, *Prosecutor v. Kayishema and Ruzindana*, Trial Chamber II, Judgement, 21 May 1999, ICTR-95-1-T, paras. 325 and 412 (https://www.legal-tools.org/doc/0811c9/).

played virtually no role in the critical part of a trial, that is, the determination of individual criminal responsibility: did the defendant play any role in the crimes and, if so, what role and to what extent?[21] Moreover, the passage of time will no doubt lead to the loss of witness evidence, as particularly older witnesses will have died. Other witnesses may have disappeared without the possibility of being located.

### 9.3.2. The Failure to Record and Document Crimes

Due to the nature of international crimes, their chaotic circumstances and post-conflict instability, they are usually not well-documented by their perpetrators or by post-conflict authorities. The last genocide that was well-documented was the genocide against the Jews by Nazi Germany, which kept meticulous records of all meetings, conversations, orders and killings, including a full administrative record of the extermination camps where the Jews were exterminated with gas. In fact, the Prosecutor at the Nuremberg trials, Robert H. Jackson, rarely used witnesses to prove the charges brought against the top-level Nazi leaders who had remained to stand trial. Instead, he presented hundreds of documents, not only to convince the Tribunal that genocide had taken place, but also that the defendants had taken part in the genocide and were criminally liable for their participation, a truly unique situation. The masterminds of the more recent atrocities, such as in the former Yugoslavia, East Timor, Sierra Leone, Liberia, Cambodia, Rwanda and South America, did not normally keep many records of the crimes being committed, let alone of the individual involvement of a particular person. An exception must be made for crimes committed by armies and army-like organizations, such as rebel groups that have assumed a military structure. The most extreme situation in this respect can be found in Rwanda, where hardly any relevant document exists on the execution of the genocide against the Tutsis and the roles of individuals therein. Even video footage of the killings and related events is extremely rare. The oral culture in Rwanda (and other parts of the region) appears to be the main determining factor in this circumstance.

The cases adjudicated in the Netherlands and listed above are no exception. Most were almost exclusively concluded on the basis of witness testimo-

---

[21] Although forensic evidence was not widely used, the Prosecutor at the ICTR and ICTY did conduct forensic investigations in the former Yugoslavia and in Rwanda. In particular, mass graves were unearthed and exhumations were performed on the remains of bodies. For a personal account, see, generally, Clea Koff, *The Bone Woman: A Forensic Anthropologist's Search for Truth in the Mass Graves of Rwanda, Bosnia, Croatia, and Kosovo*, Random House Trade Paperbacks, 2005.

ny.[22] However, in some recent cases, where the crimes were committed within the last ten years, digital evidence in the form of videos and photographs was used to convict the defendant. More importantly, evidence collected from open sources (OSINT) is increasingly collected and presented. This does not take away the fact that even in those cases, the courts still rely on witness testimony.

Therefore, in the absence of other types of evidence, trial judges have to rely almost exclusively or predominantly on witness testimony. In most cases, this means that trial judges have to determine the guilt or innocence of an individual charged with the most serious crimes known to mankind based on individual witness accounts which are given 5, 10 sometimes 20 years or even longer after the facts have occurred. Given this dependency and vulnerability, it is worth focussing the attention on issues related to witness testimony. This, in turn, gives rise to the problems associated with the passage of time on the memory of witnesses, as is addressed in the next two sections below.

## 9.4. The Different Phases of Memory: Encoding, Retention and Retrieval of Information

This section examines the different stages of a witness' memory. Such a step-by-step consideration is important because what is finally produced, as witness statement or testimony, depends on how a memory is encoded, retained and then retrieved. It has been scientifically shown that the human memory is fallible.[23] There are three phases in a memory's lifespan: the 'encoding', during which the information is recorded in a person's memory; the 'retention', during which the information is stored in a person's memory; and the 'retrieval', the moment during which the witness reproduces the information, for instance, during a witness statement or witness testimony. Each phase has its unique challenges.[24]

---

[22] With the exception of the above-mentioned case against the member of the Dergue regime in Ethiopia. The Court of Appeal convicted him partly based on letters signed by the defendant in which he ordered the execution of political opponents. See *Eshetu* case, 8 June 2022, *supra* note 17.

[23] Scientific publications in the Netherlands on witness memory were researched for this chapter. There is an abundance of foreign literature. A leading study in the United States can be found in Jennifer Dysart, James M. Doyle and Elizabeth Loftus, *Eyewitness Testimony: Civil and Criminal*, 4th ed., Lexis Law Publishing, Charlottesville, 2008.

[24] E. Rassin, *Tussen Sofa en Toga: Een Inleiding in de Rechtspsychologie*, Boom Juridische Uitgevers, The Hague, 2009, p. 87.

### 9.4.1. The Encoding Phase of Human Memory: The Selection, Impression and Storage of Memory

Part of the human memory is the autobiographic memory. Information we have personally experienced and which relates to time, place and persons is stored in our brains and can be distinct from other, more general information we have without knowing where we accrued this knowledge.[25] When being heard as a witness, one is invited to use his or her autobiographic memory. The problem with autobiographic memory is that information is only stored in a person's memory as far as it is relevant and needed. Once the memory becomes obsolete, it will disappear and be replaced by more recent information. Thus, after years, much of the memory will have disappeared. This may be problematic in view of the need during witness' hearings or testimonies where the witness is invited to recall details that occurred long before.[26] Some witnesses I have personally heard during sessions, when confronted with questions on the details of the events the witnesses were questioned about, responded by saying: 'I could never have imagined someone would come from that far to ask me that question after so many years'. The answer may be indicative of the above-mentioned phenomenon of renewal of memories based on relevance.

Research has revealed that a sequence of events is best recorded in a person's brain. The recording in a person's memory of *where* the events happened and *who* was involved in it is much less reliable. *When* an event happened is recorded the worst.[27] However, the *when*, *where* and *who* questions are particularly relevant during a criminal investigation and subsequent trial to assess a witness' reliability. Equally problematic is the fact that a victim of multiple crimes is less likely to recall the details of these crimes because he or she has difficulty distinguishing them. Someone who has been tortured once is most likely able to recall that torture in every detail: the date, the place, the person who tortured and how it was executed. Someone who has sustained multiple instances of torture over time is less likely to recall those details. They have become a blur.[28] I have heard a witness who testified that he was, as part of a group, chased on a hill in Rwanda for more than two weeks by Hutu

---

[25] Hans F.M. Crombag, Peter J. Van Koppen and W.A. Wagenaar, *Dubieuze Zaken: De Psychologie van Strafrechtelijk Bewijs*, Contact, Amsterdam, 1994, p. 271.

[26] *Ibid.*, pp. 271–272.

[27] Peter J. Van Koppen and Hans F.M. Crombag (eds.), *De Menselijke Factor: Psychologie voor Juristen*, Gouda Quint, Arnhem, 1991, p. 159; Peter J. Van Koppen, Dick J. Hessing and Hans F.M. Crombag (eds.), *Het Hart van de Zaak: Psychologie van het Recht*, Gouda Quint, Deventer, 1997, p. 319.

[28] Rassin, 2009, p. 38, see *supra* note 24.

killers. Many of his fellow refugees were killed. The witness was well able to recall the first day of the attack on the hill and, to a lesser degree, the second day. The witness' memory on the rest of the two weeks was blended together into a vague memory of snatches of attacks without recalling dates, places and persons. The multiple occurrences of attacks clearly affected the memory of that particular witness in the way described above. Although a level of detail in a witness statement is necessary to assess the credibility of that information, the lack of details does not necessarily constitute an insurmountable hurdle in assessing the truth.

We observe selectively and we store our information selectively. Everyone has a natural bias in recording what we see and hear. More importantly, our registration of events is partly because our sense organs are not capable of capturing everything we see, hear and smell, *et cetera*. Our capability to concentrate is limited.[29] Special and remarkable events are recorded and stored more accurately than normal, everyday events. Moreover, special events are more likely to be discussed and recalled shortly after they have occurred, which improves the recollection. On the other hand, this results in the danger of a personal memory blending with the stories of others, which cannot be disentangled so many years after it occurred.[30]

An excessively strong focus of our sense can lead to an impediment of our observations.[31] A widely described phenomenon is the 'weapons focus effect'. Victims of armed robbery and the like appear to be able to describe the weapon used during the robbery in great detail, while completely unable to describe the person who robbed them, including his or her features such as height, hair colour and the clothes the person wore. The trauma that victims of crimes like robbery sustained does not seem to impair the victim's recollection of such or other details.[32] The District Court in The Hague took notice of this phenomenon in its verdict against Joseph Mpambara, who was convicted of participating in the Rwanda genocide in 1994, and observed that trauma itself cannot lead to the conclusion that the witness' observation becomes unreliable *per se*.[33]

---

[29] *Ibid.*, p. 45.
[30] Van Koppen, Hessing and Crombag (eds.), 1997, p. 390, see *supra* note 27; Ingrid Candel, Harald Merckelbach and Ineke Wessel, "Traumatische Herinneringen", in Peter J. Van Koppen, Dick J. Hessing, Harald Merckelbach and Hans F.M. Crombag (eds.), *Het Recht van Binnen: Psychologie van het Recht*, Uigteverij Kluwer BV, Deventer, 2002, p. 420.
[31] Rassin, 2009, p. 46, see *supra* note 24.
[32] Van Koppen, Hessing and Crombag (eds.), 1997, p. 290, see *supra* note 27.
[33] *Mpambara* case, Chapter 6, para. 18, see *supra* note 12.

In sum: the observation of a person is determined by the combination of the impression on the senses of the observer and the personal features of the observer.[34] Clearly, a weapons expert will remember different things when fallen victim to a robbery or shootout than a victim who is the owner of the shop that was robbed.[35] Equally, physical impairments can heavily affect a witness' observations. A witness in the *Kouwenhoven* case[36] was not assessed as a reliable witness by the Court of Appeals in The Hague when he stated without explanation that he read the name on a ship when it turned out he was illiterate.

## 9.4.2. The Retention Phase of Human Memory: Remembering Over Time

Human memory is a process, stretches over time, and its content is influenced by how we interact with it over time, not only at the initial encoding stage. For example, as shown by research, our memory only records fragments of events we have observed. Yet, when we reproduce the events from our memory, we do so as a story, as if we have remembered all of what has happened. Unwittingly, we fill the gaps with information from other sources, mainly by using logical inferences based on our knowledge, expectations or even biases.[37] The involvement of a person in a certain event, recalled and reproduced by a witness, may then well be the result of a bias the witness holds against that person instead of what the witness in reality can recall as the person's involvement.

This effect is exacerbated when the circumstances under which the witness saw the events happen were not optimal, because it was dark, rainy or there were obstacles between him or her and the event unfolding before his or her eyes.[38] For these reasons, it is recommended that the witness recalls and reproduces these events shortly after the events took place. As mentioned, this will not likely be the case in investigations of international crimes. Associated with this is what is called the 'bystander effect': the witness recalls a person as the perpetrator of a crime or an act, while in reality the person was merely there.[39]

The correct and complete observation and storage of a crime or event are not sufficient for a reliable recount of the crime and event. What is needed is that the information is properly retained in the memory of the witness until it

---

[34] Van Koppen and Crombag (eds.), 1991, p. 160, see *supra* note 27.
[35] *Ibid.*, p. 162.
[36] *Kouwenhoven* appeal, paras. 9–15, see *supra* note 15.
[37] Rassin, 2009, p. 43, see *supra* note 24; Peter J. Van Koppen, "De Goede Getuige die af en toe Faalt", in *Tijdschrift voor Criminologie*, 2007, vol. 49, no. 4, pp. 411–412.
[38] Van Koppen and Crombag (eds.), 1991, p. 159, see *supra* note 27.
[39] Van Koppen, Hessing and Crombag (eds.), 1997, p. 390, see *supra* note 27.

is needed for reproduction. General recollections of events by witnesses become less reliable for this reason when the time between the event and the reproduction is longer.[40] The examples I have given above indicate that this is likely the case in investigations of international crimes. First of all, memories of a crime or event can have disappeared altogether or, in the event the information is still stored, it cannot be retrieved for reasons of time lapse. Therefore, using the right techniques to retrieve that information is critical. It may be that several attempts have to be undertaken before the information is remembered and reproduced.[41] Inconsistencies in different statements from the same witness do not necessarily mean the witness is unreliable. When the information that is sought is associated with reoccurring events, the retrieval of that information can be performed by using schemes.[42] When a murder takes place during the weekly market in the village, which the witness observed while visiting the market as he usually does every week, the witness will not recall the visit to the market that particular day, but he will remember the tragic event when he is confronted with his usual market visits.

During the retention of the information between the event and the reproduction of the information by the witness, for example during an interview or hearing, 'source blending' may occur.[43] The witness who was at a crime scene or an event may have acquired only limited information during the crime or event itself. It is not unlikely that, after the crime or event, the witness hears more about the crime or event from other sources. He will probably speak about it with others, who also may have been at the same place as the witness, or the witness may read about it in the news. When giving his statement or testimony, he will reproduce what he has seen and heard, attributing his information to his eye-witness status, while in reality he has acquired the information from *post hoc* sources. This is particularly relevant in a criminal judicial process where it makes a world of difference whether the information produced by the witness is based on hearsay or eye-witness testimony. The need to ensure that information remembered is produced effectively and adequately by witnesses leads us to consider issues of information retrieval.

### 9.4.3. The Retrieval Phase of Human Memory: Reaching Back Into the Past

A memory phase particularly relevant to this anthology's topic – old evidence – is the retrieval phase. Even though a witness has observed an event

---

[40]   Van Koppen and Crombag (eds.), 1991, p. 163, see *supra* note 27.
[41]   Rassin, 2009, p. 47, see *supra* note 24.
[42]   Crombag, Van Koppen and Wagenaar, 1994, p. 276, see *supra* note 25.
[43]   Rassin, 2009, pp. 48–49, see *supra* note 24.

accurately and recorded it accurately, there is still a need to ensure that his or her observations are accurately retrieved and presented after a significant passage of time.

The retrieval of the information from the witness is a vulnerable process, full of pitfalls. Investigators, prosecutors and judges alike always want a chronological narrative of an event by the witness with sufficient focus on time, place, persons, 'who-did-what-when', et cetera. And that is hardly ever the result of a witness statement or testimony. Always, the information needs to be aroused or triggered by what is called 'retrieval cues'. Considering how the psychology of a human works, this can be done by any means that arouses the sense organs.[44] Giving pieces of information to the witness or bringing a person to the crime scene or the place where the event took place can trigger the memory; even a specific scent can do that.

Normally during criminal investigations, it is the question posed to the witness that triggers the witness' mind and memory.[45] The witness hardly ever produces information spontaneously. I remember when asking a witness in the Rwanda case the question: 'Can you tell me what happened during the attack on 16 April 1994?', the witness just responded by saying: 'The Hutus came and attacked us. They killed all of us'. In reality, the attack lasted the whole day and the situation was so complex that it would have been easy to write a book about that attack alone. Obviously, further questioning is necessary to retrieve the information. How these questions are asked to the witness is critical. The most common pitfall in questioning witnesses is to ask suggestive questions, commonly known as leading questions. Leading questions are not only suggestive because the answer is included, but witnesses are also inclined to affirm leading questions.[46] Research has shown, for example, that when eye witnesses had to estimate the speed of a car during a collision, they indicated a higher speed for the car when they were asked what the speed was when the cars *banged* on each other than when asked what the speed was when the cars *contacted* each other. Obviously, the witnesses were led by the suggestion incorporated in the use of the word 'banged'.[47] Leading questions have not been banned at tribunals, certainly not during cross-examination, as ruled by the

---

[44]   Van Koppen, Hessing and Crombag (eds.), 1997, p. 319–320, see *supra* note 27.

[45]   *Ibid.*, p. 320.

[46]   Crombag, Van Koppen and Wagenaar, 1994, p. 383, see *supra* note 25; Gerardus P.M.F. Mols, *Getuigen in strafzaken*, Kluwer, Deventer, 2003, p. 230.

[47]   Elizabeth F. Loftus and John C. Palmer, "Reconstruction of Automobile Destruction: An Example of the Interaction Between Language and Memory", in *Journal of Verbal Learning and Verbal Behavior*, 1974, vol. 13, no. 5, pp. 585–589.

Appeals Chamber in the *Akayesu* case.[48] However, in the *Mbarushimana* case before the ICC, the Pre-Trial Chamber displayed a rare willingness to scrutinize the behaviour of the investigators towards the witnesses when it affected the probative value of the witnesses' testimonies. The Chamber expressed serious criticism of the investigation and the interview techniques of the investigators, which led, among other things, to the decision not to confirm the charges against Mbarushimana.[49]

Using the right 'retrieval cues' is critical to retrieving as much information as possible from the witness. It may be that multiple attempts to ask the same question to the witness using several and different 'retrieval cues' are necessary to retrieve the information necessary from the witness' memory. The danger of course lies in the leading nature of the questioning and the 'retrieval cues' used, which can lead to reproducing false or unreliable information.[50] Providing to the witness the name of the suspect or defendant in the ongoing investigation is certainly within the category of risky 'retrieval cues'.

In two of the cases of international crimes before the District Court in The Hague, this became an issue. In the *Faqirzada* case,[51] a particular witness, when heard in a related case, had not mentioned the name of the defendant of the concerned case. When the same witness was heard once more, now in the case of the concerned defendant, he was given the name of the defendant by the interviewing police officers and was asked: 'What do you know about him?'. The witness responded by saying this was the person who tortured him. This discrepancy was the reason for the Court to disqualify the statement as insufficiently reliable.[52] In the case against Joseph Mpambara,[53] a similar problem occurred. Five witnesses, both during the statements to the police as well

---

[48]  ICTR, *Prosecutor v. Jean-Paul Akayesu*, Appeals Chamber, Appeal Judgement, 1 June 2001, ICTR-96-4-A, paras. 320–326 ('*Prosecutor v. Akayesu*, 1 June 2001') (https://www.legal-tools.org/doc/c62d06/).

[49]  ICC, *Prosecutor v. Callixte Mbarushimana*, Pre-Trial Chamber, Decision on the Confirmation of Charges, 16 December 2011, ICC-01/04-01/10, para. 51 (https://www.legal-tools.org/doc/63028f/).

[50]  Van Koppen, Hessing and Crombag (eds.), 1997, pp. 306 and 319–321, see *supra* note 27.

[51]  *Faqirzada* case, see *supra* note 14.

[52]  *Ibid.*, the Court states:
    Because of the procedures regarding [P1]'s testimonies, and the ever changing statements made by this witness and the fact that no supporting evidence is available, the Court did not come to the conclusion that [the defendant] was the person who indeed committed one or more of the acts of violence or other criminal acts as charged. As for being a co-perpetrator regarding the charged offences, it needs to be proven that these actions were carried out by [the defendant] consciously and in cooperation with [P3] and/or [P4].

[53]  *Mpambara* case, Chapter 10, paras. 71–74, see *supra* note 12.

as during their testimonies before the investigation judge, gave extensive information on the role of the defendant during an attack on a hospital complex in Kibuye province in Rwanda on a particular date after having heard the name of the suspect or defendant. However, they had also given testimony and statements to the ICTR and even in trials in the United States and Canada on the same attack. None of the witnesses had ever mentioned the defendant's name at all in those statements or testimonies which were taken or performed prior to the statements and testimony in the Dutch case. The witnesses were all given the opportunity to comment on the discrepancies, and based on their testimony, the Court put their information aside as being insufficiently reliable in respect of the alleged participation of the defendant in the attack.[54]

Finally, research has shown that the most reliable statements are given when the witness is able to freely narrate the story of what has happened without much intervention of the interviewer. They do not make many mistakes in their statement if they are at ease and not under pressure. If, however, pressure is exerted on witnesses to come up with answers and they are thus forced to tell as much as possible, mistakes in their account will be on the increase.[55] Certainly, when leading questions are repeated over and over again by the interviewers, the impression is easily established with the witness that he or she should affirm the assertions implied in the questions.[56] Interviewers and investigators can thus try to ensure as accurate and effective an information retrieval process as possible by being aware of these issues and adopting certain procedures. An awareness of the different stages of memory, how they work and their individual challenges will help in the design of such procedures.

### 9.5. Memory and Witness Testimony in the Context of International Crimes

The section above examined how the different phases of memory work. Here, I apply this framework to analyse issues that are commonly faced when interviewers and investigators are dealing with witnesses who are victims of international crimes. These witnesses have undergone significant trauma, speak different languages and come from different cultural backgrounds. These issues impact the phases of memory in particular ways, and give rise to specific problems that need to be addressed to ensure accurate and adequate witness testimony.

---

[54]  *Ibid.*, paras. 75–135. However, the Court of Appeal accepted the testimony of those witnesses as evidence.

[55]  Van Koppen, Hessing and Crombag (eds.), 1997, pp. 300–301, see *supra* note 27.

[56]  *Ibid.*, p. 307.

### 9.5.1. The Impact of Trauma on Witness Testimony and the Requirements of a Criminal Trial

Victims of international crimes are usually greatly traumatized by their experiences. However, I believe there is no scientific proof that witnesses who suffer from trauma are incapable of credibly recounting what they have witnessed. Even for the assumption that victims of trauma are less reliable as witnesses in criminal proceedings, I have not found scientific evidence. Certainly, they will have difficulty recounting all details of the events they went through, but I believe they are in fact very well capable of supplying key elements of the events.[57] General conclusions about the reliability of witness statements by traumatized victims cannot be given, as the ICTY and the District Court in The Hague also found.[58] However, many trial judges in criminal cases have used the argument of the assumed traumatic experiences incurred by the witnesses as a reason for the impeded memory of witnesses so as to explain shortcomings or inconsistencies in the witnesses' recount of the events. A witness in the *Karera* case at the ICTR, for example, made different statements in different interviews about his hiding place during an attack. Firstly, he stated he was hiding in the bushes. Later, he stated in full detail and extensively about hiding in a banana farm. Again later, he said he had been hiding in the grass. Finally, it appeared he hid in a ditch. Confronted with these inconsistencies, he stated he had been so afraid that he could not concentrate on where he had been hiding. The Trial Chamber in the case accepted this explanation with a reference to the assumed trauma and the inconsistencies were smoothened out.[59] The question remains, however, of why the witness had concretely stated his hiding place while, in fact, he could not remember because he was too frightened to pay attention at the time. In the same way, the Court of Appeals in The Hague in the *Hesam and Jelalzoy* case[60] has accepted discrepancies in statements by referring to the "dramatic events" without giving an explanation as to how these dramatic events had impacted the memory of the witnesses. This is even more interesting as the causal relationship between trauma and incorrect statements has never been proven.[61]

---

[57] Alexander Zahar, "Witness Memory and the Manufacture of Evidence at the International Criminal Tribunals", in Carsten Stahn and Larissa van den Herik (eds.), *Future Perspectives on International Criminal Justice*, T.M.C. Asser Press, The Hague, 2010, pp. 606–607.

[58] ICTY, *Prosecutor v. Furundžija*, Trial Chamber, Judgement, 10 December 1998, IT-95-17-T, para. 102 (https://www.legal-tools.org/doc/e6081b/); and *Mpambara* case, Chapter 6, para. 18, see *supra* note 12.

[59] ICTR, *Prosecutor v. Karera*, Trial Chamber, Judgement and Sentence, 7 December 2007, ICTR-01-74-T, para. 304 (https://www.legal-tools.org/doc/7bc57f/).

[60] *Hesam and Jelalzoy* appeal, see *supra* note 14.

[61] Zahar, 2010, p. 206, see *supra* note 57.

There is a higher likelihood that the traumatic events under investigations and the trauma incurred by witnesses have a profound impact on witnesses when statements are taken or when witnesses testify in court. No doubt witnesses will become emotional when they have to again experience the events that caused their trauma, even more so when they have to tell their stories time and time again as often happens in these investigations when only few witnesses have survived. This can trigger the prosecutor or investigator not to (re-)interview the witness or even not to ask certain questions to the witness in order to protect the well-being of that witness.

Furthermore, research[62] has shown that witnesses[63] frequently are unable or unwilling to answer whole categories of questions that are crucial in criminal investigations and trials that can be referred to as the 'what', 'who', 'where' and 'when' questions. I often refer to these questions as the 'quantitative' questions that one can answer by giving a number or a short factual description. The questions are mostly simple in nature and crucial in terms of truth-finding. They are also critical because they offer opportunities to assess the reliability of the witness statement because the information can be cross-checked. The extensive study by Professor Combs gives an abundance of examples of questions that are extremely easy to answer for Western witnesses but where international witnesses have failed: witnesses could not mention their age and made many mistakes when it came to dates, times, distances and other numerical estimates. I can confirm many of these examples with my own experience.

I remember asking a witness to estimate a certain distance in the context of what the witness had seen during an event and how far he was from what he had described. When the witness responded by saying that it was two kilometres, I asked him to estimate the same distance from where he was sitting during the hearing to an object of his choice outside the room that we could all see. When he pointed to the object, a flag post in the garden of the building in which the hearing took place, my estimate was that the very distance was not more than 100 meters. There is an endless list of such examples.

---

[62]   My observations are, apart from my own experiences, to a great extent based on the research conducted by Nancy Combs, Professor of Law at William and Mary Law School in Williamsburg, United States. Her study "Fact-finding Without Facts: The Uncertain Evidentiary Foundations for International Criminal Convictions" has been published in 2010 and is the first in its kind that thoroughly analyses the use of (witness) evidence by some of the tribunals. Nancy A. Combs, *Fact-finding Without Facts: The Uncertain Evidentiary Foundations of International Criminal Convictions*, Cambridge University Press, 2010.

[63]   Professor Combs' research is limited to the work of the ICTR, the Special Court for Sierra Leone ('SCSL') and the Special Panels for Serious Crimes ('SPSC') in the Dili District Court in East Timor.

---

Similarly, any identification of time, be it dates, hours, years, and any estimation of duration, appears to be problematic for many witnesses. A clock or watch is not common everywhere in Africa or other places in the world. Many times, the witness could give an estimation by indicating how high the sun was up or by giving a reference to where the sun was above the tree or house. Asking the witness to give a precise location is often too complicated. Many witnesses asked to elucidate their account of events by means of a map or a sketch declined to draft one or read from it. It does not make sense to them.[64] I remember I struggled with witnesses for a long time to find out which room in a certain building the witness was hiding. When asked to describe where the witness entered a building and how he went along from room to room or hall to hall, the witness was not able to put together a comprehensive picture. Left, right, forward, backward, in or besides, or other prepositions were difficult to explain or maybe difficult to translate. On top of the inability of witnesses to provide such factual or quantitative type of answers, the answers also often lack description and detail. A vague account void of details or description is an account that cannot be cross-checked and that will be difficult to challenge by the defence.

### 9.5.2. Language Disconnects and Misunderstandings

The questioning of a witness in international crimes is never smooth and straightforward. Many times, witnesses do not understand the question or have no clue as to what information is sought. Much of the terminology we use is unknown to witnesses in Africa or other areas in the world. It is extremely difficult to bring a witness to a time order or chronology. And once the witness has a reference point of time and starts narrating what has happened, there is a good chance that the witness leaves the chronology within the next three to four questions and answers these questions in a completely different time frame, which is two or three months earlier or later, while the interviewer still believes that the witness is answering the question in the original time frame. The quality of the questions is paramount here. Misunderstandings are always looming and, when they appear, it takes time to straighten them out. At the end of the day, these challenges do not categorically impair the truth-finding, provided there is a check and double check with the witness, and time to do so is abundantly available.

---

[64] See, for example, ICTR, *Prosecutor v. Elizaphan and Gérard Ntakirutimana*, Trial Chamber, Transcript, 19 September 2001, ICTR-96-10 and ICTR-96-17-T, p. 9; *Prosecutor v. Kamuhanda*, Transcript, 14 February 2002, ICTR-99-54-T, pp. 4–7 ('*Prosecutor v. Kamuhanda*'); SCSL, *Prosecutor v. Fofana and Kondewa*, Transcripts, 4 November 2004, SCSL-04-14-T, p. 38 ('*Civil Defense Forces* case'); SPSC, *Prosecutor v. Marques et al.*, Case Notes, 26 July 2001, 09/2000, p. 78 ('*Los Palos* case').

Many of the inabilities and difficulties described here can be attributed to the education, illiteracy and life experience of the witnesses, or the lack thereof. It is a reasonable assumption that the lack of education and limited verbal capabilities impair the ability of many international witnesses to express themselves accurately in answering the questions posed to them. If a witness never went to school and did not learn how to read and write, how can he or she be expected to give detailed information about distances, heights, times, *et cetera*, and be asked to give accurate estimations? For the same reason, the witness will probably not know how to read a map which needs explanation, learning and practising.

### 9.5.2.1. Language Challenges: Translation and Rare Languages

Special mention must be made of language issues and translation challenges that can impair the veracity of the witness statement, at least as it is recorded.[65] When the witness has truly and accurately observed the events, recorded what he or she witnessed in his or her memory unimpaired, and is able to retrieve and reproduce that information to the interviewer or judge during witness testimony in court, it is all in vain when the translation fails. At best, the evidence becomes nebulous and the defendant is acquitted. But what if the wrong translation contributes to a guilty verdict and the defendant is sentenced based on this faulty assessment of guilt? Language interpretation is not unique to international courtrooms or cases of international crimes. Since societies have become multi-ethnic and multi-national, interpreters have entered the courtrooms and every judge in any national system acknowledges that, however professional their work and that of the prosecution and police is, they are totally at the mercy of the interpreters. Furthermore, judges equally depend on the quality of interpreters used by the law enforcement in the investigations. I do not know of any scientific or even non-scientific research conducted on the quality of the translations in the justice process in national systems.[66] In the Netherlands, the situation has evolved from one where practically anyone could practise the profession of interpreter in a court of law to the one existing today, where rules apply to the use of interpreters and quality standards are imposed on anyone who wants to work as an interpreter. That has certainly raised the

---

[65] Apart from examples within my own experiences, a comprehensive analysis of language issues in international criminal law can be found in Robert Cryer, "Witness Evidence Before International Criminal Tribunals", in *The Law and Practice of International Courts and Tribunals*, 2003, vol. 2, no. 3, pp. 411–439; and the study by Professor Nancy Combs, mentioned above, Combs, 2010, see *supra* note 62.

[66] With the exception of the limited research mentioned by Nancy Combs in her study, see Chapter 3B and the research mentioned in footnotes there. Combs, 2010, Chapter 3B, see *supra* note 62.

level of quality of the interpreters. However, it is uncertain how many mistakes are made and what the effect of this is on the judicial outcome of a trial.

These observations apply to situations in domestic courtrooms where circumstances are relatively favourable. The prevailing situation in international tribunals is, however, far worse than that of national systems and the same is true for the adjudication of cases of international crimes in national systems. The languages used in these cases and before the international tribunals are rare or extremely rare,[67] and it is often difficult to find appropriate interpreters for them. International tribunals still have the advantage of having English and French, common languages in the world, as their official court languages. But what if these rare languages spoken by the witnesses have to be translated into Dutch, Finnish, German or a national language of even smaller countries? Where can one find such translators?

Often this leads to using double translation to obtain a translation into the target language. Double translation also occurs in international tribunals. Moreover, taking witness statements and conducting witness hearings in court trials are excruciating and long for interpreters. Often, one and the same interpreter conducts the translation throughout the whole process, with the risk of being worn out and losing concentration, which will have a negative impact on the quality of the translation. Obviously, some of the languages spoken by international witnesses in international criminal cases pose huge challenges to the translation, as shown below.

### 9.5.2.2. Translation Mistakes and a Lack of Vocabulary

First of all, translation errors occur on a regular basis. Infamous is the example of German speaking witnesses used during the Nuremburg trials in 1946 who started their answer by saying 'Ja'. Interpreters would translate this word by 'Yes' as an affirmative, which is technically correct. In reality, the witnesses used the word as a filler word which should have been translated by 'Well' or 'Uhm', meaning they were pondering the answer to come.[68] In the *Mpambara* case, a witness used an expression which was translated as 'neighbour' without placing it in the cultural context. When questioned about the use of the word 'neighbour', the witness explained that he meant anyone living in his neighbourhood and village even persons up to 30 minutes away from him.[69] In Nan-

---

[67] By way of example, in Northern Uganda, where the ICC has operated, each tribe involved in the conflict has its own language: Iteso, Lwo and Langi. Similar situations appear in Eastern DRC and in Darfur. In East Timor, at least 10 different languages exist.

[68] Joseph E. Persico, *Nuremberg: Infamy on Trial*, Penguin, New York, 1994, p. 263.

[69] *Mpambara* case, para. 54, see *supra* note 12. The quote from the witness statement is:

cy Combs' study, a whole list of examples of erroneous translations is mentioned.[70]

Apart from these errors, it has appeared in various situations before tribunals and in national systems that some languages simply do not have the same vocabulary as Western languages do. Often that is the case for legal terminology and phrases. This was encountered during the ICC investigation in Northern Uganda, in which I participated. There were no analogous words in the local languages for 'judge', 'court', 'International Criminal Court', 'defendant' and the like. Solutions had to be found to circumvent these problems and determine a phrase or explanation that was closest to the original meaning. In her study, Combs points out that, in East Timor, witnesses and defendants had no understanding of the judicial concepts of equality for the law and the like. That is particularly disturbing, as it prevents judges and the defence from explaining to the defendants what the charges being brought against them are, and ascertaining with them if they understand their rights and if their arrest was legally executed.

At the ICTR trials, in an early stage, it was determined that in Kinyarwanda, the language of Rwanda that a witnesses spoke, there was not a good translation for the word 'rape'. Reversely, the expressions used by the witnesses were translated with the word 'rape', but in reality, it was debated whether or not the wording used by the witnesses did include the use of force inherent to rape. At the end, the Trial Chamber determined in the *Akayesu* case[71] that it was correct to translate using 'rape' in light of the contextual elements.

There is a long list of examples that brings to light the dilemmas of translations in a cultural context that investigators and judges are unfamiliar with.[72] Suffice it to say that these dilemmas often disrupt the quality of the translation in such cases, certainly when the contexts and dilemmas are not recognized and understood. The various trial chambers of the ICTR have, on numerous occasions, shown their awareness of the disturbing effects of language differences on the veracity of the witness statements. The Trial Chamber in the *Rutaganda* case ruled that:

> You ask me if I call him a neighbour. I have used this word to let you know I know the man. [...] I can use the word neighbour for a person who is located somewhere else. [...]. You explain that in The Netherlands a neighbour is someone living directly next door to you. I am sorry, that hardly exists here. If someone lives in a place which is 30 minutes' walk from you, you call him neighbour. When something happens to someone, for example a wedding or death, then you can obtain that information easily. That is why we say "neighbour".

[70] Combs, 2010, Chapter 3B, see *supra* note 62.
[71] *Prosecutor v. Akayesu*, 1 June 2001, paras. 152–154, see *supra* note 48.
[72] See, for more examples, Combs, 2010, Chapter 3C, *supra* note 62.

> [...] many of the witnesses testified in Kinyarwanda and as such
> their testimonies were simultaneously translated into French and
> English. As a result, the essence of the witness' testimony was at
> times lost. Counsel questioned witnesses in either English or
> French, and these questions were simultaneously translated into
> Kinyarwanda. In some instances it was evident, after translation,
> that the witness had not understood the question.[73]

I have not seen similar reflections in similar cases in national systems,
although it is likely that situations like these have occurred.

### 9.5.3. Cultural Differences

Lastly, cultural differences hugely impact witness statements and witness hearings during trial and, thus, have to be considered when administering justice in
cases of international crimes. The relevant cultures, and their distance from
Western cultures, are very much determined by the region of the world where
the crimes have taken place and the investigation is carried out. There are a
number of cross-cutting issues, however, that apply throughout the situations
that have been or are under investigation by international tribunals and national systems.

### 9.5.3.1. The Influence of Education, Social Identity and Customs on Witness Behaviour

First of all, in many cultures in Asia and Africa, or within communities in
these continents, society focuses less on individual independence and more on
communal interdependence, and values shared consensus over individual opinions. Instead, the individuals' culture determines that they are part of a homo-
geneous group, built on ethnical, national or religious features, with the objective of supporting the rules and values of that group. Most of the time, such
cultural values affect individual identity and the ability to define one's own
identity and opinion, separate from the group. When confronted with witnesses
with such cultural backgrounds, more often than not, an investigator will find
that the witnesses have an inclination not to contradict the interviewer, but instead affirm what he or she is putting to them in their questions, or to simply
supply the information that the interviewer is seeking. This effect is often exacerbated by the fact that in many countries where these types of investigations take place, the authorities, including police and judicial officers, are
feared. Witnesses do not want to create conflicts with those officers and will
try to please them by giving the information they believe is sought by the officers.

---

[73] ICTR, *Prosecutor v. Georges Rutaganda*, Trial Chamber, Judgement, 6 December 1999,
ICTR-96-3-T, para. 23 (https://www.legal-tools.org/doc/f0dbbb/).

In combination with the above-described and -explained dangers of asking leading questions, the blending of sources in the memories of witnesses and the inability of many witnesses to spontaneously recall and recount events before police or judicial authorities in the course of criminal investigations, the need to ask open questions to witnesses is paramount. The question 'was the suspect present during the attack you were a victim of?' may seem like quite a neutral question in our Western-style investigations. Yet, in light of the notions just described, a witness from a different culture will not often respond by saying 'No' as it might be sensed by that witness that the answer will disappoint the interviewer, which the witness will want to avoid. On the same notion, I sensed during some of the hearings I conducted that the witnesses wanted to know in which case and against which defendant I came to conduct the hearing. Some witnesses even asked me. This could be indicative of the process just described and is all the reason to be cautious.

Another important consequence of cultural differences can be the behaviour of witnesses during witness statement or hearings, which can be misinterpreted by the interviewer or the judges when assessing the credibility and reliability of the witness and the information provided. In many cultures, direct eye contact is considered a sign of disrespect, which will be avoided when an individual with such a cultural background is heard as a witness, certainly when there is a hierarchy between the witness and the person leading the hearing. In Western cultures, avoiding eye contact can be taken as signs of insecurity. Misunderstanding these differences can thus easily lead to the assessment that the witness and his or her testimony are unreliable while, in fact, the assessment is culturally determined. In other cultures, people communicate with much aplomb or assurance, and they testify or give their statement with positiveness. Doubt is seen as a sign of weakness. Certainly, in cultures where masculine behaviour is dominant, men can be extremely direct and strong in their communication and behaviour. Depending on how the person expresses him or herself and behaves during his or her testimony or statement-taking, this can be taken either as a sign of a reliable statement, or as strange and aggressive behaviour and, thus, as a sign of an unreliable person or statement.

I have heard a former Afghan general as a witness in a criminal investigation. The general held a high position during the communist regime in the 1980s. His testimony was taken by a foreign judge who was hosting the hearing. On my first question, he requested the local judge's permission to make a statement, which was allowed. What followed was a long and complex monologue, performed standing, where his honour and integrity as a former army general of Afghanistan was pivotal. The scene could easily be taken as a way of avoiding answers by the witness, while, in fact, what the witness did was very consistent with his culture. Having an understanding of these cultural features and showing respect to the general and his (former) position could lead to his willingness to answer the more factual questions.

### 9.5.3.2. The Need for Cultural Sensitivity to Avoid Misinterpretation

As shown above, cultural differences impact translations and how the wording of the witnesses should be interpreted. Interviewers can easily be duped by the witness about what the latter says or means to say. I remember interviewing a witness in the framework of the ICC investigation in Northern Uganda, to establish whether she was the biological mother of her son. In the first-day interview, the witness consistently spoke about her son and recounted all the highlights of her son's birth and life: his birth, his baptism, his school, *et cetera*. A day later, it turned out that she was not his biological mother. Instead, she was the co-wife of her husband and the son was, in fact, the son of the wife of that man. When the biological mother died, as culture prescribed, the co-wife had assumed the role of the mother as if she was the son's biological mother. Practice has shown us multiple such examples.[74]

Similarly, the obsessive attention to factual and precise details is not understood in many cultures, where exaggerations are not a sign of inaccuracy or even lies, but a way of expression. Our continuing and persistent questioning about exact distances, times, description of places is clearly not understood by witnesses from other cultures and these questions often lead to impossible answers or unreliable indications, as witnesses want to avoid the embarrassment of admitting they do not know the answer. A trial judge at the ICTR was sceptical towards a witness and the reliability of the answer when the witness told the judge that the perpetrator, who had raped her, had been on top of her for four hours. Questioned about this time estimation, the witness answered: "For me, it was about four hours or maybe one year because the suffering was too much".[75] Here, the time indication was in no way meant to be precise but an expression of the intensity of the suffering.

Cultural norms and taboos can also lead to a reluctance to give information at all. In many cultures, there certainly are taboos towards representatives of other cultures, or persons who are not familiar. Victims of rape are often not forthcoming about what has happened to them, and questioning the details of a rape case is an extremely sensitive undertaking from the interviewer's perspective. If victims of rape come forward and decide to speak about what happened, they incur the risk of being stigmatized by their community,

---

[74] Combs, 2010, Chapters 3C and 3D, see *supra* note 62.
[75] ICTR, *Prosecutor v. Alfred Musema*, Appeals Chamber, Transcript, 11 March 1999, ICTR-6-13-A, p. 48 ('*Prosecutor v. Musema*') (https://www.legal-tools.org/doc/baa0e9/).

which will certainly learn about it. I remember a situation in Northern Uganda where a victim of rape was being interviewed and completely denied having been raped while there were clear indications that she was. It appeared that the presence of her father during the interview, following a policy decision in the Office of the Prosecutor, caused great embarrassment for her, as she had not yet told her parents about the rape. Policies in tribunals dictate that victims of sexual crimes are first assessed before being interviewed and that counsel is present to assist the witness when necessary. Victims of sexual crimes are often offered a choice to be interviewed by a male or female interviewer.

### 9.5.3.3. Being Aware of Traditions of Oral Culture: A Lack of Sourcing

A last feature of the cultural differences already indicated above is the lack of sourcing by the witness of the information given during his or her statement or hearing. Certainly, in oral cultures, the distinction between what the witness eye-witnessed and what he or she heard from others is routinely not made. In oral cultures, the knowledge of one person is the truth for all.[76] Even when explicitly requesting the witness about whether the witness saw what was described or whether the witness had heard it from others, often the distinction is still not made. Here, however, and that is also my experience, when the interviewer respectfully but clearly and persistently requests the witness to tell whether what the witness told was seen with his or her own eyes or was told by others, the witness is very well capable of doing so.[77] The Court of Appeal in The Hague, in the *Kouwenhoven* case, observed that witnesses "have seemingly difficulties in being able to distinct between their own visual observations and what they have heard from third persons. Also for that reason a general picture emerges wherein reality and imagination seem to blend together".[78] The judges in the *Mpambara* case considered, in the framework of how to assess reliability of the witnesses, that the court will "examine whether the witnesses have been able to distinguish between what they saw themselves and what they heard from others".[79]

---

[76] See, for concrete examples of witness testimony alluding to this phenomenon, *Prosecutor v. Kamuhanda*, p. 41, see *supra* note 64; and *Prosecutor v. Musema*, para. 103, see *supra* note 75.

[77] ICTR, *Prosecutor v. Akayesu*, Trial Chamber, Transcript, 4 February 1997, ICTR-96-4-T, pp. 39–40 ('*Prosecutor v. Akayesu*, 4 February 1997') (expert witness Ruzindana).

[78] *Kouwenhoven* appeal, paras. 9–15, see *supra* note 15 (sic.).

[79] *Mpambara* case, Chapter 6, para. 17, see *supra* note 12.

In the *Akayesu* case before the ICTR, the trial judges were presented with an expert witness on language and cultural facets of Rwanda.[80] The judges took this expert testimony into considerations by ruling:

> According to the testimony of Dr. Ruzindana, it is a particular feature of the Rwandan culture that people are not always direct in answering questions, especially if the question is delicate. In such cases, the answers given will very often have to be 'decoded' in order to be understood correctly. This interpretation will rely on the context, the particular speech community, the identity of and the relation between the orator and the listener, and the subject matter of the question.[81]

Witness testimony poses certain challenges when investigating international crimes because these witnesses are traumatized, speak different languages and come from different cultural backgrounds. To effectively address this, there is a need to be aware of and to understand the underlying reasons, as set out above. There is a need for judges to openly recognize and transparently discuss this, so as to avoid further misunderstanding, which calls for a high level of professionalism and awareness on the part of adjudicators.

## 9.6. The Role of Professionals in Processing Witness Testimony in the Investigation and Prosecution of International Crimes

The sections above discussed evidential difficulties associated with the investigation and prosecution of international crimes, specifically with respect to retrieving statements or testimonies from witnesses. There are a number of professionals involved in this process, which comprises several stages. It is important to be aware of the different challenges encountered by different professionals at various stages of the investigative and prosecutorial process. There continues to be insufficient discussion on the role of the individual professional involved in the criminal procedure leading up to the trial of a defendant and the critical determinations that the judges have to make, namely, to determine the guilt or innocence of the defendant. This should be remedied because the mindset of and work done by these professionals are critical to the outcome of the investigations and prosecutions of international crimes.

---

[80] *Prosecutor v. Akayesu*, 4 February 1997, pp. 39–40, see *supra* note 77 (expert witness Ruzindana).

[81] ICTR, *Prosecutor v. Akayesu*, Trial Chamber, Judgement, 2 September 1998, ICTR-96-4-T, para. 156 (https://www.legal-tools.org/doc/b8d7bd/).

### 9.6.1. Investigators of International Crimes: The Taking of Witness Statements in a Sensitive and Unbiased Manner

Investigators are usually the first who encounter the witnesses and request their information during the interview and the taking of the statement. How they will conduct an interview may determine the outcome of a case. A witness who possesses crucial information for the case is not a guarantee of a successful prosecution if the information is not professionally taken by the investigators and recorded in a statement. It is obvious that investigators interviewing witnesses in this context need to be aware of the challenges and pitfalls as described above. If they fall into one or more of these pitfalls, the result can be devastating. If they manage well, there may be a basis for at least establishing the truth and a successful prosecution.

Investigators can suffer from bias. Certainly, during investigations in national systems, the target or suspect is known from the beginning. It is often the only reason why the investigation is carried out, as the suspect triggers the jurisdiction in his or her role as either a national or a person residing in a territory. The strong focus on the individual suspect by investigators, even unwittingly, *vis-à-vis* the crimes that have been committed, can lead to a preoccupation during an interview that influences the witness, and leads to unreliable information. A question made to the witness early on during an interview such as 'we are investigating the role of Mr. X in the crimes that have been committed in this area. What can you tell us about his role?' is clearly a disastrous question, in light of the witness-related issues described above. But mistakes in this respect can be more implied than given in the example. Furthermore, investigators need a host of other skills and qualities: excellent writing skills; cultural sensitivity; a genuine care for the witnesses, including for their safety and social and psychological well-being; gender awareness; and knowledge of the field of operations and its political and social contexts. These are all crucial to obtaining a high-quality witness statement.

### 9.6.2. Prosecutors or Trial Attorneys of International Crimes: Case Consolidation From Witness Interviews

Prosecutors also play a very important role. Prosecutors must effectively direct the investigators, including those who conduct the interviews, to avoid misunderstandings and mistakes. The prosecutor needs to set clear guidelines as to the topics to be covered during witness interviews and the information needed to build the case. The prosecutor is the pivotal individual professional in constructing the case from a legal perspective while ascertaining the information needed to build that case is acquired, for example, from witness interviews. Investigators who conduct witness interviews must have received instructions and training about the legal requirements of the case and how to collect information based on these requirements. Finally, the prosecutor needs to present the case to the trial chamber convincingly, which presupposes the prosecutor's complete knowledge of the case and of how to translate factual information into the legal charging of the defendant.

### 9.6.3. The Role of the Judges in Adjudicating International Crimes

Judges exercise several important functions in every case, one of which is ensuring the defendant's due process rights. International law guarantees certain rights of the defendant, and their exercise should be protected by the judge. These rights include the right to cross-examination or questioning of the witnesses presented by the prosecution, and the presenting of exculpatory evidence to the judges. There are various ways in which these rights are exercised in conformity with the respective legal systems. In international tribunals, the witnesses are brought before the trial chambers and questioned by the judges, the prosecution and the defence. In some national systems, the same rules apply, but in other countries, the trial judges take depositions in the field, more specifically at the location where the witness lives or resides.[82] In other, more civil law countries, an investigative judge or examining magistrate, who cannot be part of the trial proceedings, is in charge of hearing the witnesses in preparation of the trial and conducting these hearings either in his or her office or in the field, in co-operation with the state where the witness is located. In any event, these hearings and cross-examinations are critical for the outcome of the case. In all cases, these hearings will test the witnesses. Discrepancies in witness hearings and earlier statements form the brunt of the deliberations by the judges in their rulings,[83] which can lead to the disqualification of witnesses, or their acceptance with reasoning as to why the discrepancies were no reason for disqualification.

Suffice it to say that these hearings are problematic for the witnesses, as they have to be traumatized again for the purpose of the adjudication of the cases. Moreover, all the challenges described above also apply to these hearings. Consequently, the participants in these hearings, the judges, the prosecutor and the defence need to be cognizant of these challenges, and have the ca-

---

[82] An example of a trial judge taking depositions in the field can be found in the Canada, Superior Court, Montréal, *Prosecutor v. Désiré Munyaneza*, Verdict, 22 May 2009, Case No. 500-73-002500-052 ('*Prosecutor v. Désiré Munyaneza*') (https://www.legal-tools.org/doc/c9d203/). The case was adjudicated by a single judge, the Honourable André Denis, J.S.C. who conducted a number of hearings in Rwanda and Tanzania. Munyaneza was sentenced to life imprisonment on 29 October 2009 (https://www.legal-tools.org/doc/81e956/).

[83] Combs, 2010, Chapter 7, see *supra* note 62.

pability to deal with them. Clearly, there is a crucial role to be played by the judges – both trial and investigating judges, if applicable – in securing both a fair trial and the rights of the defence, as well as ascertaining that the exercise is faithful to truth-finding with respect to the witnesses, as truth-finding forms the basis of the main responsibility of the judges: to determine the guilt or innocence of the defendant.

## 9.7. The National Jurisdiction: The Dutch Effort

### 9.7.1. Introduction

The challenges described above can only be faced and properly addressed when there is an awareness of them and a well-developed system, wherein these challenges can be assessed, analysed and addressed.

International tribunals, generally, are well designed to meet those challenges and, within their institutions, resources have been created to organize the proper response to meet the challenges. National jurisdictions vary widely in scope, size and quality and, therefore, in my view, they are much more vulnerable to failing to meet the challenges described. Yes, national jurisdictions feel the need and obligation to establish universal jurisdiction and start investigations, prosecutions and trials of international crimes, but they often have to acknowledge that these efforts come with a responsibility, and realize that the journey overwhelms them. Can they meet the challenges? Let me lead the reader into the Dutch effort.

### 9.7.2. Universal Jurisdiction

As has been mentioned earlier,[84] many national jurisdictions have established some form of universal jurisdiction for international crimes, thus enabling the prosecution and adjudication of these crimes in their courts.[85] This complements[86] universal jurisdiction, established by the Rome Statute, which forms

---

[84] See *supra* note 5.

[85] Recent research shows how many countries around the world have criminalized one or more of the international crimes under the Rome Statute and whether they have established universal jurisdiction for those crimes, see the project by the Clooney Foundation for Justice, "Justice Beyond Borders" (available on its web site). TRIAL also has documented cases in national jurisdiction exercising universal jurisdiction: TRIAL International, "Universal Jurisdiction Annual Review 2023" (https://www.legal-tools.org/doc/7d9oyf/).

[86] In fact, the Rome Statute, in its Preamble, calls on all states to establish jurisdiction for the international crimes listed in the Statute and explicitly emphasizes that the ICC shall be complementary to national criminal jurisdictions. More importantly, the principle of complementarity is made an admissibility issue in Article 17 of the Rome Statute, thus emphasizing that the first responsibility for ending impunity is with the states which created and signed on to the Rome Statute.

the basis of the ICC, aimed at bringing the most responsible persons for these crimes to justice.

There is no doubt that these provisions are a critical and determining factor in bringing about a credible deterrent for perpetrators of these crimes, wherever they are. Not only will the higher-level perpetrators know that they run a substantial risk of ending up in the dock in The Hague to respond to charges of international crimes; but any person who has been involved in international crimes can be prosecuted in any country that has established universal jurisdiction over such crimes.

### 9.7.3. The Dutch Effort

### 9.7.3.1. Overview

The Dutch government established universal jurisdiction for certain international crimes in the aftermath of World War II, when the first international treaties were established. By implementing these treaties in their national law, limited universal jurisdiction was created for the crime of genocide, from 1970 onwards; for torture, from 1989; and for war crimes, from 1952. Until the beginning of the new century, no significant investigations or trials were initiated.

With the signing of the Rome Statute and the obligations that ensued from it, there was a dramatic shift. This event, but above all, the fact that the seat of the ICC was established in The Hague, made the Dutch government realize that they should be in the forefront of implementing the Rome Statute in their national legislation. This also meant that they had to be serious in enforcing the law, meaning that they needed to take measures to ensure that investigations were carried out and that trials could be held in the Dutch courts.

On 1 October 2003, the Dutch International Crimes Act became effective.[87] For crimes committed before that date, the older laws, mentioned above, remained applicable.

Since the beginning of the century, a new and specialized investigation team became operational and has carried out multiple investigations. Trials ensued in the years thereafter. Until this date, the courts have rendered verdicts in more than a dozen cases. The cases ranged from a member of the military junta in Ethiopia, the Dergue, and members of the Afghan regime in the 1970s, to Dutch businessmen charged with complicity for the delivery of weapons or chemicals, to Rwandan nationals in the context of the Rwandan genocide, and

---

[87] The Netherlands, Act of 19 June 2003 Containing Rules Concerning Serious Violations of International Humanitarian Law ('International Crimes Act'), 19 June 2003 (https://www.legal-tools.org/doc/1f99a7/).

finally to the alleged leadership of the Tamil Tigers of Sri Lanka in the Netherlands.

### 9.7.3.2. The Legal Toolbox

Any credible national system, capable of handling cases of international crimes, starts with a comprehensive and usable set of legal provisions. A filled legal toolbox is a precondition for both criminal investigations that match the seriousness of the crimes that actually took place and an effective prosecution.

Before the International Crimes Act became effective in 2003, only the crimes of torture, genocide and war crimes could be tried in Dutch courts, and with a limited jurisdiction. Although the implementation laws for war crimes and torture did not limit universal jurisdiction, the Supreme Court of the Netherlands, in the application of these laws, has limited universal jurisdiction for these crimes to cases where the defendant or the victim had Dutch nationality, or where the defendant was physically present on the territory of the Netherlands. Universal jurisdiction for genocide was limited by law to cases where the defendant or the victim had Dutch nationality.

All this changed when the International Crimes Act became effective in 2003. Now, nearly all the crimes mentioned in the Rome Statute, the crimes of torture and enforced disappearance, are punishable within the Dutch jurisdiction. Universal jurisdiction was limited by law in the sense that only when the defendant or victim was a Dutch national, or the defendant from any nationality was physically present on Dutch territory, was the Dutch court competent to try these cases, therewith creating the legal opportunity for the prosecutor to initiate a criminal investigation and use all investigative methods regulated by Dutch law.

This situation was short-lived when, in 2006, a Rwandan national living in the Netherlands was arrested for his alleged involvement in the Rwandan genocide, the above-mentioned Joseph Mpambara. There did not seem to be a *prima facie* jurisdiction in his case as the man, not a Dutch national, was charged with acts committed before the entry into force of the International Crimes Act, and the Act was not made to work retroactively. Nevertheless, the prosecutor charged him with, among other things, direct perpetration of the genocide in his area of operation, using various and complicated legal reasoning to circumvent the fact that there was no direct basis for jurisdiction to charge him with genocide. The Supreme Court of the Netherlands rejected claims by the prosecution that they were competent to try the accused for genocide and, consequently, the defendant was charged with war crimes and torture. The District Court in The Hague convicted the accused for torture, whilst acknowledging that the man *de facto* had participated in the genocide.[88] The Court of Appeal convicted the defendant of war crimes.[89]

Although the Court of Appeal reversed the ruling and convicted Mpambara of war crimes, the peculiar situation led the government to amend its legislation in this respect after it had barely existed, and made the genocide provisions in the International Crimes Act retroactive until 1970, the year in which the implementation law of the Genocide Convention finally became effective.

Another major development was the incorporation, into the International Crimes Act of 2003, of the crime of enforced disappearance as a separate crime on 1 January 2011.[90] By making this crime punishable as an international crime, the Dutch government fulfilled its obligation under the International Convention for the Protection of All Persons Against Enforced Disappearance.[91]

In 2013 a number of common crimes, such as incitement, participating in a criminal organization, handling criminal goods and money laundering, when committed in relation to international crimes, became international crimes themselves rather than common crimes, with matching maximum sentences. Certainly, it can be concluded that the legal toolbox under Dutch law is considerable.

### 9.7.3.3. Organization and Resources

### 9.7.3.3.1. Police Organization

The existence of the legal possibility to charge defendants with international crimes does not itself make a system effective. It comes down to enforcement, or real-time criminal investigations at a professional level, which enable the prosecution to lay charges and start the process of prosecution in a court of law. After a difficult start, that is exactly what the Dutch authorities have been able to do, fulfilling the obligation it felt after deciding to host the ICC and implementing the Rome Statute expeditiously.

The International Crimes Team ('TIM'),[92] which is conducting the criminal investigations of international crimes, is a separate unit within the Criminal Investigations Division of the Dutch National Police Force. The unit has

---

[88] *Mpambara* case, Chapter 6, para. 17, see *supra* note 12.

[89] *Ibid.*

[90] Since the International Crimes Act became effective in October 2003, the crime of enforced disappearance is punishable as a crime against humanity.

[91] The International Convention for the Protection of All Persons Against Enforced Disappearances, 20 December 2006 (https://www.legal-tools.org/doc/0d0674/).

[92] More information is available on the page dedicated to TIM on the web site of the Dutch Police, "Team Internationale Misdrijven".

approximately 43 staff members, and consists of a variety of criminal investigations expertise which is needed to be able to investigate the full scope of international crimes. Apart from regular investigators, the team includes financial investigators, forensic experts, analysts and a historian. Being part of the wider Investigation Division, the team enjoys the support of other investigative expertise, such as surveillance and technical surveillance, including the capacity to intercept telephone calls and other conversations, undercover operations, *et cetera*. Recently, the team has hired Arabic speakers and OSINT specialists.[93]

### 9.7.3.3.2. The Prosecution Service and the Role of Victims

Cases of international crimes are the responsibility of the national office of the Public Prosecution Service in the Netherlands. The Office also has a special team responsible for the criminal investigation and prosecution of cases of international crimes and all related matters, such as international mutual legal assistance. The team, at the time of writing, has three specialized (and senior) public prosecutors, an appeals prosecutor, two legal assistants, a legal expert, an historian and administrative staff.

I should also point out that the position of victims in criminal proceedings in cases of international crimes is paramount for the way the truth is investigated and the charges are brought. Traditionally, the position of a victim in a criminal proceeding is non-existent or, at best, weak. However, recently, such position has been strengthened. In Dutch criminal proceedings, victims can lodge a claim against the defendant for compensation for harm inflicted upon them, albeit under restrictions. Secondly, more recently, victims have been granted the right to appear and address the court in a full statement how they view the case, in particular about the way in which the crime has impacted their personal life. In court proceedings where cases of international crimes are adjudicated, victims have indeed used these rights. Courts schedule certain days during the proceedings especially for the victims, and provide ample time for the victims to express themselves and make themselves heard. Often, victims are represented by lawyers specialized in these cases. Those days are the most dramatic and impressive days of the trial.

One of the conditions, however, for a trial judge to decide upon a victim's claim for compensation, is that the claim may not be complicated because it would delay the criminal proceedings. In recent international crimes cases, the trial judges have ruled that the claims brought against a defendant

---

[93] Recently, the OSINT investigators were able to track a substantial number of missing Ukrainian children using open sources: "Missing Ukrainian Children Located in Dutch Co-ordinated Effort", *DutchNews*, 9 February 2024.

were complicated and therefore denied them.[94] Consequently, in some cases, victims of international crimes have no access to criminal proceedings for their compensation claims, and have to rely on excruciatingly slow and costly civil court cases. What makes these claims additionally complicated for courts is the fact they have to apply foreign law. With regards to victims having a role in criminal proceedings to influence the scope of the case or truth-finding, national systems are averse to accepting such a role. The ICC adopted a different approach, and the Rome Statute provides for a progressive system of victims' rights. Case law will have to show what the actual role of the victims will be.[95]

### 9.7.3.3.3. Co-operation With Other Services

More important than resources or the number of staff in a team is the idea that effective investigations and prosecutions cannot take place without co-operation with other services. One of the most valuable partners in investigating international crimes is the Dutch Immigration Service ('IND'). All requests for asylum in the Netherlands are handled by this service and the IND creates a file for every single asylum seeker in the country.

Following Dutch immigration law, based on the 1951 Convention relating to the Status of Refugees, any person against whom there is a suspicion that he or she has committed an international crime is exempted from entering the process of asylum seeking. The IND creates a file of any of these cases, and is under the obligation to transfer these files to the Prosecution Service for review.

Needless to say, these files create a wealth of information about possible cases of international crimes, and are often the basis for initiating a criminal investigation and prosecution.

The Prosecution Service has formed a task force for international crimes in which the Prosecution Service, the Police, the Ministry of Justice, the Ministry of Foreign Affairs and the IND are represented and where all issues regarding international crimes and how to co-operate are discussed.

Noteworthy in this context is the effort by the Ministry of Foreign Affairs of the Netherlands, in co-operation with other countries, to establish a Multilateral Treaty on Legal Cooperation and Extradition for International

---

[94] *Van Anraat* case, see *supra* note 16. More recently in the *Mustafa case, supra* note 19.
[95] In the ICC case against Thomas Lubanga, the victims have successfully pleaded to the trial judges to expand the scope of the case to other crimes than charged by the Prosecutor.

Crimes, which was concluded by a signing ceremony at the Peace Palace in The Hague on 14 February 2024.[96]

### 9.7.3.3.4. The District Court

Under the provisions of the International Crimes Act, the District Court in The Hague is exclusively competent to try cases of international crimes. The investigation judge, who cannot, by law, participate in the trials, is part of the District Court in The Hague. The law made the District Court in The Hague uniquely competent in these cases for two obvious reasons: one court is more capable of developing experience and expertise in these matters, and The Hague is the international city of justice. It would have been strange if the government of the Netherlands had chosen another city in the country, whose court would handle such cases.

Within the District Court in The Hague, there is not one chamber that is dedicated full-time to the trials of cases of international crimes. There just are not sufficient cases to have a permanent chamber. Instead, the District Court has chosen to select a number of the most experienced and knowledgeable trial judges who are appointed for certain cases and trials, once the prosecutor has brought the case before the court by bringing charges against the defendant.

Once the case is brought to court, the pre-trial judicial investigation, conducted by the investigation judge, commences and it is not before a date for the trial is set that the trial judges are taken out of their roster obligations, and start preparing for the trial by reading the files in the dossier. Normally, trial judges are freed of their regular duties for about six months for a case of international crimes, including the trial itself and the drafting of a written verdict. This may not seem like a lot of time, but it puts a tremendous burden on the rest of the trial judges, who adjudicate all other cases.

The trial judges have a number of court clerks, available to handle all organizational matters surrounding the trial, and legal officers specialized in international criminal law. In the appeals phase, the Court of Appeals in The Hague retries the case[97] and, if necessary, additional investigations can be performed, normally by the investigation judge. Similar arrangements are availa-

---

[96] See "Over 30 Countries Sign New War Crime Treaty in The Hague", *NL Times*, 14 February 2014. For a summary of how the Treaty works: Leila N. Sadat, "Understanding the New Convention on Mutual Legal Assistance for International Atrocity Crimes", in *ASIL Insight*, 2023, vol. 27, no. 2.

[97] Under Dutch criminal procedural law, the case on appeal is not limited to legal considerations, but the evidence is reviewed by the trial judges in full range. New evidence can be introduced by the parties, who can decide to limit the scope of the appeal.

ble for the trial judges in appeal as described for the trial judges in first instance.

Over the years, the District Court in The Hague has acknowledged that the investigation judge, whose responsibility it is to investigate the cases pretrial, which entails the hearing of most of the witnesses outside the trial, often in their country of residence, is a specialized function that requires a full-time judge. Since 2008, such an investigation judge has been appointed[98] and he or she has a staff of two legal officers, two clerks and one administrative assistant to organize the work.

Apart from requiring sufficient resources, the position of trial judges under Dutch legal rules can also be problematic in some respects. They are not competent to view the crime scenes in the countries where the crimes occurred, because the law does not allow them to travel outside their territorial jurisdiction and view the crime scene. Nor do they hear witnesses themselves in those countries, but rely on the work of the investigation judge. Again, this position very much follows from the provisions in the law, and may be different in each country even within Europe, irrespective of whether they have a common law or civil law system. For instance, in 2009, a court in Finland tried a suspect allegedly involved in the Rwandan genocide in 1994. For this purpose, the judges heard most of the witnesses themselves, in Rwanda, and moved the whole court to Rwanda.[99] In 2021 and 2023, Finnish courts travelled to Liberia to hear witnesses in a case against a Sierra Leonean rebel commander.[100] We can assume that the way in which trial judges are involved in truth-finding during trial impacts on the outcome of the case.

### 9.7.3.3.5. Defence

Truth-finding, as it stands under the Dutch legal rules, is very much the responsibility of the police investigators and the investigation judge. The defence does not play an active role. I do not envy the defence attorneys in cases of international crimes. They will feel the need to find exonerating evidence for their client to balance the investigation of the police. This evidence can only be found under the same circumstances and with the same challenges applicable to the police investigators and the investigation judge.

---

[98] I was the first person appointed as such. Earlier, several investigation judges had heard witnesses in the same case. My successor took over in 2013. Currently, there are two specialized investigation judges.

[99] "Finnish Genocide Trial in Rwanda", *BBC News*, 16 September 2009.

[100] See Thierry Cruvellier, "Massaquoi Case: Finnish Court of Appeal Arrives in Liberia", *Justice Info*, 27 January 2023.

This means, automatically, that the defence will have to access the countries where the crimes have taken place, and will need time to investigate. Under Dutch law, the defence's resources are very limited. Normally, the defendant is entitled to one defence attorney, and regulations do not provide for long, extensive investigative trips to far-away countries. As a matter of fact, the regulations concerning defence rights do not distinguish between the types of cases, and do not provide for more than one defence attorney in international crimes cases, as in any other case.[101] Consequently, the defence attorney will not be able to travel and investigate unless their clients provide the money to do so.[102] This is not the situation in every country, though, as every national system has its own rules. In an older case in Canada,[103] the defendant was provided with three counsel, funds for rogatory commissions, normal disbursements, transcription services and expense money for the attendance of defence witnesses at trial. These provisions were provided by the Attorney General of Canada based on case law by Canadian courts.[104] In civil law countries, however, the situation will resemble what is applicable in the Netherlands. It has been pointed out that this situation is quite divergent from the defendants' rights in this respect within international tribunals. There, the defendant is entitled to a defence team, including a defence investigator, as well as a budget and support from the Registry. In some tribunals, there is a defence office.

It is equally important that defence attorneys in cases of international crimes are sufficiently equipped and knowledgeable about how to handle these cases and hear the witnesses. In the Netherlands, there are just a handful of qualified defence attorneys capable of presenting a credible defence in cases of international crimes. Often, these attorneys have prior experience in these types of cases, and some even have experience before international tribunals.

The International Crimes Act mentioned above does not provide for procedural rules. Instead, the criminal procedural rules, as enshrined in the Criminal Procedure Act, are applicable in cases of international crimes as well. This means that defence attorneys can exercise defence rights similar to their rights in ordinary cases. They will not be automatically entitled to a budget or a defence team, as there is no basis for these provisions in the Criminal Proce-

---

[101] However, two defence attorneys can be appointed to the case, but they will be paid by the amount of work they do in the case based on a very complex fee system.
[102] In some cases, defence attorneys have been provided small amounts of advance money for investigative work, which they need to claim back and justify after the case is concluded with the risk it is not awarded.
[103] *Prosecutor v. Désiré Munyaneza*, see *supra* note 82.
[104] Court of Appeal for Ontario, *R. v. Rowbotham*, Judgement, 21 March 1988, CanLII 147 (ON CA) (https://www.legal-tools.org/doc/ydpw1l/).

dure Act, and their capabilities to present defence witnesses or other exculpatory evidence depends on their personal, hard work in the case, and on what the court grants them in these particular circumstances. Defence attorneys can address the investigation judge or the court itself to request additional investigations which they deem necessary in the interest of their clients and, even then, they are still dependant on what the investigation judge or the trial judges rule on their requests.

### 9.7.3.4. Expertise

As mentioned before, every participant in the criminal justice process, leading up to and including the trials, needs specific knowledge, experience and skills to effectively play his or her role, certainly when hearing witnesses. Accruing this knowledge, experience and skill is necessary, but not easy, at the same time.

First of all, it is appropriate to assess that there are no generally agreed and concluded standards of investigations of international crimes. A traditional handbook with globally agreed standards outlining how to investigate these crimes has yet to be published.[105]

Consequently, due to a lack of generally agreed standards, there is no global, authoritative training course where all investigators and any other person with a role or responsibility in international crimes can resort to, and get up to standard.[106] It is equally important to assess that, to my knowledge, there has never been a judicial body, international tribunal or national court, which has set any standard of investigations in their verdict, against which they will measure the evidence presented by the prosecution or defence.

Within the Dutch judicial system, there is a struggle to have people trained and develop expertise. The Dutch Police Academy developed a training course for international crimes and combined it with training investigators specialized in terrorism-related investigations, but it appeared hard to create the right modules and level of training. The management of the Team Interna-

---

[105] Obviously, there are a good number of investigation handbooks available. Under the auspices of the UN Office of the High Commissioner for Human Rights a number of handbooks have been published see, for example, *Commissions of Inquiry and Fact-Finding Missions on International Human Rights and Humanitarian Law: Guidance and Practice*, New York and Geneva, 2015 (https://www.legal-tools.org/doc/kj1rsd/). Many non-governmental organizations have published investigation handbooks, often dealing with specialized topics such as sexual crimes.

[106] It is fair to mention the existence of the International Institute of Criminal Investigations ('IICI'), which offer courses for investigators of international crimes. International tribunals, however, tend to train their investigators in-house.

tional Crimes at the Dutch Police has sent their investigators to the courses offered by the International Institute of Criminal Investigations.

Within the judiciary, the training institute for prosecutors and judges, known by its acronym 'SSR', developed training for every staff member, including prosecutors and judges, in the field of international crimes, where participants are also trained in judicial aspects of prosecuting and adjudicating cases of international crimes.

Lastly, some of the universities in the Netherlands have developed classes and Master's studies in the field of international criminal law, with some specializing in the role of the tribunals. The Free University in Amsterdam initiated a Master's degree in criminology in the field of international crimes,[107] and organizes workshops discussing how academic research can assist the prosecution or adjudication of these cases in international tribunals or national courts. There is a fair share of co-operation between the Prosecution Service as well as the Court with academics.

### 9.7.3.5. Challenges

The picture described above appears quite positive, and the effort that the Dutch authorities have put into creating a credible system of criminal justice to handle cases of international crimes is certainly impressive. However, there remain many challenges for all practitioners involved in cases of international crimes at the national level.

The police struggle to keep their investigators on board and ensure sufficient continuity in their investigations over a longer period of time. In reality, many investigators, for all sorts of reasons, leave the team to pursue another career and, consequently, the expertise is lost, sometimes even before it is fully accrued.

Investigations of international crimes continue over many years and trials take a long time, certainly when it is considered that there is an appeal in almost every case of international crimes. Although the efficiency of national systems seems to be a little better than the international tribunals, where cases can take up to 10 years, the length of the judicial process in these cases leads to all sorts of challenges, including the fact that investigators and prosecutors are replaced in the course of the cases, and expertise and knowledge are lost.

The management within the Police force and Prosecution Service needs to accept that any result will take many years to emerge, and will hardly con-

---

[107] The programme of the Master's is available on the web site of the Free University of Amsterdam.

tribute to the favourable statistics that nowadays dominate management and politics.

The courts equally face the challenge of working efficiently and producing as many verdicts as possible within a certain year. Cases of international crimes do not help very much to achieve this efficiency. Judges, who are taken out of a roster to work on a case of international crimes for an extended period of time, cannot produce a verdict in another case. Management, therefore, tries to limit the time that judges are given to work on such cases.

One can genuinely question whether three judges and a couple of assistants can truly process all the information produced in a case involving international crimes. First of all, there are thousands of pages of transcripts of witness hearings, and then the need to analyse them to a full extent. On top of this, judges in national courts are, more often than once, confronted with complex legal issues, no different from the ones international judges deal with. Judges in national courts also need to ascertain that they are not only proficient in national law, but also need to know the state of affairs in international criminal law and the case law of the tribunals, as they will have to interpret their national law with the help of international criminal law and international case law. This is a not a small task and responsibility. It appeals greatly to the intelligence and skills of judges and prosecutors as well, and puts pressure on their time-management.

Defence attorneys face equal challenges. Sometimes they work these cases by themselves. In many instances, they are funded to work with two attorneys on a case, but it depends on their offices whether they really can free up two defence attorneys continuously. Generally, defence attorneys are not supplied with a budget to investigate the case. As highlighted above, on rare occasions, the court will grant them relatively small amounts of money for defence work,[108] which allows the defence at least to travel and hire an investigator to approach defence witnesses. Needless to say, under national criminal procedure, the defence faces huge challenges to present a credible defence in trial.

Mention must be made of a provision in Dutch criminal procedural law which does not allow trial judges to view the locations where the crimes have taken place if these locations are situated outside the limits of the geographical area for which the court is competent, thus certainly when the locations are abroad. This leads to the extraordinary situation where the trial judges in the District Court in The Hague not only do not hear and see the witnesses testi-

---

[108] In the case before the District Court in The Hague against *Yvonne Ntacyobatabara*, see *supra* note 13, the defence was granted EUR 15,000 for their defence work.

fy,[109] but also do not have the chance to see where the crimes took place or any other relevant location in the investigation. Instead, they rely on the transcripts of the witness hearings and how the police and the investigation judge have visualized the locations relevant to the investigations.

All these observations lead to the general question of whether the lack of pertinent criminal procedural law impedes a fair and proper trial and the ability of judges, trial judges in the first place, to adjudicate cases of international crimes at a sufficiently professional level.

The government of the Netherlands, when implementing the Rome Statute in the national legislation, more specifically the International Crimes Act, chose not to implement different criminal procedural rules with the reasoning that it was not necessary, and that it would confuse the trial judges as they would have to work with two different sets of criminal procedural rules. That is certainly a serious argument, but over the years, with all the experiences in the investigations and trials of international crimes available, I could imagine this issue being revisited and reconsidered.

## 9.8. Reflections on Truth-Finding and Conclusion

I cannot conclude this chapter without reflecting on what this chapter is all about: truth-finding. Every practitioner will acknowledge that pursuing justice in cases of international crimes is ultimately about truth-finding, but we may all mean different things. Victims often speak about their desire to know what actually happened to their relatives when those relatives have lost their lives. Investigators tell witnesses, at the start of the interview, that they want to hear the truth. Witnesses sometimes swear oaths to only tell 'the truth, the whole truth and nothing but the truth'. I have heard defendants complain about the outcomes of investigations and trials, claiming that the truth had not come out. They have their truth. Historians pursue holistic truths, drawing broad lines in history.

This consideration leads to question whether there is an objective, all-encompassing truth, whose authority is it to establish it, or whether we are allowed to have our own truths. Yet, criminal justice is highly ambitious in that justice based on the truth is its *raison d'être*, the very reason it exists.[110] We

---

[109] Under Dutch law, the investigation judge will hear almost all witnesses, unless there are specific requests from the parties to hear a witness in court or when the trial judges *proprio motu* decided to hear witnesses in court.

[110] Sergey Vasiliev, in his 2014 Ph.D. thesis, has given an excellent analysis on truth-finding and international criminal justice, specifically in regard to the ambition of the tribunals. See Sergei Vasiliev, *International Criminal Trials: A Normative Theory*, Ph.D. thesis, University of Amsterdam, 2014, Chapter 5.

may risk losing ourselves in the arduous task of establishing the most comprehensive truths in criminal cases. I believe courts, specifically, need to keep their feet on the ground, their focus on the charge presented to them by the prosecution, and, first and foremost, dedicate all their intellectual powers in answering the question: can the facts alleged be proven on the basis of the evidence presented? Truth is facts in criminal cases. It seems unfairly restricted, but there is no alternative. The next question is: how do we do that?

In this chapter, I have laid out how the quest for the facts in criminal cases of international crimes is fraught with obstacles, which may prevent us from finding reliable evidence to establish the facts that matter, and blind us in seeing the truth. But that awareness, combined with applying the right techniques, can overcome these obstacles. In fact, that is merely part of the solution. We often overlook other obstacles, even personal, psychological or politically-driven impediments. I will briefly identify a few.

First, every person who pursues the truth, or the establishment of facts for that matter, needs to have the mindset, the skills and even the desire to exactly do that. It requires neutrality, impartiality and objectivity.[111] An almost unsurmountable set of qualifications.

This leads to the fascinating question of which party in a criminal trial is best positioned to pursue the truth, establish facts and conduct the investigation. There is a debate among academics about this question, pivoting at the issue of whether the parties in a criminal trial are best positioned for that task, or whether judges need to take an active role even to the extent of having an independent investigation judge leading the hearings and conducting other investigations. In other words: is truth-finding better served in an adversarial or non-adversarial legal system?[112] Being moulded in a non-adversarial system, and having served as an investigation judge in international crimes for years, I am certainly biased, but I definitely see the advantages of an investigation judge or at least trial judges conducting the hearings. Too often I have been in hearings where both the prosecutor and the defence lawyer stopped asking questions because they feared answers that would undermine their case, or that they would ask one-sided questions. I read many statements by witnesses who have been asked about what incriminates the defendant, not what exculpates him. Do prosecution cases provide sufficient facts to make a fair judgement on whether the conduct of the defendant makes him criminally liable? And even if the cross-examination of witnesses may be a routine technique in adversarial

---

[111] Neutrality as being independent from external parties, impartial as unbiased towards the parties, and objective as being unbiased towards the facts.

[112] See Nancy Combs, 2010, Chapter 9C(iv), *supra* note 62. See also Vasiliev, 2015, para. 3.3.1, *supra* note 110.

trials, it may not induce the most reliable answers, and instead prevent witnesses from providing a free narrative.[113]

But there is a much more fundamental point to make: truth-finding requires a society and an environment that induce truth-finding. A prerequisite for truth is a society where its members feel the liberty to speak openly and candidly without fear of oppression from the state, threats, restrictions of personal liberties, infringements of their rights, or even a general anxiety that speaking the truth can somehow backfire. This may sound too obvious, but in reality, many witnesses come from places where these freedoms and liberties are not a given. And I have seen examples where witnesses were unduly influenced, even under duress from their state, leaders, family, religion and others. In some hearings, I have even decided to adjourn because I was unconvinced that witnesses could testify freely. Societies where investigations need to take place must embrace the quest for truth without fear of facts that do not suit them, and be willing to face all realities, even the grim ones.

Unfortunately, in contemporary history, more and more states are driven by nationalism and use their powers to impose their will on their population. Too often states use the powers of the justice system to silence their opponents and favour their supporters. Cases of international crimes almost exclusively deal with the most heinous crimes, committed on a large scale during conflicts in which opposing political rivalries struggle for powers. It is not rare for those who win to use their judicial powers to punish their former rivals. Criminal investigations and trials are then used to shape the narrative that will dominate the history of the country. Victor's justice is the biggest enemy of truth-finding, as citizens will never be in the position of deviating from that narrative or even nuance it.

I have come to realize that the investigation and adjudication of international crimes do not prosper well in jurisdictions where the victims of the conflict rule. The same can be said in the extraordinary situations where these investigations and trials are held where the perpetrators still managed to hold on to their power.

I have experienced it during my tenure in Rwanda in 2014 and 2015, when I advised the National Public Prosecution Authority in their quest to pursue justice for the victims of the Rwandan genocide by prosecuting alleged perpetrators. Rwanda had been rebuilt, including its justice system, and it desired to have the *génocidaires*, of whom many were living abroad, extradited to Rwanda for trial. The question was whether the investigations and trials

---

[113] See the quote from Lord Justice Bonomy, formerly of the ICTY, included in Vasiliev, 2015, p. 319, see *supra* note 110.

were fair to a degree to justify extradition. To answer that question, we must first realize that the ICTR in Arusha, Tanzania, has only tried Hutus for their role in the genocide, while there was evidence that the members of the Tutsi army, the Rwandan Patriotic Front ('RPF'), may have committed war crimes during the three-months war in 1994, and even beyond that timeframe. Publications[114] have further revealed the horrific crimes being committed in Rwanda and the DRC. However, the carefully protected narrative in Rwanda is that there has been only the genocide against the Tutsi minority. When I typed a document with the phrase 'genocide' or 'Rwandan genocide', I was always urged to correct that into 'genocide against the Tutsis'. Anyone who attempted to suggest other crimes were committed or criticize the current leadership in the country risked being charged in court with genocide denial or another crime.

In June of 2015, I testified as an expert witness before the Magistrate's Court in Westminster, London, in an extradition trial against five Rwandan nationals whose extradition had been requested. After having spent a year in Rwanda, monitoring multiple trials, speaking to a number of defence lawyers, government officials, prosecutors and a few confidential sources, I had come to the conclusion that the fairness of the trials was questionable. Not because there were no judges, prosecutors or even defence lawyers assigned to the defendants – who were provided some procedural rights – but precisely because of the issues I have raised above. There seemed to be no space for anyone daring to challenge the national narrative of the genocide or question the validity of testimony by Tutsi victims. I have seen defendants and defence lawyers being reprimanded in court because they called Tutsi victims liars, defence witnesses refusing to testify at all out of fear or anxiety, and defence lawyers not challenging the court or the prosecution. Lawyers expressed fears even of taking these cases, believing it would come at the expense of their business and even their safety, because the public did not accept that they defended these cases. Additionally, I found a complete lack of material defence. The Magistrate's Court and, later, the High Court in London refused to authorize the extraditions.[115]

---

[114] See, for example, the impressive account of Judi Rever, *In Praise of Blood, The Crimes of the Rwandan Patriotic Front*, Random House Canada, Toronto, 2020.

[115] High Court of Justice, England and Wales, *Rwanda v. Nteziryayo and Others*, Judgment of Lord Justice Irwin and Mr Justice Foskett, 28 July 2017, [2017] EWHC 1912 (Admin) (https://www.legal-tools.org/doc/u27zkn/). In the Netherlands, two men were extradited to Rwanda in 2017 after the Court of Appeal in The Hague, in a civil case where defence attorneys had requested the civil court an injunction against the extradition order by the Justice Minister, decided the extradition and trial in Rwanda would not infringe on fair trial rights, applying a much narrower interpretation of these rights than the courts in London. However,

What these experiences made abundantly clear is that the lack of sufficient challenge by defence lawyers was devastating for truth-finding. Facts can be accepted as the truth when they have been tested, alternative scenarios have been presented and, after scrutiny, the charged facts still stand as true beyond reasonable doubt. It did not happen. I am afraid this is true in many jurisdictions.

Judge Christine van den Wyngaert, formerly at the International Criminal Court, in her minority opinion in the Katanga case, has eloquently expressed:

> The point of defence investigations is to give the accused a fair opportunity to challenge the charges and the evidence against him or her. Even if in the end the accused is convicted, the defence's investigatory efforts will still have made a very important contribution to the trial process, *namely by showing that the incriminating evidence was so strong that it could not be defeated by whatever evidence the defendant could – or, crucially, could not – find to contradict the charges.* In other words, defence investigations that yield no significant result play a very important role in confirming the validity of the conviction. However, if no investigation takes place at all, there always remains the reasonable possibility that evidence might have been found that could contradict the available incriminating evidence.[116]

In the end, truth-finding in cases of international crimes is not merely a technique, it is a fundamental right of a defendant to be judged fairly, and an obligation to the victims and society at large. When the facts of the field end up in the court room, and ultimately in the judge's chamber, where the fate of a defendant is determined, if evidence is unprofessionally collected, flawed, untested and then used for political purposes, turned into one-sided historical narratives, or used for personal agendas, truth is lost and justice not served.

---

courts in the Netherlands have reversed their course. In December 2023, the Court of Appeal in The Hague, in a civil case where an injunction was requested to stay the extradition signed off by the Minister of Justice, denied the extradition of two Rwandan nationals to Rwanda because of a risk of flagrant denial of fair trial rights, see Court of Appeal in The Hague, Judgment, 19 December 2023, Case No. 200.328.650/01 (https://www.legal-tools.org/doc/896x0n/). On 9 November 2022 the extradition court in the District Court of the Hague declared an extradition of a Rwandan national to Rwanda inadmissible for the same reason: District Court of The Hague, Extradition Chamber, Judgment, 9 November 2022, Case No. UTL-I-2012050151 (https://www.legal-tools.org/doc/qsmh3f/).

[116] ICC, *Prosecutor v. Germaine Katanga*, Trial Chamber, Judgment Pursuant to Article 74 of the Statute, Minority Opinion of Judge Christine Van den Wyngaert, 10 March 2014, ICC-01/04-01/07-3436-AnxI, para. 92 (italics added) (https://www.legal-tools.org/doc/3py7s8/).

---

# 10

---

# Investigating Core International Crimes in Indonesia Using Old Evidence: The Indonesian National Commission on Human Rights' 1965–1966 Investigations

## Sriyana[*]

## 10.1. Introduction

Everyone has the right to pursue and enjoy a safe, serene, peaceful and prosperous life. Hence, humans, as one of God's creatures, are blessed with a set of attached rights which must be respected, upheld and protected by the State, law and government. Every individual deserves respect from others by virtue of his or her dignity as a human being.

However, in reality, Indonesian history is marked by various events of suffering, misery and social inequality, such as those resulting from unfair and discriminatory practices between 1965 and 1966. This chapter explains how victims of the violations committed over this period of time have claimed their rights through Indonesian domestic processes. It specifically focuses on the investigatory and evidentiary work done by the National Commission on Human Rights ('Commission'), which is an essential stage in these victims' fight for justice.

I will first provide an overview of the Commission's investigative mandate, and its special role *vis-à-vis* Indonesia's Human Rights Court with regards to the investigation and prosecution of gross human rights violations. I then offer an outline of the 1965–1966 incidents, which will serve as the case study of my chapter. Next, I proceed to explain the investigatory process and the methods used by the Commission. The chapter also highlights some of the challenges which have been encountered, with particular reference to those related to old evidence, and the recommendations made so far by the Commission in that regard.

---

[*] **Sriyana** is Head of Bureau of Law, Public Relations and Cooperation of the Indonesian Witness and Victims Agency (LPSK), was previously Head of Bureau at the Indonesian National Commission on Human Rights and has been Secretary of the Inquiry *Ad Hoc* Team for the 1965–1966 incidents. He has been a prominent leader in the Indonesian human rights community for more than 25 years.

## 10.2. The Investigative Functions of the National Commission on Human Rights Based on Act No. 6 (2000) Concerning Human Rights Courts

The National Commission on Human Rights is an independent agency whose position is on par with other State agencies, and which is charged with carrying out human rights assessment, research, dissemination, monitoring and mediation.[1] It is located in the capital of Indonesia and may establish representatives in local areas. It has had six representatives in West Kalimantan, West Sumatra, Papua, Aceh, Moluccas and Central Sulawesi.

Specifically, the Commission's purposes, as set out in Act No. 39 (1999), are the following:[2] (a) to develop conducive conditions for the implementation of human rights in accordance with *Pancasila*,[3] the Constitution[4] and the United Nations Charter, as well as the Universal Declaration of Human Rights; and (b) to enhance the protection and enforcement of human rights for the full development of the Indonesian people.

The Commission's establishment and operations are conducted in line with the international standards outlined in the Paris Principles of 1991,[5] and it has been granted an accreditation of Category A by the International Coordinating Committee of National Institutions for the Promotion and Protection of Human Rights, under the framework of the United Nations Office of the High Commissioner of Human Rights. The accreditation status of the Commission may be said to amount to an international recognition of its independence, and enables its active participation in each relevant session organized by the United Nations.

In addition to the Commission's general human rights-related functions outlined above, as set out in Act No. 39 (1999), the Commission plays a specific role with respect to Indonesia's Human Rights Court. The Commission is the only institution authorized to conduct investigations of gross human rights violations, which may then be pursued before the Human Rights Court.

---

[1]  Indonesia, Legislation No. 39 of 1999 Concerning Human Rights, 23 September 1999, Article 76 ('Act No. 39 (1999)') (https://legal-tools.org/doc/abced1/).

[2]  *Ibid.*, Article 75.

[3]  The term 'Pancasila' refers to the foundational philosophical theory of Indonesian democratic thought.

[4]  The 1945 Constitution of the Republic of Indonesia, 5 July 1959 (https://legal-tools.org/doc/fad0e0/).

[5]  The Principles Relating to the Status of National Institutions, defined in Paris on 7–9 October 1991, have been adopted by the United Nations General Assembly, National Institutions for the Promotion and Protection of Human Rights, UN Doc. A/RES/28/134, 20 December 1993 (https://legal-tools.org/doc/b38121/).

The Indonesian legal system frames gross violations of human rights as extraordinary crimes, which are not to be addressed through the laws governing common crimes or by ordinary courts. The cases arising from such gross violations are to be heard by Indonesia's Human Rights Court.

The Human Rights Court was first established by Act No. 26 (2000).[6] This act is an implementation of Article 104(1) of Act No. 39 (1999), which reads "to hear gross violations of human rights, a Human Rights Tribunal shall be set up in the domain of the District Court".[7] In fact, Act No. 26 (2000) is a successor of Government Regulation in Lieu of Act No. 1 of 1999 Concerning Human Rights Courts,[8] which has been revoked by the House of Representatives because it was considered inadequate and flawed.[9]

To deal with gross violations on human rights, it is necessary to undertake distinct steps, namely investigation, prosecution and dedicated examination. To this end, Act No. 26 (2000) introduced a specific legal framework which differed from ordinary criminal law in many aspects:

a) investigators form *ad hoc* teams; *ad hoc* investigators, prosecutors and judges may be appointed;[10]

b) the act clarifies that all inquiries pertaining to gross human rights violations can only be performed by the National Commission on Human Rights as an independent institution, rather than the police or the prosecutor's investigative agency for ordinary crimes;[11]

c) the maximum duration provided by the act is different from the time limit set by the Criminal Procedure Code[12] for investigation, prosecution and examination in court;[13]

d) measures for the protection of victims and witnesses are provided in case of gross violations of human rights;[14]

---

[6]   Indonesia, Legislation No. 26 of 2000 Concerning Human Rights Courts, 23 November 2000 ('Act No. 26 (2000)') (https://legal-tools.org/doc/8d6ceb/). The linked document is an unofficial translation; the original text is also available in the Legal Tools Database (https://www.legal-tools.org/doc/fbaf18/).

[7]   Act No. 39 (1999), Article 104(1), see *supra* note 1.

[8]   Indonesia, Government Regulation in Lieu of Act No. 1 of 1999 Concerning Human Rights Courts, 8 October 1999 (https://www.legal-tools.org/doc/cdwu62/). This regulation, adopted in circumstances of emergency, was made in relation to human rights violations in East Timor.

[9]   Act No. 26 (2000), Preamble, para. c, see *supra* note 6.

[10]  *Ibid.*, Articles 18–33.

[11]  *Ibid.*, Article 18.

[12]  Indonesia, Code of Criminal Procedure, 31 December 1981 (https://www.legal-tools.org/doc/a8a8ef/).

[13]  Act No. 26 (2000), Articles 22, 24, 31, 32 and 33, see *supra* note 6.

e) no statute of limitations is provided for gross violations of human rights.[15]

## 10.2.1. Types of Human Rights Court

There are two kinds of human rights courts in Indonesia: permanent human rights courts and *ad hoc* courts which are set up on a case-by-case basis. The Indonesian permanent human rights courts have the authority to investigate and prosecute incidents occurring after the enactment of Act No. 26 (2000). Pursuant to Presidential Decree No. 31 (2001) of 12 March 2001, the government has established such courts in Central Jakarta, Surabaya, Medan and Makassar.[16]

*Ad hoc* human rights courts have the authority to examine and rule on human rights violations that occurred prior to the enactment of Act No. 26 (2000). In other words, they may examine cases on a retrospective basis. Presidential Decree No. 53 (2001) of 23 April 2001 established an *ad hoc* human rights court in the Central Jakarta District Court.[17] There was debate over retroactivity in relation to the prosecution of gross human rights violations in East Timor in light of Article 28I of the Constitution, resulting from the second amendment of the 1945 Constitution, which states that an individual cannot be judged on the basis of retroactive law.[18] Additionally, this aspect of Indonesian *ad hoc* human rights courts violates the internationally recognized principle of non-retroactivity.

## 10.2.2. The Subject-Matter Jurisdiction of Human Rights Courts

Indonesia's human rights courts have the authority to examine and rule on cases of gross violations on human rights, including the crime of genocide and crimes against humanity.

Genocide is defined in Act No. 26 (2000) as any action committed with intent to destroy or exterminate in whole or in part national, racial, ethnic or religious groups, by: killing members of the group; causing serious physical or

---

[14] *Ibid.*, Article 34.

[15] *Ibid.*, Article 46.

[16] Indonesia, Presidential Decree No. 31 of 2001, 12 March 2001 (https://www.legal-tools.org/doc/bwamme/).

[17] Indonesia, Presidential Decree No. 53 of 2001, 23 April 2001 (https://www.legal-tools.org/doc/svhfak/). *Ad hoc* human rights courts are to investigate and prosecute cases of human rights violations in East Timor in 1999 and in Tanjung Priok, North Jakarta, in 1984. The ICC Legal Tools Database offers a collection of documents, including judgments and indictments, of the Indonesian *ad hoc* human rights courts of Abepura, Tanjung Priok and East Timor.

[18] The 1945 Constitution of the Republic of Indonesia, Article 28I, see *supra* note 4.

mental harm to members of the group; creating conditions of life that would lead to the physical extermination of the group, in whole or in part; imposing measures intended to prevent births within the group; or forcibly transferring children of a group to another.[19]

Crimes against humanity, under the same Act,[20] consist of any action committed as part of a broad or systematic attack directed at a civilian population, which can take the form of: murder; extermination; slavery; expulsion or forcible transfer of population; arbitrary deprivation of independence or physical liberty in violation of international law; torture; rape, sexual slavery, forced prostitution, forced pregnancy, enforced sterilization or "other similar forms of sexual assault";[21] inflicting terror on a group or association that is based on certain similarities of political beliefs, race, nationality, ethnicity, culture, religion, gender or any other grounds, in a manner that is universally regarded as inconsistent with international law; enforced disappearances; or the crime of apartheid.

It is noteworthy that the definitions stated above largely adopt the definitions set out in the Rome Statute.[22] It may be said that Act No. 26 (2000) has adopted several provisions of the Rome Statute. However, the Rome Statute's subject matter jurisdiction is not limited to genocide and crimes against humanity, but also includes war crimes and the crime of aggression.

### 10.2.3. The Investigative Role Played by the Commission in Bringing Gross Violations of Human Rights Before Human Rights Courts

As mentioned above, investigations of gross violations of human rights are only to be done by the Commission. In conducting the investigation, the Commission may establish an *ad hoc* team which can include "public constituents".[23] In undertaking its task, the *ad hoc* team is authorized to receive reports and complaints from individuals or groups, gathering relevant evidence and statements, including hearing witnesses, the complainants, the subjects of a complaint, the victims of the alleged violations, and generally to "gather statements from the location of the incident and other locations as deemed necessary".[24] The inquiring team is specifically authorized to receive written statements and documents and to conduct documentary examinations, searches

---

[19] Act No. 26 (2000), Article 8, see *supra* note 6.
[20] *Ibid.*, Article 9.
[21] *Ibid.*
[22] Rome Statute of the International Criminal Court ('Rome Statute'), 1 July 2001, Articles 6, 7 (https://legal-tools.org/doc/9c9fd2).
[23] Act No. 26 (2000), Article 18, see *supra* note 6.
[24] *Ibid.*, Article 19.

and seizures, examinations of places of interest, and call in specialists with expertise that is relevant to the investigation.[25]

Upon concluding its investigations, the Commission is to submit the results to the Attorney General, who will then decide on further investigations and prosecutions. So far, the Attorney General has brought two cases before the *ad hoc* human rights courts based on investigations submitted by the Commission: in the case of East Timor in 1999 and in the Tanjung Priok incident in 1984. A case regarding a 2000 incident in Abepura has been heard before the Human Rights Court in Makassar, and in 2023 another case from Paniai, in Papua, was also brought to the same court.

The Commission has investigated and submitted a number of cases of gross violations on human rights to the Attorney General: the incidents of Trisakti and Semanggi I and II, the *riot* case in May 1998, the Wasior and Wamena issues in Papua, enforced disappearances and the Talangsari issue.

### 10.2.4. Provisions for the Rights of the Victims

Considering that gross violations on human rights are extraordinary crimes, the protection of victims and witnesses is particularly needed. To that end, the government has issued Government Regulation No. 2 (2002) of 13 March 2002 on Procedures for the Protection of Victims and Witnesses in Gross Violations on Human Rights.[26] Act No. 26 (2000) also provides the right of victims to obtain compensation, restitution and rehabilitation.[27] As a result, the government has issued Government Regulation No. 3 (2002) of 13 March 2002 concerning Compensation, Restitution, and Rehabilitation of Victims of Gross Violations of Human Rights.[28]

In addition, Act No. 13 of 2006 on Protection of Witnesses and Victims established the Witness and Victims Protection Agency, which is charged with providing the necessary protection to all witnesses and victims at every stage of the judicial process, including in cases of gross violations of human rights.[29]

Article 5 of Act No. 13 (2006) states that witnesses and victims are entitled to receive assistance in maintaining the security of themselves, their prop-

---

[25] *Ibid.*

[26] Indonesia, Government Regulation No. 2 of 2002 on Procedures for the Protection of Victims and Witnesses in Gross Violations of Human Rights, 13 March 2002 (https://www.legal-tools.org/doc/91b8e1/).

[27] Act No. 26 (2000), Article 35, see *supra* note 6.

[28] Indonesia, Government Regulation No. 3 of 2002 on Compensation, Restitution, and Rehabilitation of Victims of Gross Violations of Human Rights, 13 March 2002 (https://www.legal-tools.org/doc/4aea63/).

[29] Indonesia, Legislation No. 13 of 2006 on Protection of Witnesses and Victims, 11 August 2006 ('Act No. 13 (2006)') (https://www.legal-tools.org/doc/51b8a3/).

erty and their family, as well as protection from threats related to the testimony, with the specific right to participate in the selection and determination of the forms of protection to be granted. The Act provides for the possibility of obtaining new residence, new identity, legal advice, reimbursement or coverage of transportation costs and temporary living expenses until the State-mandated protective measures last. Other forms of protection include the guarantee of not being subject to pressure or to malicious questioning aimed at 'trapping'. Witnesses and victims have the right to be informed about the case, with specific regards to being notified of the release of a convict.[30]

Furthermore, Article 6 states that victims of gross violations of human rights are also entitled to medical assistance and psycho-social rehabilitation.[31] As mentioned above, such victims have the right to obtain compensation by applying to the courts.

## 10.3. Case Study: Gross Violations of Human Rights During 1965–1966

The events of 1965–1966 are a black mark on Indonesian history. These events were the result of the State's crackdown against the members and followers of the Communist Party of Indonesia, which was considered to be a resistance movement against the nation.

According to reports from the victims and their families, the 1965–1966 incidents resulted in various forms of human rights violations, including murder, extermination, enslavement, expulsion or forcible transfer, freedom and physical deprivations, torture, rape, persecution and enforced disappearances.

In addition, victims and families of victims suffered mental harm, from one generation to another, and were subject to discriminatory practices in the field of civil and political rights, as well as in the field of economic, social and cultural rights.

The victims have made various efforts to seek redress for the violation of their human rights and to obtain justice. Among others, they denounced these issues to the National Commission on Human Rights.

In response to the complaints of the victims, their families and communities, the Commission established the Soeharto Human Rights Violation Assessment Team for the events related to Buru Island. The team's mandate and responsibilities were based on Act No. 39 (1999), namely, to search for data, information and facts in order to determine whether there was an occurrence of human rights violations.[32]

---

[30] *Ibid.*, Article 5.
[31] *Ibid.*, Article 6.
[32] Act No. 39 (1999), see *supra* note 1.

As a result of its assessments, the team concluded that, in the Buru Island incident, there had been violations of human rights, such as the forcible transfer of population, placing of detainees in isolation camps, slavery in the form of forced labour, violence in detention and other inhumane acts. The team concluded that gross violations of human rights, as defined in Act No. 26 (2000), had taken place in the case of Buru Island.[33]

In order to ascertain and confirm whether the acts uncovered in the case of the Buru Island amounted to gross violations of human rights, the team submitted their recommendations to the Plenary Session of the National Commission on Human Rights for a legal analysis to be conducted on the basis of the team's recommendations and investigations. Following the decision of the Plenary Session, the Commissioner then proceeded to conduct such an assessment of the issues. Based on the results of the legal analysis, it was concluded that gross violations of human rights did indeed take place in Buru Island.[34]

The team recommended judicial investigation to the Plenary Session of the Commission, according to Act No. 26 (2000). In response to the conclusions and the recommendations of the legal analysis team, the Commission, during its following Plenary Session, set up an *Ad Hoc* Team of Gross Violations of Human Rights ('*Ad Hoc* Team') for the 1965–1966 issues, including the ones that took place in Buru Island.

### 10.3.1. Framework of the Investigation

The National Commission on Human Rights has conducted these investigations from 1 June 2008 to 2011, the results were ratified by its Plenary Session in 2012 and forwarded to the Attorney General for further investigation, but there has been no follow up at the time of writing. In order to understand the implementation of the investigation, it is useful to refer to the framework used by the Commission (see Annex 1 in Section 10.6.).

To organize its work, the *Ad Hoc* Team compiled a standard operating procedure for its investigations of the 1965–1966 incidents and a team-work organizational structure with reference to Indonesian law as well as basic principles of human rights and international law.

Additionally, before carrying out its investigations, the *Ad Hoc* Team defined the format of the interviews and undertook other preparatory steps in

---

[33] See the conclusion of National Commission on Human Rights, "Assessment Team's Report on the Soeharto Human Rights Violation", 6 August 2003.
[34] See the conclusion and recommendations of the National Commission on Human Rights, "Analysis Report on the Buru Island Incident", 5 February 2004.

order to facilitate the implementation of its tasks. The implementation process of the investigation is reflected in Annex 2 (in Section 10.6.).

## 10.3.2. Implementation of the Investigation

In addition to administrative planning, investigations must fulfil a number of requirements under Indonesian law. For example, Article 19(2) of Act No. 26 (2000) requires the Commission to inform the Attorney General of the beginning of the investigation.[35] Accordingly, the Commission informed the Attorney General that the investigation regarding the 1965–1966 incidents had started by sending a letter on 12 August 2008.

Then, as set out in Article 19(1) of Act No. 26 (2000),[36] the following investigatory procedures were implemented.

a) *Receiving Complaints*: Since its formation, the *Ad Hoc* Team tasked with the 1965–1966 incidents received 51 relevant reports or complaints from the public.

b) *Examination of Witnesses and Victims*: In carrying out its duties, the *Ad Hoc* Team called 349 witnesses to give testimony. These testimonies are recorded, sometimes using video recordings as well. The investigators use computer technology that is connected to a projector, so witnesses can directly follow the interview by looking at the monitor. Upon the completion of the interview, the witness is given the opportunity to read the statement. After his or her agreement, the interview document is printed and then signed by the witness and the concerned investigator. A copy of the witness' identification is attached to the document.

   Witnesses and victims have the right to obtain protective measures, and significant care was taken to explain to those coming forward that they had the right to request such measures. However, none of the witnesses and victims in this case requested such protection. The law provides that witnesses have a right to a diverse set of protective measures, such as obtaining a new identity, a new residence, and temporary coverage of living costs for the duration of the protective measures. They also have the right to be provided with medical assistance and social rehabilitation. Witness requests for such forms of protection are processed and assessed by the Witness and Protection Unit; nonetheless, the Commission's staff is generally trained on the rights of victims and witnesses. The Commission has a Memorandum of Understanding with the Witness and Protection Unit, ensuring co-ordination between the two

---

[35] Act No. 26 (2000), Article 19(2), see *supra* note 6.
[36] *Ibid.*, Article 19(1).

bodies when the Commission makes requests for the protection of witnesses or victims.

In other cases dealt with by the Commission, witnesses have requested protection. For example, in the case of Ahmadiyah, based on the Commission's recommendations and request to the Witness and Protection Unit, a witness was placed in a safe house and provided with protection when leaving the house. In the case of murder and torture by the military in Atambua, West Nusa Tenggara, witnesses were accompanied throughout the entire military court process to ensure their safety and a sense of security.

Victims may also request restitution or compensation. To do so, they need to apply to the Commission and obtain its letter of support. Upon obtaining the letter from the Commission, they may submit the document along with their request to the Witness and Protection Unit, which processes such claims.

Witnesses are guaranteed confidentiality by the law, and, to this end, the full investigative report is not made public. Only an executive summary is published, and it does not make references to the names of witnesses or victims. When a witness or victim requests protection, codes are employed in order to protect his or her identity. Care is always taken to explain to witnesses that they have a right to confidentiality, as well as to obtain protection. For example, if witnesses object to being video recorded, the investigative team will transcribe the interview or only record the audio feed instead.

To ensure accuracy, pursuant with the Commission's independent nature, investigative teams are conscious of the need to verify and cross-check the information provided by witnesses. In general, teams start with interviewing witnesses and victims. The information and data obtained is then cross-checked with what is subsequently obtained from the alleged perpetrators, or any institution related to the case.

c) *Review and Scene Inspection*: The *Ad Hoc* Team reviewed and gathered information from crime scenes, altogether 30 times, as represented in the chart below. In general, a single site visit lasts for about five days in total. However, the duration of a site visit may be extended depending on the number of individuals to be interviewed, their location and other factors. Witness interviews are conducted in a variety of places, depending on the witness' own preference. For example, interviews have been conducted in the homes of witnesses, in hotels or in the Commission's office.

d) For these cases, the *Ad Hoc* Team determined that excavations were necessary. Excavations, however, may only be conducted with the approval of the Attorney General. A request was made, but the Team had not received a response at the time of writing. Such sites are identified on the basis of witness interviews.

| No. | The Scenes |
|-----|-----------|
| 1. | Palembang – South Sumatera |
| 2. | Surakarta – Central Java |
| 3. | Solo – Central Java |
| 4. | Maumere – NTT |
| 5. | Bali |
| 6. | Jakarta |
| 7. | Manado – North Sulawesi |
| 8. | Medan – North Sumatera |
| 9. | Palu – Central Sulawesi |
| 10. | Palembang – South Sumatera |
| 11. | Bangka – Bangka Belitung Islands |
| 12. | Bangka Selatan – Bangka Belitung Islands |
| 13. | Kutai Kertanegara – East Kalimantan |
| 14. | Balikpapan – East Kalimantan |
| 15. | Buru – Maluku |
| 16. | Maumere – NTT |
| 17. | Bali |
| 18. | Kendari – South East Sulawesi |
| 19. | Bukitinggi – West Sumatera |
| 20. | Medan – North Sumatera |
| 21. | Pekanbaru – Riau |
| 22. | Samarinda – East Kalimantan |
| 23. | Makassar – South Sulawesi |
| 24. | Balikpapan – East Kalimantan |
| 25. | Solo – Central Java |

| | |
|---|---|
| 26. | Jakarta |
| 27. | Jakarta |
| 28. | Blitar – East Java |
| 29. | Surabaya – East Java |
| 30. | Bau – Bau – South East Sulawesi |

**Table 1: Sites identified by the *Ad Hoc* Team.**

e) *Collecting Documents*: In addition to testimonies, the Team also obtained and analysed secondary material, such as historical texts and non-governmental organizations' ('NGO') reports. Historical texts are usually obtained from formal institutions. Reports prepared by local NGOs or grassroots organizations such as Kontras, Pakorba and others are often collected and studied.

f) *Focus Group Discussions*: In order to obtain optimal results of the investigation, focus groups were organized by the Commission. Team members were grouped into teams of 15, according to certain topics or expertise. For example, a group dealt with legal matters and other historical matters. One discussion was organized for each focus group. Group discussions were recorded.

### 10.3.3. The Challenges of Using Old Evidence

In investigating the incidents in the scope of its mandate, the Commission's work has encountered some of the unique challenges related to the use of old evidence. However, the passage of time has also the potential to ease other issues that are common to investigations of international crimes. For instance, the Commission could count on many secondary sources of knowledge, such as existing research and books, which have been completed in the decades between the facts and the investigation. Furthermore, certain confidential documents may become public only with the passage of time.

Not all sources of evidence are necessarily affected by deterioration to a point that they cannot be employed. In its investigations pertaining to the 1984 Tanjung Priok incidents, the Commission sought the assistance of the Indonesia University in forming a forensic team tasked with the analysis of a mass burial site. The bodies in the grave were exhumed, pursuant to the authorization of the Attorney General, and their analysis led to successful identifications by a part of the forensic team. With regards to witnesses, and the specific question of the conservation of their memory of relevant events, the Commission found most victims to have sufficient and precise capacity for recalling the facts, more so when the victims' groups had been adequately empowered by civil society organizations. Likewise, the Commissions capacity to gather relevant documentary evidence was not particularly hampered by the passage of time.

Physical forms of evidence may indeed be lost, if displaced or forgotten. In this regard, the Commission has found that the knowledge of the location of mass graves was often preserved within the surrounding communities, which informally tasked individuals with 'remembering' the locations; such processes were helped by other common practices, such as victims marking mass graves with stones or trees. As a result of these practices, burial sites were located, and their positions conveyed to the Attorney General along with requests for exhumation which, unlike in the Tanjung Priok inquiry mentioned above, were not granted frequently.

Political and societal will to uncover, investigate and prosecute mass atrocities can also be influenced by the passage of time, positively or otherwise. While the Commission did not generally find the victims to be reluctant to provide information, it encountered forms of adversarial pressure from society, such as from the wider Indonesian Muslim society through its capillary organization. Political considerations are likely the grounds for the willingness of institutional actors, national and foreign, to provide documents in their possession; such considerations are naturally bound to change with the passage of time, which may then prove to be both beneficial and detrimental, depending on the timing of the investigation.

## 10.4. Results and Findings

Based on data obtained during the investigations and the Commission's own synthesis and analysis, the Commission came to the following conclusions on the types of human rights violations that took place.

| No. | Crimes | Notes |
|-----|--------|-------|
| 1. | Murder | At least 1,956 people |
| 2. | Extermination | At least 85,483 people |
| 3. | Enslavement | At least 11,500 people |
| 4. | Forcible Transfer of Population | At least 41,000 people |
| 5. | Arbitrary Arrest or Detention | At least 41,000 people |
| 6. | Torture | At least 30,000 people |
| 7. | Rape, Sexual Slavery | At least 32 people |
| 8. | Persecution | At least 85,000 people |
| 9. | Enforced Disappearance | At least 32,774 people |

**Table 2. Results and findings of the Commission based on investigations.**

The Commission's analysis of raw data has been facilitated by its use of the ICC Case Matrix system.[37] The Case Matrix helped by organizing and providing easier access to the concerned data, and highlighted the areas in which more information was needed in order to prove whether gross violations of human rights were committed during the 1965–1966 incidents.

Upon completing these various investigatory and analytical processes, the Commission then prepared its report. The report comprises of two parts: the final and complete report which describes the investigative process and its results in detail and the executive summary of investigation results. The final report is confidential and may only be used by the Attorney General in the implementation of further investigations. The executive summary is made for the benefit of public information and can be divulged.

The Commission had completed its report, concluding that there was enough evidence of gross violations of human rights during the 1965–1966 incidents. The report had been sent to the Attorney General in 2012, to follow up with further investigation and to be brought to the *Ad Hoc* Human Rights Court. As this chapter went to press, after more than 11 years, there has been no progress from the Attorney General, with victims waiting for justice for a long time. In January 2023, the President of the Republic of Indonesia, Joko Widodo, made a public statement recognizing 12 gross violations of human rights, including the incidents of 1965–1966.[38]

---

[37] See Case Matrix Network, "The ICC Case Matrix", available on its web site.
[38] Kelly Ng, "Jokowi Acknowledges Indonesia's Past Human Rights Violations", *BBC News*, 12 January 2023.

## 10.5. Conclusions

Pursuant to internationally recognized values and legal principles, gross violations of human rights should be followed up by investigations and prosecutions. Such investigation and prosecution are essential for human beings, so this should be seen as an obligation of concerned authorities to the international community as a whole.

Such processes are an effort to break the chain of impunity and deliver justice to the victims. The duty to seek justice for gross human rights violations is an obligation that must be upheld as a commitment to international law. Therefore, if a State or a government does not investigate and prosecute those who commit such violations, the international community should be prepared to assume the responsibility of conducting investigations and prosecutions.

Despite the existing limitations, the Commission has done its utmost to implement its functions and duties as mandated by Act No. 39 (1999) and Act No. 26 (2000). This has particularly been true in its investigations, disclosure and resolutions with regards to the cases related to the 1965–1966 incidents.

The Commission has been aware that, in performing its functions and duties, it still falls short of meeting the expectations of society, especially those of the victims. All suggestions, criticism and input that will improve the quality and quantity of performance of the Commission are therefore welcome. The promotion, protection, enforcement and fulfilment of human rights are for everyone.

I wish to conclude this chapter with an important reminder, quoting what former United Nations Secretary-General Kofi Annan stated regarding the International Criminal Tribunal for Rwanda: "there can be no peace without justice; and there can be no justice without respect for human rights and the rule of law".[39]

---

[39] "Secretary-General Welcomes Rwanda Tribunal's Genocide Judgement as Landmark in International Criminal Law", Press Release, UN Doc. SG/SM/6687, 2 September 1998.

## 10.6. Annexes

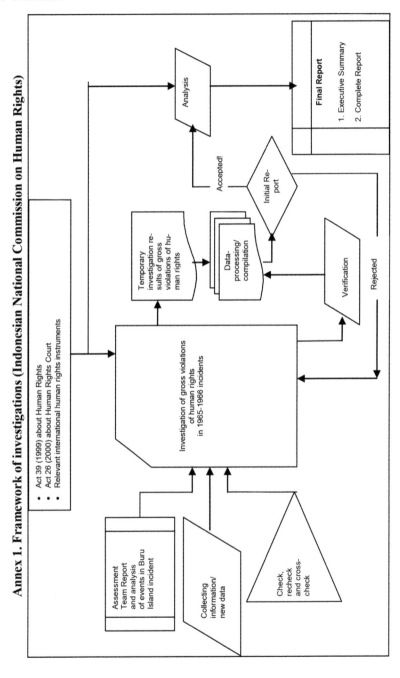

**Annex 1. Framework of investigations (Indonesian National Commission on Human Rights)**

- Act 39 (1999) about Human Rights
- Act 26 (2000) about Human Rights Court
- Relevant international human rights instruments

Assessment Team Report and analysis of events in Buru Island incident

Collecting information/new data

Check, recheck and cross-check

Investigation of gross violations of human rights in 1965-1966 incidents

Temporary investigation results of gross violations of human rights

Data-processing/compilation

Verification

Initial Report

Rejected

Accepted!

Analysis

**Final Report**
1. Executive Summary
2. Complete Report

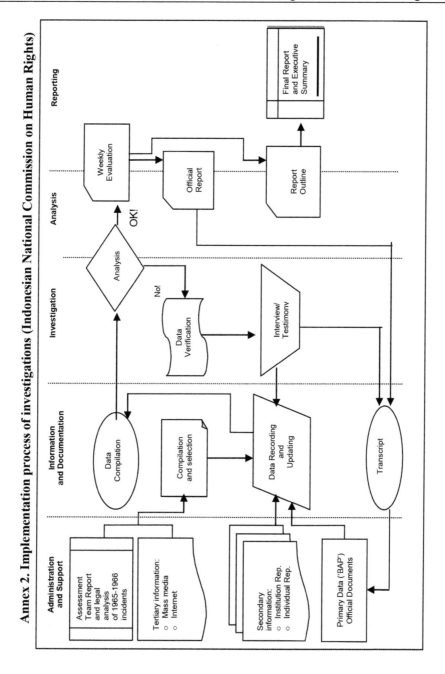

**Annex 2. Implementation process of investigations (Indonesian National Commission on Human Rights)**

# 11

## 'The Messaging Effect': Eliciting Credible Historical Evidence From Victims of Mass Crimes

### Mahdev Mohan*

### 11.1. Introduction

The 1971 Liberation War (or the 'war of independence') of Bangladesh was an armed conflict that pit then East Pakistan and India against then West Pakistan. It led to the secession of East Pakistan and the formation and recognition of the independent State of Bangladesh. The conflict claimed countless lives,[1] and displaced 10 million people.[2] The atrocities committed in 1971 have been described as "selective genocide" by the United States ('US') embassy in Dhaka in a cable in March 1971, revealed in declassified documents in 2002.[3]

The current administration led by the Awami League in Bangladesh established an International Crimes Tribunal ('ICT-BD') within its domestic court structure to try those accused of crimes against humanity, genocide and war crimes during that tragic period in the country's history. The ICT-BD's first trial commenced on 20 November 2011, almost four decades after the conflict took place. The ICT-BD's affiliates opine that justice delayed is better than having it denied. The former ICT-BD prosecutor Advocate Zead-Al-Malum stated that the "international community had never any reason to be concerned about the standard of Bangladesh's legal system [...] my team

---

\*    **Mahdev Mohan** is regional policy lead within the Global Policy and Standards team at Google. At the time of the submission for the first edition, he was Assistant Professor of Law at the Singapore Management University ('SMU') and Director, SMU School of Law's Asian Business and Rule of Law programme ('ABRL'). The author wishes to thank Ms. Geetanjali Mukherjee, Research Fellow at SMU's ABRL at the time of submission, for the invaluable research assistance.

1    The Rahman Commission estimated 26,000 died in the conflict, see War Inquiry Commission, "Supplementary Report", 28 October 1974 (https://www.legal-tools.org/doc/iacqir/). Others have estimated that the number is closer to three million; see, for instance, Bina D'Costa, "Frozen in Time? War Crimes, Justice and Political Forgiveness", in *Nation Building, Gender and War Crimes in South Asia*, Routledge, London, 2011 ('D'Costa, 2011').

2    D'Costa, 2011, p. 145, *ibid.*

3    US Consulate in Dacca, "Selective Genocide", 27 March 1971.

---

members and I are committed to do our best to ensure justice, that is not for the victims only, but also for the accused".[4]

The trials have been criticized as being politically charged, and as facing significant challenges in terms of their legitimacy, due process and procedural fairness.[5] US-based Human Rights Watch stated, in a letter to Prime Minister Sheikh Hasina, that without significant amendments to the International Crimes (Tribunals) Act of 1973 ('1973 Act'), the judicial process would fail to meet international standards of fair trial.[6] In March 2011, then US Ambassador-at-large for War Crimes Issues Stephen J. Rapp drafted a series of recommendations suggesting amendments to the rules of the ICT-BD, which may help to ensure that the ICT-BD's proceedings are fair and transparent.[7]

Ambassador Rapp recommended that provisions enshrining the right to appeal against interlocutory orders be incorporated, along with provisions adopting the International Criminal Court's ('ICC') Elements of Crimes,[8] an interpretative tool which assists the ICC in the interpretation and application of the crimes of genocide, crimes against humanity, war crimes and the crime of aggression – all crimes within the jurisdiction of the ICT-BD as well.[9] He also suggested that the accused should be ensured the rights under Part III of the International Covenant on Civil and Political Rights of 1966, and benefit from provisions detailing the detention of the accused similar to that used by the International Criminal Tribunal for Rwanda ('ICTR'). He further recommended the inclusion of rules on the presumption of innocence and placing the burden of proof on the prosecution. He additionally suggested incorporating rules on witness protection and granting visas to foreign counsel whose advice has been sought.[10]

---

[4]  Zead-al-Malum, "Meeting on Bangladesh: Exchange of Views on War Crimes Trials and on Accountability Issues", Delegation for Relations for the Countries of South Asia, European Parliament, Brussels, 31 January 2012 (https://www.legal-tools.org/doc/obposm/).

[5]  John Cammegh, a British lawyer advising the defense, argues that the trials "mak[e] a mockery" of the principle of accountability against impunity, due to the inadequate protections and safeguards for the defense of the accused. See further, John Cammegh, "In Bangladesh: Reconciliation or Revenge?", *The New York Times*, 17 November 2011.

[6]  Human Rights Watch, "Letter to Prime Minister Sheikh Hasina Re: International Crimes (Tribunals) Act" (available on its web site).

[7]  "Recommendations Made by Stephen J Rapp, US Ambassador at Large, War Crimes Issues and the Extent of their Implementations by the International Crimes Tribunal and the Government of Bangladesh", *ICT-BD Watch*, 28 November 2011 ('Rapp's Recommendations').

[8]  ICC, Elements of Crimes, 11 June 2010 (http://www.legal-tools.org/doc/3c0e2d/).

[9]  See Rapp's Recommendations, 28 November 2011, *supra* note 7.

[10]  *Ibid.*

## 11.2. Message as Medium in Bangladesh?

With justice processes that seek accountability for core international crimes, it is not enough to merely denounce alleged perpetrators, as the credibility and legitimacy of such processes are locally perceived and assessed – that is, by the very local constituents they are meant to vindicate and serve.[11] As Rama Mani observes, "[i]f ideas and institutions about as fundamental and personal a value as justice are imposed from the outside without an internal resonance, they may flounder, notwithstanding their assertions of universality".[12]

Ambassador Rapp has remarked:

> these trials […] are of great *importance to the victims* of the 1971 war of independence from Pakistan. What happens in Bangladesh today will *send a strong message* that it is possible for a national system to bring those responsible for grave human rights abuses to justice.[13]

Ambassador Rapp appears to view the trial as, among other things, an expressivist exercise for victims of the war: a process that is designed to tell a story and, through trial, verdict and punishment, affirm the value of law, strengthen social solidarity, and incubate a moral consensus among victims.[14] His view accords with the United Nations ('UN') Secretary-General Ban Ki-Moon's definition of 'legacy' as:

> a court's lasting impact on bolstering the rule of law in a particular society, including by conducting effective trials to contribute to ending impunity, while also strengthening domestic judicial capacity.[15]

Put differently, expressivism is less concerned with whether the law deters or punishes, than it is with the message victims get from the law. Diane Marie Amann reminds us, however, that for the law to have expressive value, the "message understood, rather than the message intended, is critical".[16] To

---

[11]  Mark Drumbl, "Rights, Culture and Crime: The Role of Rule of Law for the Women of Afghanistan", in *Columbia Journal of Transnational Law*, 2004, vol. 42, no. 2, p. 349.

[12]  Rama Mani, *Beyond Retribution: Seeking Justice in the Shadows of War*, Blackwell Publishers, 2002, p. 49.

[13]  "Bangladesh International Crimes Tribunal: The Judges, at the First Opportunity, Must Define What the Term 'Crimes Against Humanity' Means", *Voice of America*, 6 December 2011 (emphasis added).

[14]  Mark Drumbl, *Atrocity, Punishment, and International Law*, Cambridge University Press, New York, 2007, p. 17.

[15]  UN Secretary-General, "Guidance Note of the Secretary-General on the United Nations Approach to Transitional Justice", 10 March 2010 (https://www.legal-tools.org/doc/kr8dl5/).

[16]  Diane Marie Amann, "Message as Medium in Sierra Leone", in *International Law Students Association* ('ILSA') *Journal of International and Comparative Law*, 2001, vol. 7, p. 238.

send the right message, justice processes and their affiliates must be attentive to their primary constituents: their victims. This attentiveness can pave the way for justice and reconciliation, which are maximized when undertaken in a manner that resonates in local cultures and communities, the environs in which law matters most and where the actual abuses take place.[17]

Ambassador Rapp's recommendations are consistent with international law and practice and should be applauded. But further research should be undertaken to consider contemporary Bangladeshi sentiments about the ICT-BD and Rapp's recommendations. In order to have resonance and to be properly understood and received, any proposed legal reforms to the ICT-BD must be context-sensitive, and not simply adopt a one-size-fits-all approach to transitional justice.[18] As Ambassador Rapp himself concedes, it is crucial to "keep in mind that different countries have different procedures and different courts have had different procedures".[19] After all, victims of massacres that transpired nearly four decades ago often have an astute appreciation of the historical and political baggage that hinders efforts to secure accountability. Survivors of the war of independence are no different. Furthermore, the adjudication of crimes committed decades before trial face the peculiar challenges of working with old evidence, which warrant adequate and specifically tailored measures.

Drawing on lessons the author has learnt from litigation at the Extraordinary Chambers in the Courts of Cambodia ('ECCC'),[20] including gathering victim evidence in relation to its *Cases 003* and *004*, this chapter considers: (i)

---

[17] See, generally, Drumbl, 2004, see *supra* note 11; Elizabeth S. Anderson and Richard H. Pildes, "Expressive Theories of Law: A General Restatement", in *University of Pennsylvania Law Review*, 2000, vol. 148, p. 1503; and Dan M. Kahan, "The Secret Ambition of Deterrence", in *Harvard Law Review*, 1999, vol. 113, no. 2.

[18] Increasingly, research is being undertaken to explore innovative and contextual approaches to transitional justice, including research and writing by this author in collaboration with others.

[19] Stephen J. Rapp, Ambassador-at-Large, War Crimes Issues, Press Conference, 13 January 2011, p. 20.

[20] The ECCC is a hybrid tribunal established on 6 June 2003 by a bilateral agreement between the UN and the Cambodian government as an "Extraordinary Chambers within the existing court structure of Cambodia for the prosecution of crimes committed during the period of Democratic Kampuchea", albeit with international assistance. See "Agreement Between the United Nations and the Royal Government of Cambodia Concerning the Prosecution under Cambodian Law of Crimes Committed during the Period of Democratic Kampuchea", 6 June 2003 (https://legal-tools.org/doc/3a33d3/). The KRT was recognized by the Cambodian legislature with the Law on the Establishment of Extraordinary Chambers in the Courts of Cambodia for the Prosecution of Crimes Committed During the Period of Democratic Kampuchea, 27 October 2004 (https://www.legal-tools.org/doc/88d544/), when it ratified and implemented the agreement through the adoption of enabling legislation (named the Law on the Ratification of the Agreement, 5 October 2004).

---

the inherent challenges of eliciting non-contemporaneous or 'old' evidence from victims or witnesses; (ii) how to gather and verify old evidence from victims or witnesses; and (iii) what courts should take into account when applying for and enforcing protective measures for them.

These considerations are critically important to the fair administration of justice by the ICT-BD and the sober reality that the Tribunal is, and should be, only one component of transitional justice processes in Bangladesh. Such processes ought to respond to the country's context while anchored in international norms and standards to address the impact of large-scale past abuses in order to ensure accountability, serve justice and achieve reconciliation, which may include non-judicial mechanisms.

## 11.3. The 'War of Independence', Politics and Elusive Justice

The seeds of a conflict as complex as the war of independence of Bangladesh did not begin with the armed attacks of 1971, but can be traced to deep-seated grievances, politicking and unrest. The declaration by Muhammad Ali Jinnah as early as 1948 of Urdu as the official language of Pakistan as a whole was deeply resented by East Pakistanis (whose Bengali language community was one of the largest in the region), and led to an uprising in 1952 and the deaths of several demonstrators. Conflict mounted with economic and political grievances in East Pakistan. Although East Pakistan's population was larger, West Pakistan received the lion's share of fiscal support and opportunities in government.

Additionally, in 1970, a cyclone devastated large parts of East Pakistan, with a reported death toll between 300,000 and 500,000.[21] Pakistani President General Yahya Khan mismanaged the relief efforts and tried to suppress the magnitude of loss, leading to protests against the regime in Dhaka. In the same year, the Awami League led by Mujibur Rahman ('Mujib') achieved a landslide victory in East Pakistan, obtaining an overall majority of parliamentary seats in Pakistan. However, Zulfikar Ali Bhutto was unwilling to allow Mujib to become Prime Minister, and proposed a joint Prime Ministership solution, which was not received well by the East Pakistanis. Subsequently, Bhutto and Yahya Khan travelled to Dhaka to seek a solution.

However, unrest was brewing, and West Pakistan secretly flew a number of soldiers to East Pakistan. On 25 March 1971, the Pakistani army launched 'Operation Searchlight', an attempt to quash the movement for liberation by the then East Pakistanis. The army began to gun down students, intelligentsia and Bengali members of the military, especially targeting the Hindu areas. Mu-

---

[21] Nicholas D. Kristof, "Cyclone in Bangladesh Tests the Fragile New Democracy", *The New York Times*, 19 May 1991.

jib was arrested, but not before he reportedly declared the emergence of the State of Bangladesh in the early hours of the next morning.

Over the next nine months of conflict, an estimated three million people were killed,[22] although the Hamoodur Rahman Commission estimates only 26,000 victims.[23] Also, it is estimated that there were about 10 million refugees crossing the border into India.[24] Around 200,000 women were raped by West Pakistani soldiers, leading to a generation of 'war babies'.[25] The international community failed to stop the atrocities, although the UN condemned the human rights violations. India finally intervened, sending arms and soldiers into East Pakistan and training guerrilla fighters, resulting in a war between the two countries. The West Pakistani army surrendered on 16 December 1971. General Yahya Khan was subsequently ousted, and Zulfikar Ali Bhutto was declared the Prime Minister of Pakistan.

Prime Minister Bhutto negotiated with India for the return of land lost by Pakistan as well as the release of Pakistani prisoners-of-war ('POWs'). India held 90,000 POWs, the highest number since World War II. Pakistan refused to recognize the new State of Bangladesh, and thus Bangladesh and India refused to settle the issue of POWs. Mujib wanted to try 1,500 of the POWs for alleged war crimes,[26] although later the number was reduced to 195 accused of genocide and other serious crimes, and the other 90,000 POWs were given amnesty and returned to Pakistan. On 17 April 1973, the government decided to convene war crimes trials; however, political factionalism within the country and the compromises struck with Pakistan led to them being shelved indefinitely. Mujib and his family were assassinated in 1975 after the Awami League was removed from power,[27] and Bangladesh went through 15 years of martial law, poverty and economic hardship.

In the aftermath of the war, the new government was unable to prosecute alleged war criminals. In 1972, the Bangladesh Collaborators (Special

---

[22] D'Costa, 2011, p. 145, see *supra* note 1. Although it is difficult to independently confirm this figure.

[23] The Hamoodur Rahman Commission was appointed by the President of Pakistan in December 1971 to inquire into the circumstances of the surrender of the Pakistani forces to India. The Commission examined 213 witnesses and its report was submitted in July 1972, see D'Costa, 2011, *supra* note 1. See also Ziauddin Ahmed, "The Case of Bangladesh: Bringing to Trial Perpetrators of the 1971 Genocide", in Albert Jongman (ed.), *Contemporary Genocides: Causes, Cases, Consequences*, Pioom, Leiden, 1996, pp. 95–115.

[24] D'Costa, 2011, p. 145, see *supra* note 1. See also Susan Brownmiller, *Against Our Will: Men, Women and Rape*, Simon and Schuster, 1975.

[25] D'Costa, 2011, see *supra* note 1.

[26] *Ibid.*, p. 145.

[27] *Ibid.*, p. 149.

Tribunals) Order came into force, to indict those who collaborated with the Pakistani forces.[28] There are conflicting reports on the number of arrests and trials conducted by the tribunals.[29] However, it is generally believed that evidentiary difficulties held up the trials.[30] Pressing humanitarian and economic concerns also derailed any plans for legal proceedings.[31]

The promulgation of the International Crimes (Tribunals) Act of 1973 ('1973 Act') was the only concrete legislative step taken towards accountability.[32] In November 1973, however, the government granted a general amnesty and released most of the detainees.[33] Organizations that were previously labelled as collaborators and banned were permitted to participate in politics, and many of their members were appointed to influential positions in government, making the establishment of a tribunal even less probable.[34]

The assassination of Mujib and the political events that followed forestalled all accountability processes for the next several years. In the 1990s, powerful civil society advocates, movements and campaigns called for erstwhile alleged collaborators to be removed from power and brought to justice.[35]

## 11.4. New Parliamentary Resolve and a Push to Prosecute Core Crimes With an Old Statute

The Liberation War Museum, located in Dhaka, was established on 22 March 1996, and it has since been archiving documents and testimonies of the independence war.[36] At the time of writing, the Museum was located in two buildings, with a total of six galleries.[37] The collection had over 10,000 artefacts, including rare photographs, documents and pamphlets. The Museum had an outreach programme that educates students who visit it,[38] as well as a large bus mounted with 360 photographs and objects, acting as a mobile exhibition, which travels to different parts of the country.

---

[28]  Suzannah Linton, "Completing the Circle: Accountability for the Crimes of the 1971 Bangladesh War of Liberation", in *Criminal Law Forum*, 2010, vol. 21, no. 2, p. 204.

[29]  Some reports state that 11,000 suspects were in custody and 73 tribunals constituted.

[30]  Linton, 2010, p. 205, see *supra* note 28.

[31]  D'Costa, 2011, p. 151, see *supra* note 1.

[32]  *Ibid.*, p. 150.

[33]  Linton, 2010, p. 205, see *supra* note 28.

[34]  D'Costa, 2011, p. 151, see *supra* note 1.

[35]  *Ibid.*, pp. 151–152. For example, Jahanara Imam's campaign against Golam Azam and the Ghatok Dalal Nirmul Committee.

[36]  Liberation War Museum, "About Us" (available on its web site). The Museum was directed by Mr. Mofidul Haque at the time of writing.

[37]  Liberation War Museum, "About the Museum", *ibid.*

[38]  *Ibid.*

The process of pursuing justice for the victims of the 1971 atrocities moved forward in April 2008, with the War Crimes Fact Finding Committee releasing a list of 1,597 war criminals involved in the 1971 war.[39] The list included Pakistani Army officers, political collaborators and members of the Jamaat-e-Islami, a junior coalition partner in the previous government.[40] In a bold move in 2009, the Bangladesh Parliament adopted a resolution to try persons accused for crimes under the 1973 Act.

The Resolution provides for individuals and groups to be tried, institutes an appeal process and includes English as an official language of the court along with Bengali.[41] While these amendments are designed to ensure that the ICT-BD's process accords with international standards, there is still a long way to go. Several provisions of the 1973 Act have been criticized for being insufficient with regards to ensuring that international standards of fairness and due process are met.[42]

The demands for fairness and justice should not centre exclusively on victims, with scant regard to the corollary rights of alleged perpetrators. In order to achieve a justice system free of what has been termed an "impartiality deficit", its statutory foundation must allude to the defence function, equal in status, resources and respect to the judicial, administrative and prosecutorial functions.[43]

The temporal jurisdiction[44] of Article 3(1) is wide, stating that the Tribunal has jurisdiction over any individual who has committed any of the crimes listed "before or after the commencement of [the] act". The subject matter jurisdiction[45] of the 1973 Act has also been called into question. It permits prosecution for "genocide, crimes against humanity, war crimes and *other crimes under international law*" (emphasis added).

---

[39] D'Costa, 2011, p. 153, see *supra* note 1.

[40] Members of this group under the name Al-Badr allegedly rounded up approximately 150 academics and journalists and killed them the day before Pakistan's surrender. Mark Dummett, "Bangladesh War Crimes Stir Tension", *BBC News*, 30 June 2008.

[41] The International Crimes (Tribunals) Act, 20 July 1973 (https://www.legal-tools.org/doc/c09a98/).

[42] Human Rights Watch, "Bangladesh: Upgrade War Crimes Law", 8 July 2009 (available on its web site).

[43] See William A. Schabas, Ramesh Thakur and Edel Hughes (eds.), *Atrocities and International Accountability: Beyond Transitional Justice*, UN University Press, Tokyo, 2007.

[44] 'Temporal jurisdiction' refers to the jurisdiction of a court of law over an action in relation to the passage of time.

[45] 'Subject matter jurisdiction' refers to the authority of a court to hear cases of a particular type or cases relating to a specific subject matter.

Commentators have argued that the statute lacks precise definitions of war crimes, crimes against humanity, genocide and sexual violence.[46] The extant statutory definitions of these crimes are adapted from the International Military Tribunal (Nuremberg) Charter, with certain amendments. For instance, crimes against humanity in the 1973 Act include imprisonment, abduction, confinement, torture and rape. Ethnicity is contemplated as one of the grounds of discrimination, though it is unclear if this reflects customary international criminal law in this regard.[47] The last provision, "any other crimes under international law", is vague and may not be held to be consistent with the principle of specificity, an important tenet of international criminal law.[48]

It is noteworthy that the ICT-BD conceded that it was bound to enforce domestic legislation which gives effect to international treaties to which Bangladesh is a State Party. However, the Tribunal held that it saw no reason to borrow definitions of crimes within its subject matter jurisdiction from "fairly recent international tribunals", and that it may only "take into account jurisprudential [and normative] developments from other jurisdictions should it feel so required in the interests of justice".[49] With respect, this is unsatisfactory: though the ICT-BD is a national tribunal, it should have recourse to relevant case law and international standards which are widely accepted at both national and international courts.

It is unclear from the first decision of the ICT-BD, from the way in which the charges are described, in the context of the pronouncement "that there is a *prima facie* case against the accused", whether the judges are merely reciting charges by the prosecutor for the accused to hear, read and understand, or whether they have agreed that these charges form the exclusive and unchallengeable scope of the trial.[50] It appears that it is the latter – that since a *prima facie* case has been made against the accused, the defence is now being called to answer, which raises significant concerns of perceived impartiality or lack of it.

---

[46] Jyoti Rahman and Naeem Mohaiemen, "1973 War Crimes Act: Getting It Right", *The Daily Star*, 10 July 2009.

[47] See Linton, 2010, pp. 231–239, *supra* note 28, for an exhaustive treatment on the differences between the provisions for the definition of 'crimes against humanity'.

[48] *Ibid.*, p. 268.

[49] ICT-BD, *Prosecutor v. Delowar Hossain Sayeedi*, Order No. 23, 3 October 2011 (https://www.legal-tools.org/doc/r9dt67/). The ICC Legal Tools Database contains an excellent collection on the ICT-BD (https://www.legal-tools.org/).

[50] There is indication to say that not all the charges were accepted: 20 out of 31 submitted by the Prosecutor.

In addition, certain charges name suspected victims of rape in connection with a crime against humanity, without taking into account whether such identification would adversely affect the physical and psychological security of the victim. This is inconsistent with international standards and best practices.

Strikingly, the 1973 Act also fails to guarantee the independence of prosecutors and the judiciary or the protection of victims and witnesses. In response to these and other criticisms, the 1973 Act was further integrated by the International Crimes Tribunal Rules of Procedure[51] and their 2011 amendment ('2011 Amendment Act'),[52] which includes provisions guaranteeing the rights to: the presumption of innocence,[53] not be tried twice for the same offence,[54] a fair and public hearing with a counsel of his choice,[55] trial without undue delay,[56] be heard in his defence,[57] not be compelled to testify or confess his guilt against his will,[58] have access to the judgment at no cost,[59] to be released on bail at any stage of the proceedings subject to certain conditions being fulfilled.[60]

Importantly, the 2011 Amendment Act also provides for the protection of victims or witnesses.[61] The ICT-BD is authorized to ensure the physical well-being of victims and witnesses and to order *in camera* proceedings to preserve the anonymity of victims and witnesses if that is in their best interests. Such measures are vital to the proceedings as well, as victims and witnesses are particularly sensitive sources of evidence, increasingly so with the passage of time.

The establishment of the Tribunal and the earlier amendments to the 1973 Act should be applauded, and these changes have been heralded as posi-

---

[51] *Ibid.*
[52] International Crimes Tribunal Rules of Procedure (Amendment), 28 June 2011 (https://www.legal-tools.org/doc/92fb50/).
[53] International Crimes Tribunal Rules of Procedure, 15 July 2010, Rule 43(2) ('International Crimes Tribunal Rules of Procedure') (https://www.legal-tools.org/doc/efe1e7/).
[54] *Ibid.*, Rule 43(3).
[55] *Ibid.*, Rule 43(4).
[56] *Ibid.*, Rule 43(5).
[57] *Ibid.*, Rule 43(6).
[58] *Ibid.*, Rule 43(7).
[59] *Ibid.*, Rule 43(4).
[60] *Ibid.*, Rule 34(3).
[61] *Ibid.*, Rule 58(A). I understand that drafters of the 2011 Amendment Act benefited from the expertise of, among others, the University of California Berkeley's International Human Rights Law Clinic and Clinical Professor of Law, Laurel E. Fletcher.

tive steps by some legal experts.[62] Article 58(A) of the 2011 Amendment Act, for instance, states that the ICT-BD may order government authorities to "ensure [the] protection, privacy and well-being" of victims and witnesses, and to maintain the confidentiality of this protective process.[63] The government shall also be required to "arrange accommodation", ensure "security and surveillance" during their stay in connection with the protective process, and take "necessary measures" to ensure that law enforcement officials "escort" victims and witnesses to the courtroom.[64] Where proceedings are held *in camera*, the prosecution and defence counsel are also required to maintain the confidentiality of the proceeding and any related information, including the identity of the victims and witnesses.[65]

Before assessing the potential efficacy of these recent amendments in facilitating the gathering of old evidence from victims and witnesses, it would be appropriate to consider another historical conflict and attendant ongoing justice process which may offer useful lessons – the ones of the Khmer Rouge crimes and the ECCC.

### 11.5. Failure to Keep Therapeutic Promises May Lead to Victims Losing Respect and Confidence

Led by Pol Pot, who died in 1998, the ultra-Maoist Khmer Rouge emptied Cambodia's cities in a bid to forge an agrarian utopia in the 1970s. Up to two million Cambodians died of starvation, overwork and torture or were executed during the regime's 1975–1979 reign. Khmer Rouge prison chief Kaing Guek Eav, alias 'Duch', was convicted for overseeing the torture and execution of around 17,000 detainees at Tuol Sleng prison, also known as 'S-21'. Four other former senior Khmer Rouge leaders are currently being tried for core international crimes at the UN-backed ECCC, which was formed in 2006 after nearly a decade of wrangling between the UN and the Cambodian government.

Cambodia, like Bangladesh, has endured its share of seemingly intractable political impasses amidst allegations that high-ranking officials of the ruling government bear responsibility for having ordered or permitted large-scale human rights violations between 1975 and 1979. Notwithstanding this, the establishment of the ECCC in 2003, the conclusion of its first trial in July 2010, and its trials of senior Khmer Rouge leaders, one of whom was formerly

---

[62] See, generally, Rapp's Recommendations, 28 November 2011, *supra* note 7. For the history of the framing of the 1973 Act, see Wali-Ur Rahman, *A Brief History of the Framing of the International Crimes (Tribunals) Act 1973*, Bangladesh Heritage Foundation.

[63] International Crimes Tribunal Rules of Procedure, Rule 58(A)(1), see *supra* note 53.

[64] *Ibid.*, Rule 58(A)(2).

[65] *Ibid.*, Rule 58(A)(3).

granted a royal amnesty for his crimes as part of a political compromise, is expected to attest to the fact that there may yet be hope for accountability in Cambodia.

Under the 2011 Amendment Act, a victim refers to a person who has suffered harm as a result of crimes under the ICT-BD's jurisdiction, without limitation as to whether such harm is physical, material or psychological.[66] Like the ICT-BD, anyone who has suffered from physical, psychological, or material harm as a direct consequence of the crimes committed by the Khmer Rouge between 1975 and 1979 is considered a victim and may apply to become a 'civil party' to the proceedings at the ECCC.

The ECCC's procedural rules permit an unprecedented degree of victim participation, surpassing even the Rome Statute.[67] By allowing victims to participate in the trials as 'civil parties', the ECCC also seeks to involve Cambodians in the pursuit of justice and national reconciliation.[68] Civil parties enjoy rights at trial akin to the prosecution and the defence. The ECCC's civil party process thus derives from a victim-oriented approach to punishment, which suggests that a victim needs to tell her story before an impartial judge within the framework of a formalized process in order to feel better.

Commentators have applauded the ECCC for giving victims a robust role, saying that it is a long overdue "recognition, after fifteen years of international and hybrid courts like [the ECCC], not to exclude victims from the justice that is being dispensed on their behalf".[69] Kheat Bophal, the former Head of the ECCC Victim's Unit, claimed that participation has the potential to transform Cambodian victims into both agents and beneficiaries of a rule of law culture:

---

[66] Article 2(26) of the 2011 Amendment Act states that "'Victim' refers to a person who has suffered harm as a result of commission of the crimes under section 3(2) of the International Crimes (Tribunals) Act, 1973".

[67] Rome Statute of the International Criminal Court, 17 July 1998 ('Rome Statute') (https://www.legal-tools.org/doc/7b9af9/).

[68] On 12 June 2007, the ECCC's Judicial Committee on the Rules of Procedure, composed of both national and international judges serving in their capacity as rule-makers, issued Internal Rules ('Internal Rules') that, *inter alia*, provided for civil party action purporting to confer on victims extensive participatory rights. These Internal Rules will guide the investigation and trial process and help ensure that the court meets international standards for fair trials. Note that the Internal Rules have been amended several times since, and are currently at the tenth revision (https://www.legal-tools.org/doc/z3ae4o/).

[69] Seth Mydans, "In the Khmer Rouge Trials, Victims Will Not Stand Idle By", *The New York Times*, 17 June 2008. Mydan states: "Diane Orentlicher, Special Counsel of the Open Society Justice Initiative believes that the Tribunal marks the evolution of international criminal justice".

> It is essential for the effectiveness and legitimacy of the Court that victims are part of the [Khmer Rouge Tribunal's] process, and that they have their own voice.
>
> Participation restores faith in the justice system and provides the first hand-satisfaction of making public the harm suffered.
>
> The process of participation also allows victims the opportunity to denounce the crimes committed against them and support norms and laws that prohibit such actions and events.[70]

In theory, the notion that victims benefit from participation is difficult to dispute, but, as we shall see, in practice, victim participation has significant limits. Participation is not always a 'panacea', nor should the trial function as a sort of modern-day 'degradation ceremony'.[71] As Morten Bergsmo has noted, "victims' interests are variegated": victims want "not only to have someone convicted, but also to have a court verify what exactly the facts were and whether the accused is responsible for those acts", and if others may have been complicit.[72]

While not perfect, *Prosecutor v. Kaing Guek Eav* ('the *Duch* case') is noteworthy also in this respect. Significantly, the ECCC Trial Chamber did not merely pronounce on Duch's guilt, but upheld his due process rights, ruling that his pre-trial detention for more than eight years by the Military Court of Cambodia was illegal and merited a reduction in his sentence.[73] This reduction, however, was quashed by the Supreme Court Chamber in the Appeal Judgment, which sentenced the accused to life imprisonment.[74]

The *Duch* case is of great importance to stability in Cambodia in the long run. In Cambodia the test of legitimacy is not arrests – the Cambodian government knows how to arrest people it does not like – but whether 'fair trials' can be carried out, allowing Cambodian victims to see that justice is possible in their country.

---

[70] "Interview with Kheat Bophal, Head of the Victim's Unit at ECCC", in *Access Victims' Rights Working Group Bulletin*, 2008, vol. 11, p. 4.

[71] See, generally, James Cockayne, "Hybrids or Mongrels? Internationalized War Crimes Trials as Unsuccessful Degradation Ceremonies", in *Journal of Human Rights*, 2005, vol. 4; and Harold Garfinkel, "Conditions of Successful Degradation Ceremonies", in *American Journal of Sociology*, 1956, vol. 61, no. 5, pp. 420–424.

[72] Morten Bergsmo, "Using Old Evidence in Core International Crimes", FICHL Policy Brief Series No. 6 (2011), Torkel Opsahl Academic EPublisher, Brussels, 2011, p. 4 (http://www.toaep.org/pbs-pdf/6-bergsmo).

[73] ECCC, *Prosecutor v. Kaing Guek Eav*, Trial Chamber, Judgment, 26 July 2010 (www.legal-tools.org/doc/dbdb62/).

[74] ECCC, *Prosecutor v. Kaing Guek Eav*, Supreme Court Chamber, Appeal Judgment, 3 February 2012 (http://www.legal-tools.org/doc/681bad/).

Bergsmo has added a cautionary note about balancing victims' interests for truth and justice through adherence to the highest legal professional and evidentiary standards in court:

> A people should be entitled to its own history, even when every detail is not documented. Yet, in comparison higher standards of evidence should apply to core international *crimes processes, where penalties are particularly severe. If old evidence should not be an excuse not to prosecute, it requires greater caution. The fact that it relates to events carrying highly emotional burdens may render it more fragile.*[75]

Complexities arise when this caution is cast aside. They are compounded when promises are made to victims about their role in formal accountability and truth-telling processes which are not honoured. These complexities have occurred at the ECCC, and should be carefully examined. In particular, I have encountered significant problems in connection with victim-oriented approaches being misunderstood or misapplied at the ECCC, which the ICT-BD's affiliates may wish to consider.

The ECCC's civil party process derives from a victim-centred approach to punishment, which suggests that a victim needs to tell her story before a decision-maker within the framework of a formalized process in order to feel better.[76] Suggestions abound about the soothing effects of participation.

To Naomi Roht-Arriaza, victims gain "a sense of control, an ability to lessen their isolation and be reintegrated into their community, and the possibility of finding meaning through participation in the process".[77] For Jamie O'Connell, participation may also restore a victim's dignity by giving him "a sense of agency and capacity to act that the original abuse sapped".[78] More than testifying as a witness, playing a role in the prosecution is said to "assist victims to take back control of their lives and to ensure that their voices are

---

[75] Bergsmo, 2011, see *supra* note 72 (emphasis added).

[76] Naomi Roht-Arriaza, *Impunity and Human Rights in International Law and International Law and Practice*, Oxford University Press, 1995, p. 21. The author notes: "more formalized procedures, including the ability to have an advocate and to confront and question their victimizers, may be more satisfying for victims than less formal, less adjudicative models".

[77] *Ibid.*, p. 19; see also Raquel Aldana-Pindell, "An Emerging Universality of Justiciable Victims' Rights in the Criminal Process to Curtail Impunity for State-Sponsored Crimes", in *Human Rights Quarterly*, 2004, vol. 26.

[78] Jamie O'Connell, "Gambling with the Psyche: Does Prosecuting Human Rights Violators Console Their Victims?", in *Harvard International Law Journal*, 2005, vol. 46, no. 2. The author quotes from a telephone interview with Mary Fabri, clinical psychologist.

heard, respected, and understood".[79] Leila Sadat notes that war crimes trials "will not only provide a forum for the particular defendant but also an arena in which the victims may be heard".[80]

In short, participation is equated with 'truth-telling', which is held out as being fundamentally and necessarily beneficial, validating the victims' experience and permitting them to heal.[81] Yet, legal justice is often too 'thin' to support therapeutic goals. The notion that victims benefit from participation is powerful, but it should be closely examined if tribunals wish to send the right message to victims.

Based on conversations with and observations of Cambodian victims and civil parties at the ECCC, it is my view that unless modestly conveyed and properly managed, the message of victim participation can devolve into a rhetorical device:[82] a device that soothes the ECCC's affiliates and donors, but not all victims, some of whom complain that their token participation in the ECCC trial proceedings has "revive(d) memories, bitterness and misery", and engendered a "loss of faith in the ECCC".[83]

Despite being a hybrid court based in Phnom Penh, the ECCC has at times externalized justice away from Cambodian victims. The ECCC's promise that victims have a place in the proceedings results in heightened disillusionment for victims when the process turns out to be unreceptive to and incompatible with their subjective impressions, general reminiscences, emotions

---

[79] Yael Danieli, "Victims: Essential Voices at the Court", Victims' Rights Working Group, London, 2004, p. 6.

[80] Leila Nadya Sadat, "Redefining Universal Jurisdiction", in *New England Law Review*, 2001, vol. 35, pp. 241–263.

[81] Judith Lewis Herman, *Trauma and Recovery*, Basic Books, New York, 1992, p. 181. The author notes that the "fundamental premise of psychotherapeutic work [with survivors of severe trauma] is a belief in the restorative power of truth-telling".

[82] See, generally, Mahdev Mohan and Vani Sathisan, "Erasing the Non-Judicial Narrative: Victim Testimonies at the Khmer Rouge Tribunal", in *Jindal Global Law Review*, 2011, vol. 2, no. 2; Mahdev Mohan, "The Paradox of Victim-Centrism – Victim Participation at the Khmer Rouge Tribunal", in *International Criminal Law Review*, 2009, vol. 5, no. 5, pp. 733–775.

[83] Victims' Press Conference at the ECCC, "Victims Voice their Hopes and Concerns about ECCC", 3 December 2009, press release (on file with author):

We hope participation in this process will provide us with some relief, a sense that justice has been done and an understanding of our history; but it also revives memories, bitterness, and misery. We began with hope that the ECCC would provide some satisfaction, but we are now concerned about the delays, the allegations of corruption, the sufficiency of available resources, and the lack of information on the progress made by the ECCC and prospects for our involvement. These problems prompt many of us to lose hope and faith in the ECCC.

---

and renditions of truth.[84] This has happened to, for instance, some Cambodian civil parties. Others who have applied to become civil parties but have been told that their applications are inadmissible for jurisdictional reasons – for instance, because the crimes they suffered took place outside the 1975–1979 timeframe – have felt affronted because their status and identity as victims has been questioned. Still others wish to speak in their own voice in court rather than through prosecutors and are distraught when the evidence they take pains to re-tell does not make their way into the official record.[85] Preventing affected communities from joining the proceedings may also have, as already mentioned, the unintended consequence of alienating potential sources of evidence.

Historically, the indigenous lowland Khmers or 'Khmer Krom' have been a marginalized minority group due to their geographical, historical and cultural ties to both Cambodia and Vietnam. Their distinct identity also made the Khmer Krom community the target of crimes during the Khmer Rouge regime. In the Khmer Krom heartland of the Bakan district, Pursat Province, up to 80 per cent of the community was singled out and slaughtered *en masse* by the Khmer Rouge, who considered them to be traitors associated with the Vietnamese – persons with 'Khmer bodies but Vietnamese minds'. This was a calculated mass murder with some chilling parallels to the notorious Srebrenica massacre of 1995 in Bosnia and Herzegovina.

Yet, for two years, the Khmer Krom community remained a blind-spot for the Investigating Judges and Co-Prosecutors at the ECCC, who had repeatedly failed to acknowledge their evidence. In January 2010, the ECCC's Co-Investigating Judges decided to charge the suspects for crimes against Cambodia's Cham Muslim and ethnic Vietnamese minorities, but not the Khmer Krom (ethnic Khmers with roots in southern Vietnam). This omission stemmed in part from the prosecution's exclusion of the Khmer Krom from its investigations, which left the Court's judges unable to pursue such charges, despite compelling evidence of mass killing and forced displacement of the Khmer Krom throughout Cambodia.[86]

---

[84] Marie-Benedicte Dembour and Emily Haslam, "Silencing Hearings? Victim-Witnesses at War Crimes Trials", in *European Journal of International Law*, 2004, vol. 15, no. 151, p. 156.

[85] See, generally, Mohan and Sathisan, 2011, see *supra* note 82.

[86] The ECCC based its decision partly on a technicality. Months earlier, prosecutors had sent a memorandum to the Co-Investigating Judges about possible genocide against Khmer Krom in Pursat Province. They entitled the memorandum an "investigative request" rather than a 'supplementary submission'. The latter title would have triggered a judicial investigation.

---

However, Khmer Krom survivors continued to press their case with the ECCC, submitting extensive evidence of the atrocities they suffered and detailing prison sites and mass graves. These efforts paid off.

On 13 June 2010, former ECCC's International Co-Prosecutor Andrew Cayley reached out to Khmer Krom survivors. Meeting for the first time with nearly 200 of them in Pursat Province, on the grounds of a pagoda where Khmer Krom had been executed, Cayley acknowledged the need to present to the Court the atrocities committed against the Khmer Krom people.

On 17 June 2011, Cayley lived up to his word. He filed a "Request for Investigative Action and Supplementary Submission" which adds additional crimes to a new case at the Court (*Case 004*), including crimes committed against the Khmer Krom population in Takeo and Pursat provinces, based primarily on civil party evidence. Subsequent developments, such as *Case 002/02*, have enshrined the relevance of the evidence provided by this group. In July 2018, Cayley's successor, Nicholas Koumjian, issued a summary of the statements in *Case 004* against accused person Yim Tith. The summary acknowledged that the accused met the requirements for most responsible to fall under the jurisdiction of the Court, and in his positions, Tith "ordered and facilitated crimes that resulted in large-scale atrocities in the Northwestern Zone [and] should be tried for the genocide of Vietnamese and Khmer Krom groups in Cambodia in addition to murder charges".[87]

The fate of *Case 004* is uncertain at the time of writing. Regardless, evidence provided by initially excluded groups, and which is yet to be documented, plays a central role in *Case 004*.

As one civil party eruditely put it when speaking to court officials:

> Give me, give us [civil parties] the voice that you promised. Do not play with the hearts and the souls of the victims and my (dead) parents. Justice must be transparent, if not it will be for nothing, and you will have a real problem on your hands.[88]

For its part, the ECCC – fearing an onslaught of more than 3,800 Cambodians who have been admitted as civil parties, all jostling for an opportunity to address the court – has back-pedalled on several of the rights it originally conferred on civil parties. All in all, the civil party process promises far more than it can deliver. Legal accountability processes can buckle under the strain of supporting ambitious therapeutic or restorative goals. The ECCC and other accountability processes should instead abide by their foundational goal of

---

[87] See "Prosecutors at ECCC Issue Summaries of Case 004 Statements", *Phnom Penh Post*, 3 July 2018.
[88] Mohan, 2009, p. 26, see *supra* note 82.

delivering accountability under the law. To ask more of it may be asking too much of any criminal trial. Restorative justice may better reside with complementary processes that can be more receptive to strategies that commemorate victims in the non-legal arena using pre-existing traditions that are communicated in a manner that resonate with victims.

As we shall see, practice at the ECCC offers important lessons on the inherent challenges of eliciting 'old evidence' from victims or witnesses; how to gather credible old evidence from them; and the protective processes that ought to be supported and strictly enforced when seeking to inspire victims and witnesses to come forward to share their traumatic narratives with the tribunal.

## 11.6. The Importance of Sending the Message That the Trials Are Independent

The involvement of victims in justice processes for core international crimes present significant challenges related to how such processes are perceived by victims and witnesses. This is not because international justice actors, affiliates and lawyers have to deal with victims who are powerless, helpless innocents whose naturalist attributes have been negated. As Mutua notes, that presumption, which has at times unwittingly informed the larger international criminal justice process, is often as flawed as it is offensive.[89] On the contrary, victims or witnesses are keenly aware of the possible risks that their testimony may involve. After all, piecemeal investigations or purported laws promising protection that may not be enforced are problematic, particularly in the eyes of Bangladeshi victims, who have historical reasons not to trust any exercise that resembles official information gathering, and whose victimization goes back in time to 1971.

Victims of mass crimes which transpired over three decades ago and who have not benefited from timely justice processes and legal remedies are necessarily aware that the promise of such processes and remedies may be but a mirage. Despite the due-process guarantees that have been introduced by the above-mentioned legislative amendments, other extant constitutional provisions send a different message.

Under Article 47(A) of the Bangladesh Constitution, traditional fair trial rights which are accorded to all other citizens have been deliberately withdrawn from persons detained, suspected or charged in connection with crimes within the scope of the 1973 Act. Linton highlights additional difficulties undermining due process, as well as concerns over the retention of the death pen-

---

[89] Makau Mutua, "Savages, Victims, and Saviors: The Metaphor of Human Rights", in *Harvard International Law Journal*, 2001, vol. 42, no. 1, p. 201.

alty.[90] As Linton notes, "such considerations could have enriched and improved the Bangladeshi law in the amendments of 2009, in a way that is consistent with the overarching principle of legality".[91]

Steven Kay, too, has been moved to lament as follows:

> The overall effect of these measures was to put persons questioned, detained, suspected of committing crimes or charged with crimes within the International Crimes (Tribunal) Act 1973 outside the norms of the national legal system. For the first time inequality has been introduced into the Bangladesh justice system by the Constitution that claimed to promote equality.[92]

War crimes courts cannot apply justice selectively and all applicable legislation undergirding the ICT-BD's judicial process should be harmonized. The process and the victims it seeks to vindicate are not helped by anything which may resemble a 'degradation ceremony', regardless of how heinous the alleged crimes may be. In fact, the greatest danger to such a process is the perception that it may be denouncing certain groups, whilst implicitly condoning others that are equally or more culpable. Such a perception robs the court of its legitimacy in the eyes of local and international stakeholders and undermines its goals. This is precisely what happened when Pol Pot and Khmer Rouge Foreign Minister, Ieng Sary, were tried *in absentia* for genocide and other international crimes in 1979, by the so-called People's Revolutionary Tribunal ('PRT') established by the Vietnamese-installed Heng Samrin administration.[93]

Although foreign lawyers had been invited to serve as prosecutors and defence counsel in order to 'reflect international standards of justice' and thereby enhance the legitimacy of the proceedings, the PRT was not well received by local and international stakeholders. The short duration of the trial, the denial of due process rights to the defendants who were convicted *in absentia* and a poor defence combined to create the impression of mob justice. These factors created the impression of "primitive political justice" which was seen to be "akin to the Stalinist show trials of the 1930s".[94] Many Cambodian victims of the Khmer Rouge regime saw the trial as an assertion of Vietnamese sovereignty over Cambodia. The reaction in the West to the verdict was con-

---

[90] Linton, 2010, see *supra* note 28.
[91] *Ibid.*, p. 209.
[92] Steven Kay QC, "Bangladesh War Crimes Tribunal – A Wolf in Sheep's Clothing?", *International Criminal Law Bureau*, 2010.
[93] US Bureau of Citizenship and Immigration Services, "Cambodia: Information on P.G. Jail in Phnom Penh from 1979–1981", 13 May 2003 (https://www.legal-tools.org/doc/xrzxbg/).
[94] Peter Maguire, *Facing Death in Cambodia*, Columbia University Press, 2005, p. 65.

spicuous silence – all it commanded was two square inches in the back pages of *The New York Times*.

In contrast, the UN-backed ECCC was established by virtue of a great deal of patience and skilful negotiation. Throughout the 1980s, Cold War politics and competing national interests impeded the establishment of a tribunal to try Khmer Rouge leaders. Painstaking negotiations among the UN, various member states and Cambodia over much of the ensuing decade reflected a mixture of ambivalence, conflicting priorities and active hostility to the Court, depending on the government in question.

Despite this, Cambodian Prime Minister Hun Sen, himself formerly a Khmer Rouge cadre, was moved in 1997 to request the UN to assist in bringing senior Khmer Rouge leaders to book through war crimes trials. Mr. Hun Sen invited international participation in the trials due to the weakness of the Cambodian legal system and the international nature of the crimes, and to help meet international standards of justice.

Until the requisite political will and donor support aligned to permit the creation of the ECCC, the idea of a UN-backed tribunal was kept alive by a variety of diplomats, UN actors, international non-governmental organizations ('NGOs') and Cambodian NGOs. Prominent actors included, among others, the UN Office of the High Commissioner for Human Rights, US Senator John Kerry, US Ambassador-at-large for War Crimes David Scheffer, the Director of Genocide Watch Gregory Stanton, academics from the Yale Genocide Program and Cambodian civil society leaders such as Youk Chhang, Director of the Documentation Centre for Cambodia ('DC-Cam').

International negotiators and experts, such as the Group of Experts which was established by the UN Secretary-General in 1999, were instrumental in laying the foundation for the ECCC. At times, they settled for a compromise, such as when the UN decided against the Group's recommendation to establish an *ad hoc* tribunal pursuant to the UN Security Council's powers under Chapter VII of the UN Charter to restore international peace and security, and instead established a hybrid tribunal situated in Cambodia so that local communities could better identify with the process.

On other occasions, negotiators stood firm, such as when the UN withdrew from negotiations with Cambodia in 2002 because they had not yet yielded the result of impartiality and independence required for UN cooperation. Finally, the ECCC was established in 2003 with UN's chief negotiator, then Under-Secretary General for Legal Affairs Hans Corell, stating that the ECCC's foundational documents and processes were "designed to ensure a fair and public trial by an independent and impartial court".[95]

Mr. Corell's faith in the ECCC was vindicated when the ECCC's Trial Chamber delivered its first judgment in the *Duch* case – a well-reasoned decision which has been praised for its sound treatment of the facts before the Court. Had the ECCC been rushed into action ahead of its time, rather than through a phased-in approach over several years, or had international negotiators caved in to pressure to allow national judges to have greater say in deciding cases rather than ensuring that decisions will require a 'super-majority' to be conclusive, it is likely that chances of securing justice would have been scuttled or led to results that would not have been viewed as credible, fair or impartial by national and international stakeholders alike.

It is striking that despite the more than 40 years that have elapsed since the fall of the Khmer Rouge, the trials are broadly considered meaningful and important by the Cambodian public. Despite the long delay, the general public followed the *Duch* trial with great interest, as indicated, among other things, by the very large television viewing audience the trial attracted. While a delay in justice is hardly advisable as a matter of course, it is important to bear in mind that justice delayed is not necessarily justice denied – war crimes trials that come long after a conflict may nonetheless enjoy very considerable public support and may operate to promote reasoned reflection upon the past. Having said this, it may still be too early to tell whether, as some ECCC affiliates argue, the trials will in themselves make a significant contribution to societal reconciliation by 'healing' survivors.

Tribunals such as the ECCC have grand ambitions of delivering 'justice', in the broadest sense of the word. Judging by continued obstacles to accountability at the ECCC, however, it appears justice does not come easy or cheap. Cambodians have faced a long road to justice. At the time of the submission of the chapter for the first edition of this book, the final two cases pending before the ECCC, referred to as *Cases 003/004*, were submitted for judicial investigation in September 2009, concerning former Khmer Rouge cadres who were part of or closely associated with the ruling political party and the Hun Sen administration.[96] Unsurprisingly, little has been achieved since, due in part to the reluctance of national investigators to co-operate.

---

95  "UN and Cambodia Reach Draft Agreement for Prosecuting Khmer Rouge Crimes", *UN News*, 17 March 2003 (https://www.legal-tools.org/doc/8brxc5/).

96  See, generally, Robert Carmichael, "Tribunal's Credibility Under Threat as Controversial Cases Head for Closure", *Radio Australia*, 11 May 2011 (https://www.legal-tools.org/doc/57pn8d/); James A. Goldston, "Justice Delayed and Denied", *The New York*

The reluctance of the ECCC's top Cambodian investigators to proceed with *Cases 003/004* is likely in response to statements from high-ranking Cambodian officials indicating that these trials should not go forward. The clearest example of ostensible interference came from Prime Minister Hun Sen when he told the UN Secretary-General, "Case 003 will not be allowed [...]. The court will try the four senior leaders successfully and then finish with Case 002".[97] The International Co-Investigating Judge resigned from his post, ostensibly in protest against his inability to make headway in *Cases 003/004* (or their mini-trials).[98] Both cases have attracted an overwhelming amount of criticism from commentators due to the serious and consistent allegations of political interference by the Cambodian government. In the past years, several senior ECCC officials have resigned from their posts, citing, in some instances, the government's interference as making it impossible for them to carry out their functions.[99]

Despite the success of the first trial before the ECCC, the controversy aroused by the Prime Minister's remarks, and similar happenings, has become a threat to the Court's legitimacy. If, in fact, the case still before the ECCC is not permitted to go forward because of political interference, the Court will be seen as having failed both to provide accountability and to serve as a model of the rule of law for Cambodia. The lesson we can glean from this is that if the independence, impartiality and effectiveness of an accountability mechanism cannot be guaranteed at its inception, the expectations of victims may be disappointed and the culture of impunity may be reinforced rather than overcome. Being forced by the circumstances to work with old evidence is no excuse to not seek accountability, or to not do so appropriately; importantly, the victims' views do matter in this regard, especially if their will to provide evidence depends on the perceived legitimacy of the jurisdiction.

This lesson is particularly apposite in Bangladesh as genuine concerns have been expressed by victims that the ICT-BD trials could be advanced by the current administration to gain political or electoral mileage, and if there is

---

*Times*, 13 October 2011; see also Sok Khemara, "Alleged Genocidaire Could See Case Dismissed at Khmer Rouge Tribunal", *Voice of America Cambodia*, 3 March 2018.

[97] "Hun Sen to Ban Ki-moon: Case 002 Last Trial at ECCC", *Phnom Penh Post*, 27 October 2010.

[98] See the following reports by civil society actors that called for (and achieved) this resignation due to the fact that the ECCC had not made any progress on *Cases 003/004*, see Open Society Justice Initiative, "Recent Developments at the Extraordinary Chambers in the Courts of Cambodia: June 2011 Update", 14 June 2011 (available on its web site); Human Rights Watch, "Cambodia: Judges Investigating Khmer Rouge Crimes Should Resign", 3 October 2011 (available on its web site).

[99] See Human Rights Watch, 2011, *supra* note 98.

a change in power, the ICT-BD may be strangled at birth. Like the suspects in *Cases 003/004* at the ECCC, many of the suspects and accused persons at the ICT-BD have long-standing political ties.[100] Bangladeshi victims would not be alone in harbouring such suspicions, as expert commentators too have argued that the trials may be politically motivated, calculated to shift focus away from other issues which impair the current administration's political control.[101]

As former Ambassador Rapp noted, it is "important that the trials be carried out in a way that will stand the test of time".[102] While this is far easier said than done, no effort should be spared in order to insulate the Tribunal from political interference. The best tool for such insulation is for the Tribunal to adhere to domestic and international legal standards which will help it make clear that it is a separate and independent body within the judicial branch of government that is beyond executive interference.

It is important, therefore, that the ICT-BD's affiliates entertain modest ambitions when it comes to devising and calibrating its process. In view of the current political climate in Bangladesh and the historical lens through which the ICT-BD may be viewed by victims and the international community, it would be beneficial if the ICT-BD ensured that its legal and judicial officials possess the requisite training and resources to see the process to fruition, in compliance with Bangladeshi law and international law and standards.

For a start, the ICT-BD's practical challenges and capacity constraints should be anticipated and addressed. It has been reported that approximately USD 1.5 million has been approved by the Cabinet for the trial.[103] Yet, the elements of the legal process covered by the budget are unclear and the sheer scope of crimes and alleged criminals within its jurisdiction are staggering.[104] The ECCC has done well to have planned for similar exigencies[105] so that it could have deployed its resources more effectively in the last five years.

---

[100] "War Crimes and Misdemeanours: Justice, Reconciliation – or Score-settling?", *The Economist*, 24 March 2011.

[101] D'Costa, 2011, pp. 158–159, see *supra* note 1.

[102] Rapp, 2011, p. 22, see *supra* note 19.

[103] D'Costa, 2011, p. 159, see *supra* note 1.

[104] See Linton, 2010, p. 309, see *supra* note 28; D'Costa, 2011, see *supra* note 1; D'Costa and Hossain, "Redress for Sexual Violence before the International Crimes Tribunal in Bangladesh: Lessons from History and Hopes for the Future", in *Criminal Law Forum*, 2010, vol. 21, no. 2, pp. 331–332.

[105] The ECCC planned to spend close to USD 200 million to try five defendants, a big increase from the court's initial three-year budget of USD 56.3 million – an amount unfathomable to many ordinary Cambodians who live on less than USD 1 a day. Such plan proved to be unrealistic, as the ECCC has spent USD 357.5 million since its inception: however, it was far closer to the mark than the initial budget. The Court's spokespersons have emphasized that

As intuitive as it may be to commence war crimes trials, absent systematic investigations, sufficient resources and sustained political will, or an adequate mandate and principled completion strategy, such trials may be mired in challenges. This is particularly true when there are additional concerns related to old evidence, or engagement with victims and witnesses. Flawed trials may also divert precious attention and resources from achievable restorative goals. Criminal prosecution is just one element in a toolbox of post-conflict justice and accountability. In any given context, those who seek accountability must closely examine their objectives to ensure that the mix of tools they select is best tailored to the particular need. Exaggerating what just one tool – prosecution – can reasonably accomplish may mean that other avenues which are more meaningful and effective are not explored or are prematurely foreclosed.

## 11.7. Investigating, Documenting and Preserving: The Role of Civil Society

Another innovative way to bolster the legitimacy of a judicial institution prosecuting atrocities would be for it to make appropriate reference to and rely on other independent and complementary transitional justice processes that may be well-received by the victims. The experience in Cambodia points to the key role that civil society may play. The lessons from these contexts indicate that international practitioners who wish to engage in investigation and documentation of alleged mass atrocities are more likely to succeed if they engage and work with local experts who enjoy the trust and confidence of victims and, in some cases, of at least some governmental actors. In my experience partnering with local experts in a respectful and constructive manner is a necessary prerequisite for gaining a sound legal and forensic understanding of the nature of the mass atrocities, their scale and their geographical sweep. This sets the foundation stone for proper documentation of victim narratives, which will in turn form the basis for comparative assessment and corroboration of new testimonial evidence of old crimes which may emerge in the course of the investigations and trials.

In Cambodia, leading local NGOs have assisted in interviewing vulnerable survivor communities and put forward data that has assisted the ECCC to charge defendants for crimes such as genocide and forced marriage, which were hitherto unknown to ECCC prosecutors.[106] Valuable insight can be obtained by looking at NGOs in Cambodia such as DC-Cam, which was first es-

---

Cambodia's hybrid court looked like a bargain compared with tribunals in Rwanda and the former Yugoslavia, which have cost about USD 150 million a year.

[106] Similarly, in Timor-Leste, for example, it was national NGOs that led the way in documenting systematic sexual violence, providing a report that spurred investigation into such crimes.

tablished by international funding and supported by academic research to conduct research, documentation and training on the Khmer Rouge regime. DC-Cam and the Tuol Sleng Museum serve as the principal sources of evidentiary material for the ECCC. DC-Cam's very inception can be traced back to a statute passed by the US Congress in April 1994 – the Cambodian Genocide Justice Act – that led to the establishment of the Yale Genocide Program in the US, and to the birth of DC-Cam in 1997.

The organization's motto, "searching for the truth", gives it the aura of an investigative entity tasked with finding, corroborating and recording facts. DC-Cam's Director, Youk Chhang, emphasized this when he told the press, "They say that time heals all wounds, but time alone can do nothing. You will always have time. To me, research heals. Knowing and understanding what happened has set me free".[107] In its methodical approach to gathering data, DC-Cam is "analysing an oral text, and correlating it with other, written documents and other pieces of information" to "'restore' the text to its 'original' version, and situate this version in its social context, establishing the particular perspective on the past that the 'oral document' takes".[108]

As the nation's primary repository of documents relating to the Khmer Rouge that provided the ECCC with its secondary evidence, we ask how the very act of 'searching for the truth' has been significantly influenced by DC-Cam. The lesson to be learnt here is that under the right circumstances a limited and well-calibrated mandate to document and preserve old evidence can achieve success in establishing the truth, while a broader mandate might well undermine it, regardless how noble its intentions.

Nevertheless, despite the best efforts of archives and libraries in Cambodia and elsewhere, over the years much evidence of and witnesses to the Cambodian 'killing fields' have been destroyed, disappeared or perished and unfortunately will not form part of Cambodia's historical record.[109] For victims of mass violence who have now come forward to give evidence, including their testimony in the ECCC's legal record or in some other virtual space which acts as a repository of their important narratives and aspirations may become the only formal acknowledgment they will receive of the atrocities

---

[107] Stefan Lovgren, "Documenting Cambodia's Genocide, Survivor Finds Peace", *National Geographic News*, 23 January 2008.

[108] James Fentress and Chris Wickham, *Social Memory*, Blackwell Publishers, Oxford, 1992.

[109] Tuol Sleng has been in a state of gross disrepair, with inadequate facilities to house and archive old primary documents, despite its status as a 'museum'. Observers have noted that its staff lack training in the proper preservation of such material, and little has been done to fulfil the wishes of survivors who were interred there, to refurbish it and turn it into a proper memorial site.

they endured under the Khmer Rouge regime.[110] Former ECCC International Co-Prosecutor Andrew Cayley puts it well:

> [I]t is crucial that evidence be documented as soon as possible and as regularly as possible thereafter. This documentation should be preserved in a form which will permit it to be understood and interpreted. Also it is very important that original documents be retained and that chains of custody are able to be proven.
>
> With regard to crimes committed decades ago [...] the above circumstance may not be present; however those prosecuting international crimes should seek out interested persons and organizations that have been collecting evidence from the relevant period. Furthermore, electronic data systems and other advanced technologies should be used to discover, preserve, organize, analyze and disseminate evidence of crimes. These are invaluable tools to both those who are prosecuting and defending.[111]

Civil society can complement the work of the judiciary by interviewing potential witnesses, identifying and analysing narratives of survival, securing important primary evidence, implementing measures to prevent the destruction of documents and forensic evidence, and providing a basis to begin to confront the conflict and its consequences. By identifying and preserving evidence, both through traditional and electronic means, such archives may yet make a significant contribution to the success of future prosecutions.

## 11.8. Accounting for the Distinction Between Judicial and Non-Judicial Actors

Investigation and documentation of alleged mass atrocities can be led by formal or informal truth and reconciliation commissions and referenda, by civil society, or by researchers at academic and documentation institutions dedicated to contemporaneous data collection and analysis. Where effective formal judicial accountability mechanisms are stalled, transitional justice processes devoted to truth and reconciliation can nonetheless provide a foundation for sustained accountability, not to mention strengthen local legal capacity and justice institutions which maintain the rule of law.

---

[110] A Victims Register or *Kraing Meas* ('Golden Book') whereby victims' information and narratives will be maintained in physical and online formats by the ECCC in co-ordination with NGOs. The online format of the register could be an important component of the Virtual Tribunal, an online educational legacy tool chronicling the regime and the work of the ECCC developed under the leadership of Professor David Cohen at Stanford University.

[111] As summarized in Bergsmo, 2011, p. 2, see *supra* note 72.

The lessons from Cambodia show how important the role of civil society can be in locating and preserving the documentary record of a conflict, a crucial source of old evidence. Ideally, collaborative civil society and court initiatives can make use of that documentary record and victim testimonies and narratives for educational purposes as well, for assisting victims to come to terms with the past, and for fathoming how to prevent and deter mass atrocities. Yet, compulsory truth-telling is not always effective or well-received in Asian or non-Judeo-Christian societies, where speech may be seen as performative and not necessarily consistent with justice and reconciliation.

An initiative spearheaded by a Cambodian NGO a few years ago is instructive in this regard. From 2006 to 2008, the Centre for Social Development ('CSD') sought to create an outreach programme that was one of the most ambitious and far-reaching efforts by any NGO at that juncture. Its then Executive Director, Theary Seng, stated during one such public forum that "the goal is to broaden the conversational space and to put down the burden of the past, which many have carried silently for too long. In that sense, ours is an informal truth and reconciliation commission".[112]

The combined effect of these informal public forums and the legal outreach work of civil society organizations in the context of the ECCC is to extol 'truth telling' and positivist ideas of the law as the main paths to reconciliation. As one Cambodian victim said during one of these forums: "We need *clear and exact facts/cases* from Cambodian people. In the past they did not collect written evidence but they can tell what they have suffered. But in law it is not enough to be regarded as evidence, so it's not relevant".[113]

Several difficulties arose in the course of this civil society organization ('CSO') initiative, which typify legal outreach and informal transitional justice processes that CSOs have conducted in Cambodia.

First, as the victim's quote above demonstrates, the discourse of truth-telling has become synonymous with 'facts' established within the court of law, rather than 'truth' and is evidenced by the sorts of impassioned remarks made by victims at non-judicial *fora*: in the course of public forums, press interviews and civil society meetings. If allowed to overreach themselves, CSO-led non-judicial truth-telling processes may often become freighted with the same baggage that weighs heavily upon judicial war crimes trials – *id est*, a desire to compel a population that preferred to heal through forgetting into "truth-telling

---

[112] Theary C. Seng, "Opening Speech at the Phnom Penh Public Forum", 14 November 2007.
[113] On file with the author.

subjects who would, after adequate sensitization, recognize their 'need' to talk about the violence".[114]

However, when CSOs take a legal tone, it has a profound impact on how people are expressing their memories; how they understand justice and the law. As Rosalind Shaw aptly stated with regards to the Truth and Reconciliation Commission in Sierra Leone:

> Different regions and localities, moreover, have their own memory practices and often their own techniques of social recovery that may have developed during the course of their own history. How do these practices intersect with public truth telling during a truth commission?[115]

In the case of Sierra Leone, Shaw indicates that local practices were largely focused on 'forgiving and forgetting' and that "valorizing verbally discursive remembering"[116] was problematic as a result.

Shaw's words are apposite in the ECCC context as well. Even if she was referring to a truth and reconciliation commission and not a tribunal as is the case in Cambodia, the combined effect of these informal public forums and the legal outreach work of CSOs in the context of the ECCC is to extol 'truth telling' and positivist ideas of the law as the main paths to reconciliation. Non-judicial initiatives which seek to establish a historical record and smooth out the creases of conflicting versions of the truth or collective memory in the public's mind can be antithetical to the victim's desire to disclose vital nuanced truths and layered memories which depart from the 'standard total view'.[117]

Insisting on forming or adhering to collective memory can also run contrary to the judicial endeavour. In other words, judges cannot presume to accept 'facts of public notoriety' which have not been established as agreed or probative facts in accordance with the applicable standard of proof.[118]

---

[114] Rosalind Shaw, *Rethinking Truth and Reconciliation Commissions: Lessons from Sierra Leone*, US Institute of Peace, February 2005, Special Report No. 130, p. 4.

[115] *Ibid.*, p. 3.

[116] *Ibid.*, p. 12.

[117] Michael Vickery, *Cambodia 1975–1982*, South End Press, Boston, 1984.

[118] Bergsmo, 2011, p. 3, see *supra* note 72; ECCC Supreme Court Chamber Judge Agnieszka Klonowiecka-Milart states:

> [Beware of] the danger of collective memory, as forged through secondary sources such as reports or books. First the demonstration of individual criminal responsibility should clearly be distinguished from the establishment of the background of facts. Second, tribunals should be very careful in addressing what might be presented to them as 'facts of public notoriety'. Such concepts might serve the economy of the trial, but they de facto lower the standard of proof.

In order to elicit credible evidence, especially when much time has passed from the commission of the crimes, one must keep in mind what remembering and recounting traumatic and deeply personal events entails. After all, to remember is to have a 'reading' of the past, which:

> requires linguistic skills derived from the traditions of explanation and story-telling within a culture and which [presents] issues in a narrative that owes its meaning ultimately to the interpretative practices of a community of speakers.[119]

A key problem in Cambodia has been the lack of adequate investigation into what local practices are in this regard. Cognizant of this *lacuna* at the ECCC and its attendant processes, any judicial initiative should explore the non-judicial arena when considering victim-oriented measures premised on restorative justice, regardless of how alien that may seem to lawyers. Non-judicial initiatives which run or will run parallel to the ECCC's trials give victims confidence that restorative justice can be meted outside the courtroom at a spiritual ceremony or ritual, through testimonial therapy, on a dramatic stage or through the arts.[120] With regards to the ICT-BD, there are informal transitional justice mechanisms like the *Shalish* in Bangladesh, arguably akin to the *Gacaca* in Rwanda, which can also be further researched and explored.[121]

Second, by taking on the mantle of the court when speaking to victims about their evidence and using and encouraging the language of the law, CSOs externalize their greatest strength – their roots in and connection to the community and the trust and confidence that this connection inspires and the narratives it elicits. Without this connection, victims or witnesses will look upon civil society as an extension of the court or the government, which is not always beneficial. The proposition that the involvement of judges necessarily makes proceedings more accessible to local constituents is doubtful. It has been my experience that Cambodian victims are generally more suspicious of justice initiatives that are linked to local authorities and judges, some of whom are regarded as corrupt.

Third, inexperienced or untrained local CSOs can also miss the point and undermine the legal process. Speaking extra-judicially, ECCC Supreme Court Chamber Judge Agnieszka Klonowiecka-Milart remarked as follows:

> [Beware of] the frailty of contemporaneously adduced evidence, especially in relation to its physical availability and credibility.

---

[119] David Bakhurst, "Social Memory in Soviet Thought", in David Middleton and Derek Edwards (eds.), *Collective Remembering*, Sage, London, 1990, pp. 209.

[120] For further details on the sort of initiatives which can be supported, see Mohan and Sathisan, 2011, *supra* note 82.

[121] See, generally, Banglapedia, "Shalish" (available on its web site).

---

> The latter is especially salient when civil society participates in the collection of evidence as its lack of adequate training may impede the process. This is one of the reasons why the adversarial nature of the proceedings should be enhanced, if necessary through international involvement.[122]

Non-judicial processes must therefore retain their independence and separation from the judicial arena. Justice actors should be wary of civil society-led or entirely national commissions of inquiry, surveys, referenda or truth commissions which profess to deliver healing: however noble the intentions of such commissions or processes may appear, they are, as mentioned earlier, inherently problematic in complex political contexts such as most post-atrocity societies.

## 11.9. Retooling Law and Ethnography: Victims Deserve Proper Presentation

What then of the adversarial judicial processes, such as the ICT-BD, as a method to elicit credible old evidence from Bangladeshi victims? Noting that old evidence is not necessarily bad evidence, Judge Alphons M.M. Orie (of the former International Criminal Tribunal for the former Yugoslavia) has advanced the following instructive suggestions for ICT-BD judges:

> When drawing inferences from the evidence presented, what matters the most is to understand the psychological mechanisms underlying such a process, beyond a mere legal approach. The story of the criminal event needs to be tested in all its details, even when conclusions seem easy to draw. The search for positive and negative indicia should aim at verifying or falsifying the elements of the story. This sounds even more imperative when inferences rely on witness statements, considered as the most 'vulnerable' evidence.[123]

Yet, the judicial arena too is not without its inherent constraints which, if lawyers and judges are not careful, results in critical old evidence being compromised and the victims who possess them being scarred. The experience of civil parties in the *Duch* case is noteworthy in this regard. The judicial endeavour of the ECCC to maintain a legally authoritative account of what happened, crippled the participation of the civil parties as they were excluded from the process of asking questions that were vital in aiding them deal with their post-conflict trauma. Several civil parties were also forced to leave the stand as their identities as victims were questioned by the Tribunal. During the testimo-

---

[122] As summarized in Bergsmo, 2011, p. 3, see *supra* note 72.
[123] *Ibid.*, p. 2.

ny of civil party Ly Hor,[124] an alleged survivor of S-21, inconsistencies in his account led Duch to publicly challenge his identity as a victim.[125] Such an experience, scholars and trial monitors assert, may "defeat the positive outcomes of participation and instead lead to re-traumatization".[126] Civil party Ly Hor took the stand only to have his oral testimony and credibility come under fire as it deviated materially from both his written statement and the written confession purportedly produced at S-21 that he insisted was his own. Ly Hor's lawyers,[127] who appeared none the wiser, were unable to offer any satisfactory reason for why the ECCC Trial Chamber should nevertheless regard the documents as supportive of Ly Hor's claim.[128] "I suppose you would agree with me that this civil party has been very poorly prepared for this morning's experience", was Judge Sylvia Cartwright's wry admonishment to Ly Hor's lawyers,[129] after a morning of questioning that saw Ly Hor become visibly and increasingly distressed.[130] Also taken to task by the Chamber were the lawyers for civil party Nam Mon[131] for her belated disclosure of new allegations, which were eventually rejected.[132]

But to Ly Hor and Nam Mon, the inaccuracy of the written statements was arguably peripheral to the fact that Phaok Khan was able to recount his "very interesting" experiences before the Trial Chamber.[133] The applications of Ly Hor and Nam Mon were ultimately rejected by the Trial Chamber.[134] By

---

[124] Labelled civil party E2/61.

[125] See KRT Trial Monitor, "Report Issue No. 12: Week Ending 9 July 2009", 9 July 2009, p. 2 ('KRT Report No. 12').

[126] Michelle Staggs Kelsall *et al.*, "Lessons Learnt from the Duch Trial", Asian International Justice Initiative, KRT Trial Monitoring Group, p. 34.

[127] Ly Hor was represented by lawyers from Civil Party Group 1.

[128] ECCC, *Prosecutor v. Kaing Guek Eav*, Trial Chamber, Transcript of Trial Proceedings, 6 July 2009, pp. 58–59 ('*Duch* case, Transcript') (https://www.legal-tools.org/doc/22aae2/). According to one of Ly Hor's lawyers, the use of an informal instead of official translation resulted in the true purport of his client's documentation being unclear.

[129] *Ibid.*, p. 55. Ly Hor had informed the Trial Chamber that the last time he spoke to his lawyers was a month before his Court appearance, see *ibid.*

[130] KRT Report No. 12, p. 7, see *supra* note 125.

[131] Labelled civil party E2/32, who was represented by lawyers from Civil Party Group 2.

[132] Nam Mon's new allegations pertained to her alleged rape at S-21. According to Nam Mon's lawyers, Nam Mon had not informed them of these allegations until just before her court appearance. Nam Mon's lawyers subsequently filed a written request for these allegations to be put before the Chamber. This was rejected on the ground that the allegations were belated. See ECCC, *Prosecutor v. Kaing Guek Eav*, Trial Chamber, Decision on Parties Requests to Put Certain Materials Before the Chamber Pursuant to Rule 87(2), para. 14 ('*Duch* case, Decision') (https://www.legal-tools.org/doc/9e8c9c/).

[133] *Duch* case, Transcript, pp. 94–95, see *supra* note 128.

[134] *Duch* case, Decision, see *supra* note 131, para. 14.

rejecting their non-judicial narrative – those parts of their stories which did not comply with the legal and evidential requirements of the court – the judges gravely underestimated the cost to survivors of laying bare their personal histories in open court, having their stories publicly undermined and their efforts potentially laid to waste. The credibility of the civil parties' testimonies was, in their presence, questioned by the Chamber, and more fiercely, by Duch himself, and ultimately discredited.[135]

Attempting then to create a space for victims in the judicial arena alone is misguided. Victims recount their stories of pain and distress to an audience that is more interested in seeing how these facts neatly fit evidentiary matrices. In that process, victims' non-evidentiary voices, claims and desires for vindication, are unfortunately not heard and taken into account, but carelessly sidelined and silenced.

Rosalind Shaw notes that when interacting with victim communities, "it is important to examine, through ethnographic rather than quantitative survey methods, the range of practices of conflict resolution and reconciliation that people and communities are adapting and retooling now".[136]

Like Shaw, I find that ethnography, which mainly consists of extended periods of participant observation and informal interviews with victims, is the most appropriate approach to eliciting genuine narratives and evidence from victims on their terms. Piecemeal investigations that 'get in, extract information, get out' are undoubtedly problematic in contexts in which victims are emerging from mass violence and have historical reasons not to trust any exercise that resembles official information gathering. In my experience as a civil party lawyer gathering old evidence from Cambodian victims in relation to *Case 002* and *Case 004*, I have found that investigation that respects ethnographic field research and its subjects could give access to a very different body of knowledge from that accessible to someone who examines, documents and evaluates stories of historical trauma from mass crime victims.[137] In order to find out what my client communities wanted, my legal team and I had to

---

[135] For example, with regard to Ly Hor's testimony, Duch, after bringing the Trial Chamber through certain documents, insisted that Ly Hor was wrongly claiming as his own a written confession of a different S-21 detainee who had already died. *Duch* case, Transcript, pp. 83–87, see *supra* note 128.

[136] Shaw, 2005, p. 4, see *supra* note 114.

[137] Scholars have pondered whether memory can be distilled, with all of the chaff of personal inhibitions, prejudices and inaccuracies sloughed off, so that one can arrive at an accurate picture – indeed, a virtual photographic snapshot – of a particular moment in time, at how such stories and narratives remain unclassifiable, incomplete and marred with controversy. See, generally, Maurice Halbwachs, *The Collective Memory*, Harper and Row Colophon Books, New York, 1980.

look beyond the physical space of the hearings, evidentiary documents or victim information forms prepared by CSO intermediaries and spend time in rural provinces talking to people who have never met investigators or prosecutors, or in villages from which they had been driven, as well as those in which they were welcomed. Ultimately, this form of ethnographic investigation and lawyering is a useful approach to dealing with victims of mass crime as it entails spending time with ordinary people (as opposed to court affiliates) and listening to them on *their* terms – not through the medium of our survey forms, in our sensitization workshops, or through local NGOs and intermediaries. With this general ethos in mind, these are my specific recommendations for justice actors seeking to meet with and elicit credible evidence from vulnerable mass crime victims.[138] The following recommendations are particularly suitable for the Bangladeshi context.

1. *Work with Local Partners*: Work with local organizations, which enjoy the community's trust and confidence. Based on the indications of this intermediary organization, investigate, trace and interview victims who are keen to be civil parties and may be in a position to provide valuable evidence or testimony. Nonetheless, however good the local NGOs are, it bears mentioning that over-reliance can marginalize victims who do not wish to speak the lingo of NGOs, human rights and humanitarian assistance.

2. *Identify Focal Sites*: Identify geographical locations and sites that have been recognized in the existing literature or data currently housed at documentation centres and archives that evince a targeted attack against the victims. Trace and map these sites on physical documents and note any patterns of alleged crime and relevant conduct which may emerge. This will serve as a good starting point when speaking with victims and ultimately help establish or corroborate charges relating to core international crimes.[139]

---

[138] For further details, see, generally, Mahdev Mohan, ""Re-constituting the Un-Person": The Khmer Krom and the Khmer Rouge Tribunal", in *Singapore Yearbook of International Law*, 2008, vol. 12.

[139] See John Ciorciari, "The Khmer Krom and the Khmer Rouge Trials", Documentation Center of Cambodia ('DC-Cam'), August 2008. For example, documents recovered from the Khmer Rouge's infamous Kraing Ta Chan prison in the Takeo province, one of the few provincial prisons to leave behind a large trove of paperwork, suggest that the Khmer Krom were frequently suspected of espionage and other counter-revolutionary activities and were singled out for torture and imprisonment. According to Dr. Ciorciari, Senior Legal Advisor of DC-Cam, roughly 1,000 pages of documentary material from the Kraing Ta Chan prison are on file at DC-Cam.

3. *Adopt a 'Thick Description'*:[140] Adopt a qualitative approach that views members of the victim community as subjects rather than objects and allows time for interviewers to roll up their sleeves and properly document the victims' genuine historical narrative, examine their desires and reservations regarding reparations, and answer their questions about the process. Only then can we hope to arrive at, in Clifford Geertz's words, a "thick description" of the community that includes information about who they are as a people, the context of the crimes they suffered, and their present plight and desires for social change.[141] Social scientist Roger Henke cautioned me against relying on using quantitative surveys in group settings as a data source; Henke believes that country-wide surveys that do not have a qualitative element were prone to distortion, bias and mimicry of opinions – "getting them altogether in a dreadful focus-group to fill forms is counter-productive; they may not be forthcoming, some who have been made to fill surveys may have rehearsed answers and others may echo popular sentiments, leading to a distortion of data".[142]

4. *Further Systematic Research*: Design concise and clear interview questions, in consultation with experienced social scientists who have conducted empirical research in Cambodia's rural and urban provinces. Future researchers and investigators should investigate the data you have collected in a scientific manner. With more reliable field-data, researchers could seek to refine the typology presented and sharpen the explanations of individual dynamics.

5. *Representation and Reparation*: Provide independent legal representation to victims. Victims need to have lawyers looking out for their rights which may not always coincide with the interests and obligations of investigators and prosecutors of a judicial institution. Victims' lawyers' communications with their victim-clients are clothed with confidentiality and their role would include conducting interviews with victims, pre-

---

[140] Clifford Geertz, *The Interpretation of Cultures: Selected Essays*, Basic Books, New York, 1973.

[141] *Ibid*. As noted by Joseph Ponterotto, "Brief Note on the Origins, Evolution, and Meaning of the Qualitative Research Concept", in *The Qualitative Report*, 2006, vol. 11, no. 3, p. 538:
> Thick description accurately describes observed social actions and assigns purpose and intentionality to these actions, by way of the researcher's understanding and clear description of the context under which the social actions took place. Thick description captures the thoughts and feelings of participants as well as the often-complex web of relationships among them.

[142] Author's interview with Roger Henke, Institutional Development Specialist, Phnom Penh, Cambodia, 5 December 2008.

paring victim impact statements, collecting and analysing evidence where appropriate, and taking instructions from and keeping victims informed of the legal proceedings as they unfold and with a view of supporting the prosecution of the alleged crimes and identifying possible forms of judicial and non-judicial reparation measures. Having their own legal counsel gives victims confidence and insulates them to a degree from the clinical rigour of transitional justice processes. It reminds them that there are those whose duty it is to have their best interests at heart.

## 11.10. Protecting Vulnerable Victims

For victims of mass crime to feel confident that they can come forward and speak to official authorities about traumatic events which may be attributable to persons who occupy or may have occupied political office, it is important that they know that the law will be their guardian. The law must guarantee their safety, security and well-being before, during and after their testimony. It is also essential that vulnerable victims are given protection not just from physical violence, but also from social pressures and stigmas, which can often be far more damaging to their identity and place in society.

A precursor to the ICT-BD, the Peoples' Tribunal for Trial of War Criminal and Collaborators ('Gono-Adalot'), was infamously unable to insulate victims and witnesses who gave evidence before it from ostracization and remains a cautionary tale to victims and witnesses who may wish to come forward to provide evidence. Held in 1992, the Gono-Adalot in Dhaka drew close to 200,000 participants from across the country. It comprised of several retired and respected judges and heard evidence from a cross-section of the community, including four women from a remote area in the Jessore District who publicly testified about the sexual crimes that they had endured and other attacks against their community.[143] The testimony of the women contained sensitive allegations which illustrated the 'failure' of the men in the community to protect them and thus their collective honour. In a different context, this testimony and the courage which it took these women to come forward to present it, would have been hailed as a local and international touchstone for victim-centred justice. Yet, due to a government-sponsored attack on the tribunal, the victims or witnesses who testified were brought into harm's way. Unlike the other victims or witnesses, these four women were especially socially and economically vulnerable. Nonetheless, their photographs were printed in the newspapers, and a documentary filmmaker who visited their village subse-

---

[143] D'Costa, 2011, p. 152, see *supra* note 1. For further details, see Partha S. Ghosh, "Bangladesh at the Crossroads: Religion and Politics", in *Asian Survey*, 1993, vol. 33, pp. 697–710.

quently discovered that as a result of the exposure of the women in the press, they were ostracized by their community and faced problems such as being barred from using the local well or difficulty finding a suitable match for their daughters.[144]

These and other vulnerable victims and witnesses of the 1971 sexual violence experienced "their own narratives being taken over by a broad based social movement, without any comprehension of the impact of violence on their lives, and the failure to provide them with any concrete, legal, financial or moral support".[145] Bina D'Costa and Sara Hossain point out that gender sensitivity needs to be maintained even while referring to the crimes committed against women during the conflict.[146] The crimes committed against the women have been largely described in terms of the loss to the community, rather than the individual. Additionally, the question of whether giving evidence leads to re-traumatization needs to be addressed.[147] The language and cultural context within which rape and sexual offences is couched is also significant and has a marked expressive effect. Mujib coined the term 'Birangona' to depict the 'sacrifice' of the women for their country,[148] through the roles women played during the war, even when this alluded to them being raped or forcibly impregnated. Whilst the term was ostensibly intended to provide honour and confer a special status on these women, instead it just singled them out for further ostracization.[149] Quite clearly, the message understood was far from what was intended, but it is the former that sticks and unwittingly leads to victims being 'othered'.

Unfortunately, these victims are not alone. Chin Met, one of the few female survivors of Duch's notorious Tuol Sleng torture centre in Cambodia, underwent a similar fate. In July 2007, a group that was on a tour of Tuol Sleng, organized by CSD, identified Chin Met's photo – one of the countless haunting black and white faces of prisoners interred there during the Khmer Rouge period. They knew the woman, they said, and furthermore that she was still alive. A photo-journalist caught wind of the conversation and arranged to have Chin Met brought to Tuol Sleng, where she stood beside her photo and verified that, in fact, she had survived torture at Tuol Sleng and much more. CSD quickly tasked us with drafting a press release to state that CSD, through its ground tours and outreach activities, had succeeded in finding the "sole fe-

---

144 D'Costa and Hossain, 2010, p. 347, see *supra* note 104.
145 *Ibid.*, pp. 347–348.
146 *Ibid.*, p. 333.
147 *Ibid.*
148 *Ibid.*, p. 340. The term means 'war heroine' or 'valiant woman'.
149 *Ibid.*, pp. 340–341.

male survivor of Tuol Sleng".[150] Chin Met was thrust into the public domain, her original name and identity revealed to the world. In a matter of days, she became the metaphorical 'site' of conflict between a journalist associated with a well-known European news agency and CSD on the issue of who had the authority to claim they had 'discovered' her.[151]

If the "resequencing, decontextualizing and suppressing of social memory in order to give it new meaning is itself a social process",[152] I witnessed a victim undergo a profound process. In a brief period, Chin Met experienced both the terror of public scrutiny and the peculiar sense of righteousness that comes from the 'duty to remember'. Her case seems to hinge a great deal on how accessible the ECCC is to a witness like Chin Met and on whether the witness can continue to have her voice heard, long after the media has switched off its tape-recorders and video cameras. In other words, her evidence has to be made to matter and the sacrifices inherent in coming forward to give it should be respected. It is not enough that it is intrinsically important in the courtroom; victims and witnesses like Chin Met must be protected beyond it if they are to feel comfortable in coming forward.

The ICT-BD's statutes provide only one crime of sexual violence, rape, as a core crime within the definition of crimes against humanity; and omit other offences, as well as a definition of 'rape'.[153] Additionally, in Bangladesh, the stigma associated with these crimes has led to the suppression of evidence, and social problems associated with forced pregnancies.[154] In such cases, where the testimonies provided by vulnerable victims and witnesses may be sensitive, especially where women are testifying, the court needs to ensure adequate and sustained protection that goes beyond just physical protection. D'Costa and Hossain advocate gender-sensitivity training for the Tribunal staff, as well as

---

[150] Bronwyn Sloan, "Unique Pol Pot Survivor", *DPA Wire News Agency*, 24 July 2007; Veasna Mean, "Purported Survivor Claims She Was Tortured in Tuol Sleng", *Voice of America Khmer*, 3 August 2007; Rosemary Righter, "A Paralysed Nation, Afraid to Unlock its Tortured Past", *Times Online*, 3 August 2007.

[151] After her interview with the press, CSD staff I had accompanied in our visit to Chin Met's home said that her mannerisms and her statements regarding her experiences suggested that there were significant personal reasons for why she had been wary to reveal any of these experiences to family. But these nuances were lost on the media and, importantly, the ECCC which viewed her as another repository of information and evidence. Chin Met was called to testify as a witness in *Case 001*, the '*Duch* case' (the name has been spelled 'Chim Math' in various sources). See ECCC, *Prosecutor v. Kaing Guek Eav*, Trial Chamber, Transcript of Trial Proceedings, 8 July 2009 (https://www.legal-tools.org/doc/42f140/).

[152] Fentress and Wickham, 1992, p. 201, see *supra* note 108.

[153] D'Costa and Hossain, 2010, p. 343, see *supra* note 104.

[154] *Ibid.*, p. 344.

---

caution and sensitivity when interviewing witnesses and victims, with which I wholly agree:

> If the Tribunal is to deal with sexual crimes, then an informed review of the available evidence and an exploration of possible gender-friendly approaches is urgently needed.
>
> While the Tribunal does set up a possibility for some form of accountability, the investigation and trial process is a particularly thorny one in cases of sexual violence, and needs to be navigated with care and caution, given the risk of repercussions for the survivors.[155]

These observations are important and should be carefully heeded as the first judgement of the ICT-BD contains names of suspected sexual violence victims and makes little or no meaningful effort to provide them with adequate witness or victim support and protection.

As vulnerable victims (such as survivors of sexual violence) have the potential to contribute to justice processes, their needs should be cared for incisively. This is even truer, if we consider that such victims can be very valuable sources of evidence, especially when other kinds of evidentiary material – such as DNA samples – have been weakened by the passage of time.

## 11.11. Conclusions

As for most national efforts to hold perpetrators of core international crimes accountable, the ICT-BD's legacy will depend on its ability to contribute to building the capacity of Bangladesh's justice sector, and the degree to which it harmonizes its justice system with international rule of law norms.

This entails transferring knowledge, skills and practices from the ICT-BD to the rest of the national justice sector, and fostering local ownership of judicial and legal reform. As Diane Marie Aman has observed, while "conveying a concrete message of accountability may begin to break [the] cycle of violence, that message must be managed with the utmost care and respect for victims of mass violence".[156] Without guarantees of fair trial, accessibility, protection and sensitive communication, victims may feel that their role in a tribunal is a token one and may not be prepared to provide genuine and independent evidence, thereby significantly diminishing the legitimacy of the institution itself. Victim and witness protection, in particular, is critically important to eliciting and preserving the veracity of both 'old' and 'new' evidence. Its central relevance to old evidence, however, is sometimes underestimated as the

---

[155] *Ibid.*, p. 338.
[156] Aman, 2001, p. 245, see *supra* note 16.

common misconception is that victims or witnesses of old evidence have come to terms with their past or are no longer under threat.

As we have seen, real and perceived threats are often not diminished by the passage of time: they may remain unchanged or sometimes take on heightened dimensions due to changed political realities. In order to elicit credible evidence from victims and witnesses who have suffered so much, the law must send them the right message and, more importantly, it must have the modesty of ambition and live up to honour these messages, lest victims and witnesses lose what little confidence they may have in the process.

As a national initiative to prosecute politically sensitive international crimes, the ICT-BD's process should match available resources and political will from local and international actors, and its mandate should be tailor-made to suit operational realities. Consideration of the Cambodian experience shows that it is important not to create a flawed mechanism and then try to patch it up with quick fixes in response to criticisms levelled against it. Finally, any international justice actor should be mindful that prosecution is just one element in a toolbox of accountability. Both political and judicial stakeholders, such as the Bangladeshi government and the ICT-BD, must closely examine their objectives to ensure that the mix of tools they select is best tailored to the particular need. Exaggerating what just one tool, prosecution, can reasonably accomplish may mean that other avenues that are more meaningful and effective are not explored or are foreclosed.

# 12

---

# Towards the Prosecution of Core International Crimes Before the International Crimes Tribunal

## M. Amir-Ul Islam[*]

I deem it a great honour and a privilege to have co-hosted the international expert seminar entitled "Old Evidence and Core International Crimes" organized by the Centre for International Law Research and Policy (CILRAP), a knowledge-transfer international platform that has extended support to Bangladesh. Activities such as the seminar and the publication of this anthology assist the prosecutors and investigators engaged in the trials of perpetrators of genocide and crimes against humanity committed in Bangladesh upon innocent men, women and children in 1971, causing death and destruction, rape and rampage, arson and extermination, the killing of three million civilians and the violation of 200,000[1] women during an army occupation of nine months (25 March–16 December 1971).

The support and co-operation of CILRAP – its capacity-development department Case Matrix Network ('CMN') – in the field of law and its concern

---

[*]  **M. Amir-Ul Islam** is Senior Advocate, Bangladesh Supreme Court, and Senior Partner in the leading Bangladesh firm Amir and Amir Law Associates. He was a Member of the Drafting Committee of the Bangladesh Constitution (1972) and served as Minister of Food (1973–1974). Having been in the Chambers of Mr. John Platts-Mills QC (1961–1963), he has later founded the Continuing Legal Education Program ('CLEP') for lawyers; served as Vice Chairman of the Bangladesh Bar Council; Chairman of the Legal Education Committee of LawAsia and Chairman of the Legal Education and Training Institute ('LETI'); Founder and Honorary Secretary General of the Bangladesh Institute of Law and International Affairs ('BILIA'); President of the Asia Pacific Organization on Mediation; President of the South Asian Association for Right to Development; Country Chairman of the Union International Des Advocates; President of SAARCLAW; Vice Chairman of the International Law Association, Bangladesh and IFA Bangladesh; Country Correspondent and Contributor for Lloyd's International Ship Arrest and Euromoney's Laws on International Banking and Security; Special Envoy (1972–1973) and Law Officer (1977–1979), United Nations ('UN'), New York, and worked for the UN Commission on International Trade Law. He was a Visiting Member of the Faculty of National Law School University of India (1995) and of Law and Development at Tufts University (1977). This chapter shares an important contextual perspective from Bangladesh as it faces challenges of old evidence in its domestic prosecutions of the crimes of 1971.

[1]  This is according to a conservative estimate of The Economist while the unofficial estimate is double the number, see "War's Overlooked Victims", *The Economist*, 13 January 2011.

about the trials of core international crimes, such as genocide and crimes against humanity, is based on international and universal commitments as duly resonated in the Preamble of the Rome Statute. One of the objects of the Rome Statute is that perpetrators of core crimes must not go unpunished. It further reiterates that "their effective prosecution must be ensured by taking measures at the national level".[2] CILRAP's co-operation and support thus fit well within the object of the Rome Statute, which emphasizes measures to be taken at the national level for fair and effective prosecution to be ensured. Bangladesh thus finds a perfect match by developing a collaborative effort and initiative "by enhancing international co-operation" for holding the trial in Bangladesh at the national level, this being an integral part of the universal concept and commitment stated in the Rome Statute, as well as one of the objects of Bangladesh's International Crimes (Tribunals) Act of 1973.[3]

I, on behalf of my colleagues and friends, with great appreciation and gratitude, would particularly like to acknowledge the most timely initiative taken by CILRAP, with special tribute to Professor Morten Bergsmo[4] who, besides being endowed with knowledge and expertise in his field of discipline in international law, is gifted with tremendous capacity, dedication and energy in mobilizing experts and resources to ensure support for national initiatives in various countries, like the one extended to Bangladesh.

This chapter will provide a background to the crimes which took place in 1971 in Bangladesh, linking them to more recent instances of violence. In doing so, it will illustrate how the enduring impunity of the perpetrators of the 1971 crimes affected the country for decades. Time may have caused evidence to become old, but the need for justice persisted: facing the additional challenges presented by old evidence has been the subsequent duty of the International Crimes Tribunal ('ICT') of Bangladesh.

## 12.1. Background of the International Crimes (Tribunals) Act of 1973 and Its Content

After the liberation of Bangladesh from Pakistan's occupation army, there rose a human cry for the trial of perpetrators. The father of the nation, Bangabandhu Sheikh Mujibur Rahman, asked, at the very early stage in 1972 in his speeches, that an international tribunal be instituted in Bangladesh to try war criminals. Unfortunately, there was no one able and willing to set up such a

---

[2]    Rome Statute of the International Criminal Court, 17 July 1998, Preamble ('Rome Statute') (https://www.legal-tools.org/doc/e5faa8/).

[3]    International Crimes (Tribunals) Act, 1973, 20 July 1973, amended in 2009 (https://www.legal-tools.org/doc/c09a98/).

[4]    For information on Morten Bergsmo, see the note on the first page of Chapter 1.

tribunal.[5] Due to a then-existing void in the world of international machinery to prosecute perpetrators of international crimes, Bangladesh, in consultation with international jurists and experts, enacted a special law, namely, the International Crimes (Tribunals) Act, 1973 ('the Act'). The International Crimes (Tribunals) Rules of Procedure, 2010 ('ICT Rules of Procedure') was also framed as provided under the Act.[6] The above-mentioned Act was considered by international jurists at that time "as a model of international due process". "It is a carefully prepared document", as commented by the International Commission of Jurists, which covers:

> [...] the legal ramifications of the "detention, prosecution and punishment of persons for genocide, crimes against humanity, war crimes and other crimes under international law", affording appropriate legal protections to those accused of such crimes.[7]

This Act assured that the trial of perpetrators would be conducted in accordance with international legal and human rights standards, and by an independent tribunal. Some amendments were also made to the Act in order to achieve the desired standard, transparency and due process. According to the Act, the accused would be given the full opportunity to defend themselves at trial. Persons convicted of crimes specified under Section 3 of the Act and sentenced by the Tribunal shall have the statutory right to appeal under Section 21 of the Act to the Appellate Division of the Supreme Court of Bangladesh, the highest court of the country.

---

[5]  Niall MacDermot QC, "Crimes Against Humanity in Bangladesh", in *International Lawyer*, 1973, vol. 7, no. 2, pp. 483–484. If there is to be a trial, what kind of court should there be? Sheikh Mujibur Rahman asked this at an early stage in public speeches that an international tribunal should be sent to Bangladesh to try war criminals. Unfortunately, there was no one able and willing to set up such a tribunal. The efforts within the UN to promote the establishment of an international criminal court had, for the time being at least, foundered. Even more modest proposals, such as that of the UN High Commissioner for Human Rights, so sturdily promoted by Ambassador Rita Hauser, had been blocked. There were, it seems, too many governments with too many skeletons for them to agree to any effective enforcement machinery for human rights. The Commission's purpose in Bangladesh was to try to persuade the government that, if they do hold such a trial, they should themselves constitute an international court for the purpose, much in the way that the victorious allies did at Nuremberg and Tokyo after World War II.

[6]  International Crimes (Tribunals) Rules of Procedure, 15 July 2010, amended 28 October 2012 and 28 June 2011 (https://www.legal-tools.org/doc/efe1e7/).

[7]  Jordan J. Paust and Albert P. Blaustein, *Human Rights and the Bangladesh Trials: A Legal Memorandum to the People's Republic of Bangladesh*, Editorial Correspondents Ltd., New York, 1973, p. 65.

## 12.2. Background of Core International Crimes Committed in 1971

The crime of genocide was perpetrated in Bangladesh by Pakistan's occupation army with their cohorts, *id est*, the Rajakar, Al Badr, Al Shams and various local killing squads in 1971. Although the killing of unarmed civilians in early March seemed abrupt and sporadic, it soon became a systematic act of violence with 'Operation Searchlight' enforced at midnight on 25 March 1971, as part of the central planning and conspiracy hatched at Larkana[8] and reinforced at Rawalpindi by Pakistani General Yahya Khan and other generals. The operation was prepared and executed in collaboration with their quislings under the umbrella of a politico-religious military alliance, creating the formation of local militia as an auxiliary force for perpetrating 'the cleansing process'.

Peter Hazelhurst, writing in *The Times* on 4 June 1971, also accused Pakistani President Yahya Khan of having perpetrated a 'holocaust' in Bangladesh, and Mr. Zulfikar Bhutto as well, for their role in the events leading up to the massacre on 25–26 March 1971.[9]

## 12.3. Genocide in Bangladesh and Its Aging Evidence

The object of the operation was to eliminate the Awami League and its supporters in former East Pakistan, in order to crush the will of the majority earlier demonstrated in the general election, and to turn a majority people of the then East Pakistan (now Bangladesh) into a minority forever by creating terror through indiscriminate killing, rape, arson and looting, thus forcing 10 million people to leave their country, and to seek shelter and succour in the neighbouring states of India. In this mayhem, the members of the Hindu community were the major target. Within the first 48 hours, the massacre ravaged Dhaka and all the major towns and cities in Bangladesh. All foreign journalists were expelled by Yahya Khan's government, leaving only those who managed to

---

[8]    S.A. Karim, *Triumph and Tragedy*, The University Press, 2009, pp. 172–176, quoted Mohammed Asghar Khan, *Generals in Politics: Pakistan 1958–1982*, Croom Helm Ltd, 1984, p. 28:

> In the middle of 1970, only a few months before the scheduled general election, Bhutto had suggested privately to Yahya that the two of them would make a very good team and could together run the country. Yahya had replied that "this made sense" and asked what he proposed to do about East Pakistan. Bhutto replied: "East Pakistan is no problem. We will have to kill some 20,000 people and all would be well." This story was recounted by Yahya to Air Marshall (Retd.) Asghar Khan and it is quite in line with Bhutto's well-known pet theory that the Awami League was a bourgeois party and it had no stomach for a confrontation with the military. What was dismissed by Yahya as a pipe dream a year before was now apparently embraced by him.

[9]    Muhammad Zamir, "Global Response to Our War of Liberation", *The Daily Star*, 16 December 2009.

---

remain in hiding. Simon Dring,[10] being one of these very few, recounts how within the first 24 hours, the Pakistani army slaughtered approximately 70,000 people in Dhaka alone, along with another 15,000 all over Bangladesh. Old evidence referring to Dring's description of the attack on Dhaka University reads as follows:

> Led by American-supplied M-24 World War II tanks, one column of troops sped to Dhaka University shortly after midnight. Troops took over the British Council library and used it as a fire base from which to shell nearby dormitory areas.
>
> Caught completely by surprise, some 200 students were killed in Iqbal Hall, headquarters of the militantly antigovernment students' union, I was told. Two days later, bodies were still smouldering in burnt-out rooms, others were scattered outside, more floated in a nearby lake, an art student lay sprawled across his easel.
>
> Army patrols also razed nearby market area. Two days later, when it was possible to get out and see all this, some of the market's stall-owners were still lying as though asleep, their blankets pulled up over their shoulders.[11]

The military launched its offensive on the nights of 25 and 26 March 1971 with 'Operation Searchlight'. Dhaka University was among the targets of this first attack on Bengali nationalism. On 29 April 1971, Ohio Republican Senator William Saxbe placed a letter from a constituent, Dr. Jon E. Rohde, in the Senate record. Dr. Rohde had served in East Bengal for three years as a physician with the United States ('US') Agency for Independent Development. His letter contained the following account of what he witnessed before he was evacuated from Dhaka:[12]

---

[10] Simon Dring is an award-winning foreign correspondent, television presenter and producer, who alerted the whole world about the massacre in Dhaka by the Pakistani Army. He has worked for Reuters, the Daily Telegraph of London, BBC Television, Radio News and Current Affairs.

[11] See Bangladesh Genocide Archive, "History" (available on its web site).

[12] Rohde's letter is reprinted from the Record of the US Senate as "Recent events in East Pakistan", in Sheelendra Kumar Singh *et al.* (eds.), *Bangladesh Documents*, vol. 1, BNK Press, Madras, 1971, pp. 349–351:

> My wife and I watched from our roof the night of March 25 as tanks rolled out of the Cantonment illuminated by the flares and the red glow of the fires as the city was shelled by artillery and mortars were fired into crowded slums and bazaars [...]. On the 29th we stood at the Ramna Kali Bari, an ancient Hindu village of about 250 people in the centre of Dacca Ramna Race Course, and witnessed the stacks of machine gunned burning remains of men, women, and children butchered in the early morning hours of March 29 [...]. At the university area we walked through [...] two of the student dormi-

> The law of the jungle prevails in East Pakistan where the mass killing of unarmed civilians, the systematic elimination of the intelligentsia, and the annihilation of the Hindu population is in progress.[13]

Another US citizen evacuated from Dhaka, Pat Sammel, wrote a letter to the Denver Post, which was placed in the House record by Representative Mike McKevitt of Colorado on 11 May 1971. Sammel wrote:

> We have been witness to what amounts to genocide. The West Pakistani army used tanks, heavy artillery and machine guns on unarmed civilians, killed 1,600 police while sleeping in their barracks […] demolished the student dormitories at Dacca University, and excavated a mass grave for the thousands of students; they've systematically eliminated the intelligentsia of the country, wiped out entire villages – I could go on and on. It's hard to believe it happened.[14]

Further reports of a massacre at Dhaka University can be found among James Michener's interviews in Tehran with US citizens who were evacuated from the East Pakistani capital. Several evacuees reported that they had seen Pakistani leaders with specific lists containing the names of Bengali professors who were slated for execution. They also reported seeing mass graves of students who had been killed.[15]

## 12.4. Murders, Extermination, Widespread and Systematic Attacks Against the Civilian Population of Bangladesh

The 'old town' quarter of Dhaka city was targeted and demolished largely due to the strong Awami League support there, but also because there were many Hindu residents[16] in the area. In Simon Dring's words:

> The lead unit was followed by soldiers carrying cans of gasoline. Those who tried to escape were shot. Those who stayed were burnt alive. About 700 men, women and children died there that day between noon and two pm, I was told. […]

---

tories at Dacca University [were] shelled by the army tanks. All inmates were slaughtered […]. A man who was forced to drag the bodies outside, counted one hundred three Hindu students buried there […]. We also saw evidence of a tank attack at Iqbal Hall where bodies were still unburied.

13   *Ibid.*, p. 351.
14   Reprinted from the Record of the US House of Representatives in *ibid.*, p. 357.
15   James A. Michener, "A Lament for Pakistan", *New York Times*, 9 January 1972.
16   Particularly in the Jagannath Hall, which is a full resident hall exclusively for Hindu and non-Muslim students, teachers and professors of the University of Dhaka.

> In the Hindu area of the old town, the soldiers reportedly made the people come out of their houses and shot them in groups. The area, too, was eventually razed.

> The troops stayed on in force in the old city until about 11 pm on the night of Friday, March 26, driving around with local Bengali informers. The soldiers would fire a flare and the informer would point out the houses of Awami League supporters. The house would then be destroyed – either with direct fire from tanks or recoilless rifles or with a can of gasoline, witnesses said.[17]

After having massacred 15,000 unarmed civilians in a single day, the Pakistani soldiers bragged about their invincibility to Simon Dring:

> "These bugger men," said one Punjabi lieutenant, "could not kill us if they tried."

> "Things are much better now," said another officer, "Nobody can speak out or come out. If they do we will kill them – they have spoken enough – they are traitors, and we are not. We are fighting in the name of God and a united Pakistan".[18]

Pakistani journalist Anthony Mascarenhas was permitted to tour East Bengal in April 1971. His reports indicate that the government's policy was to eliminate the Hindus by death or expulsion. The comments made by Pakistani military officials in Bengal are eerily reminiscent of Nazi notions of purification and the weeding out of bad elements from society. According to Mascarenhas, senior government and military officials in East Bengal stated:

> [W]e are determined to cleanse East Pakistan once and for all of the threat of secession, even if it means killing off two million people and ruling the province as a colony for 30 years.[19]

The Pakistani army carried out this ruthless genocide with military precision, employing tanks, artillery, mortars, bazookas and machine guns against the unarmed civilian population of Dhaka. Although their prime targets were students, local police, intellectuals, political leaders, Awami League supporters and Hindus, they still killed ordinary citizens indiscriminately.

## 12.5. Forcible Transfer of Ten Million People and Persecutions

Bangladesh suffered the crimes perpetrated on the entire people. By some estimates, three million of the civilian population were killed. Women and chil-

---

[17] Simon Dring, "Dacca Eyewitness: Bloodbath, Inferno", *The Washington Post*, 19 March 1971.
[18] *Ibid.*
[19] Anthony Mascarenhas, *The Rape of Bangladesh*, Vikas Publications, 1971, p. 117.

dren were raped and violated. There was indiscriminate killing of the civilian population, including professors, doctors, engineers, lawyers, teachers, political activists, Awami League leaders and supporters, and members of the religious minorities, particularly those of the Hindu community, who were subject to killing, torture, arson, rape and looting. Ten million people[20] of whom 70 per cent were Hindus, had to leave the country to seek succour and shelter in the refugee camps of India. Leadership layers in all fields, such as politics, education, business and professions were the main targets, with the intention of making the country leaderless in every sector. This was done with a view to destroying the nation, with an intent to make the targeted victims a numerically and electorally a permanent minority without leadership. They would thus be crippled politically and economically, and be easily exploited under Pakistan's military-backed autocracy.

## 12.6. Independence of Bangladesh and Prisoners-of-War Returned to Pakistan

The scheme of Pakistan's military regime, which denied the right of the majority people, through their elected representatives, to frame the constitution and form a government of their own choice as so expressed through the election of 1970, was to be frustrated by any means. The election was held under the Legal Framework Order ('LFO').[21] The resort to crimes of genocide and crimes against humanity, and the holding of another sham election to constitute a so-called parliament consisting of the perpetrators of crimes and their cronies, were part of the military regime's well-knit agenda. Candidates were hand-picked, and having no contestants, the results were published by the military junta to install a rubber stamp parliament.[22] After nine months of resistance against the Pakistani occupation army, victory was achieved in December 1971 following an effective resistance and mobilization by the people of Bangladesh. The occupation army of Pakistan surrendered on 16 December 1971 following a short-lived war declared by Pakistan, while an operation conducted under

---

[20] MacDermot, 1973, p. 479, see *supra* note 5. The result of this systematic repression was a flood of refugees to India on an unprecedented scale. We have no reason to think that the Indian estimate of 10 million refugees is exaggerated.

[21] According to LFO, if the Constitution could not be framed within 120 days, the Parliament was to be dissolved for the holding of another election. See Story of Pakistan, "Legal Framework Order", 1 June 2003 (available on its web site).

[22] The Parliament was without any rival candidate nor was any poll to be held. See "Reforming Pakistan's Electoral System", in International Crisis Group, *Asia Report*, March 2011, no. 203–230.

India-Bangladesh's joint command was formed on 3 December 1971.[23] This brought an end to Pakistan's occupation of the country, which emerged as Bangladesh through a blood bath of nine months.

Following the victory, initiatives were taken for the trying of 195 prisoners of war ('POWs') against whom there was specific evidence and proof of core international crimes. Under the pressure of Pakistan's Western allies[24] and Islamic states headed by the strong lobby of Saudi Arabia, and ultimately on the assurance of Mr. Bhutto that he would ensure the trial of those 195 POWs in Pakistan, which was given to both Bangladesh and India, they were so returned.

## 12.7. Old Evidence Revealed Before the Enquiry Commission in Pakistan

The Hamoodur Rahman[25] Commission was constituted by the Pakistani government to obtain credibility in the eyes of the international community and the governments of Bangladesh and India by indicating Mr. Bhutto's willingness to hold the trial before those 195 POWs were returned. He was also to use it as leverage on Pakistan's military junta in order to secure his political power. The Commission so constituted inquired into the atrocities committed during the nine months of occupation. The Commission examined nearly 300 witnesses and hundreds of classified army signals between East and West Pakistan.[26] Generals Yahya, Niyazi and Tikka's own admissions, along with those of their cohorts and collaborators, are evident from the available Commission reports and documents. Let us refer to some of this old evidence that is available and which has been established before the Commission as admitted by those army officers themselves. According to the allegations generally made, the excesses committed by the Pakistani Army and their collaborators, as summarized by the Commission, fall into the following categories:

> a) Excessive use of force and fire power in Dacca during the night of the 25 and 26 March 1971 when the military operation was launched.

---

[23] "Gen. Tikka Khan, 87; 'Butcher of Bengal' Led Pakistani Army", *The Los Angeles Times*, 30 March 2002.

[24] MacDermot, 1973, p. 483, see *supra* note 5. In the Western world, there seems to be a considerable body of opinion which thinks there ought not to be any trials of those alleged to be responsible.

[25] Justice Hamoodur Rahman was the Chief Justice of the Supreme Court of Pakistan and Vice Chancellor of Dhaka University.

[26] Government of Pakistan and War Inquiry Commission, Hamoodur Rehman Commission of Inquiry into the 1971 War, 23 October 1974 ('Hamoodur Rahman Report') (https://www.legal-tools.org/doc/iacqir/).

b)  Senseless and wanton arson and killings in the countryside during the course of the "sweeping operations" following the military action.

c)  Killing of intellectuals and professionals like doctors, engineers, etc., and burying them in mass graves not only during early phases of the military action but also during the critical days of the war in December 1971.

d)  Killing of Bengali Officers and men of the units of the East Bengal Regiment, East Pakistan Rifles and the East Pakistan Police Force in the process of disarming them, or on pretence of quelling their rebellion.

e)  Killing of East Pakistani civilian officers, businessmen and industrialists, or their mysterious disappearance from their homes by or at the instance of Army Officers performing Martial Law duties.

f)  Raping of a large number of East Pakistani women by the officers and men of the Pakistan army as a deliberate act of revenge, retaliation and torture.

g)  Deliberate killing of members of the Hindu minority.[27]

Indefinite identification of responsibility as revealed from the Hamoodur Rahman Report is as follows:

> It is, however, clear that the final and overall responsibility must rest on General Yahya Khan, Lt. Gen. Pirazada, Maj Gen. Umar, Lt. Gen. Mitha. It has been brought out in evidence that Maj. Gen. Mitha was particularly active in East Pakistan in the days preceding the military action of the 25th of March 1971, and even the other Generals just mentioned were present in Dacca along with Yahya Khan, and secretly departed there on the evening of that fateful day after fixing the deadline for the military action. Maj. Gen. Mitha is said to have remained behind. There is also evidence that Lt. Gen. Tikka Khan, Major Gen. Farman Ali and Maj. Gen. Khadim Hussain were associated with the planning of the military action [...].
>
> At the same time there is some evidence to suggest that the words and personal actions of Lt. Gen. Niazi were calculated to encourage the killings and rape.[28]

---

[27]  *Ibid.*, pp. 22–23.
[28]  *Ibid.*, p. 34.

## 12.8. An Impunity Culture Begins, Contributing to the Destabilization of the Constitutional Regime

Following the Report, the lack of political will originated the decades-old impunity of the major perpetrators of the 1971 crimes, while the available evidence invariably aged. Mr. Bhutto did not keep his promise and desecrated his international obligation to try these criminals. Following such default, impunity grew in all directions and on all dimensions. In 1977, Mr. Bhutto and his party secured the majority's vote and won the parliamentary elections held in Pakistan, but the military took over power in a successful *coup d'état* led by General Muhammad Zia-ul-Haq under code name 'Operation Fair Play'.[29]

The history that followed is a series of tragedies backed by extra-constitutional regimes and the destabilizing of democracy, not only repeating the frustration of the electoral verdict of 1977 in Pakistan, but also leading to the killing of Mr. Bhutto himself as the elected Prime Minister, who was hung by a court verdict widely believed to be a judicial killing.[30] The rule of law and constitutional governance was thus destabilized, and Zia-ul-Haq, who patronized the religious-militant groups as part of his agenda for Pakistan to be eventually transferred into a theological state, was killed in an air crash on 17 August 1988. His military transport aircraft, a C-130, exploded mid-air a few minutes after take-off from Bhawalpur Airport, killing all passengers aboard including the President.[31] The power in Rawalpindi rolled from one general to another, except for some interruption by elected governments that were then toppled by the military.

Failure to try the perpetrators of core crimes by the Pakistani Army thus caused disaster, followed by a series of killings and frequent constitutional derailment on the one hand, and the rise of core militancy and extremists under the patronage of the military wing on the other. Under the Pakistani military's direct patronization, the Taliban[32] were raised and trained, and used in the Afghan War. There is need therefore for proper and systemic research and analysis by academics and experts, taking Pakistan and Bangladesh as a case study,

---

[29] Mohammad Hanif, "Pakistan's General Problem", *Open*, 11 June 2011.
[30] See Chagatain Kahn, "Judicial Murder of Zulfikar Ali Brutto, Judiciary and CJ [R] Nasim Hasan Shah", 25 February 2010 (available on the Blogspot web site).
[31] See Story of Pakistan, "Death of General Zia Ul Haq", 1 June 2003 (available on its web site).
[32] Pierre Tristam, "History of the Taliban: Who They Are, What They Want", *Thoughtco*, 24 January 2018:

> They were schooled in Pakistan's *madrassas*, religious schools which, in this case, were encouraged and financed by Pakistani and Saudi authorities to develop militantly inclined Islamists, which raised another military reign, known as Talibans which later transformed into various groups such as al Qaeda, Harkat-ul-Jihad-al-Islami (Huji), etc.

to identify the relationship between the omission and default in trying the perpetrators of crime, and the destabilization of the constitution, democracy and the rule of law as well as the rise of a religious-military oligarchy that has a close relationship with militancy, that is patronized by the military or military-backed regimes, and that has formed under the shelter of political party. The tragedies which followed in the form of coups, counter-coups, killings and assassinations, the destabilizing of the constitutional regime, the subverting of the electoral process, and the rise of extra-constitutional regimes, can be traced back to the failure and omission to hold trials and punish the perpetrators of the original crimes committed in Bangladesh in 1971, giving rise to a culture of impunity. This seems to be the core causation between the repetitious derailments of constitutional regimes followed by the rise of terrorism spreading all over the globe. The seed of this lies in the failure to try the perpetrators of core crimes of genocide and crime against humanity in Bangladesh in 1971. As illustrated below, the need for justice survived the culture of impunity, and its consequences are found in the challenges to national peace and stability Bangladesh faced in the following decades. The troubled aftermath of the 1971 crimes shows how the call for justice must try to overcome the challenges of old evidence.

## 12.9. Violent Aftermath of the Impunity

Although Bangladesh's 1973 Act is the first written statute on core international crimes, the trial could not be held due to the hijacking of state power by the killing of the father of the nation, Bangabandhu Sheikh Mujibur Rahman and his family, which included Begum Mujib and children, including the young child Russel, newly-wed Jamal and Kamal, along with their wives, on 15 August 1975. Two other families of close relations to the President, one being a cabinet member, Mr. Serniabad, and his family, met the same fate as his son-in-law, Sheikh Moni, along with his pregnant wife, who was killed around the same time in their respective residences in the city. It was followed by the killing of the four national leaders[33] in prison on 3 November 1975 in another orgy operated by the same military group at the Dhaka Central Jail who killed the President on 15 August 1975.

---

[33] In the absence of the President Sheikh Mujibur Rahman (in Pakistan prison), Mr. Syed Nazrul Islam was the Acting President of the government in exile in 1971, Mr. Tajuddin Ahmed was the Prime Minister, Mr. M. Mansur Ali was the Minister of Commerce and Trade, and Mr. A.H.M. Kamruzzaman was a cabinet minister. They lead the liberation movement as the lawful and constitutional government. "Jail Killing Day Today", *The Daily Star*, 3 November 2010.

This would reveal genocide and crimes against humanity surfacing often thereafter, all part of the same scheme to destabilize Bangladesh by making Bangladesh leaderless, thus subverting and derailing its Constitution and democracy so that this nation may not sustain its constitutional values, the values of the war of liberation and democracy. Thus, in the process, the fruits of freedom are left to the future generation. The killings of 1975 were protected from any trial by an indemnity ordinance decreed by the usurpers, after having hijacked the state power. The killers were patronized by the new military-backed regime under which some of the killers were given diplomatic assignments abroad, and others were encouraged to form a political party and to become members of the parliament. The Constitution was changed by decree in order to change the secular character of the republic, introducing Islam as the state religion.

The passage of time proved how dire the consequences of the lack of justice for such crimes can be. During subsequent regimes, cultural workers, artists, public leaders and judges also became targets of bomb attacks by the religious-militant groups which were allowed to grow and operate under the umbrella of the military-backed regime. This threatened the national peace and stability of the country several times. Systematic terror and violence occurred through the targeting of cinema halls, public meetings and cultural functions, and the killing of innocent people, which created public scares. All court premises in the country, including the Supreme Court, became targets of bomb blasts on 17 August 2005, simultaneously also causing the death of judges in Jhalakathi and some advocates in Gazipur on 14 November 2005.[34] Election and post-election violence following the general election in 2001 was another manifestation of such crimes, as reported in various newspapers and documented by a commission of inquiry set up by the government and headed by Judge Shahabuddeen. Based on newspaper reports, during the 87 days of the caretaker government in 2001, there were about 2,483 incidents of atrocities in which 906 were killed and 15,616 injured. After the assumption of the four-party Alliance[35] to power, several hundreds were killed, more than a thousand injured, about 41,000 tortured, and several hundred raped as part of the post-electoral violence.[36] The figures continued to swell each day as the reports appeared in the dailies.

---

[34] "2 Britons Funded JMB to Carry Out Bomb Blasts", *The Daily Star*, 9 February 2006. See Wikipedia, "Jamat ul Mujahideen Bangladesh" (available on its web site).

[35] "A major rightist alliance of B.N.P. along with Jamat-e-Islami and two other parties", see Bertil Lintner, "Bangladesh Extremist Islamist Consolidation", in *Faultlines*, 2003, vol. 14.

[36] Such incidents have been reported in various newspapers such as:

Such violence and atrocities in the form of killings, rape and looting were committed on Hindu communities and on Awami League leaders and supporters at the grassroots level, repeating the same syndrome perpetrated in 1971 against the party which won the election in 1970 and which led the liberation movement to a victory in December 1971.

On 21 August 2004, there was an attack on Prime Minister Sheikh Hasina while she was the leader of the opposition and holding a rally protesting the killing of a senior leader of her party, distinguished statesman Mr. Shah A.S.M. Kibria, the former Finance Minister of the country, who was brutally assassinated in a grenade attack on 27 January 2005 in his constituency at Sylhet.[37] The leader of the Awami League, Sheikh Hasina, was protected by a human shield built around her against a repeated grenade attack at the venue of the meeting. Though she miraculously survived (with an impairment of hearing), her other colleagues, including Begum Ivy Rahman, the wife of later President of Bangladesh (2009-13), Mr. Zillur Rahman, along with 21 other active members of the Party, were killed, and more than 100 wounded, many still carrying the pains of splinters in their body. Investigations reveal that this

---

- *The Daily Sangbad*, 19 September 2001: Father and daughter named Dulal Chandra Das and Akhi Rani Das of a family of Hindu minority were killed by a terrorist group in the village of Haroshshor, Allahabad Union, Debiddar Upazila of Comilla District.
- *The Daily Prothom Alo*, 5 October 2001: Terrorist groups attacked in 20 Districts of Bangladesh the supporters of Awami League and the Hindu Minorities. Nine persons were killed and 217 persons were injured in that incident.
- *The Daily Star*, 11 October 2001: Attacks on Awami League leaders and workers and the minority community continued in Pabna and Barisal districts.
- *The Independent*, 17 October 2001: Houses of minority community ransacked in Keshabpur. The members of the minority community of the district left their homes for safer places following terrorism let loose by the armed miscreants.
- *The Daily Star*, 30 October 2001: Hindus who fled to India tell tales of torture. Hundreds of Bangladeshi Hindu families have fled across the border into India because they say they have been 'tortured' since an Islamist-allied government came to power.
- *The Daily Star*, 11 October 2001: Minorities in 3 Pabna Upazilas flee houses. Torture and arson alleged. Members of the minority community in some areas of three upazilas in the district are allegedly being subjected to attacks and threats by 'terrorists', following the October 1 election. The Upazilas are Chatmohor, Sujanagar and Bera.
- *The Daily Star*, 13 October 2001: Hundreds of minority people flee Agailjhara in Barisal. Hundreds of members of the minority community including local public representatives in the neighbouring Agailjhara Upazila of Barisal fled their homes and took shelter in villages in Kotalipara Upazila. They left their houses to escape the wrath of hoodlums under the banner of Bangladesh Nationalist Party.

37    See the recollection of events in "Fact Sheet" (available on the *Kibria.org* web site).

massacre and orgy was planned and conspired under the patronage of the then government in power.

It is difficult to fathom the Bangladesh Rifles ('BDR') massacre on 25–26 February 2009. The manner of killing of the officers and the wife of the Director General of the BDR, and the looting and mutilation of dead bodies, show conduct which cannot simply be dealt with and described under the definition of mutiny or murder alone. It resembles crimes against humanity. In tracing the above-mentioned mayhem and mass murder, there seems to be a thin veil between the definition of mass murder and crimes against humanity. I crave the indulgence of experts, drawing their attention to the continuing repetition of serious atrocity: specifically, whether this has any criminological connection with impunity for core international crimes; whether mass murders as perpetrated on 11 September 2001 in the US or in Bangladesh or Pakistan, which repeatedly recurs in the name of religion or otherwise, should be considered as crimes to be included in the definition of crimes against humanity, as they have the characteristics of achieving the same or similar object.

Under the heading "Mass Killing", Blair wrote: "Looking ahead over the next five years, a number of countries in Africa and Asia are at significant risk for a new outbreak of mass killing". He defined 'mass killing' as "the deliberate killing of at least 1,000 unarmed civilians of a particular political identity by state or state-sponsored actors in a single event or over sustained period".[38] Former US President Barack Obama and other senior policy makers believe preventing mass killing, genocide and other mass atrocities is important. Upon his acceptance of the Nobel Peace Prize, President Obama stated: "[m]ore and more, we all confront difficult questions about how to prevent the slaughter of civilians by their own government [...] When there is genocide in Darfur, systematic rape in Congo, or repression in Burma-there must be consequence".[39]

What happens if the perpetrators are let go and the culture of impunity grows? It will endanger the democratic polity, the stability of the country and its constitutional continuity, as we have seen in Bangladesh more than twice since 1975. The survival of the cultural and civilizational base for democracy and the rule of law can be jeopardized by unconstitutional usurpation, making society vulnerable to terror, violence and militancy. Putting an end to impunity for atrocities must not stop the pursuit of justice, even if it entails prosecuting decades-old crimes.

---

[38] Lawrence Woocher, "A Smart Use of Intelligence: Preventing Genocide of Mass Killing", in *Georgetown Journal of International Affairs*, 2010, vol. 11, p. 43.

[39] Barack Obama, "Remarks by the President at the Acceptance of the Nobel Peace Prize", The White House, Office of the Press Secretary, 10 December 2009.

Notwithstanding the challenges of working with old evidence, the trials before the ICT in Bangladesh are held against the background of the suffering of Bangladeshi people in 1971. Threats of similar crimes in different forms and shapes still persist.

## 12.10. Lessons From History

I need not elaborate on these trails of tragedy except for the purpose of reminding ourselves of the lessons of history. History teaches us that actions or omissions to act have definite consequences. The cost of sparing evil has always been very heavy. To prevent genocide, the UN adopted the Convention on the Prevention and Punishment of the Crime of Genocide in 1948.[40] The Convention deals with issues related to the "crime of crimes".[41] The Convention codifies the prohibition against genocide, which has occurred throughout history.[42] The definition of genocide is, however, intensely contested terrain.[43]

Despite the adoption of the Convention 60 years ago, genocides[44] have occurred in various places,[45] including, arguably, in Burundi, Paraguay, Cam-

---

[40]   The Genocide Convention had been ratified by 153 states as of 2024. See, generally, Frank Chalk, "Genocide in the 20th Century: Definitions of Genocide and Their Implications for Predication and Prevention", in *Holocaust and Genocide Studies*, 1989, vol. 4, no. 2; Leo Kuper, "The Prevention of Genocide: Cultural and Structural Indicators of Genocidal Threat", in *Ethnic and Racial Studies*, 1989, vol. 12, no. 2, p. 157; Ervin Staub, "The Roots of Evil: The Origins of Genocide and Other Group Violence", in John A. Berry and Carol Pott Berry (eds.), *Genocide in Rwanda: A Collective Memory*, Harvard University Press, 1999.

[41]   This is not a new term, but for a discussion on the term's use, see Robert D. Sloane, "Sentencing for the 'Crime of Crimes': The Evolving 'Common Law' of Sentencing of the International Criminal Tribunal for Rwanda", in *Journal of International Criminal Justice*, 2007, vol. 5, no. 3, pp. 713, 713–734. Genocide was an international crime before Raphael Lemkin designed the word in the early 1940s. See Jeremy Sarkin, "The Historical Origins, Convergence and Interrelationship of International Human Rights Law, International Humanitarian Law, International Criminal Law and International Law: Their Application from at Least the Nineteenth Century", in *Human Rights and International Legal Discourse*, 2007, vol. 1, pp. 125–172 (hereinafter 'Historical Origins').

[42]   *Ibid.*

[43]   See, for instance, George Chigas, "The Politics of Defining Justice After the Cambodian Genocide", in *Journal of Genocide Research*, 2000, vol. 2, no. 2, pp. 245–265.

[44]   Barbara Harff, "No Lessons Learned From the Holocaust? Assessing Risks of Genocide and Political Mass Murder since 1955", in *American Political Science Review*, 2003, vol. 97, no. 1, p. 57.

[45]   Benjamin A. Valentino, *Final Solutions: Mass Killing and Genocide in the Twentieth Century*, Cornell University Press, 2004.

---

bodia,[46] Iraq, Rwanda[47] and in the Darfur region of Sudan.[48] In this regard, a major failure of the Convention has been the absence of an institution to oversee the work of preventing genocide from occurring and to intervene where genocide is taking place.[49]

There are certain conditions under which a moral agent may be held morally accountable for his or her actions or omissions. According to the two 'negative' Aristotelian principles, an agent should not be ignorant of the facts surrounding his or her actions, and those actions should not show undue force.[50] Equally, the principle of 'alternate possibilities' implies that "a person is morally responsible for what he has done only if he could have done otherwise".[51]

In addition to crimes of genocide, a sense of moral and ethical duty accompanies the trial of past crimes of genocide, crimes against humanity and war crimes. These cases encompass a utopian vision of seeking justice through restitution. For example, through his tenacious pursuit of justice, Simon Wiesenthal demanded that the European nations bring Nazi criminals to trial after World War II.[52] In a world that would prefer to forget, Wiesenthal hounded both criminals and States to remember and reaffirm the meaning of justice.[53]

---

[46] See, generally, David Cohen, "'Hybrid' Justice in East Timor, Sierra Leone, and Cambodia: 'Lessons Learned' and Prospects for the Future", in *Stanford Journal of International Law*, 2007, vol. 43.

[47] UN Economic and Social Council, Sub-Commission on Prevention of Discrimination and Proto of Minorities, Whitaker Report: Revised and Updated Report on the Question of the Prevention and Punishment of the Crime of Genocide, UN Doc. E/CNA/Sub.211985/6, 2 July 1985 (prepared by Benjamin Whitaker) ('Whitaker Report') (https://www.legal-tools.org/doc/99c00c/).

[48] See UN Secretary-General, Report of the International Commission of Inquiry on Darfur, delivered to the Security Council, UN Doc. S/2205/60, 1 February 2005 (https://www.legal-tools.org/doc/1480de/).

[49] See Jeremy Sarkin, "The Role of the United Nations, the African Union and Africa's Sub-Regional Structures in Dealing with Africa's Human Rights Problems: Connecting Humanitarian Intervention and the Responsibility to Protect", in *Journal of African Law*, 2009, vol. 53, no. 1, p. 1.

[50] John Martin Fischer and Mark Ravizza, *Responsibility and Control: A Theory of Moral Responsibility*, Cambridge University Press, 1998; Michael Zimmerman, "Moral Responsibility and Ignorance", in *Ethics*, 1997, vol. 107, no. 3, p. 411.

[51] David Copp, "Defending the Principle of Alternate Possibilities: Blameworthiness and Moral Responsibilities", in *Nous*, 1997, vol. 31, no. 4, p. 441.

[52] Michael Berenbaum, "The Uniqueness and Universality of the Holocaust", in John K. Roth and Michael Berenbaum (eds.), *Holocaust: Religious and Philosophical Implications*, Paragon House, 1989, pp. 82, 83.

[53] *Ibid.*

---

In seeking justice by holding trials, there is the obvious need to deal with old evidence. There is a need to critically evaluate historical records and victim recollections as well as to deal with collective memories. Such an evaluation will avoid inaccurate submissions or oversimplified comparisons. Additionally, it helps contextualize both when the events took place and the span of time that has elapsed since the events occurred. Such litigation aims to present the untold suffering and injustice of "those who have endured and suffered great injustice, [who] often have a powerful sense that what they experienced must not be forgotten, but must be cultivated both as a monument to those who did not survive and as a warning to future generations",[54] so that a nation can be free from these crimes and atrocities. However much a government tries to bury these crimes by default, the crimes continue to haunt the nation from the debris of the history in countless ways.

There is no scope to be ambivalent, hesitant or even half-hearted in one's resolve to try and punish those perpetrators through proper investigation and by conducting a fair trial. On this issue, there is no scope for being in the middle of the road either (the "ones who are in the middle of the road are in danger of being knocked down").[55] Besides its philosophical significance, it is important to remember that the failure to bring criminals to justice has statistically contributed towards generating future crimes, some of which have been mentioned earlier. This is another argument for pursuing justice notwithstanding how long ago were the atrocities committed, or how old the evidence is. The past has a curious habit of recurrence unless dealt with in an appropriate manner. The German writer Jurgen Fuchs once said: "If you do not solve this problem in a definite way it shall haunt us".[56] In Bangladesh, the series of past persecutions is a recurring nightmare even after its fortieth year of independence, largely because the burden of the past cannot be shaken off.

## 12.11. Conclusion

The trial of perpetrators of core international crimes under international law was one of the prime agendas incorporated into the election manifesto of the Awami League, the present ruling party in Bangladesh. It was partly a re-

---

54  See, for instance, Michael R. Marrus, *Some Measure of Justice: The Holocaust Restitution Campaign of the 1990s*, University of Wisconsin Press, 2009 ('Marrus'). Marrus discusses the "wave of Holocaust-era restitution" in the late 1990s.

55  The full quote, commonly attributed to Margaret Thatcher, is: "Standing in the middle of the road is very dangerous; you get knocked down by traffic from both sides".

56  Dr. Zia Uddin Ahmed, "Justice After Genocide: Ways to Deal With the Past", *Mukto Mona*, 27 October 1997. The German writer Jurgen Fuchs once said to Adam Michnik, a leader of the Polish opposition to communist rule, about crimes committed during the communist regime in East Germany: "if we do not solve this problem in a definite way, it will haunt us".

sponse to the demand of the new generation for such trials, re-confirmed by the unanimous resolution of Parliament following victory in the national elections in 2008. It also accorded with the objectives and declaration of Rome Statute:

> Affirming that the most serious crimes of concern to the international community as a whole must not go unpunished and that their effective prosecution must be ensured by taking measures at the national level and by enhancing international cooperation.[57]

The people of Bangladesh share the resolve of the Rome Statute by taking measures at the national level as the government has done, notwithstanding the challenges of trying decades-old international crimes. It is evident that the people, the government and the international community, trusting and believing in the rule of law, are "[d]etermined to put an end to impunity for the perpetrators of these crimes and thus to contribute to the prevention of such crimes", and "[r]ecalling that it is the duty of every State to exercise its criminal jurisdiction over those responsible for international crimes".[58]

In concluding, let me say how grateful I am to the international jurists who have contributed to this anthology, thereby sharing their expertise and their exposure to the international trial process related to the prosecution of crimes against humanity and genocide. In the process of doing so, we exchange and share a common commitment and aspiration to end impunity so that we may thus prosper in peace, united by common bonds and determined to contribute to the prevention of such crimes in my country and elsewhere.

---

[57] Rome Statute, Preamble, see *supra* note 2.
[58] *Ibid.*

# 13

_____

# The International Crimes (Tribunals) Act of 1973 and the Rules: Substantive and Procedural Laws

## Md. Shahinur Islam[*]

At the outset, I would like to express my gratitude to the Centre for International Law Research and Policy ('CILRAP') and the Torkel Opsahl Academic EPublisher ('TOAEP') for the opportunity to contribute to the seminar held in Dhaka, Bangladesh, and this anthology. I also wish to note that I consider it a great honour to share this undertaking with Judge Alphons M.M. Orie, Judge of the International Residual Mechanism for Criminal Tribunals ('IRMCT'); Judge Agnieszka Klonowiecka-Milart, formerly also Judge of the Supreme Court Chamber, Extraordinary Chambers in the Courts of Cambodia ('ECCC'); Mr. Andrew Cayley, previously also International Co-Prosecutor, ECCC; and other distinguished experts. My special thanks go to Professor Morten Bergsmo whose laudable efforts have made this anthology and the project conference in Dhaka possible. This chapter was first presented when I served as the Registrar of the International Crimes Tribunal of Bangladesh ('ICT-BD' or 'Tribunal') at the CILRAP Seminar entitled "Old Evidence and Core International Crimes".

The aim of this chapter is to briefly highlight the ICT-BD and its governing legal framework, its work involving evidence which had come to age before the Tribunal became operational, as well as to express a considered view on some fundamental issues.

_____

[*] Justice **Md. Shahinur Islam** is the Chairman of the International Crimes Tribunal-1 in Dhaka. He is a senior member of the Bangladesh Judicial Service, which he joined in 1983. He has served as a district and sessions judge and as the judge of the Administrative Tribunal, Dhaka. In March 2012, he was appointed judge of the second ICT-BD. He also served as a director (on deputation) in the Office of the Prime Minister (2000–2001), dealing with anti-corruption matters. He is also an adjunct faculty of the Department of Law, Stamford University Bangladesh, a Fellow of the National Defence College (Dhaka), and has published in Bangladesh law journals. At the time of publication of the first edition, the author served as Registrar at the ICT-BD. Many parts of this chapter offer an institutional perspective on the ICT-BD and have been kept given the project conference occurring in Dhaka and that 'old evidence' has been a challenge in Bangladesh as it also has in, for example, Cambodia, East Timor and Indonesia.

## 13.1. Introduction

We know of the notion that the perpetrators of crimes of a universally abhorrent nature are *hostis humani generis* – enemies of humankind. These crimes include war crimes, genocide, crimes against humanity and aggression. Irrefutably, the war crimes and crimes against humanity committed during the 1971 Bangladesh Liberation War ('1971 War', also known as Independence War of Bangladesh) exceeded the brutalities and dreadfulness of war crimes committed in contemporary times. With the aim of establishing a durable peace and justice and bringing the perpetrators of atrocities committed during the 1971 War to justice, a law titled the International Crimes (Tribunals) Act of 1973 ('ICTA') was enacted by Bangladesh's sovereign Parliament.[1]

## 13.2. Composition of the Tribunal

Bangladesh considers that victims of war crimes should have the right to a remedy. The State has an obligation to remedy serious human rights violations. Bangladesh recognizes Article 8 of the Universal Declaration of Human Rights ('UDHR') and Article 2(3) of the International Covenant on Civil and Political Rights ('ICCPR'), which guarantee the right to an effective remedy for violations of human rights. To this end, after making significant amendments to the ICTA in 2009, the ICT-BD was finally established on 25 March 2010. The decades that had passed after the commission of the crimes rendered much of the evidence old, while the commitment to justice – along with the force of law of the ICTA – persisted.

Under Sections 6(1)–(2) of the ICTA, the Tribunal is composed of one Chairman and two Members. The Chairman and the Members serve as judges of the Bangladesh Supreme Court.

## 13.3. The International Crimes Tribunal of Bangladesh: A Domestic Tribunal

The ICT-BD is a purely domestic tribunal. In other words, it is a national judicial mechanism that has been established to try crimes of an international nature which have been criminalized pursuant to Bangladeshi domestic legislation, described in further detail in the chapter below by Otto Triffterer. While the Tribunal's name includes the word 'international' and it possesses jurisdiction over crimes such as crimes against humanity, crimes against peace, genocide and war crimes, it would obviously be wrong to assume that the Tribunal should be treated as an 'international tribunal', as the International Criminal

---

[1]    The International Crimes (Tribunals) Act, 20 July 1973 ('ICTA') (https://www.legal-tools.org/doc/c09a98/).

Tribunal for Rwanda ('ICTR'), the ICTY, the Special Court for Sierra Leone ('SCSL'), the ECCC or the International Criminal Court ('ICC').

The legitimacy of the ICTA stems from its adoption by an overwhelming decision of the Bangladesh Parliament, which is a democratically elected body of representatives and constitutionally mandated to enact legislation. As such, the ICT-BD should be interpreted in light of the framework set out by the ICTA and not international legal instruments (beyond the international legal obligations of Bangladesh, as per the constitution). ICTA, however, refers to and expressly adopts a variety of international legal standards. Nevertheless, respect for a country's domestic sovereignty and the democratic will of its people require ICTA to be considered as the first and predominant point of reference.

## 13.4. Independence of the Tribunal: Section 6(2)(A)

Independence is key and fundamental to a judicial body's functions and to ensure a fair trial. It is the statutory obligation of the Tribunal to ensure fair trials by maintaining fundamental and universally recognized procedures. Section 6(2)(A) of the ICTA expressly recognizes this by providing that "the Tribunal shall be independent in the exercise of its judicial functions and shall ensure fair trial". This guarantee of judicial independence reflects international standards. In practice, the Tribunal has been sensitive to the need to protect the interests of the defendant. For example, it has not hesitated to grant the defence additional time if needed for further preparation: the Tribunal has tended to accept requests made by the defence for further time.

## 13.5. Personal Jurisdiction and Powers of the Tribunal

The Tribunal has jurisdiction over both civilians and individuals from the military. Section 3(1) of the ICTA provides that the Tribunal shall have the power to try and punish "any individual or group of individuals, or any member of any armed, defence or auxiliary forces, irrespective of his nationality, who commits or has committed, in the territory of Bangladesh, whether before or after commencement of the 1973 Act, any of the crimes mentioned in subsection (2)".

Several of ICTA's provisions address the responsibility of individuals of a certain institutional rank. This is particularly important given the fact that the systemic and large-scale nature of international crimes often involves institutional actors with the necessary resources. Section 5 expressly recognizes that the "official position" of an individual does not free him or her from responsibility nor will it mitigate punishment.[2] However, Section 5(2) notes that if the

---

[2]    ICTA, Section 5(1), see *supra* note 1.

accused acted "pursuant to his domestic law" or the "order of his Government or of a superior", while it does not free him or her from responsibility, may be considered for punishment mitigation purposes if "justice so requires".[3]

Section 4 of ICTA also recognizes a variety of ways by which superiors may be linked to, and held liable for, crimes committed by their subordinates "in the same manner as if it were done by him alone".[4] The first category of superiors applies to the person "who orders, permits, acquiesces or participates in the commission of any of the crimes". The second refers to those "connected with any plans and activities involving the commission of such crimes". The third is the person "who fails or omits to discharge his duty to maintain discipline". The fourth are those who fail "to control or supervise the actions of the persons under his command or his subordinates". The fifth refers to an individual "who fails to take necessary measures to prevent the commission of such crimes".

### 13.6. Definition and Elements of Crime

Before examining ICTA's subject-matter jurisdiction, it would be useful to recall present-day jurisprudence regarding the definition of crimes against humanity as developed by an *ad hoc* international tribunal, the ICTY. The fundamental thing to be noted is that a crime against humanity must be part of a "widespread or systematic attack".[5] The ICTY concluded that the term 'widespread' refers to the scale of the attack and the number of victims. Thus, it could relate to the broad magnitude and a series of acts or one act of very wide effect. In the same case, it was also held that the term 'systematic' relates to the 'organized nature of the conduct' concerned, which will often be evidenced by the 'planning' or 'organization' undertaken by the accused. That is to say such 'planning' or 'organization' will often fulfil the 'systematic' requirement. 'Planning' is one of the key components of 'conspiracy'. According to ICTA, conspiring to commit any of the crimes enumerated in Section 3(2) is punishable. Additionally, committing offences enumerated in Section 3(2)(c) "with intent to destroy", in whole or in part, a national, ethnic, racial, religious or political group explicitly qualifies as the offence of genocide under Bangladesh law.

---

3    *Ibid.*, Section 5(2).
4    *Ibid.*, Section 4.
5    An attack would include, but is not confined to, acts of violence. See ICTY, *Prosecutor v. Kunarac et al.*, Trial Chamber, Judgement, IT-96-23-T and IT-96-23/1-T, 22 February 2001 (https://www.legal-tools.org/doc/fd881d/); *Prosecutor v. Tihomir Blaškić*, Trial Chamber, Judgement, IT-95-14-T, 3 March 2000 (https://www.legal-tools.org/doc/e1ae55/).

The ICC will probably continue to draw on the jurisprudence developed by the ICTY and the ICTR.[6] The two earlier tribunals have developed their understanding of customary international law relating to crimes against humanity and have systematized a very extensive functional juridical framework for the prosecution of these crimes.

According to Section 3(2)(a), the crimes described as 'crimes against humanity' must be committed "against civilian population", persecution must be committed on "political, racial, ethnic or religious grounds", "whether or not in violation of domestic law of the country". While Section 3(2) of ICTA does not replicate word-for-word the crimes against humanity definition adopted by other international tribunals, there are shared fundamental notions. The ICC Elements of Crimes document, as noted in the Rome Statute, is not, in fact, binding on the ICC itself; instead, the document "shall assist the Court" in interpreting the various crimes.[7] It should also be noted that while the ICT-BD is not obligated to follow the definitional standards applied by other international tribunals, it is not to be precluded from seeking guidance from universally recognized references.

Undeniably, the old evidence perused by the ICT-BD shows how the context and extent of atrocities committed in the 1971 War in Bangladesh itself amply prove that they were directed in a 'systematic' manner and based on 'planning' against 'civilian non-combatant population' or 'members of civilian population'. The attack – which must be either widespread or systematic or both to be tried as a crime against humanity – must also be primarily directed against a 'civilian population'. With regards to the context, since the specific offences of crimes against humanity which were committed during the 1971 events are tried under ICTA, they are obviously alleged to have been committed in the context of the 1971 War. Such context would in itself suffice to establish a 'widespread and systematic attack' against the Bangladeshi self-determined population in 1971 at the ICT-BD. Additionally, the Tribunal does not require proof of facts of common knowledge, as per Section 19(3) of ICTA; it shall take judicial notice of such facts.[8] So, there can be no arguable room to say that the offences enumerated in ICTA are not well-defined or devoid of their constitutive elements.

---

[6] Guénaël Mettraux, "Crimes Against Humanity in the Jurisprudence of the International Criminal Tribunals for the Former Yugoslavia and for Rwanda", in *Harvard International Law Journal*, 2002, vol. 43, no. 1, p. 237.

[7] Rome Statute of the International Criminal Court, 17 July 1998, Article 9(1) (https://www.legal-tools.org/doc/7b9af9/).

[8] ICTA, Section 19(3), see *supra* note 1.

## 13.7. Prosecution, Investigation, Trial Proceedings and Rules of Evidence

The proceedings before the Tribunal shall commence upon submission of the formal charge by the prosecution, prepared on the basis of the investigation report submitted by the Investigation Agency established under ICTA. As illustrated by this anthology, the challenge of collecting and organizing evidence may not be insurmountable, even after a passage of 40 years. The need to work with old evidence should be matched by adequate practices and rules in order to serve the interests of justice while upholding the rights of the accused. The ICT-BD considers all probative evidence regardless of its format unless the rights of the accused are deemed to be prejudiced by the admission of the said evidence. Section 19 of ICTA notes that the Tribunal "shall not be bound by technical rules of evidence",[9] and provides for the possibility of admitting reports, photographs, films and other materials carrying probative value as evidence. This provision has been supplemented by Rule 44 of the ICT Rules of Procedure, which notes the Tribunal's discretion to "exclude any evidence which does not inspire any confidence in it".[10]

All proceedings before the Tribunal are public, but the Tribunal may, if it deems fit, take proceedings *in camera*.[11] The ICTA also states that no oath shall be administered to any accused person.[12] Further, the statement made by an accused to an investigation officer during interrogation shall not be admissible in evidence, except for that part of the statement leading to the discovery of incriminating material.[13] Providing at least three weeks – after the framing of a charge – for the preparation of defence explicitly offers a key element of due process which appears to be broadly consistent with the settled criminal jurisprudence.[14] This time frame aims to strike a balance between the accused person's rights and ensuring expeditious trials. There is a need to be motivated by both justice and pragmatism, bearing in mind the conditions and general resource constraints faced in Bangladesh and the evidentiary challenges of prosecuting decades-old crimes.

---

[9]   *Ibid.*, Section 19(1).

[10]  International Crimes Tribunals Rules of Procedure, 15 July 2010, amended 28 October 2010 and 28 June 2011, Rule 44 ('ICT Rules of Procedure') (https://www.legal-tools.org/doc/efe1e7/).

[11]  ICTA, Section 10(4), see *supra* note 1.

[12]  *Ibid.*, Section 10(5).

[13]  ICT Rules of Procedure, Rule 56(3), see *supra* note 10.

[14]  *Ibid.*, Rule 38(2).

## 13.8. Presumption of Innocence

No one can be convicted unless the charge brought against him is proved beyond reasonable doubt. This is the normal and universally settled criminal jurisprudence that all the courts constituted under valid legislation will follow. This norm, due to its settled nature, does not need to be embodied in ICTA for the Tribunal to remain bound to respect it.

The Tribunal's legal framework reflects this commitment to proof beyond reasonable doubt. Rule 50 of the ICT Rules of Procedure requires the burden of proving the charge to lie upon the prosecution.[15] After its establishment, the Tribunal adopted Rule 43(2) which states that a person charged with crimes as described under Section 3(2) of the Act shall be presumed innocent until found guilty.[16]

## 13.9. Pre-Trial Arrest and Detention: Permitted Even Internationally

There is no international legal rule expressly prohibiting pre-charge detention, which is itself practiced in many countries. The ICTA does not contain explicit provisions on pre-charge arrest and detention. But if we have a careful look at Section 14(1) of ICTA, there will be no disagreement that pre-charge detention is permitted. Section 14(1) recognizes that any magistrate "may record any statement or confession made to him by an accused person at any time in the course of investigation or at any time before the commencement of the trial". If pre-charge arrest and detention is not permitted, how can the confession of an accused, at any time in course of investigation, be recorded by a magistrate?

Investigation is the key to prosecuting the offences defined in Section 3(2). Considering the time which has lapsed since the commission of the crimes, there is a need to take effective steps to preserve or prevent the destruction of any evidence that may be already compromised by the passage of time. The framework set out in Rule 9 of the ICT Rules of Procedure aims to facilitate effective and proper investigation.[17] This rule supplements Section 14(1) of ICTA. By setting out distinct stages of the investigatory process, Rule 9 aims to prevent arbitrary arrest consistent with international norms. Checks are built into Rule 9's framework. For example, for accused persons already in custody for another offence or case, the Tribunal is to be "satisfied" that a detention order is "necessary" for the "effective and proper investigation" prior

---

[15]  *Ibid.*, Rule 50.
[16]  *Ibid.*, Rule 43(2).
[17]  *Ibid.*, Rule 9.

to directing that the person be detained.[18] In addition, investigations are required to comply with certain time limits.[19]

## 13.10. Bail

With respect to the question of bail, the ICT Rules of Procedure provide that, upon the production of the accused before the Tribunal, he shall be sent to prison if he is not enlarged on bail.[20] At the pre-trial stage, and even at any stage of proceedings, the accused has the right to seek release on bail, and on hearing the matter, the Tribunal shall pass the necessary orders.[21] The Rules also provide for the release of the accused person, if investigation is not completed within a specified time.[22]

## 13.11. Rights of the Accused During the Interrogation

Through its framework and practice, ICTA has sought to provide for various rights of the accused person during the investigation process. These aim to protect the accused by preventing coercion, torture and other grave violations of his or her human rights. The Tribunal has adopted a number of practices to enhance protections afforded to accused persons despite the absence of explicit rules. For example, at the time of writing, the Tribunal has ensured that at the time of interrogation, both defense counsel and a doctor are present in a room adjacent to that where the accused is being interrogated. The accused is permitted to consult them during breaks in the interrogation. According to the Jail Code, as and when ordered by the Tribunal, upon a request made on behalf of them, accused persons are duly allowed to meet their respective counsel. The accused persons have the opportunity to have privileged communication with counsel that may last over a couple of days and for consecutive hours on each day. Their family members are also allowed to meet them, according to the Jail Code which is applicable to the prison management system of Bangladesh.[23]

## 13.12. Interlocutory Appeal

The ICTA does not provide for appeal against an interlocutory order. The absence of such a procedural rule should not be said to automatically result in a greater likelihood of injustice for the accused. The Tribunal retains the ability

---

18  *Ibid.*, Rule 9(4).
19  ICTA, Section 9(5), see *supra* note 1.
20  ICT Rules of Procedure, Rule 33, see *supra* note 10.
21  *Ibid.*, Rule 33(3).
22  *Ibid.*, Rule 9(5).
23  The 'Jail Code' refers to several laws governing the prison system, though mainly Bangladesh, Prisons Act, Act No. IV of 1894, 22 March 1894 (https://www.legal-tools.org/doc/daab7d/).

to intervene to correct any injustice upon viewing the process as a whole. The accused is able to raise any judicial error at the final appeal from conviction before the Appellate Division under ICTA Section 21.[24] Thus, as such, ICTA, when appreciated in a holistic manner, adequately ensures that the accused is not without any recourse, even in the absence of a specific provision for appeal against interlocutory orders. Additionally, a rule has been embodied authorizing the Tribunal to review its order on request of either party or its own motion.[25]

## 13.13. The International Crimes (Tribunals) Act and Rules of Procedure: The Key Rights of the Defence, Witnesses and Victims

Pursuant to ICTA Section 22, the Tribunal has formulated the ICT Rules of Procedure.[26] These Rules and their subsequent amendments implement significant changes aimed at ensuring the highest degree of defence rights and fair trial. Despite the absence of any explicit provision relating to witness and victim support measures in ICTA, the Rules set out provisions aimed at ensuring the protection, privacy and well-being of the witnesses and victims.[27]

The Rules explicitly set out a number of provisions aimed at preserving the accused's interests. Taken as a whole, they aim to prevent the arbitrary arrest or detention of an accused; any prosecution on a frivolous charge; coercion, duress or threat of any kind; and self-incrimination through confession. Further, a failure to prove an *alibi* itself will not *ipso facto* prove the guilt. Additionally, the accused is recognized to have the following rights:

- the right to examine witnesses (Section 10(1));
- the right to an interpreter (Section 10(3));
- the right to expeditious trial (Section 11(3));
- the right to have counsel engaged at the expense of the government (Section 12);
- the right to remain free from compulsion in making confession (Section 14(2));
- the right to inspect documents (Section 16(2));
- the right to conduct his own defence (Section 17(2));
- the right to cross-examine prosecution witnesses (Section 17(3)); and
- the right to appeal (Section 21(1)).

---

[24] ICTA, Section 21(1), see *supra* note 1.
[25] ICT Rules of Procedure, Rule 26(3), see *supra* note 10.
[26] ICTA, Section 22, see *supra* note 1.
[27] ICT Rules of Procedure, Chapter VI(A), see *supra* note 10.

## 13.14. Witness and Victim Support Measures

As mentioned above, the main statute remains silent on the aspect of witness and victim protection measures. But, undeniably, the protection and co-operation of victims and witnesses is essential for fair and successful prosecutions; the evidence they provide becomes more crucial with every passing decade. Yet, in post-conflict situations, individuals very often do not want to co-operate out of fear, and the passage of time may or may not ease such concerns. Offering protection is further justified by the age of many witnesses and victims of crimes perpetrated in 1971, who become old along with the evidence they may relate. Providing witness protection is therefore both an expedient for law enforcement as well as a fundamental legal obligation. However, the ICT Rules of Procedure introduce significant provisions regarding witness and victim protection. The amendment states:

> The Tribunal on its own initiative, or on the application of either party, may pass necessary order directing the authorities concerned of the government to ensure protection, privacy and well-being of the witnesses and/or victims. This process will be confidential and the other side will not be notified.[28]

The government shall arrange and pay for the accommodation of witness(es) and victim(s), and ensure their security and surveillance during their stay as directed by the Tribunal. Witnesses and victims shall also be escorted to the courtroom by the members of law enforcement agencies. Additionally, the government has taken initiatives to enact legislation in this regard.

In the case of holding proceedings *in camera* under Section 10(4) of ICTA, both the prosecution and the defence are required to respect the confidentiality of the proceedings, and shall not reveal any information arising out of such proceedings, including the identity of the witness concerned.[29] Any violation of such undertaking shall be prosecuted under Section 11(4) of ICTA.[30]

## 13.15. Procedural Fairness

There can be no disagreement that the entire trial process is to be conducted by maintaining acceptable and settled standards of procedural fairness and by affording fundamental rights of defence. What is procedural fairness? Fairness should not be neither a 'bull in a China shop' nor a 'bee in one's bonnet'. In essence, fairness aims for a good conscience in a given situation, nothing more and nothing less. A fundamental element of procedural fairness is the principle of equality of arms. It means that a person must be afforded a reasonable op-

---

[28]   *Ibid.*, Rule 58(A)(1).
[29]   ICTA, Section 10(4), see *supra* note 1.
[30]   *Ibid.*, Section 11(4).

portunity of presenting his case to a court under conditions which do not place him at a substantial disadvantage in relation to his opponent. The ICTA and the ICT Rules of Procedure aim to achieve this by setting out key safeguards of the accused person, notwithstanding the added challenges of prosecuting on the grounds of old evidence.

Procedural fairness, as we see in the ICT-BD, covers the key and fundamental safeguards to the accused person before the Tribunal, including adequate time to prepare his defence and that he shall be presumed innocent until found guilty. Procedural fairness as recognized by the ICT-BD covers many rights of the accused which shall appear to be quite compatible with international human rights law, *id est*, the right to know of the offense charged, the right to trial within a reasonable time and the right to safeguards against double jeopardy. All these fundamental rights, as already mentioned, have been duly guaranteed by ICTA and the Rules as well. The rights of the defence and the procedure set out in ICTA and the ICT Rules of Procedure are manifestations of the due process of law and fair trial which make the legislation of 1973 jurisprudentially resonant.

It would be relevant to emphasize that the International Bar Association ('IBA') Committee, in a report, is of the opinion that the "1973 Legislation, together with the 2009 amending text, provides a system which is broadly compatible with current international standards".[31] It is to be borne in mind too that each war-crimes trial is unique and different. A procedural standard followed in one may or may not be worthy of adoption in another. Lessons from contemporary war-crimes trials suggest that procedural aspects are usually tailored to suit the specific circumstances of a given trial, and that this is an evolving process. Finally, I would like to add that the mere incorporation of provisions in either the legislation or the Rules does not ensure the maintaining of standards and fairness of the trial process. The implementation of provisions contained therein has to be maintained by the acumen of the judges based on settled judicial norms and rational logic which shall appear to be globally compatible.

## 13.16. Conclusion

The Convention on the Prevention and Punishment of the Crime of Genocide of 1948 has defined genocide as an international crime, and spelled out obliga-

---

[31] International Bar Association and War Crimes Committee to the United Kingdom Parliament Human Rights Group, "Consistency of Bangladesh's International Crimes (Tribunals) Act 1973 with International Standards", 29 December 2009, presented at the 16 April 2010 Conference on the Legality of the International Crimes (Tribunals) Act 1973, organized by the National Forum for Protection of Human Rights.

tions upon States Parties in terms of prosecution.[32] It is thus significant to observe that the demand of trying the war crimes of the 1971 War only received impetus in recent times. Regardless of how many decades have passed, victims of wars or atrocities need justice to heal.

War victims need justice to heal. Bangladesh considers that the right to remedy should be granted to the victims of war crimes as well, pursuant to the State's obligations under the UDHR and ICCPR as mentioned in Section 13.2., and said remedy must be effective.

The consistency between the crimes as described in ICTA and international law would enable the ICT-BD to draw upon the steady stream of jurisprudence and judicial precedents of international criminal law in conducting its trial. While speaking at a workshop on the ratification of the ICC Statute in Bangladesh, Sang-Hyun Song, a former ICC President, said that the "judicial system and legal experts of Bangladesh are adequate with considerable competence and knowledge to deal with the war crimes of 1971".[33]

To conclude, I sincerely hope that the result of this anthology will be the furthering of our fruitful interactions and thought-provoking discussions with distinguished judges and experts so as to benefit from their knowledge and wisdom through the exchange of ideas.

---

[32] Convention on the Prevention and Punishment of the Crime of Genocide, 9 December 1948 (https://www.legal-tools.org/doc/498c38/).
[33] "Ratify Rome Statute to Fight Crimes Against Humanity", *The Daily Star*, 2 December 2009.

# INDEX

## A

Afghan War, 285
Afghanistan
  Military Intelligence Service, 176
  Pul-e-Charkhi prison, 177
Ahmed, Shafique, ix
Al Badr, 278
Al Shams, 278
Aman, Diane Marie, 237, 272
analysis
  qualitative, 15, 90, 94, 268
  quantitative, 90, 91, 93, 266, 268
Angotti, Antonio, i, 1
Annan, Kofi, 231
Arbour, Louise, 61
areas of evidence
  analytical evidence, 56
  crime scenes, 50
  documentary evidence, 54, *See* main entry
  *documentary evidence.*
  expert evidence, 56
  witnesses, 38, 52, *See* also main entry
  *witness.*
Aristotelian principles, 291
*Auschwitz,* 18
Awami League, 280, 292

## B

Babić, Milan, 130
Ban, Ki-Moon, 237
Bangladesh, ii
  Bangladesh Collaborators (Special Tribunals)
  Order, 241
  Bangladesh Rifles, 289
  injustice (1973 Act), 15
  interlocutory appeal (1973 Act), 15
  International Crimes (Tribunals) Act, 1973,
    x, 39, 40, 41, 155, 236, 241, 276, 277, 296
  Jail Code, 15
  Legal Framework Order, 282

Liberation War (1971), ii, ix, x, 56, 235, 237,
  239, 240, 242, 275, 278, 282, 296, 299,
  306
Liberation War Museum, 241
Operation Searchlight, 239, 278, 279
Rome Statute, ix
Rules of Procedure (1973 Act), 244, 305
Supreme Court, x
War Crimes Fact Finding Committee, 242
Bassiouni, M. Cherif, 151
Bengali nationalism, 279
Bergsmo, Morten, i, x, 1, 248, 295
Bhawalpur Airport, 285
Bhutto, Zulfikar Ali, 278, 283
Birangona, 270
Bosnia and Herzegovina
  Srebrenica Massacre, 45, 250
burden of proof, 31, 32
  agreed facts, 158
  contextual elements, 159
  judicial notice, 158, *See* also main entry
  *judicial notice*
Burundi, 290
Butenschøn Skre, Alf, ii

## C

Cambodia, 15, 291
  Ampe Phnom, Samrong Tong District, 50
  Dang Tong District, 50
  First January Dam, 52
  Khmer Rouge, 53
  Khmer Rouge atrocities, 245–50
  Koh Phal, Kampong Cham Province, 51
  People's Revolutionary Tribunal, 53, 253
  Phnom Srok District, 50
  Prek Thnoat River, 51
  Sang Prison, 51
capacity development, 11
case selection, iv
Cayley, Andrew, 12, 47, 89, 251, 295
Central African Republic. *See* CAR
Centre for International Law Research and
  Policy, 1, 3, 295

# TOAEP TEAM

# VOLUMES IN
# THE *PUBLICATION SERIES*

Morten Bergsmo, Mads Harlem and Nobuo Hayashi (editors):
*Importing Core International Crimes into National Law*
Torkel Opsahl Academic EPublisher
Oslo, 2010
FICHL Publication Series No. 1 (Second Edition, 2010)
ISBN: 978-82-93081-00-5

Nobuo Hayashi (editor):
*National Military Manuals on the Law of Armed Conflict*
Torkel Opsahl Academic EPublisher
Brussels, 2023
Publication Series No. 2 (Third Edition, 2023)
ISBN print: 978-82-8348-226-3
ISBN e-book: 978-82-8348-225-6

林 伸生（主编）：
国家武装冲突法军事手册研究
Torkel Opsahl Academic EPublisher
Brussels, 2023
Publication Series No. 2 (Chinese Edition, 2023)
ISBN print: 978-82-8348-119-8
ISBN e-book: 978-82-8348-120-4

Morten Bergsmo, Kjetil Helvig, Ilia Utmelidze and Gorana Žagovec:
*The Backlog of Core International Crimes Case Files in Bosnia and Herzegovina*
Torkel Opsahl Academic EPublisher
Oslo, 2010
FICHL Publication Series No. 3 (Second Edition, 2010)
ISBN: 978-82-93081-04-3

Morten Bergsmo (editor):
*Criteria for Prioritizing and Selecting Core International Crimes Cases*
Torkel Opsahl Academic EPublisher
Oslo, 2010
FICHL Publication Series No. 4 (Second Edition, 2010)
ISBN: 978-82-93081-06-7

Morten Bergsmo and Pablo Kalmanovitz (editors):
*Law in Peace Negotiations*
Torkel Opsahl Academic EPublisher
Oslo, 2010
FICHL Publication Series No. 5 (Second Edition, 2010)
ISBN: 978-82-93081-08-1

Morten Bergsmo, César Rodríguez Garavito, Pablo Kalmanovitz and Maria Paula Saffon (editors):
*Distributive Justice in Transitions*
Torkel Opsahl Academic EPublisher
Oslo, 2010
FICHL Publication Series No. 6 (2010)
ISBN: 978-82-93081-12-8

Morten Bergsmo, César Rodriguez-Garavito, Pablo Kalmanovitz and Maria Paula Saffon (editors):
*Justicia Distributiva en Sociedades en Transición*
Torkel Opsahl Academic EPublisher
Oslo, 2012
FICHL Publication Series No. 6 (2012)
ISBN: 978-82-93081-10-4

Morten Bergsmo (editor):
*Complementarity and the Exercise of Universal Jurisdiction for Core International Crimes*
Torkel Opsahl Academic EPublisher
Oslo, 2010
FICHL Publication Series No. 7 (2010)
ISBN: 978-82-93081-14-2

Morten Bergsmo (editor):
*Active Complementarity: Legal Information Transfer*
Torkel Opsahl Academic EPublisher
Oslo, 2011
FICHL Publication Series No. 8 (2011)
ISBN print: 978-82-93081-56-2
ISBN e-book: 978-82-93081-55-5

Morten Bergsmo (editor):
*Abbreviated Criminal Procedures for Core International Crimes*
Torkel Opsahl Academic EPublisher
Brussels, 2017
FICHL Publication Series No. 9 (2017)
ISBN print: 978-82-93081-20-3
ISBN e-book: 978-82-8348-104-4

Sam Muller, Stavros Zouridis, Morly Frishman and Laura Kistemaker (editors):
*The Law of the Future and the Future of Law*
Torkel Opsahl Academic EPublisher
Oslo, 2010
FICHL Publication Series No. 11 (2011)
ISBN: 978-82-93081-27-2

Morten Bergsmo, Alf Butenschøn Skre and Elisabeth J. Wood (editors):
*Understanding and Proving International Sex Crimes*
Torkel Opsahl Academic EPublisher
Beijing, 2012
FICHL Publication Series No. 12 (2012)
ISBN: 978-82-93081-29-6

Morten Bergsmo (editor):
*Thematic Prosecution of International Sex Crimes*
Torkel Opsahl Academic EPublisher
Brussels, 2018
Publication Series No. 13 (Second Edition, 2018)
ISBN print: 978-82-8348-025-2
ISBN e-book: 978-82-8348-024-5

Terje Einarsen:
*The Concept of Universal Crimes in International Law*
Torkel Opsahl Academic EPublisher
Oslo, 2012
FICHL Publication Series No. 14 (2012)
ISBN: 978-82-93081-33-3

ترج آينارسن:
مفهوم جرايمجهانيدر حقوقبينالملل
Torkel Opsahl Academic EPublisher
Brussels, 2023
Publication Series No. 14 (Persian Edition, 2023)
ISBN print: 978-82-8348-202-7
ISBN e-book: 978-82-8348-203-4

莫滕·伯格斯默 凌岩(主编):
国家主权与国际刑法
Torkel Opsahl Academic EPublisher
Beijing, 2012
FICHL Publication Series No. 15 (2012)
ISBN: 978-82-93081-58-6

Morten Bergsmo and Ling Yan (editors):
*State Sovereignty and International Criminal Law*
Torkel Opsahl Academic EPublisher
Beijing, 2012
FICHL Publication Series No. 15 (2012)
ISBN: 978-82-93081-35-7

Morten Bergsmo, Cheah Wui Ling and Antonio Angotti (editors):
*Old Evidence and Core International Crimes*
Torkel Opsahl Academic EPublisher
Brussels, 2024
Publication Series No. 16 (Second Edition, 2024)
ISBN print: 978-82-8348-228-7
ISBN e-book: 978-82-8348-229-4

Yi Ping:
戦争と平和の間――発足期日本国際法学における「正しい戦争」の観念とその帰結
Torkel Opsahl Academic EPublisher
Beijing, 2013
FICHL Publication Series No. 17 (2013)
ISBN: 978-82-93081-66-1

Morten Bergsmo and Song Tianying (editors):
*On the Proposed Crimes Against Humanity Convention*
Torkel Opsahl Academic EPublisher
Brussels, 2014
FICHL Publication Series No. 18 (2014)
ISBN: 978-82-93081-96-8

Morten Bergsmo and Carsten Stahn (editors):
*Quality Control in Fact-Finding*
Torkel Opsahl Academic EPublisher
Brussels, 2020
Publication Series No. 19 (Second Edition, 2020)
ISBN print: 978-82-8348-135-8
ISBN e-book: 978-82-8348-136-5

Morten Bergsmo, Cheah Wui Ling and Yi Ping (editors):
*Historical Origins of International Criminal Law: Volume 1*
Torkel Opsahl Academic EPublisher
Brussels, 2014
FICHL Publication Series No. 20 (2014)
ISBN: 978-82-93081-11-1

Morten Bergsmo, Cheah Wui Ling and Yi Ping (editors):
*Historical Origins of International Criminal Law: Volume 2*
Torkel Opsahl Academic EPublisher
Brussels, 2014
FICHL Publication Series No. 21 (2014)
ISBN: 978-82-93081-13-5

Morten Bergsmo, Cheah Wui Ling, Song Tianying and Yi Ping (editors):
*Historical Origins of International Criminal Law: Volume 3*
Torkel Opsahl Academic EPublisher
Brussels, 2015
FICHL Publication Series No. 22 (2015)
ISBN print: 978-82-8348-015-3
ISBN e-book: 978-82-8348-014-6

Morten Bergsmo, Cheah Wui Ling, Song Tianying and Yi Ping (editors):
*Historical Origins of International Criminal Law: Volume 4*
Torkel Opsahl Academic EPublisher
Brussels, 2015
FICHL Publication Series No. 23 (2015)
ISBN print: 978-82-8348-017-7
ISBN e-book: 978-82-8348-016-0

Morten Bergsmo, Klaus Rackwitz and Song Tianying (editors):
*Historical Origins of International Criminal Law: Volume 5*
Torkel Opsahl Academic EPublisher
Brussels, 2017
FICHL Publication Series No. 24 (2017)
ISBN print: 978-82-8348-106-8
ISBN e-book: 978-82-8348-107-5

Morten Bergsmo and Song Tianying (editors):
*Military Self-Interest in Accountability for Core International Crimes*
Torkel Opsahl Academic EPublisher
Brussels, 2015
FICHL Publication Series No. 25 (2015)
ISBN print: 978-82-93081-61-6
ISBN e-book: 978-82-93081-81-4

Wolfgang Kaleck:
*Double Standards: International Criminal Law and the West*
Torkel Opsahl Academic EPublisher
Brussels, 2015
FICHL Publication Series No. 26 (2015)
ISBN print: 978-82-93081-67-8
ISBN e-book: 978-82-93081-83-8

Liu Daqun and Zhang Binxin (editors):
*Historical War Crimes Trials in Asia*
Torkel Opsahl Academic EPublisher
Brussels, 2016
FICHL Publication Series No. 27 (2015)
ISBN print: 978-82-8348-055-9
ISBN e-book: 978-82-8348-056-6

Morten Bergsmo, Mark Klamberg, Kjersti Lohne and Christopher B. Mahony (editors):
*Power in International Criminal Justice*
Torkel Opsahl Academic EPublisher
Brussels, 2020
Publication Series No. 28 (2020)
ISBN print: 978-82-8348-113-6
ISBN e-book: 978-82-8348-114-3

Stian Nordengen Christensen:
*Counterfactual History and Bosnia-Herzegovina*
Torkel Opsahl Academic EPublisher
Brussels, 2018
Publication Series No. 30 (2018)
ISBN print: 978-82-8348-102-0
ISBN e-book: 978-82-8348-103-7

Stian Nordengen Christensen:
*Possibilities and Impossibilities in a Contradictory Global Order*
Torkel Opsahl Academic EPublisher
Brussels, 2018
Publication Series No. 31 (2018)
ISBN print: 978-82-8348-104-4
ISBN e-book: 978-82-8348-105-1

Morten Bergsmo and Carsten Stahn (editors):
*Quality Control in Preliminary Examination: Volume 1*
Torkel Opsahl Academic EPublisher
Brussels, 2018
Publication Series No. 32 (2018)
ISBN print: 978-82-8348-123-5
ISBN e-book: 978-82-8348-124-2

Morten Bergsmo and Carsten Stahn (editors):
*Quality Control in Preliminary Examination: Volume 2*
Torkel Opsahl Academic EPublisher
Brussels, 2018
Publication Series No. 33 (2018)
ISBN print: 978-82-8348-111-2
ISBN e-book: 978-82-8348-112-9

Morten Bergsmo and Emiliano J. Buis (editors):
*Philosophical Foundations of International Criminal Law: Correlating Thinkers*
Torkel Opsahl Academic EPublisher
Brussels, 2018
Publication Series No. 34 (2018)
ISBN print: 978-82-8348-117-4
ISBN e-book: 978-82-8348-118-1

Morten Bergsmo and Emiliano J. Buis (editors):
*Philosophical Foundations of International Criminal Law: Foundational Concepts*
Torkel Opsahl Academic EPublisher
Brussels, 2019
Publication Series No. 35 (2019)
ISBN print: 978-82-8348-119-8
ISBN e-book: 978-82-8348-120-4

Morten Bergsmo, Emiliano J. Buis and Song Tianying (editors):
*Philosophical Foundations of International Criminal Law: Legally-Protected Interests*
Torkel Opsahl Academic EPublisher
Brussels, 2022
Publication Series No. 36 (2022)
ISBN print: 978-82-8348-121-1
ISBN e-book: 978-82-8348-122-8

Terje Einarsen and Joseph Rikhof:
*A Theory of Punishable Participation in Universal Crimes*
Torkel Opsahl Academic EPublisher
Brussels, 2018
Publication Series No. 37 (2018)
ISBN print: 978-82-8348-127-3
ISBN e-book: 978-82-8348-128-0

Xabier Agirre Aranburu, Morten Bergsmo, Simon De Smet and Carsten Stahn (editors):
*Quality Control in Criminal Investigation*
Torkel Opsahl Academic EPublisher
Brussels, 2020
Publication Series No. 38 (2020)
ISBN print: 978-82-8348-129-7
ISBN e-book: 978-82-8348-130-3

Morten Bergsmo, Wolfgang Kaleck and Kyaw Yin Hlaing (editors):
*Colonial Wrongs and Access to International Law*
Torkel Opsahl Academic EPublisher
Brussels, 2020
Publication Series No. 40 (2020)
ISBN print: 978-82-8348-133-4
ISBN e-book: 978-82-8348-134-1

Morten Bergsmo and Kishan Manocha (editors):
*Religion, Hateful Expression and Violence*
Torkel Opsahl Academic EPublisher
Brussels, 2023
Publication Series No. 41 (2023)
ISBN print: 978-82-8348-141-9
ISBN e-book: 978-82-8348-142-6

Gavin E. Oxburgh, Trond Myklebust, Mark Fallon and Maria Hartwig (editors):
*Interviewing and Interrogation: A Review of Research and Practice Since World War II*
Torkel Opsahl Academic EPublisher
Brussels, 2023
Publication Series No. 42 (2023)
ISBN print: 978-82-8348-200-3
ISBN e-book: 978-82-8348-201-0

Mark Klamberg, Jonas Nilsson and Antonio Angotti (editors):
*Commentary on the Law of the International Criminal Court: The Statute*
*Volume 1*
Torkel Opsahl Academic EPublisher
Brussels, 2023
Publication Series No. 43 (Second Edition, 2023)
ISBN print: 978-82-8348-204-1
ISBN e-book: 978-82-8348-205-8

Mark Klamberg, Jonas Nilsson and Antonio Angotti (editors):
*Commentary on the Law of the International Criminal Court: The Statute*
*Volume 2*
Torkel Opsahl Academic EPublisher
Brussels, 2023
Publication Series No. 44 (Second Edition, 2023)
ISBN print: 978-82-8348-206-5
ISBN e-book: 978-82-8348-207-2

Mark Klamberg, Jonas Nilsson and Antonio Angotti (editors):
*Commentary on the Law of the International Criminal Court:*
*The Rules of Procedure and Evidence*
Torkel Opsahl Academic EPublisher
Brussels, 2023
Publication Series No. 45 (2023)
ISBN print: 978-82-8348-208-9
ISBN e-book: 978-82-8348-209-6

All volumes are freely available online at http://www.toaep.org/ps/. For printed copies, see http://www.toaep.org/about/distribution/. For reviews of earlier books in this Series in academic journals and yearbooks, see http://www.toaep.org/reviews/.